+THE THRESHOLD

Part I: New York—The Mystery Struggle
and
Part II: California—The Goals, Grinds, and Joys

MICHAEL D. ROURKE

VOLUME ONE

WestBow
PRESS
A DIVISION OF THOMAS NELSON

WestBow Press books may be ordered through booksellers or by contacting:

WestBow Press
A Division of Thomas Nelson
1663 Liberty Drive
Bloomington, IN 47403
www.westbowpress.com
1 (866) 928-1240

Because of the dynamic nature of the Internet, any web addresses or links contained in this book may have changed since publication and may no longer be valid. The views expressed in this work are solely those of the author and do not necessarily reflect the views of the publisher, and the publisher hereby disclaims any responsibility for them.

This work is a memoir. It reflects the author's present recollection of experiences over a period of years, and may not coincide with what others depicted in the story experienced or remember. The author recreated dialogue from memory and a few scenes were restructured. Therefore, in consideration of that fact and in the interest of protecting identities and privacy, I have changed relationships, names, cities, states, and other locations. Any resemblance to actual persons, living or dead, events, or locales is entirely coincidental.

Any people depicted in stock imagery provided by Thinkstock are models, and such images are being used for illustrative purposes only.
Certain stock imagery © Thinkstock.

Scripture taken from the New King James Version. Copyright 1979, 1980, 1982 by Thomas Nelson, Inc. Used by permission. All rights reserved.

All lyrics are original and written by Michael D. Rourke.
Front cover design by Michael D. Rourke.
Front cover artwork by Bill Carney.

ISBN: 978-1-4497-6190-5 (sc)
ISBN: 978-1-4497-6191-2 (hc)
ISBN: 978-1-4497-6189-9 (e)

Library of Congress Control Number: 2013917132

Printed in the United States of America.
WestBow Press rev. date: 11/13/2013

Contents

New York—The Mystery Struggle 1

Chapter 1: Dyslexia 2

Chapter 2: Latchkey Kids. 24

Chapter 3: Off the Treadmill 42

Chapter 4: Farewell, Love: Travel-Bound 62

Chapter 5: Brain Trauma 80

Chapter 6: The Lyric Muse 93

Chapter 7: Optimism Found 107

Chapter 8: Old Thunder. 121

Chapter 9: Texas Tenacity 128

California—The Goals, Grinds, and Joys 147

Chapter 10: West Coast Flight of Perseverance 148

Chapter 11: Still Not Thirty. 168

Chapter 12: The Business, the Bible, and the Bust 188

Chapter 13: Garage Life 215

Chapter 14: Chance Went to Church 239

Chapter 15: The Bottom. 251

Chapter 16: The Dead Life Ends 266

Chapter 17: Born Again 285

Chapter 18: Alone on the Range. 304

Chapter 19: Charismatic Twist or Trendy Oddity 321

Chapter 20: Learning Truth, and Fighting Lies and Vices 340

Chapter 21: One Year Born-Again 369

Chapter 22: Blessings of the Lord 379

Chapter 23: Stay to Learn 394

List of Lyrics

Outside 10

Out Those Windows 14

Satisfied 26

Down In General 49

Manual Labor 65

Bound Free 69

Can't Frame the Wind 72

Circles and Lines 84

The Man in the Moon Is Laughing 88

Jump-Start My Heart 95

Whether to Love 99

The Substitute 102

The Devil Lives in America 104

Dog Gone 106

Electric Light Man 108

September Fifth 118

Torn Threads 119

A Breed 127

Everything in Texas 132

Crowded 135

Songwriter 144

If 145

The Player 166

A Home 170

Shadow People 191

Hang On, Hurricane 195

The Big Muse 197

Love in the Zodiac 198

The Garage. 224
When God Calls You. 230
Certain Design. 247
Only Prayer 265
Your Time 265
To Make a Mark 270
Melissa. 277
Time 284
King of Kings. 303
Living In His Way 315
Beyond and Within 319
Black 328
Chaos Drafted 331
Lord Jesus 333
In His Honor on My Guard. 336
Be Separate, Says the Lord 338
Standing Firm in the Lord 348
Basil's Diner. 355
The Early Stage 355
Great Physician 361
A Living Light 372
A Proverb a Day. 379
Circus of Sin 404
The Good News. 419
The Threshold 420

Preface

Reminiscing through the first two decades of my life flushed out what had influenced me for sixty years and still does. Recalling the times of my youth brought clarity and gave more meaning to my foundations.

Born with a learning disability I saw many situations in life differently. I am dyslexic. What made sense for me didn't always fit in society's box called normal. As a young adult deciding what were good for me and my creative imagination I chose to jump off the traditional treadmill of obligations in life. I turned away from marriage and job security. I began beating down my own artistic path as a diarist and then a lyricist in the beautiful lands of up-state New York.

Continuing life as an artist in California I was a laborer with two lives. I worked at different jobs only to enhance my writing and even lied to make my way in life. The temporary joys of physical life are what occupied my mind. Ending up in a grave was going to be the end result of whatever I did, so why not party? What I didn't know much about was the eternal soul within. I did not know my soul was spiritually dead, lifeless without the eternal life of Jesus. It was a soul destined for eternal suffering in hell. When Christ came into my life it was His love that united real joy in this life and life in all eternity. Time is once – reach for hope.

Acknowledgements

Thanks to my small family, extended family and friends for all the memories. My warmest thanks are especially for those wonderful loving times with my Father and Mother and Brother. Love you Ma.

Introduction

God didn't have to create me He did so for His good pleasure. Born in 1953 on a path of time designed by God, He was always the Potter shaping me as His piece of clay. As my young life unfolded I didn't know God for thirty six years. On August 20th 1989, He let me know Him, the love of His Son and that I was heaven bound. But those first twenty one years were filled with searching, and finding and then loss.

In 1974 I began writing a diary using longhand to regain my damaged memory from a traumatic brain injury. As the pen met the paper I critiqued my thoughts scratching out and adding words. The concussion kept causing me to forget and then remember. I enjoyed the labor of learning how to process a thought. The time it took a thought to travel down my arm and come out of my fingers to push the pen and see it on the paper was like a medicine. Holding those thoughts before my eyes rethinking and reshaping the words became therapeutic. Recalling memories and projecting new ideas began a thirty nine year friendship with the diary.

My hidden dyslexic condition had made consistent accurate school work impossible. Mistakes in life were mysterious. But with the diary accuracy was no longer a problem. I didn't need to consider what was grammatically proper in the construction of a sentence. I had no rules in reaching my main objective which was to capture and communicate my thoughts onto paper. Unbeknown to me my dyslexia also gave me an uncommon ability to look at life differently. The gift of dyslexia only added to my growing artistic way of expressing me. Along with my ever increasing writer's voice I expressed verbally to friends and family my feelings and viewpoints.

My West Coast years began in 1982 as an amateur lyric writer seeking to be a professional. At twenty nine years old I was told I was dyslexic for the first time. A woman I learned to love as one of my closest friends spotted my disability because she was dyslexic also. The mystery of decades of wondering why I made mistakes was solved. I wasn't stupid there was a reason why the numbers and words moved when I read them. There was no fixing it but I knew to avoid it.

My first seven California years were lived out with the goal of soliciting the music industry for a record deal. During those times my thoughts of grandeur and of life being a big deal, I drove a women's expensive Mercedes Benz and met some of the rich and famous. While possessing nothing of value but still holding a dream I worked at telemarketing jobs and acted on stage and for the camera in efforts to reach a dream. In truth I was a poor artist bunking on a plywood bed living in a garage in North Hollywood.

After hearing my lyrics sung live in Hollywood nightclubs and all the solicitation for a record deal came to a close the momentum of a dream slowed to nothing. After all the wooing words into all the ears of beautiful women they were but sweet nothings and they too left. All those thirty six years of so called 'living it up and living a dream' is my back story before a new life came for those last four years West coast sun.

The miracle of being born again was God's gift of salvation through faith in Jesus and I became spiritually alive. In my new life I was given bible truth and joy in this life with a growing faith to believe in heaven's eternal life. Old bad habits collided with new truth as the Holy Spirit established His new foundation in biblical teaching. After learning from the bible and learning from the Christian radio preachers I was led to the best of all churches. I learned of the spiritual strength and struggle of good and evil within. My greatest lesson came in knowing God would never leave me and He would finish what He started. My path through life is God's gift and heaven is just ahead.

Every true Christian's life is different but with the same calling. The Christian life is the most dynamic, most exciting and by far the greatest exhilarating gift God gives through His Son. He welcomes all to come and drink the water of salvation and His truth will cleanse and set you free.

Part I

New York—The Mystery Struggle

Chapter 1: Dyslexia

I was surrounded by fences in my very small backyard. My kneecaps massaged the grassless plot as I plowed paths through the dirt with my pudgy fingers. Scooping up the tiny granules of sand, I pushed and smoothed out trails, then flat roads for plastic, two-and-a-half-inch-tall World War II soldiers. Their mission was to safely escort the northeastern homemade wagon train west. A month earlier, my hands were full of earth and stained Popsicle sticks as I shaped and constructed an elaborate raised-road system. But it was destroyed during the struggle of Godzilla versus King Kong. I wasn't able to prevent my brother's feet from stomping my project back into the earth.

I whistled while I worked. As a recently accomplished whistler, I whistled everywhere I went. It was a comfortable, solitary source of amusement. I had a good thing going, and I quickly grew accustomed to rearranging my solo variations. I puffed my cheeks and blew *O* shapes over the heads of the infantry while on my knees surveying ahead. Notes flew out like little invisible parachutes as I wondered which way to twist the terrain and where to lead my convoy.

I considered creating a lake to cross, and then great mountains to overcome beyond. *Yes, to battle across the water and build a frontier fort. Of course, there'll be Indians. First I'll fight with the mighty Mohawks, then the Cherokee, and then onward through Apache territory.* As an eight-year-old seeking adventure, my thoughts varied. *If I dig deep enough, I might find an arrowhead.* My father knew someone who'd found a Mohawk Indian arrowhead. Our city had an Indian name: Schenectady. I didn't know what the name meant, but I knew the Indians had burned down the fort near the river. The early settlers lost that fight.

I dug a small trench fashioned after the Mohawk River. Peering from the hilltop at the end of Hamilton Street, I could almost see the river and the Erie Canal. My dad and mom drove us over the river when we went for ice cream. We watched speedboats with skiers jumping off the giant ramp. Yachts and ocean liners crawled along slowly, like turtles rolling in calm ripples. We scrutinized the floating luxury and licked our dripping cones along with the crowd as waves slapped the shoreline.

Blowing notes in sequence and variation, I reached for the garden hose. Maybe when it got hotter, my brother would come outside. I would squirt him, and we would have a hose fight with water balloons. My plan of action was worthy, and with the sun at my back, I knew I had time; I had all day.

I thought and worked and whistled all the while, making my own tunes. I breathed deliberately, shaping my lips for more than surrounding the food on a fork or crying out *uncle*. Uncle was the one word that could coax my brother into releasing me from his Tarzan scissor-lock leghold. I was always the alligator in his vise grip.

Suddenly I was no longer alone. I heard my whistle repeated. An echo? No, a person! I stood up to look around. The water kept running. I searched for someone who was moving. My whistle had a shifting shadow. It was with me, but it moved about. I was the hunter, but I was being hunted.

Cautiously, with small steps, my curiosity advanced into the only escape route: the alley. Step by step I tweeted between the double skyscraping houses. Twin two-story flats loomed over me like walls of a Colorado canyon. I craned my neck and peered into the rectangular tunnel of blue skies that only Sky King could fly through. That was one of my favorite Saturday-morning shows. Sky and his plane named the *Songbird* were the heroes, and always just a few days away.

My feet were planted next to my granny's small garden. We were never to mess it up. It was like a miniature grave site, but instead of a grave, there were four spectacular flowers and one tiny, twelve-inch pine tree.

My lips pinched out a longer, clearer call, declaring my new position. The reply bounced back instantly from up high. I was being observed from above. I turned and tilted my head straight back, peering upward. There, under the house's eave, thirty-five feet high, was a tiny, bright yellow bird. The bird took a little hop and bobbed its head slightly, giving me a cockeyed look as birds do. The mysterious echo was found. I was in awe. My gaze relaxed. The bird cocked its head and looked at me with its other eye. I turned my head and held my other eye to its eye. It was a duel of stares.

So far we spoke the same language, so I shot first with a simple whistle of chirp chat. The bird's chirp chat echoed exactly and faster. A challenge! The contest was on; the line was drawn. My new talent and pride were at stake. Like Little John and Robin Hood exchanging blows in broad daylight, we did it again and again: whistle, chirp, whistle, chirp. As this small bird and I ping-ponged our communication, I realized I was outmatched.

I blew what must have been a sincere note of trusting surrender. The victorious yellow bird willingly flew down and crowned my head. Again I was in awe! I held my breath. My lower jaw and lips shaped another donut hole. I wasn't tall enough to see its reflection in the window glass, but the little life stayed with me.

Tiny scratching fingers kneading my hair and scalp for a grip were searching for something else. I thought of our home for this new feathered friend. My *O*-shaped lips whispered a soft whistle, an answer to the bird's gentle questioning: "Yep, we're friends."

Inch by inch, chirp by chirp, I crept like a glacier down the cement walk. Uh-oh! I was walking in the overflowing water from the hose. Soldiers were lying on their backs; some were facedown in the stream and bumping off my toes. I stood on enormous pillars, hulking against the raging waters, determined to overcome life's changing obstacle course. The bird hung on.

I reached carefully for the invisible handles of balance. More tiny green soldiers floated down the walkway among the wagon train debris. My very own stream was heading for the sewer in the street. *Will the soldiers get to the river?* I wondered. I waded to the porch steps and through our downstairs doorway with the bird still clutching my hair.

The yellow barnacle began to peck my head. I resisted the urge to slap it. Ever so slowly, so as not to alarm the fowl, I tiptoed into the kitchen like a burglar, spy, or secret agent. My mom's small lunch party was hushed in amazement. Suddenly Aunt Susie's uncontainable exclamation, "Mikey's got a bird on his head," launched the bird into flight.

Finding each other from whistling may have been a small wonder, but a wonder just the same. My very first pet and I had communicated. The winged beauty was much more than the turtle. The turtle was a joint project, but neither my brother nor I took responsibility for its disappearance. A few weeks after it vanished, we discovered that its slow, determined walk carried it under the living-room rug. I was reaching for a toy under the couch when I felt the bump of its shell. I can't remember if the turtle was still breathing.

My new, airborne friend was named Kee-Kee Bird for his frantic *chirp, chirp, chirping*. He was the golden-feathered pilgrim, a yellow parakeet who found a home: a cage inside our cage. He rode on my finger or my head, and liked walking from shoulder to shoulder nipping at my earlobes. Turning my head brought us eye to eye, and we would bob our heads together. Hearing first his wings flapping at takeoff, I then felt a slight breeze and watched his feathers slice the air.

That memory has lived on ever since, and I hope it never gets lost. From then on, I've always looked up wondering what I could see or find. I still speak to birds, whistling flexible variations of *O's* and *U's,* with my lifetime friends answering.

✝

It was 1960. At seven years old in second grade, there were the usual ups and downs for me, same as for all kids. But something going on inside of me would often cause mistakes on the outside. When I played marbles, sometimes my inattention would hit my own colored marble out of the circle. Then my brother and my cousin would laugh and ask why I was doing that. I didn't know why. They'd call me stupid or retard. Those names hurt even though we were kids kidding around.

Simple mistakes appeared, like passing food in the opposite direction at the table during supper. If someone asked for the salt, I'd pass the pepper sometimes—but not all the time. Or I'd open a can of soda with the can opener at the wrong end of the can. I knew better, but somehow I made the wrong choice anyway. My mom would correct me, and life went on. But I saw what I did. I felt the wrong, and I would often pause in a blank stare. I knew the difference between salt and pepper, but why I grabbed the wrong one I didn't know.

The way I thought or saw things, the way I used my hands, either independently or combined, often resulted in mistakes. Though not always bad, gaffes would appear, sometimes with and sometimes without a pattern. Like turning the knob on the TV the wrong way or running the wrong way while playing tag.

At times my vague perception of knowing that mistakes would somehow pop up made me feel isolated. My own disappointment and the comments or laughter of others somehow marred me on the inside. My sense of awkwardness unexpectedly broke in and took away some space from my inner comfort. I never knew the cause; I could only feel the discomfort. I stood gawking at a stupid mistake I made that left me feeling alone as I meandered in the halls of childhood. No one else realized I was hurt.

Reading out loud in school was confusing. Answering wrongly on math questions would often cause snickers or even loud laughter. How could fifteen plus six be anything but twenty-one? My answer of twelve was so much more than just wrong. But I was labeled as a kid not trying hard enough. My so-called carelessness was really my undiscovered dyslexia.

Dyslexia was a live alien relative secretly living within me and causing sporadic trouble. So close within and so fast was its strange power that it would switch the words my eyes saw with a different image. Words coming out of my mouth weren't what were written on the page. Like a phantom, dyslexia breathed with me closer than a shadow, and yet it remained as elusive as passing time. School was at times like being tied to a whipping post. Each student in each row would read aloud.

With my turn nearing, my eyes would scan ahead and estimate my portion of sentences. While the student ahead of me read aloud, I drilled my eyes onto my words and read silently. I tried to hurry so I could reread my portion, but I could hear and see my mistakes in my head. I tried to appear calm, but my breath was small. I could feel the heat under my shirt. I read aloud and got through the first sentence, but then the soundless inner disorder exploded to the surface. Words that were there were not read, and words that were not there were read in their place. The chaos and panic covered me. Again I was trapped in a cage with my strange secret troublemaker. My face felt hot. I was stuck between classmates snickering and the teacher asking me to read it again, this time more slowly.

There were questions never asked, and therefore the answers were never looked for. So the unexplainable, obviously stupid school mistakes became a source of amusement for the class. Snickers and grinning kids pushed my frantic eyes and forehead into the floor. The grains in the hardwood became competing rivers running side by side, carrying me anywhere from there. When the last bell rang, I was up and out, swiftly moving away from the war zone. Some relief came playing in my small, fenced-in, dirt, grassless backyard surrounded by two-story houses.

But lingering embarrassment from school often made the backyard feel like a fishbowl and I was the fish. The neighbors' accusing faces looked down from their windows. Eyes staring down at me, or noisy curtains closing, caused an ill feeling of being under surveillance. But that same awkwardness and self-consciousness became a passage in which I found my escape into imagination. It's a curious thing, the imagination. It could become a loose cannon that might find a way to sink those thoughts into darkness or blast free the possibilities of artistic talent.

✝

For Christmas we got new shiny bicycles and rode them in our stone-walled basement until spring. The old house had a foundation carved out of rock. The dark place was so black I felt the scary madness mounting the walls. One bright light bulb over my dad's cluttered workbench hung and swung as shadows jumped. A few other bulbs would flicker along a flimsy black wire to the corner full of old piled coal. Several feet below the ground and without windows, we held flashlights looking for arrowheads within the walls themselves. We knew our city once had a fort filled with pilgrims and Indian fighters. Downtown by the river in the stockade area, there was a tall iron statue of an Indian named Lawrence, of the Mohawk Nation. In one battle the Mohawk Indians fought back hard enough to win the fort and then burned it down. The cellar at night was definitely the worst scariest place to be. When someone turned off the light from upstairs and you were down there, you just screamed for mercy. Tripping through the cobwebs running up the steep wooden stairs was the only escape route back to normal. Linoleum floors never felt so good. Once the snow was gone, so were my brother and I, on bikes.

Spring air powered through our lungs and gave new life to our pedal-pushing legs blasting off cabin fever. As we grew, so did the city. Our area of travel increased, and we explored new streets with excitement. I always had to catch up to Ken, who was two years older and ten times stronger. There were just the two of us weaving and bobbing on and off the sidewalks. In the 1950s and early 60s, the streets were safe places to enjoy and learn about life. We were careful dodging between hot rods and crossing streets that sounded like drag strips. Sharpening our instincts, we were always looking ahead.

The slow- or high-speed balancing act on two wheels with no hands would launch inner and outer harmony. We were off our feet and flying. Finding the easiest route to keep moving, always to keep moving was our way and mean between adventures. We coasted down hills on sunshiny days with as much fun as a hands-free high-wire act at the circus. Reaching the pond or a stream to cool off near Central Park was like a brief oasis akin to the lake. We soaked our feet and talked about the sights on our ride; it was so cool and time went slowly.

Returning, we slowly pushed the pedals down as we went uphill.

Each leg thrust turned the tires inches as we fought to be balanced getting closer to the top. A few times we needed to walk. Back on top saddled on our bikes again made riding more worthwhile. With wind at our backs or in our faces, we loved the freedom. Living the adventure of finding the next new place always brought us back home hungry.

†

In third grade in 1961, the silent dyslexic foe remained anonymous and would often ambush me in school. Its stealth subtly produced outward errors without a steady pattern. My troubles went untended to. My foundational years of learning were built on a shifting stone of uncertainty with mysterious effects.

The flip side of dyslexia is the gift of intuitiveness. I could see through a situation quickly and determine if it were interesting or not. When my interest wasn't enticed and captured, boredom was found easily. Then drifting into thought came naturally as I turned my head to look out the windows and imagine. Life's windows of possibilities were more fascinating than just the twelve glass panes in the tall classroom windows.

One wall in each of the old fourteen-foot-high schoolrooms was nearly all glass. Just outside the glass in my third-grade room, there were large trees, with active moving branches and birds fluttering among the leaves. The great outdoors was a launchpad for me to dream. Castles in the sky were my escape route, holding only the good that I remember from that room. Like the long narrow cloakroom, with thirty kids taking off winter boots and coats with swinging arms and legs. Laughing, and falling was great fun before we sat on our wooden chairs trying to give attention.

†

OUTSIDE

When I recall my daze as a youth,
Learning was law, like telling the truth.
Sin was to look out through the window;
Eyes on the book, don't let your mind go.

> Some kids aren't content dreaming at night;
> Some will dream in school, dream in the light.

Smoke rings and birds' wings, they rise Outside together,
Oh a cloud to ride, Outside in the weather.

Moonbeams and day dreams, they rise Outside together,
Oh, a cloud to ride, Outside like a feather.

> Some kids aren't content dreaming at night;
> Some must dream in school, dream in the light.

With my supply of total unrest,
Wiping my eye, turn out in protest,
Start again new, fly up in the sky,
Away I flew, drifting, drifting by.

That summer after failing third grade, I lived in denial with my family in our home at the lake. My denial was a bomb, with a long fuse burning slowly. My parents hoped I wouldn't become a serious problem by acting out in rage the reality of my setback. We all wanted to enjoy the time away from the city. My rides up to camp were captured and dipped in gold. Our family's seasonal drives shine as some of my best memories. The lake was the best place on earth, a land of challenge and fun.

Our nature home was surrounded with the sweet smell of pines. Bolting out of our back door after breakfast was our routine. Then my brother and I would climb the easy limbed trees. We pushed past branches going up or lay on the fallen needles to hide and seek. The pine pitch always found my brother and me and stayed with us. Running through the yellow sands of Cowboy Country, we were Lone Ranger and Rin Tin Tin. Even playing baseball in the vacant sandlot wasn't pitch-free. Somehow the sticky pine sap would show up on the foul ball. The week of the Fourth of July, our hands were washed extra clean. We didn't want the firecrackers sticking to our fragrant pine-pitch fingers or the lit matches. Cherry bombs and ash cans were the scariest and the loudest, and the most desired.

Hot-dog picnics with watermelon-juice smiles led to rocking sleepily in the hammock under the pines. As long as we were outside, we were happy. Roasting marshmallows with quiet snapping fires under the blanket of blackness, we saw faraway snowflake stars. We laughed as we tried to count them all, and the white specks filled my eyes before sleep. In the still-quiet hour of exhausted darkness, Pa's arms scooped us up and we sailed to the bunk beds. Ma rubbed cool Noxzema cream on our sunburns.

It was the water, Galway Lake, that held the most power to draw us into fun and adventure. I outgrew and exchanged the city's concrete trouble with playing in the beach sand and wearing a snorkel and face mask. The shimmering water played tag with my breath at eye level. Treading like a unicycle on a high wire, I was Tarzan, halted by the invented submerged crocodile for combat. Twisting in circles, kicking, bobbing for air, tail-whipped, I was sunk for dead. With the light of life above flickering through the shade of clean freshwater, hope surged, and freely my inner call for salvation was answered. I floated above the fluid earth; I grabbed a breath to fight yet other unknown deepwater foes. The jungle warrior cut through the unknown ocean like a catamaran on our freshwater lake. I recouped, sucking in deep flat breaths and shifting my sandy back on the shore of safe sunburns.

I gazed about, searching colonial blue skies with plate-sized gum-ball clouds. I saw smiling whipped cream-fringed Santa Claus faces. My squinting eyes filtered sunshiny diamond sparkles darting off bathtub-warm water. Returning waves to waving sails on silent boats, I basted my bronze body. Wisps of syrupy orange tufts caught the burning balls' beauty before sinking. With Marco Polo eyes, I searched the gathering, the unfolded glimpses of heaven's delicacies digesting my contentment. Sunset Beach satisfied the sweet tooth on the day's menu for action heroes.

Running to the beach and diving in or jumping from the dock into the freshwater became my world. Nearly sleeping on the hot sand, turning red or rolling to the water's edge, we were always on the move. We were one of many families continually cycling in and out of the water for relief. I lounged between camp and the beach as one more chapter filled in the story of innocent youth. Summer seemed endless until our last big party on Labor Day arrived. Then we cleaned up, packed up, and drove past all the farms down to the city. The ride was like watching the slowly rolling credits of a great movie as we saw familiar landmarks. The summer had passed; it was the end of the good times. It was time to start school.

I didn't know the elements involved with rational and irrational thinking; all I knew was what I did. I suppose as the preparation with new clothes and supplies was undertaken, there were also discussions. I'm sure reality was discussed, along with encouragement. But the truth that I failed third grade was still pushed down deep inside of me. I did not want to look at the fact that I needed to repeat it.

✝

In September 1962, the first day of school came. Even though I had rehearsed the truth of repeating third grade with my mother, I still didn't accept it. My brother and I walked together like we always did, but we were silent. My defiance was mine alone.

I stood firm in the fourth-grade line outside of school. Students were pointing and whispering words that carried shame and hopelessness around my downcast eyes. I stood in line, at the back of the line, in the line for the fourth-grade students. Between the third- and fifth-grade lines, my shifting eyes could not be lifted up; my face was down like a plow sunk into concrete. I did not want to see the reality, but I could hear the familiar whispers and giggles. Some students gathered eagerly, happy to see each other after the summer's fun and adventure. Boys and girls anticipating the next rung on the learning ladder of life listened as the nuns commanded obedience to stay in your lines. One of the sisters marched up to me, grabbed my arm, and pulled me over to the third-grade line. Not one word was said. I stood there until she left and then stepped back into the fourth-grade line.

That confrontation was witnessed by the priest across the street. He stood on the church steps smoking a cigarette and blowing out smoke. Perhaps someone in the cars passing by saw me in my disobedience and contrasted it with the good report cards of his or her child. I didn't think about God watching. Any fear about God that was drilled into me by the nuns was not applied. My rejection of the truth had been reinforced all summer long. I was firm, and then like a teakettle whistle blows at boiling, the bell rang. It was suddenly not an immediate issue because all the doors were opened and a few hundred excited children entered the building and climbed the stairs. Going up, I wanted to move on and be like everybody else.

I wanted to be in the fourth-grade classroom, so I walked in and sat down. I sat there sweating, waiting for something to happen, sitting on a volcano of truth. A nun came in and without a word grabbed my arm and began pulling me. I was within myself; she couldn't pull me out. I could hear noises but not hear voices; I was there in my shell. I stiffened my body, my fingers frozen to the wooden chair. She said, "You don't belong here." Everyone heard her, but I sat staring down like a lifeless mannequin. Another nun came in, and the two of them pried my hands loose, lifted me up to my feet, and then forced me out of the room. I alone heard my inner scream. My face of fear froze my arms and legs, which moved at first but then resisted. Those black and white legless figures without feeling returned me to the third-grade classroom. They pushed me down into my last year's seat and desk in my exact old spot. Bending over, one of the guards uttered through her clenched teeth, "Stay here." I could smell the stale cigarette smoke on her breath and garb. Both stood outside the door with their invisible arms folded in the shroud.

I was swirling in shame. Breathlessly I sucked in air and hated tasting the truth. The wall of windows, where I had many, many times cast my eyes and thoughts, once again became a harbor of tranquility. Once again I looked at the large tree, with the familiar seasonal green leaves soon to be changing color to a burned orange. I found my old friends, the leaves, and the birds waved at me. There were no pains in those huge twelve-foot windows. The sky welcomed me and released my thoughts into the great outdoors. That passageway was the freedom of inspiration that led me to engage my imagination. That tree was more than a tree; it was independence, it was climbing, it was outside, it was fun, and it was where I wanted to be. But the sharp voice of the nun, the taskmaster, cracked.

My head bobbed up. Naked history was repeated before me. My old classroom walls hung last year's lessons like sour meals ready to be dished out again. Familiar collages hung and nodded, and the same jungle animals caught in a photo remained silent and stared. They were bitter leftovers. It was good to see the backs of the new students' heads and not their eyes. I was alone and staring down. The delayed movie of summer fun had passed, and the new movie of truth was hard to watch. When I heard laughter, I glared. My rage burned the remaining fuse on the bomb of my denial. My inner explosion caused truth to surface. My view turned away from reality, and looking out and up, I wanted to fly.

✝

OUT THOSE WINDOWS

Turning from details on blackboards,
Daydreamers find their own rewards.
Looking beyond dyslexia,
Blueprint school, so hard to see ya.

Where to go somehow, Out Those Windows,
Looking out windows, past the framework of shadows,
Still looking out windows, past pains separate me now,
Where to go somehow, Out Those Windows.

Treetop castaways, neighbor's laundry waves,
Mash-potato clouds, quietly out loud,
Restless baggage sails Out Those Windows.

Search for grades; in the twilight sun,
Clues fade, homework is never fun,
Mistakes made, third grade twice, he's lazy,
Potential, but hazy, that summer I went crazy.

Where to go somehow, Out Those Windows,
Looking out windows, past the framework of shadows,
Still looking out windows, past pains separate me now,
Where to go somehow, Out Those Windows.

—————————— † ——————————

I sat sulking until my mom came and got me before lunch. We went home and we both cried. I screamed and kicked. She held me with a mother's love and told me that it would be okay and that she and Pa would make it better. The mess did not immediately go away; I was soundly stuck in it. There was no outward escape from my daily embarrassment, my stupidity, and my failure. I wanted something else but didn't know what. I was someone I did not want to be. There was nowhere to go to get away from my inner mystery struggle. The alien within and I were a life lived together. I was a square peg, and all the other kids were more rounded pegs, with far fewer edges. Everyone was being steered or trying to be fitted in round holes. The education system took the shape of a mallet. Daily poundings hurt some of us more than others. School was a place where they were going to fit us kids in.

For me, it was impossible to fit in. Encouragement or embarrassing ridicule, nothing could trim off my corners and help me to be installed into the pegboard of life. Living meant being a daily misfit who couldn't find where he belonged. It doesn't matter who determined it or why I was classified a failure. What mattered was the F mark. Being branded with an F was what kids made fun of and parents' voices got low when they spoke of it.

Time dragged on. There was no fun or new adventures; each day was a season. In that school I would see my old classmates every day above and beyond me, smiling, laughing, and enjoying life. My parents tried to help and paid a high school girl to tutor me. The only thing that got help was the answers on my homework. But I was not happy. There was no getting away from the day-to-day despair of going to school. When the last school bell rang out each day, I rose up like a shot thundering through the battle. A little relief came with my hands rubbing the earth in the backyard, shaping a path.

✝

Two decades would pass before I even heard the word *dyslexia* spoken for the first time. I would be far away from the timely youthful years when defects could be considered, handled, and adjusted for. My slipups were brushed off as childish quirks that were still yet to be worked out. Nothing to be alarmed about—that's what they thought. Arguably dyslexia's impact as an elusive broken cog in the gears of my thinking process carried over into all areas of my life. Dyslexia is certainly an alien relative still causing sporadic trouble in my life, but it has also been a vehicle of creative blessings.

How I processed information was just as important a foundation as schooling itself. In 1962, the help I needed wasn't offered in schools. My awkwardness in learning sharpened my self-consciousness. Shaky primary steps in education grew into strength-forming perseverance. Imagination helped in blasting me away from trying to fit into the traditional "thinking in the box." Where my thoughts were going wasn't as important as the reconciliation I found in the escape. My mind's eye or imaginings were planted. Learning challenges and "thinking out of the box" were on my young path toward the threshold.

✝

The twelve-foot-wide alleyway between houses emptied onto the sidewalk and then into the narrow, two-lane Hamilton Street. When cars parked on both sides, traffic was very tight. Large, long painted metal and shiny chrome sedans passed by like railroad cars with big windows. Sleek hot-rod coupes wormed through the slow flow, revving their engines. With just two seats, no fenders, roof, or motor cover, they gunned the motor and shot off in the straightaways. Everything was crowded. Houses were full of families who clustered on their porch and steps. Joe Public walked, stood, or sat in the doorways up and down the cramped street day or night. The urban scene was a larger fishbowl. I was just one quiet kid in the spotty bunches of noisy people.

Once there was a man with a pinto pygmy pony walking in the neighborhood taking pictures. The small horse packed a small kid's cowboy outfit and a white or a black hat. Ma had our Polaroid pictures taken, and I was a real cowboy sitting in the saddle like the Lone Ranger. It was a thrilling one-shot miniature movie start to finish. I wanted to ride that pony, not just sit on it. A few houses later, the same scene took place with another little kid. The man and the pony traveled; they weren't stuck or in a store selling photos. The old man earned his money and kept going. I liked watching their motion of coming and going. I liked the idea of moving on and that the man had his friend, a small pony.

There were no trees along the street. Anything natural was replaced with cement and blacktop. The only sky was above me, mostly in rectangle shapes except for the hill. Down the street at the edge of Hamilton Hill was the highest point in the city of Schenectady. With the exception of the hill at the end of the block, where tall trees stood, there was no other outlet for my eyes to drift and find peace. I was lured by the hills' view of the millions of trees in the distant forests. The hilltop still sticks out in my memory as one of my favorite places to visit.

Looking out far beyond the Mohawk River into hundreds and hundreds of miles of green and colored treetops was a peaceful adventure. There were no people, no racial divides, no tension with prejudicial words, just constant trees in a natural setting of tranquility.

How often I would look back to my childhood and visualize that great and wonderful view. That outlook was the starting point from which I traveled with my thoughts to the other life over the river. Out there was my family's summer home; Galway Lake was my only escape from the city and the alien within. Like from a tunnel, I peered out of the increasing and changing population year after year. The trees grew opposite the chattering arena of public affairs.

From the hilltop I could see past and above Schenectady with great expectations. Knowing for sure when school was out we would move was a helpful attitude adjustment. Each spring and autumn, we all raked pine needles at camp and jumped on the itchy piles. Pa would burn mountains of brown needles blazing red-hot, and thick white smoke rose. The smoke smell hung in the boughs. As he threw more on the pile of needles, the snowy cloud would burn our eyes.

There was lots of love in our family. Driving the country roads laughing as we rolled, turning into curves or feeling flighty, going fast over hilltops was fun. Going for giant dishes of ice cream was the best. Those times we all rode together, just the four of us, created unforgettable memories. At times there was just Ma, my brother, and me, without my dad. When my dad would arrive to round out the four-unit family, another scene would often play out—a more dramatic scene than anything on the local TV channels.

My worried mother, who carried the weight of the world, had her worst assumptions come true as Pa walked in late drunk again. In would totter my father, three sheets to the wind, as happy as an Irishman leaving the pub and landing on his doorstep could be. He swayed in with a cap on his head and a cheery grin beaming complete happiness. He was ambushed by my brother and me. We would wrap ourselves around his tall legs, securing our holds like rodeo cowboys. He rubbed his bowling-ball knuckles against our heads saying, "Time for knuckle-dusters." We were hauled through the shadowy hallway laughing and getting tickled and then thrown up on the living room couch by his vine-like arms. We laughed with him and repeated the toss, happily answering yes to his question, "Are you being good?"

As loving as my father was, he was defenseless. My father warred against the relentless overpowering disease of alcoholism. He got lots of help from my mother, who was strong in her resolve to have a happy family. She learned it from her mom. Granny lived in the upstairs flat alone. I never knew my real grandfather, who was also an Irishman; I did get to love his replacement, PaPa. PaPa was a thoroughbred horse trainer's assistant from the Ukraine. He traveled the racetrack circuit in America, returning with baskets of fruit and silver dollars. A few times he came back from his seasonal travels with a puppy for us. But they wouldn't last. They ran out of an opened door into the traffic twenty feet away. We only heard the tires screech and saw the door close.

The promise of another puppy always came with the future condition known as someday. For me to hear the phrase "when the time is right" always gave me hope. It was also a comfort to see Ma and Pa hug and show love. Their love brought harmony to the jagged edges of our family. Ma would find peace of mind in the kitchen cooking. Baking was her specialty; she would sing along to her favorites on the radio like "You Only Hurt the One You Love." My brother and I would be listening to Elvis singing "Hound Dog" while we played with toys or games on the floor. Over and over I played that record, singing and jumping on the bed. I loved it, and I loved the idea of having a dog. *Old Yeller* was my favorite movie. The dog and the boy grew up together. The dog gave unconditional love and protection but finally got hurt to save the boy. Then the boy had to destroy the very dog he loved because of an incurable sickness. They both did what they had to do out of love. That part of the movie always made me sad. The dog's sacrifice for the boy I understood, but how the boy could shoot the dog was too difficult to accept.

✝

Sunday morning in my youth brought some good, along with an annoying irritant of a different type. Like coming in out of the rain, but you track mud on the rug. There would be my mother telling us not to drag our feet and get ready for church. In due course, she'd have to push the legs of my brother and me into the nice pants with creases. My resentment of my mother's cattle prodding was nothing compared to my father's.

Hearing his mix of mumbled cursing to jovial commands to "get ready" bellowing from the bathroom was funny. His voice carried seriousness, but with the tone of standing calmly in line at a clambake. Smelling his cigarette smoke mixed with the shaving cream fragrance boosted my senses in the weekly ritual. Sink water gurgled down the drain, leaving a few thousand fallen black beard specks behind. He emerged a victorious casualty. My eyes fell on his face, a calculated patchwork of tissue—perhaps the engineering was learned in the field of war from a medic of a MASH unit? The beard fought back and caused injuries before its daily defeat. Pa's attempts to cover the shaving nicks looked like strawberries on vanilla ice cream. A new cigarette on fire hanging from his lips was pinched with his big fingers. He smiled at us boys, blowing out a victorious smoke ring.

He looked like the picture on *Life* magazine of a true war veteran, which he was. His fight was never with us; he always tried to be a good dad when we were around. Behind my mother's back, he would hand us dollar bills or pockets of change with a whispered, "Don't tell your mother." But once Ma and Pa were out of our sight, we could hear the bickering, the protests, the dos and don'ts of drinking. Their disagreement found a way to travel with time, as it constantly ran parallel to change.

My mom and dad married for love. And she loved and married a man who didn't drink. It was the operation he had on the GI Bill that tipped the balance. Surgery fixed his stomach's bad wiring, which then allowed him to drink. After the honeymoon period, they both found my dad fighting in another war with a silent enemy on the inside. And for the first time, in his late twenties he could have a drink with the boys. The bad guy in the battle was called Misery, and he was waiting to happen. Misery's specific name in our household was called beer. Maybe it was my dad's Irish gene or memories of World War II that demanded a drink. Whatever Pa's causes were, the effects of Misery were seen and felt by us all.

Perhaps it was a similar scenario that had been played out for centuries with soldiers. Or was it even bigger than a human battle? Was it sin? All we could do was watch and wonder. We three men bonded with moans against my mother's marching Sunday crusade to the Catholic Church. Pa was handsome and liked looking good and wearing nice clothes. But the idea of pretending to be good and look nice irritated him. He didn't like to do that, and he didn't like phonies; and at church, he had both. If there was any time of the week when the most chaos would accumulate, it was on Sunday mornings in our house before church. It was as if Satan himself were standing there throwing grenades of discord among us as we scurried about. We were fighting against ourselves, against time. Unfortunately Sunday felt like a sliver that got squeezed into the rest of the week. The annoyance didn't feel right until you got it out of the way and got back to normal.

I never resented the clock more than with its face screaming go, go, go, and its hands pushing us out the door. Ma was beautiful. All dressed up and with her family in tow, that's what she loved. We were the dolls in her house, ready to be taken out for show-and-tell. City streets were serene back then on the first day of the week, and the Sunday blue laws were enforced. Businesses shut their doors, and the whole city was slowed down to take a rest. It was nice. Church families walked slowly together, and mothers wore corsages. Everybody was seen in their Sunday best and on their best behavior, at least for a few hours.

Somehow "our best" was an expectation seldom met. Time whipped by and lashed out increased levels of confusion. Muttering tones of resentment shuffled along with us into the car as we sped away toward the ringing bell. The church bell was attention-grabbing. We joined streams of nicely dressed families with their nice kids in tow. All the pants had creases. All were filing into the open doors like southbound dark specks of geese in the high sky answering an unheard call. Pa sucked a cigarette one last draw with other men near the doors. A few still had red dotted tissue on their faces. I watched for more smoke rings as the last ring of the church bell rang and the doors closed.

All were slipping into pews ready to begin the outward calisthenics of worship. Sitting there searching the stained glass and wondering why we did not have any in our house wasn't enough to keep me occupied initially. Even if my brother and I were separated, we still managed to negotiate some kind of duel fidgeting. That prompted my mother's stern looks and her sharp "schuss's." Being told to fold our hands and pay attention did not make listening to Latin any easier. Whatever chaos erupted at our house and then got crowded into the car was ushered into the church. The mysterious mass of confusion was all trying to stand up at the same time and then sit all at once. There was no choice; there was just duty to be performed. Church was an extraordinary fishbowl, a gathering of supposed seriousness. At times it did feel like God was watching.

I was to stay in God's good favor. I was told that God was always watching. That is not a bad thing to be told. But I was only taught to fear Him. It was an unhealthy fear of punishment. All I knew was that God punished people for their black marks, or sins. My instructions were to work hard to keep my soul white, not spotted with black sins.

But I never could, no matter how hard I tried. I was always looking on the inside at my spots. That's all I knew. I never knew the love of God, how He gave His Son as a sacrifice on the cross to pay the penalty for my sins. I may have heard it, but I didn't know it. The statue of Jesus on the cross would always get my attention. It was kind of scary; the fear would flicker on and off at times and eventually wore off. My conscience would speak, and I would listen to the warnings. But I never understood God's love or how to live a life of loving Him back. In church, we were supposed to be quiet and good. We were flanked by strategically placed nuns, all called Sisters, a show of force to instill perpetual goodness. The mission of the Sisters was to observe children and point with wagging fingers.

I must admit there was something special about Sunday. Every family had a place to be together for a while. I believed then that the calm design was intended for families to be together and eat a big meal. I never understood the cross or its power to change lives.

✝

When I tried to repeat third grade that September into October 1962, it didn't work. My brother moved further ahead. Staying behind crushed me. He did not have the same wiring upstairs as I carried. Being learning disabled was my injury in life, and it had to be accepted. But I didn't know that. I had no way to deal with the mysterious wound that wouldn't heal. Mistakes on the outside continued, and I learned to lower their impact. But the scar on the inside never did heal. School left a bad taste, with many more bitter meals ahead of me. The mystery of it all was mine alone. However, my problem became everyone's problem in autumn of 1962. Soon my mother's words telling me that she would fix it were coming true.

Our family moved away like the Pilgrims. We moved away from persecutions of the city into a suburban house of our own, a new world. We had a big yard in the back and one in the front. We even had land between the houses. Trees were all around us, and there was another promise of a soon-to-arrive puppy. Best of all was the news that I would be going to a new school, where no one knew me. I stood at the top of the hill at the end of my old street. Staring out over the distance, I looked long into the magnificent New England landscape of living color. Something out there gave me tranquility and rest again and again. Serenity always drew closer with that view. We were moving, and that view I would take. That emotion of peace I would carry with me always.

There never seems to be one reason why something is right or wrong. Reasons add up, and the scales tip toward decision. My stay in the city came to a close due to a combination of rights and wrongs. My mom and dad needed to be out on their own, not living in a flat beneath my grandmother. Schenectady's population was increasing and changing the traditional neighborhoods. There was a hostility talked about among parents. More residents and differences of values caused some homeowners to sell and move out. To my parents' surprise, Aunt Susie's husband, Uncle Shawn, offered to cosign on my parents' mortgage. At my baptism, Uncle Shawn was my godfather. Their house was our favorite family place to visit. Aunt Susie always hid candy for Ken and me to find.

In 1962, we were standing on our new property. The sun shone bright and golden elm tree leaves were dropping like leaflets of good news and joy. My mom's promise came true, and Christmas was only seven weeks away. In our new house, we all were excited and enthusiastic. I unpacked my old stuff with exhilarating thoughts of where to put it. Even my feelings of going to a new school held anticipation. At the same time as I unpacked hope, the sad truth of my mystery struggle was there. With it on a shelf of its own in my thoughts, I'd wonder how it would be in school. That winter, the white fell graciously from the sky. Several times I looked up high through the branches of our trees, and the feeling of peace fell on me. I loved the sensation of a fresh clean start covering the dirty hurts.

Chapter 2: Latchkey Kids

We were not a praying family or people who read the Bible, so we did not know what the truth of God was. Our reasons and choices why we tried to think good or do something good were not guided by wisdom. Moving was the good means of staying together and getting second chances, with a fresh start closer to the trees. We unpacked our boxes higher up over and beyond into the suburbs on the edge of rural America. Our property had a dozen tall trees, with lawns circling the house. Grass was ours, and not just in a park. It seemed like a country garden and a white picket fence for Ma. The occasional car passing by wasn't noticed much in all of the quiet. Our suburban community bordered farmlands with long winding roads without streetlights. The sense of freedom was in the clean air, over the quiet land, and the space consumed me. Joy and relief were planted in my new views, and the call for adventure flourished.

Thirty feet past the house stood the most interesting building: a large six-stall garage, with five inviting barn doors. As big as the house or bigger, the garage was a haven, with seven nine-paned windows that swung in on hinges. The openness was like having a roof over the great outside, with the breeze rushing through at the same time. I marveled at the mix of being within walls and nearly outside, shade and sunshine, a fort and a playground. We could hear train whistles far off but not so far off, calling our ears to attention. Closer and closer came the clanking and then rumbling over tracks. Pa took us down the street a quarter mile or so from our house to stand near the rolling steel boxes. "I'm telling you guys never, never go any closer than we are now," he taught us. Like an abrupt summer storm, the massive chaos jangled out of sight. We could hear the train's whistle far off calling out good-byes.

Geese honking in the cloudless blue pierced the placid residential atmosphere. The wedge of harmony waved overhead and pulled my eyes with their southbound magnet. Tops of giant elms, maples, and pine trees made me crane my head back to see the source of their shedding foliage. Birds darted and squirrels leaped; pinecones fell and we dove into hills of brown pine needles and wrestled. I gazed up, gaping at those red and yellow, bright orange, shiny autumn parachutes. Leaves surfed sideways and downward as gravity slowly pulled, landing them with a faint swishing sound. Calm, quiet, breezy branches transferred their peace to me. I breathed in the all-new world, which brought a sense of healing. The weight of an excruciating time in my life was lifted. My mom and dad said they would make things better, and they did.

The transplant came and the newness started just weeks before Christmas in 1962. It was a thrill to think of different adventures bike riding. Would we get another dog and new school friends? Excitement went beyond all our expectations. We were drawn to life's party. There was happiness in our home. We were a family at dinner and at night with our new portable black and white TV. Ma was home all day baking and singing with the music on the radio. She talked on the phone to relatives and old friends about all our excitement and news updates. Each version of events contained the storybook white picket fence out front.

A big change came in with the next new year in 1963. Ma kept her promise and brought home one more puppy. This one was black and easy to spot in the snow. When my dad came home from work each evening that week, he was met at the door by the thundering barking of a puppy. Its tail hammered against the trash container drumming out a joyful surprise faster and faster the closer my dad got. Opening the door my dad exclaimed, "It sounds like Thunder," and the name stuck on the dog for the next seventeen years.

✝

SATISFIED

Sunday morn ease, low traffic tide,
Smiles, nods, and waves on my side,
Childlike warming summer fun,
Harmony rides, carousels run.

Enchanted feet, semi-dancing gait,
Streams of electric eyes can't wait,
Bubblegum pops, picks, and chews,
Inside brew all the ah's and ewoo's.

Satisfied, I'm so Satisfied.
A circus size, happy life, ice cream dome,
I got a dog, we run and play, I've got a home,
Satisfied, I'm so Satisfied, Satisfied, I'm so Satisfied.

My number shines on bingo calls,
School yards scream for red bouncing balls.
I pray, "Thank you, Lord," each sunrise,
Looking up for today's surprise.

✝

Thunder brought more than just new life into our family. Somehow he equaled out whatever was missing. His friendship smoothed out my rough places when alone. He brought harmony after my parents' outbursts from alcohol's chaotic cause and effect. He was always a tail-wagging, happy-go-lucky puppy. Being the fifth family member, he possessed the sage-like quality of a soothing balm. We could all love him and be loved by him unconditionally. He was with us in our worst times and always gave his best.

Walking and training Thunder both on and off a leash was necessary for lots of good safety reasons. The last walk in the evening, we found that the suburban streets at night were without people. The avenues of white dotted streetlights were contrasted by the yellowish warm glow from indoor house lights. Walking by those front yards and glancing into the windows, I saw picture frames hanging on the walls and things positioned to be seen. A TV's silent flickering glow looked familiar. A dog barking for attention at a window would pause and stare, wishing it were Thunder. Only the late winter and spring cold nights would cause us to get home faster. Sometimes I'd be coming home from a friend's house, and Thunder would find me. He'd been out walking and came running up to me all happy, and then we would race with each other all the way home.

The change of seasons brought warmer spring days for our bikes to hit the new territory. Adventure began with simple pleasures, like seeing a friendly face from school in a front yard. Finding railroad tracks that led to dirt paths to follow took Ken and I exploring. Our time after school was one discovery after another.

The increased pressure for more money to pay more bills fell on my mother. I saw how money issues caused her to hold her head and face with her hands. Pa's intentions to tip the scales toward doing something good fell short of real change. My father had become someone else, someone not himself. I heard muffled arguing, and we all felt the loss and heartache that come from being in debt. His inadequacy to be the guiding, providing leading member of the family became apparent. The alcohol kept him away from home.

When my mother announced her upcoming absence, it was with love and much regret. In 1964, when I was in fifth grade, my brother and I became latchkey kids. I was eleven years old when Ma gave up some of her home life and went to work. We tried the new American connivance of TV dinners, but to our family, they were a joke. Ma was a cook and loved doing it. We loved her cooking, so she cooked on weekends and worked on school days. The quality and quantity of my mother's love for her children was bargained away by meeting obligations. Her heart was not in being absent from us, but she wanted a good home for her boys so more time was exchanged for more money. We went from being a family together sharing the morning to getting rushed hugs and good-byes with love from Ma and Pa. Money came and left as did Ma and Pa, but the bills stayed. The white picket fence was just for show. It didn't keep good in or bad out.

Being alone more meant Ken and I were tested with being responsible. Aside from our chores, I grew with less guidance and accountability in my trials and errors. My time became a self-centered experiment without feedback or concern due to the absence of a parent's watchful eyes.

Ken and I passed the test of responsibility. We went through thick and thin together up to then. That was pretty cool because it made us almost equal, and even better than that, it kept us as a team. But he was two years older, so when his classes started earlier, he left earlier. That made me the last one home. I quickly noticed the first alarming senses of loneliness. They were there if I thought about them. So I amused myself.

Within seconds of him walking out of sight, all the house radios went on loud. Singing along and not noticing I was alone became okay with me. My first stereo was having four different radios playing. When commercials came on, I'd run from room to room changing stations and finding music. Sliding in my socks and sometimes crashing on the hardwood floors would bring on the laughter. Rolling on the area rug, my comrade, Thunder dog, was persistent in nudging through my huddled armadillo position. He was determined to lick my face, and he did as I roared into louder laughter. We became the new team. The black beast Thunder chased my heels and jumped on the mountain of furniture to see who was king. It was like living in a two-man riot. If the songs were slow, I would kneel on the floor, calm the dog down, and consider what was being sung. I felt the loss in the words of someone else's loss. Those were my first lyric studies.

When the sixties' rock-and-roll music rocked, I rolled through the house absorbing the words and letting the music move my feet. But those minutes, like a carnival ride, ended too quickly. The last few minutes of my morning alone would come to a close. A bit more than sorrow would come over me. I left the radios on till just before I put the key in my hand. Turning off the last radio caused an avalanche of alarming ringing quiet. It was the final pause when I would become aware that I was alone. The truth of our new family situation came with the solitary silent space of seriousness. The always on-time public bus paused in the street for passengers before moving along. I also rolled to a stop.

Holding Thunder's head next to mine kneeling on the floor tugged at my emotions. Rubbing Thunder's ears I'd whisper, "I love you, be a good boy," and then I would turn, slam the door locked, and hide the key. Locking up the house and hiding the key wasn't as simple as it sounds. There was something more in the moment than just a door latch and key. Leaving my barking Thunder was punishment for both of us. His bark told me he was hurt as I walked away. It was time to toe the line at school.

School was no party for me. My dislike for it had bitter roots in the past, pain in the present and future dyslexic disasters. I watched the classroom clock like a demolition expert, pacing my eyes from the windows to the door and back to the minute hand. There was nothing more exciting than the blast of the bell. Trying to learn by reading words and numbers correctly was good. Trying to understand why they somehow moved was bad. Hurrying away from it all was good.

Arriving to my empty home was sweet and sour. The afternoon unlocking of the door meant the letting out of a loud hello-barking event of laughter. But it was followed with a questioning slight pause of silence. Is anyone there? The afternoon's silent emptiness was realized before turning on the radio. It was the second time total quiet spoke each day. A space within me recognized vacant solitary emptiness. I learned that lingering in the aloneness wasn't good and moving on was better. The consolation for being alone was the freedom to do whatever I wanted to do. Within seconds of singing along with the radio music, I noticed I wasn't alone. I was with my dog, and I had songs to sing and feel good with. For the next seven years, my morning and afternoon routines evolved into more of me feeling good. I realized that being alone was just a different part of my world. Alone was also a lot of fun and worth keeping. Over time, lingering in the vacant solitary emptiness or moving on always meant a choice to move on. I was learning the responsibility of managing my feelings.

Another ingredient that the mysterious unknown alien within had was the power to make me lose my attention or focus. Outwardly I was labeled "accident prone." Accidents, negligence, inaccuracies were all seen as part of me, but never explained by my understanding parents. Minor hurts or carelessness breaking things were shrugged off and blamed on being young. I always did my chores and learned to keep an eye on the clock.

As the need for money increased, so did my time without parents. Some mornings, the last few minutes alone were with a bit more of the void than usual. I don't know why. It was as if I couldn't move past the truth of our new family situation. The truth always came with a silent space of solitary seriousness. Out in the street, the public bus would stop and go with passengers. I could hear the engines and exhausts of cars moving near and away. All radios were off but the one near the door. But even the best of songs come to an end, and then click. Kneeling I'd whisper, "I love you, be a good boy." I would slam the door reluctantly, hide the key, and start walking toward school one more day.

Even after years of the routine, it never became just a routine. Thunder would go from window to window, jumping up to see me, barking, protesting, and not accepting the arrangement. In my mind, I disagreed with my feet going toward a school. My heart was turning back. I continued through the morning tug-of-war exercise, and soon my footsteps were beyond his fading bark. There were times I ran back, unlocked the door, hugged my friend, and said good-bye again. Those were the most silent of spaces to live in. I felt bad leaving him. I know my mom felt bad leaving us kids.

Long before I started writing this book, my mom told me of her struggles with herself in those days. She was going head-to-head with Pa about money. Their plunge into debt wasn't working out as they'd planned. She made the difficult decision to go to work and keep our home for us boys. She told me how guilty she felt for leaving us. She deeply regretted not being there in the morning when we left for school and then the afternoon as well. All she ever wanted was to be a mother and to be at home for her family. My mom was all mom and looked forward to a big family, with lots of visits babysitting her grandchildren and lots of family events. We both relived the witnessing of how my father enjoyed and abused alcohol. His consistent mishandling of our household forced her to take action.

I told her of what it was like living in the midst of their arguing and how I perceived my path to alcohol. I would hear about or see my brother and his friends at seventeen having drinking parties. They laughed and joked about how they got away with it. Ma and I could see how the seeds were planted for my path in that sin. I was only a trigger pull away from my inward callings of an alcoholic child. But at that time, I grew to accept my increased time alone and continued to develop as an individual. I had no idea when or what my first can of beer would unleash.

✝

I had been blessed with the gift of above-average coordination. My life changed in a big way once a basketball backboard and hoop hung on our garage. Having the backyard convenience of twenty-four-hour basketball 365 days a year was awesome. The floodlight allowed me to shoot hoops at night. Sometimes it was best to get out of the house no matter the time or season of the year. I was good at the mechanics of dribbling, jumping, and shooting. Sinking the ball in my own world that I controlled fulfilled me. Commentating like a radio announcer, I'd put myself in various crowd-pleasing situations. Shooting the winning shot, I would save the game. The court, the ball, and the crowd in the arena I played in were mine. The yard was an extension of my "house." I'd do what I wanted when no one was home. Basketball games with several friends helped lose that fishbowl of a thousand eyes' self-conscious grip that windows once held over me. There were still houses and windows, but neighbors were far enough away to remove the edge. The backyard attraction was not mine solely. Friends came over and enjoyed our hospitality, which enabled Ken and me to sharpen our hoop skills and camaraderie even more.

Being alone at 7:15 a.m. was both lonely and liberating for me at fourteen years of age. That's where my square peg of rebellion got legs and climbed Mount Independence. The catalyst for most of my unbridled excitement was the songs on the radio. Those sixties' tones of rebelling guitars and lyrics against authority helped agitate my life toward wanting to be unsupervised. Songs promoted on the radio became my sponsors for self-confidence and self-reliance. Being alone increased the value of trusting and exploring my self-centeredness. The mysterious alien within wreaking dyslexic havoc in school also worked to be creative. Growing more comfortable with the sixties' radio songs, I interacted more freely with them. Top-forty rock-and-roll lyrics formed ideas and images tutoring my adolescence. They were an additional source of happy and sad times, bringing real feelings of life. Feelings that came with the music ushered me along my emerging path. Song lyrics' values were subtle substitutes filling any voids left by my busy parents. Rock and roll became a part-time faceless alternative for family hours at a time, twice a day five days a week year after year.

Perhaps the sixties' lyrics guided millions of other kids in their values as well. Perhaps latchkey kids can collectively say we were just alone more than the tight-grouped families. Either way, ours was another household in debt. Thank God we had a house. But without the biblical anchor of genuinely knowing God, I was in a house empty of worshiping Jesus as Lord. Even though my parents didn't choose to adhere to God's teachings, His plans and purposes still unfolded; He is God Almighty. By God's grace, He kept me safe—that much I know beyond any doubt.

✝

It wasn't just me being young and waiting for the change to be older; change was happening all around. There was something new and impatient happening in the sixties. America continued to move away from its beginning roots in Christianity. A more liberal social agenda advanced disapproval of traditional values such as marriage. Live-in situations with men and women were a strong popular form of protest. A younger culture also protested against the value of owning a home. They wanted to live in automobiles or communes. The music scene was evolving with more diverse sounds, intensely driven by the electric guitar. Animated rock and roll was on the Saturday morning cartoons. People wore anything from rags to multicolored outfits head to toe. Whatever opposed customary uniforms, suits, and dresses was considered a legitimate expression of rebellion. There were social wars and other wars over this and that. There was a big far-off war going on in Vietnam. Killing and death were brought to our living room on the

TV every night. Talk of death and seeing body bags of death became so real that death seemed to increase the desire to live.

✝

My mom and dad fought bitterly. At one point, Ma took my brother and me on a train ride to southern California. We were to stay at Ma's brother's house for a few weeks to help my aunt with the birth of number five of seven kids.

The train ride was fantastic, churning across the country watching pieces of America go by. As we constantly moved, studying the land and sky was so peaceful. Not knowing what was ahead was okay. After twenty-four hours of movement, we transferred in Chicago to the Santa Fe Chief. Seeing the red deserts and the authentic cowboy country were far more satisfying than scenes on TV; the real west was alive. Our first round-trip train ride was the greatest adventure of my life. The size and speed of the iron vessels in which we lived drew open our ears and eyes. Passing through the canvas of America's big top, we saw a different show of life. Faster than the human cannonball and with the ease of the greatest trapeze maneuvers, we glided coast to coast. Trains passed so close my breath was held without noticing my eyes were riveted to the glass.

Charging by cities and towns of various populations, Ken and I were like royal princes at ages fourteen and sixteen on a journey of discovery. Lounging in the club car ordering cokes and playing cards became magical, as if two of the four kings came alive. Red sand mountains that seemingly rose without permission locked our eyes in full spellbound wonder. They just stood up out of nothing and nowhere. Turquoise horizons in bleeding blue orange skies cast long black shadows from the flat crepe-top castled plateaus. I could easily accept the flat desert floor, but how did the red sand mountains get their flat tops? The sunsets were a second-to-second unfolding beauty. Shouts of "look at that" were repeated with pointing fingers on the glass. That was real cowboy country with Indian villages. Small groups of trailers or shacks appeared briefly. Figuring out how they got there became more puzzling than seeing the TV antennas sticking out of huts. All those small hamlets had old pickup trucks parked in a deserted desert with nothing else around. These scenes were not on TV; this was a glimpse of what I would learn to call surreal.

The journey of rumbling days into nights ended in Los Angeles. The climate was one of sunshine and no humidity. The sky was always nice and comfortable. There were sweet smells in the air, presumably from the strange-looking flowers on the never-seen-before plants. Palm trees came alive from the episodes of the *Beverly Hillbillies,* adorning the spacious homes of flat roofs. Southern California was like a movie made real, like the first half of a *Twilight Zone* show, before the crazy part took over.

We rode on what was called a freeway; with cars everywhere and roads in the air, it was like another planet. Kids moved on things called skateboards, and everybody wore short pants and T-shirts with flowers on them. All the girls had long, long straight blond hair, and even the boys had blond hair. And their hair was long, too—*what was that all about?*—and they road little bikes with little wheels. They leaned back on the rear wheel, pedaling with the front wheel in the air—how strange a sight. They called it a "Wheelie." These bikes were for tricks, not speed. They were for looks, not for traveling a distance.

Walking at night in the neighborhood was warm and friendly. There were lights in the ground of the front yards or the backyards or both yards. There was so much life that it did not seem to stop just because it was dark; there were swimming pools and more lights. Driveways had cars without rust and yards had sprinkler systems. Even the highway plants and trees were getting watered—the idea of it being a desert never registered.

Ma was a big help to my aunt and uncle. A few times, I could hear the hushed talk about Pa and Ma maybe moving out there. Being there made me think I was new, or maybe it was just that there was new, everything was new. I thought about Pa. I felt bad for him; he was left out of our fun, which had never happened before. He was back there at home with Thunder. To think of home and the stories to tell was good, too. Our stay came to an end, and there was another train ride home, but now we were experienced. That journey dipped to the south near Texas before heading north. We enjoyed the club car—more of the ordering soda, playing cards, and the great windows looking north and south heading into the east. Pa and Thunder were waiting for us. Things had changed a little. Everybody grew up faster, it seemed.

✝

After two years had passed, our bicycle days were over, and my brother got a motorcycle, I got a mini motorbike. Gas-powered speed increased the thrill and freedom of riding faster. Whoever I grew up into, my "self" became accelerated with my independence. My impulsive compulsive behavior never learned caution well. I was just a young snowball at the top of Pleasure Mountain waiting to roll off. Perhaps I was a small shadow of a larger American picture.

Several months later, it was as if our California experience seeing the fashions and trends was unfolding in my neighborhood as well. Boys were growing long hair and wearing peculiar clothes. The girls were transforming their clothes and hair too. There was talk about it, and some people liked it and some didn't. The times of good or bad were troubled with talk of the Vietnam War. That didn't matter much to me: I was sixteen and more concerned with just my neighborhood.

Of course, a lot of the top-forty music in 1969 was all about boys and girls and this thing called love. Many more songs were about freedom and being free. Divisions in high school based on the way kids dressed were just that to me, divides in the taste of clothing. I was still not turned on to the social climate of the sixties. Bell-bottoms, sandals, head bans—it was all about outward expressions. But they weren't mine. I had enough of my own stuff to work out. I didn't know who I was, so how could I change?

Then my brother got his own car and left for school earlier to first pick up his friends. Then he stayed later after school for sports practice. He was a fast runner and loved all sports, and our time was being separated. As our family began fading, my unchecked rebellious latchkey seeds grew into teenage mischief. Misbehaviors would grow into wrongdoings and sin. I grew up to follow in my brother's footsteps of weekend beer parties and maybe my father's lifestyle.

Going to weekend parties in high school meant more than just hearing about students getting drunk; I saw it. Seeing my peers was what began my desire to try it. When the opportunity to drink cracked open my shell, the dormant alcoholic within broke out. Swiping a few six-packs with my friends was a spontaneous chance I took. I snuck the cans out and was no longer an innocent young observer. I became involved with the disease, guzzling and hiding in the shadows of night.

✝

My best friend Timmy and I first drank together in the streets of suburbia. With our friend Don, we concocted a daring plan to acquire some cold beer on a freezing winter night. Since I was the tallest, I bought a used army green fatigue coat to appear like a young veteran. As we stood in the dark street under a lamplight, my friends gave me more respectability and darkened my blond eyebrows with a dark pencil. Adding a shadowy type of mustache to my thin hairless upper lip, we all laughed with anticipation. Before walking in, we rehearsed the scene and prepared my mind. To top off the charade, Don lit a cigarette, and I hung it in my mouth.

The old corner store was called Peddlers and was run by an old man who lived in the back with his aging wife. His shelves held only the basic commodities, like bread in plastic bags, cans of beans, cat and dog food, and milk in the cooler. I strolled into the well-lit store and went straight for the cooler with beer and grabbed three quarts, turned, and set them on the counter. As the cigarette burned my eyes, the old man walked in from the back, stood opposite me, and stared at my face. He was old, big, and tall, with a butt in his mouth burning his eyes. He had experience holding the torch flopping between his lips and said,

"That's it?" I pressed my lips, held the white Marlboro tight, and out of the side of my mouth simply said, "Yep."

Once I passed the dare and illegally bought beer, I couldn't go back to being blameless. Gliding on the streets of suburbia in the dark of night with my friends became one of my favorite classes in a teenager's school of life. As I learned to live with the subtlety of growing sin, its mischievous attacks made me become an uncommonly intoxicated teenager. That sin's evil spirits made rowdy noises and roared throughout my youth well into adulthood. After Satan placed his saddle of alcoholism on my naive Irish heritage, he rode my weakness long and hard.

That summer into autumn of 1969, I began dating more and wound up with a surprise named Robin. She was a year older and rode horses; despite my hay-fever flare-ups, I liked her. School dances were never part of my social life going into tenth grade until Robin, a twelfth-grade chick, and I became close friends. She was gorgeous, with a figure that made anything she wore breathtaking. One night my friends and I took our time walking along the railroad tracks getting drunk before the dance. I reluctantly showed up awkward, without any experience courting at dances, but happily less inhibited. With her in my arms dancing slowly, my emotions flowed with more than friendship. We moved slowly head-to-head, and I held her in my arms tightly and we rocked. When her long, sweet-smelling, beautiful blond hair touched my face, I closed my eyes and held her closer. The song ended. Then it happened quickly.

The very special moment shattered like glass. The gum I was chewing to hide my alcohol breath somehow got mixed with her hair. She pulled away with a big smile. My gum hung in her hair. I looked at it, and she saw the concentration on my face and the direction of my eyes. When she reached up to feel what was there, she mixed more hair with the blob of gum. Her tugging fingers sent the panic message to her brain instantly. Her smiling face fell into horror. She yelped and freaked out, pulling at it. Then her face held fear with tears. Her chattering friends shuffled to her side. I stood with my speechless open mouth gaping in shock. I heard the words *scissors* and *cut off*, then more gasps of unbelief.

Watching them turn to enter the ladies' room, I realized my presence was a mistake. I waited a bit and then drifted outside to watch the bonfire. I stood near the tree line drinking one of the beers we had hidden. The flames were high; the blazing light showed the happy circle of students. Embarrassed, I turned for the road and tried to hitchhike but wound up walking home.

————— ✝ —————

The racial unrest nationwide had been and was being expressed, absorbed, and released on the TV news. The United States had lived past the assassinations of King and the Kennedys. Our white high school had only four black males come in at that time. They were older than me and well accepted from what I could see. These guys played sports with my brother and were an asset to our teams. I didn't know just how much rebellion was ripping our country apart, but the news on TV showed it continuing.

The Vietnam War and social change were hot topics in our land, but to me they were just stories filling the news shows at night. Showing soldiers shooting guns and dead bodies and other social unrests was important, but the news events coming alive in the living room were easily turned off. Unless the drama was live playing out before me like Ma and Pa, it was far away.

The war was an old war, already in place with the French fighting there. There was no shortage of opinions why America should be involved. I'm sure those think tanks tried to consider every angle. The consequence of war was death for some, and that's what we saw on the news every night. The shock and awe of Vietnam forced different people to different things. If young men didn't leave the country, they stayed and made one commitment of responsibility or another. Perhaps the war changed the view of marriage and raising a family for some. The war was good for all kinds of business. Colleges filled up to avoid the war. Educating far too many young and placing them in debt shrank our workforce and jobs went overseas. Losing factory jobs might not work out in the long run. Some of the rebellious youth organized protests. Some got shot and were killed. The Vietnam War was one of authoritative usefulness. America had been the world's peacekeeper since the Korean War. It seems like the war was a means to justify several ends.

Rebellious women waged another kind of war; they wanted free sex without the obligation to care for babies. They wanted to have bedroom fun and freedom like irresponsible men. The abortion issue raged on. Again, it was the media bringing the true-life situation into living rooms for discussion. Abortion was the murder of a baby, and our laws defended the babies. That was pretty basic, pretty much common sense. But that reasonable responsibility was being swept under the rug. The wisest of judges and the highest court could no longer find the goodness to defend innocent babies. Some women wanted change from tradition at any cost, even by murdering their own. Oh, to be a fly on the wall of the think tanks and hear the thoughts. It was probably good for the business of making money somehow.

But voices of change kept rumbling under gathering storm clouds planning social war. Hope in God as He is found in the Bible was a blessed course of America's founding fathers, but now was a path less taken. The commingled insurrectionists cried together for revenge on Christian values that limited sin. America was towering on the pinnacle of blessed time, not falling but teetering. The proven pillars of strong biblical hope and goodness that guided America to the top were weakened as they steadily lost support. Those who held tightly to the teaching of God's Holy Bible watched America slide faster into liberalism. In 1970, America and I were like two snowballs. We had gotten to a point far away from guidance. It was time to start rolling down Pleasure Mountain and gathering more selfishness. The sixties released many worthy restraints holding back those three rebel sisters: Me, Me, and Me. Their lust of pride wanted to shed the restraints of established family values. The inner sin of self-first shouted louder for social revolution. Murdering babies was wanted in society. America's Supreme Court, the wisest in the land, was having a discussion about life and death. Should they continue their wisdom in the law and protect the lives of babies, or remove their responsibility? How could America continue to be a great nation if the wisest allowed the murder of its young? How could Americans then say, "God bless America"? Only God hears the cries of innocent blood. Was the fact that the courts were considering the reversal of their so-called wisdom to protect babies already a judgment from God? How long would God wait to bring His justice on a nation that legalized the murder of the innocent?

✝

In 1970 my brother's high school graduation brought his chance to sprout his wings. My home had been diminished by one. Ken was briefly there on occasion only to shower, change his clothes, make a peanut butter and jelly sandwich, and leave eating it. I watched him stay away and far off at his college a few miles away. His girlfriend was in another college, and his mind was anywhere in-between and no longer at home. The past few years of growing distance between him, and me and Ma and Pa grew. He wanted to cut out a slice of the American dream pie. Who could blame him? Unfortunately his cutting us out hurt the three of us who were left and me the most.

The same old house scenes prevailed, with Ma and Pa having mostly good days and repeated bad days. They were locked in their values of what they would allow and what they wouldn't. They were poised for the great divide of divorce, but love was their glue. College for me was a kind of future option, but never really an alternative. School was generally okay, but frequently a struggle academically. Each high school summer I'd be one of the people repeating classes in summer school. The mysterious unknown working inside my thinking remained an alien in the shadows. That vampire who stole my clarity was called dyslexia, and it sucked much fun out of learning. My only hope for a college education was to get a basketball scholarship to a two-year school, perhaps out west.

The tests that involved multiple-choice answer sheets were the trickiest. I knew I knew the answer. The teacher knew I knew the answer. But no one knew why I penciled in the wrong number or letter. The unknown parasite dyslexia was a mysterious foe that was always in a murky haze. I was always blamed for my lack of concentration.

Dyslexia's disorder always came disguised as normal. Its subtle ambush causing chaos would always escape as unidentified. I got very good at concentrating, but never good enough. Often I would just barely pass or fail on test day. There was nothing I could do. I think the fruitless attempts to try more and harder only caused my "I don't care" attitude to mature. My attitude was fertile with the seeds of discontented thoughts. Only God knew what would grow alongside my strengthening perseverance.

Chapter 3: Off the Treadmill

In the autumn of 1970, I was seventeen, a junior, and for the most part life was pretty good. I was a likable guy, I had a girlfriend, and I loved to play basketball. I could jump and move with the ball, scoring when others couldn't. My brother had talent also, and he was much more serious about sports now in college. I didn't have as strong a competitive nature; I had more fun with my skill. I was a natural when it came to using my body. A year earlier, my brother and I were like two knives sharpening off each other playing ball in our backyard. But I was headed for change; with two years left in high school, the path my life would take was still in question.

My brother was with his girlfriend, Carole, so much it dislocated him from our family. Once he was gone, he stayed mostly at college, in love and out of sight. He faded away and faded fast, only showing up once in a while with Carole. When he came, we all shot baskets and laughed. When he came alone, his visit was short, and he was constantly on the phone with his girlfriend. We would only shoot a few hoops, and he had to go, taking a peanut butter and jelly sandwich. Carole was well liked by our family, and it was always good to see them so happy.

My parents were nearly separated. My mother was carrying on as the head of the household and working one major job and one or two part-time jobs. Pa was hanging in there, but slipping closer to the edge of losing a lot. Their love had become weary. They fought with and against the currents of social peer pressure and materialism to keep up with the Joneses. But they weren't a team. They fought in a ring from separate corners, standing against life's known and unknown assailants. Their wedding band wasn't keeping them together; it was the house that brought them face-to-face.

I was in the middle a lot and uneasy at times. I'd see them before and after work, sometimes both, and talk with one parent or the other. Either before or after one of their fights, I'd eat with them or watch TV. When I visited in my friends' homes, I saw peace between their parents, and I wanted it in my house. Wishing for more peace and for the fighting to go away didn't work. With my friends I drank beer at night on weekends; it was what Pa liked, and I liked it too. All of Ma's working kept her away; she never returned home till early evening. Weekends she'd hostess at a nice restaurant. Pa came home earlier, around dinnertime. He'd shoot some baskets with me and my friends. I'd be embarrassed because of his condition. I could tell if he'd been drinking just seeing him walk. As soon as he said something, I knew about how bad it was. It was just a matter of time before Ma got home and things blew up. If I was watching TV with Pa, I got out as soon as Ma started yelling. Outside I could hear the argument and doors slamming. When Ma left for her other job, she'd tell me how sorry she was for me to have to see and hear all the bad. I just kept shooting baskets.

As time went on, I was spending more time out of the vocal arena of accusations and denials called home. Nights on the suburban streets were finding me and friends drinking beer and becoming more mischievous. It was fun to drink. I suppose the apple didn't fall far from the tree.

I watched TV until the volume in the house was too loud, and then slipped outside to shoot hoops. After seventeen years of living in the mix of inner and outer war and peace, I wondered more often what life was all about. More and more I leaned with wider eyes toward looking for answers to my inward queries of life. Some relief came watching a TV show about a guy and a motorcycle. Faithfully every week I saw *Then Came Bronson*. That man and his Harley-Davidson traveled freely, working wherever and at whatever he wanted. That lifestyle started to fill my inner void. My questions about how I fit into the greater scheme of things found visible answers in the show. The appeal to be mobile, on wheels and free to go places, was a story I could live out. The idea satisfied me in a powerful way, especially since winter was near. Leaving on a motorcycle and finding new adventures somewhere was a very tempting dream to chase.

Then I got some news from my friend Buddy, who had a cousin selling a stock 900 Harley-Davidson motorcycle. I borrowed $1,500 from my grandmother, giving my promise I'd flip burgers to pay her back. Against my father's wishes, I was loaned the money and I brought the beast home. The 1968 900cc XLH Harley-Davidson was mine. That autumn I'd ride that Harley up the railroad tracks to school. Illegally one morning on the highway, I sped up to a hundred miles an hour before parking it in the school lot. I was jazzed from the speed and from not being caught by the law. Come winter, I would keep the battery charged by zipping up and down in front of the house. That power and speed were a new thrill beyond any previous experience on wheels. The cycle was a new bad habit added to the suburban streets. Drinking with the boys on weekends became more exciting with plans to travel. With winter came the cold time and extra time on my hands. I would start the engine and prowl around the yard, up and down the driveway like a caged tiger. Time was my tormenter, and the snow teased my longings for southern travel.

Before Christmas, a small group of classmates and I were chosen to shop for a tree to decorate in the school lobby. What a crew! An older student drove, someone had a bottle of liquor, and we all got loaded before lunch. Returning, we chose to drive by the front entrance of the school blowing the horn, leaning out the windows laughing. Two of us were key members of the basketball team, so the repercussions were small. Sports came first, so drinking was put aside for the season. Nearly at the end of winter, it had been a good year for our school basketball team. Post season for me and my friends was like a green light into our temporarily restrained youthful bad habits.

✝

A new year rolled around, and 1971 in our house had the same stage setup for drama as last year. All that winter, like every season, I delivered newspapers in the morning. Just I and Thunder dog would walk and talk, planning for the great thrills on the bike, the powerful beast. I was shy without any real workplace experience, but I kept my word to pay back Granny and began flipping burgers at Burger King. After school and on weekends, I'd clean greasy tables, loaded freezers, and made monster sandwiches for myself.

My manager was a relocated surf bum from Southern California who had a way with the ladies. His attitudes toward life and the amount of time he gave toward pleasure were an eye-opening education for me. He was twenty-five and free with telling me his desires to travel and how he fulfilled them. Sometimes he'd hitchhike or drive cars to Florida for old people. Not only would he drink on the job; he would also smoke pot and hit on the girls working there. He was fearless. I watched him enjoy himself interacting with girls like a nice guy, but then talk trash behind their backs. But he always took pleasure in being agreeable with them. His inhibitions were natural and unfamiliar to me.

His other habit was going across the street into Uncle Bill's Bar, slamming down a few drinks, and coming back to play manager. Drinking alcohol was something I did have a desire for. I was still under eighteen, the legal drinking age, so bars were off-limits. This guy loved to party, so he would stash cans of beer outside in the snow for us to drink. Within my first month, we were both drunk on the job. Sliding frozen boxes off a delivery truck ramp into the freezer was done fast and with laughter. I'd be whistling while wiping tables, and smiling at girls smiling at me, life was more than amusing. Work became fun, and hearing his beach stories set my yearnings toward the west coast.

✝

A few months later, with great expectations of warmer weather soon to arrive, I could be found anytime polishing the motorcycle. Within the garage walls, my youthful freedom fueled my cabin fever with restlessness. Scenes of riding my Harley south or to California rolled around in my head. At the same time, there were new thoughts of love. I was attracted to one of the cheerleaders. Her long brown hair graced her slim figure as she twirled the baton. I found my first sincere heartfelt relationship with my new girlfriend, Hope. She was two years younger and was the first girl I could easily talk with. The young woman was very pretty, very shapely, extraordinarily kind, and most impressionable. By simply holding her hand, I felt a good sense of being grounded and more complete. My inquisitive nature was freely expressed, and we talked more and more. Hope understood me when I tried to explain what I felt. She extended her loving nature, and we spent hours on the phone fashioning our friendship into love. Thoughts of harmony were first forged in my adolescent outlook. Our young lives began to center on the idea of being together more and more. Over the winter and into 1971, our bonding increased, and we soon found devotion. Hope and I loved to laugh; we loved being together. For the first time in my life, I said, "I love you," and I heard those words told to me.

The early signs of spring were upon the northeast. Without a driver's license, I hatched a plan to take a joyride. I smashed a dark blue Maxwell House coffee can so flat it resembled a New York license plate. I screwed it on the rear of the Harley and called my friend Timmy. Neither of us made the leap from alcohol into drugs; we were jocks. He was gleaning a good education and expecting to go to college. Tim leaned more toward customary thinking, but had a touch of Irish adventure that merged with mine. The Harley idled with a low growl. As it warmed up, exhaust smells circled the garage walls. We climbed on and coasted to the end of the driveway. Turning onto the highway, I bolted; shifting the gears, we roared into the night uphill north to the lake.

In five fast minutes on a road without lights, we were at a considerably higher elevation. Attacked by freezing cold, we turned around at the intersecting roads in retreat. Driving back in the dark with just the headlight beam bouncing, I plowed ahead faster. Blinded with teardrops and wind forcing my eyes tight, I held the handlebar grips firmly. Peering into the blackness with one half-opened eye frozen, tears ran down my face. I leaned low to avoid the freezing wind, going faster, thundering like a rocket to reach the downhill warmth and home. The bend in the road at ninety—or maybe it was sixty—miles per hour turned into a very tight corner. I hit black ice, and the motorcycle dropped to the road. Like torpedoes, we slid off the blacktop, splashing in the muck and murky black-ice water.

The machine stuck into the roadside drainage ditch like a javelin. We were catapulted forward at full speed, flipping over into ice, snow, spring sludge, and complete quiet. The ride was no longer a joy. Looking up at the stars in the sea of black night sky, I heard the trickling water and felt the wet slush with my fingers. Timmy's moan from behind me alerted me. Pain registered next. I moaned. Tim's voice came from a snowbank. I lay in the water upside-down against the front of a large rock. My legs hung over it. The small boulder I smashed onto was the size of a pygmy pony. Oh boy, did my right hip and lower back hurt! Tim said he was okay and helped me up. With much effort in severe agony, I stood in the roadside water, shivering. Tim wiped off the melting snow. I leaned on him as we climbed out of the ditch slowly. We stood alone on the dark road, helpless and desperate.

The Harley lay silently like a dead body in the muddy snow. I was afraid the bike would be seen and reported to the police. This time being outside the law meant trouble. There was no way to hide or drive away; I couldn't stand without Tim. Our teeth were chattering as we ambled away from the scene of the crash. Quivering in pain, my small determined steps fought for survival. The nearest farmhouse light got closer as we got colder. We stood knocking in frozen wet clothes before a mother cautiously let us in the door. The surreal laughter of small kids in the other room watching TV surrounded my agony. Somehow I sat and called home for help. Ma was worrying about the opened garage door and missing bike. "I'll be right there," she said.

The farmhouse heat thawed away the numbing effect of the frozen wet clothing. As I sat dripping, increasing pain and then the shock climbed all over my back up to my face. The extraordinary pain almost overtook my consciousness. I was nauseous and given some water. Tim brought me a snowball. I rubbed that cold ice on my face and breathed shallow breaths. The pain was so great my desperation changed into fear. I couldn't imagine how bad the damage was.

Ma came up and got us. She and Tim got me into the car somehow without me passing out. Ma took me to the hospital. I was afraid I would be given a ticket if the bike were found. I didn't want a suspended license before I got a license. She swore a blue streak, hating the bike and the day I got it. All she cared about was my health. While I was being examined, the scene of the crash was found. Apparently the nearby fire department volunteers drove by and saw the bike in the mud. They were searching the woods for lost riders. The cops showed up at the hospital. Even my brother came by. Everybody wanted answers. I was glad to see him. I missed being with him. Our house wasn't the same without him. Ken explained to the police that I would probably be crippled for life. No tickets were issued. He was right about the damage done to my back: it was permanent. I stayed in the hospital and was measured for a full back brace.

My lower back, the "lumbar" region, suffered from direct impact. The right hip bone was chipped. My momentum and gusto toward the fun in life hurt me but did not kill me. It was the biggest of accidents in an accident-prone life; thank God it only hurt. That spring there was nothing but time crawling by and me in bed watching the dirty melting snow.

---

†

DOWN IN GENERAL

Down In General, what a way to go.
Life's transmission is stuck in low.
I tried to shift, I couldn't find
The regular pattern in my mind.

    Sometimes I feel like an automobile,
    Spinning around the same old town.
    Streets where I raced now look two-faced.
    I go around bends, avoid dead ends.

Down In General, what a way to be.
Can't start my engine, careless took the key.
I loved to ride and hold tight.
Bad luck burned me, all in one night.

Down In General, what a way to look.
Gonna need a tow, put me on a hook.
Stuck in a ditch, the world drives by.
No one stops to offer a ride.

---

†

The confines I faced forced my mother and father into a position of making sacrifices. Compromises were made, and our family pulled apart some more before pulling together. There was tension between my dad, who never wanted me to have the cycle, and my grandmother, who gave me the money. But my grandmother came to our house daily. I needed a nurse, and she was the perfect caregiver. Everybody gave up something.

Granny stayed with me while I recuperated very slowly and learned how to walk again. Lying flat in bed, I would strap on the back brace before the long process of rising to make my way to the bathroom and totter about. Painfully the very slow recovery shined a light on Hope's sacrificial love. She was so special, so dedicated to our relationship. Our intimacy grew, and her faithfulness eased my wounded spirit. It was weird how a tragedy caused me to come closer to and genuinely love my granny. Hope and I talked with her every day. Granny told stories of the thirties and how hard it was just to eat. When someone had food they shared it, and food came back to her when she had none.

Lying flat in bed, I watched the world pass by one sunset at a time. Several hours a day, all I could do was stare up and out windows. The tall treetops and birds waving were the only movements. Mornings I'd look out and recall being a paperboy and the year-round strength I needed. The sunshine's early yellow and orange brilliance rising up with the birds' chirping hellos were great signs of hope. Leaning toward the windowsill till it hurt, I saw what little I could see. It seemed sweeter, and the sounds were closer. Thunder jumped on and off the bed, and it was worth the pain to pet my old comrade. I missed several weeks of school but was able to manage the little homework I was given. Early summer was a slow-motion time for my body to heal. The doctors' pain pills helped and let my mind wander before I drifted off to sleep several times a day. The smashed and bent front end of the Harley leaned over in the garage and looked as bad as I limped. There was no hurry to do anything. The mending was measured by the minutes I was not in pain. That summer I was a cripple in a back brace sitting outside in a wheelchair parked in a sad cartoon. What does a kid think about that's always learned the hard way?

Sometimes my friend Buddy came by. I could hear his high-speed motorcycle shifting down the street and breaking rubber, then racing down the driveway. He would light up a joint outside the window and encourage me to try it. His motives came from a good heart. He was trying to help ease the pain, but I was stuck on an alcohol-only routine. I frowned on drug use, and besides, I hated cigarette smoke. Lying there in bed through the hot, humid summer months healing seemed small and precisely measured, but I was moving better.

It was the first of June 1971, and the rock-and-roll radio was too busy, too jumpy, for my immobility. I grew to hate radio commercials, which forced their materialism into my ears and thoughts. At night another station, WRPI, had a bizarre sound of slow electric guitars and wavy keyboard sounds. A new friend was found flying over the radio waves. I also began listening to classical music day and night on WAMC. I discovered what was soothing and without commercial interruption or much talk. I didn't know anybody who liked classical music. People just looked at me when I mentioned how I loved the many sounds of an orchestra playing. A fresh new appreciation for the highest form of music eased my imagination further toward remaining a square peg. I found the support coming from the radio like a door leading to warm water to relax in. Like an alleyway, with great and interesting music letting me dream into a bright pasture or an ominous approaching storm.

With my eyes open, lying still, medicated with pain relievers, staring at the ceiling, I repeatedly questioned life. I was forced to think and kept considering my future with so few options. I was channeled into making some value judgments on what was important and not important. The literal baby steps I repeatedly walked were accompanied with slow, serious thoughts. It was as if at seventeen, I was being reborn and seeing adult questions for the first time. That inward, strained thinking caused me to see how basic my changed life had become. I learned the great value of just being able to walk, to sit, and to rise. Time and the simple things became so precious. My mind began the process of eliminating lesser things of value.

I was without a clear understanding of God. I was rudderless without the truth of God as it is found in the scriptures. I had no idea of divine truth, and no one had ever explained it. All I could conceive was without much guidance and were my few experiences. Asking questions of others was never a big part of my personality. Too many times my stupid questions were laughed at. So I did what I always did:

I tried figuring out life on my own. Lying still and picturing happy lives, then shattered lives, and what was considered normal was a poor pattern of missing pieces. Everywhere were paths of how others changed or spent their time reaching their long-range views. They didn't appeal to me. Some of those patterns of life's expectations went in the same direction as those of my parents and grandparents. Divorce-broken families with unhappy lives were in the picture. Life's molds were lined with customary anticipations waiting to be filled by the next generation. My perception of what everybody else was doing with their time became tainted and indigestible. The thrill was missing.

In the social flow of people, they did not have satisfaction with enough. Like Ma and Pa, everybody was keeping up with the Joneses next door and buying things. It was adult peer pressure. Everyone wanted more than enough. Satisfaction was just out of reach and kept most people on the treadmill of desire. Life's hustle and bustle was all about people trying to fill themselves up with things and hang on. Love, work, church, kids, and no one knew what tomorrow would bring. Accidents happened. Like school, it was another pegboard of getting fitted into a hole until you die—and then what? I sprouted a yearning to do anything other than accept what I saw as a common practice of gathering more and more. Life was both simpler and fuller than that. I was unable to care for the idea of one job for thirty years in debt without change. I called it "being on the treadmill of life."

The greater mass of people formed a herd on the treadmill of normal routine called life. I saw tradition all around me with marriages and families. I saw my brother charging ahead doing it. He, too, was going on the treadmill of life. He bought into the sale of your time in exchange for money to buy what was called normal. Higher learning was supposed to not only reward the student; it would increase affluence in our society. Success was measured in dollar signs to buy a more expensive kind of normal. And time was always exchanged for money. Going into debt was normal. I saw my mother and father, who had bought that plan but were falling out of place into broken pieces. They hoped that life would be falling into place while they collected things and not be so broken up. I saw all my aunts and uncles and cousins doing it. Some were still in place, and others were falling apart also. And there were failures and there were accidents and there was a lot of pain.

Then there were those not in the herd. I saw on the news teenagers and young people protesting the war and not wanting to do what was expected of them. I heard the rock-and-roll lyrics telling me I was born to be wild. The war seemed to force or pressure young people into college, into marriage, or out of the country. Some of my own young rebellious seeds of nonconformity were getting watered. Insubordination was in my mix. Some of the necessity and the options for alternative thought came subtly with the dyslexic challenges. All the times I would try harder to think of ways to get to the answer were exercises in unconventional thinking. If a math question was in words, I'd picture the problem several ways. How long it would take to climb over a 7,920-foot-high mountaintop at five minutes a mile lost me. Not only did I think a mile had 2,580 feet, but I took into account how tired I'd be and a rest. The words were more distracting than just seeing numbers. My picture of a mountain wasn't as simple as theirs. Mine had trees. My thoughts were searching for worthy purposes for my climb. And a major question: why not go around the mountain?

In the recovery process, my thinking was growing roots out of the traditional box of social issues. What were the other varieties of living, and how would they be discovered? Still in painful mending, I yearned to travel and ride a motorcycle again someday. The latchkey-morning radio lyrics I loved of the early sixties were also seeds getting watered. The abundance of lyrics suggesting change and rebellion still played on the seventies' radio. Was I crazy? It was my unfulfilled plan to travel. I didn't consider a bigger plan because I didn't have much to build on.

Winter had long passed, and my expectations to travel became a spring of sore reality, leading to a summer of discovering my mind's eye. Painful limping and meditative exercises continued opening a pod of wonder within. I found the cousins If and Possible had emerged from that fertile bed of forced stillness. The metamorphosis of more imagination grew all summer. A greater lust for life and searching for a way to live was a rising conflict within. Yet I was in love with my beautiful young Hope; she was a nurse, an angel, a woman. We were already whispering words of walking toward a traditional life together. But that rip of selfish wondering came with if and possible and started to tear a doubt in me. I wanted to want her and to hold her when Hope was near. But alone, I wondered about tearing away from her and what I would find.

The treadmill of society was before me, and the option to think differently was beside me. I was torn. I didn't know of other ways of life off the treadmill, like those of artists or inventors. Were they casualties of the treadmill like hoboes and bums? But I knew what happened to my parents: they split. What good I thought I saw in other families didn't outweigh the bad I knew. Without knowing what I wanted, I stepped with one foot off of the treadmill. Testing the water of change without a direction to go in was okay to think about. The night music drifted without words; it didn't need processing. This classical music appreciation was growth and seemed to balance out the very business of rock and roll. I just squeaked by in school with some passing grades before I got the summer off.

✝

In mid-June of the summer of 1971, I turned eighteen. Failing third grade meant I was older than my classmates. It meant I was of legal age to buy alcohol and drink in bars. It also meant I could be drafted into the military. After I registered for the draft, my status arrived in the mail. I was classified 1-HS, "High School" status. It was too early to tell for sure, but failing third grade may have had another benefit with much greater significance than drinking in bars.

Standing alone, my first afternoon drink at the pub wasn't as big a deal as I thought it would be. The dark room was quiet and poorly lit. Sunlight found its way in through the windows hanging their lit neon signs. I wasn't even asked for my new driver's license ID. The news was on a small TV above the bottles on the top shelf. Older men were talking about the war, and I was listening. These guys were strangers to me, but similar to my father. They sat on stools, with elbows forward on the bar, smoking cigarettes. Their hands worked the butts, and glasses of foamy cold beer were raised and sipped as casually as eating lunch. I asked if they were veterans and about their feelings toward the war. Serious faces brought lower-toned voices and shaking heads. Up and down yes, the heads bobbed. Sideways no, no talk, heads shook in silence. They stared before they spoke of how bad the World War II memories were.

My circular thoughts of the Vietnam War were TV pictures and didn't have faces like these guys. I was a year away from graduating. Ideas of war or going away to play basketball in a two-year college out west were both so surreal. Getting a job was a good option, but less appealing with my sore back. My teenage love added more confusion to the mix as I sat sipping on a glass of beer. I didn't know what to value. There were so many things to like or dislike. I couldn't understand girls, and what was that makeup all about? The values that most girls placed on their external appearances were confusing. Modestly well-dressed girls like Hope, with no or little makeup, were nice. Others who wore more suggestive clothing and shined more always caught my eye. Inside my canister of youth, feelings were tumbling. Being older only made getting a drink easier.

✝

The pain in my right hip was manageable, but it was still very sensitive to the touch. Any kind of repetitive bending raised my pain level to the moon. In several ways, I was changed for life. From now on, my lower-back exercise program was three times a day. Lying with my back on the floor and raising my knees to my chest while breathing slowly was the medicine I needed. Unintentionally the twenty-minute routine became an excellent form of meditation.

Living with a physical impairment is like dragging a weight around until you learn to use what's left. The forced limits and my reevaluated values focused my thoughts on time lost and time left. Seeing time lost wouldn't make up for my loss. I had healed well and was done being forced to wait. I needed to look at what was beyond, but didn't know how or where to leap. Throwing the basketball in the backyard helped my spirit. Slowly and steadily I worked through the pain and began running and jumping. That summer of mixed painful pleasure skipped right into the early autumn and a nightmare yet to come.

✝

September 1971, school, change, and the hands of time all rolled around. My final year in high school was before me, and I was still without any plans. The girl I was in love with was one in ten million. But I wasn't yet in the spot to know and live real and true commitment. Feelings of tradition and being pinned down were like an itch without a scratch.

Basketball practice started up for our fourth and final year as a team. My injury was healing well. The doctor advised me to avoid repetitive motions that would cause pain. As long as I kept away from bending over without bending my knees, I was good. I was there practicing with the team for one of the few constant elements in my life. Our senior basketball team had potential to be first again, like we were as freshmen. School expectations for a great season were high. So were the plans being made by the students for their futures. Anticipated excitement for the season's challenges began swelling up inside of me. Practicing in my backyard gave me added confidence. Things were going good again. The healing process continued, and good times were right on track. Then for the first time in four years of playing, something went wrong.

In early October, my male desires overwhelmed my dedication to the sport I loved. One warm Indian summer afternoon, my priorities got out of focus. I rebelled against the coach's authority and went home to my house with Hope. My guilty conscience spoke up about missing practice, but not loudly enough. My pride as a key member of the team probably gave me security in my ill-fated decision. Our make-out session was all I had hoped it would be on that bright balmy afternoon. The compulsive act of disobedience to skip basketball practice was the first and last time. My lust, pride, and home-alone opportunity all collided the next day with the coach's pride. He was determined to make a more aggressive player out of me and reign in that season's glory. In his eyes, he saw more for me than just the fun and high scores; he wanted me to be dedicated, like him. He wanted the team to win, and we all wanted to make the same good memory and bring home the trophies.

The consequences of my impulsive behavior to forgo practice were quick and devastating. The next day when I arrived for practice, I was face-to-face with the coach and told to turn in my uniform. I was off the team. I can only surmise that the coach's action was to provoke a greater-than-genuine desire to play. After all, missing just one practice doesn't deserve total annihilation. He wanted me to fight for what was mine. But his intentions backfired. I turned in my uniform and dealt with another major bout of rejection, condemnation, setback, and disappointment. I tried to roll with another punch, but that blow really hurt. Once again I came home with bad news for my mother. My father had little to say about the matter. He was very upset and mad at the coach. He and Ma wanted me to ask to be back on the team, but I guess I had a pride issue. I don't know why I didn't ask; I just backed off. That was that.

No one stood up for me. No one tried to make it right. No one intervened on my behalf with the school or by pleading with the coach. Except Hope—she took half the blame and tried to reason with the coach, but to no avail. That time should have been different with regard to someone participating in my best interests. I can honestly say that there is no bitterness. The coach's pride kept him from negotiating with me, and my pride did the same toward him. When two immovable objects collide, things get broken. College was not where I wanted to go after graduating anyway. Being on the team was a privilege; it was what I knew and part of my normal. My only equalizer among my peers was taken away. I was reduced to being just another guy in school; I had never thought I would be. A streak of confidence in me never suspected the worst. Maybe the thrill I got from breaking the law or being rebellious manifested itself again that sunny afternoon. Maybe it was just hormones, a libido thing. Whatever the thing or combination of things was, one mistake brought a big change.

In the halls between classes, I felt the looks and the embarrassment of another failure. I let my team, my school, and my friends down. Once the sport was taken away, school became worthless, and good grades were still unattainable. My world of loving the sport and having teammates was gone. Hope was still a cheerleader and went to every game. I never went to another game. I felt more locked up than ever in my broken home, broken body, and broken dream of leaving my hometown. My shame and embarrassment was before me every day I went to school. My dislike and inability to cope with school were elevated to a degree of disgust. After the summer school sessions in ninth, tenth, and eleventh grades, I longed for the end of it all in June. A half year to go, and then I would be done with it. With the draft board looming in the shadows waiting for me to graduate, I was without any optimism that winter of 1971.

✝

It took six months to adjust out of what I was and into the nothingness I became that spring of 1972. My adolescent identity search was floundering big-time. My prospects for livelihood dropped to the outlook of a factory worker. I felt cheated, with no one to blame but me and no recourse. I was growing, changing, shifting, thinking who, what, and why me. My adolescent years fell into sulking self-loathing from severe identity loss. Questions were long, without even one good short answer in sight. I was without traction and without wheels to spin. Everybody wanted to know what everybody was doing, everybody but me. I knew I would be going to work somewhere. Solitude was an unwanted friend, but one I was becoming more familiar with.

Without the team status, I saw things and people differently. My fall from having a position caused me to be friendlier to other kids in school. I was in the halls more, with a lot of time on my hands after school. Just when I wanted to get away from the pressure—bingo!

My friend Buddy, who offered me a joint while visiting me during my back's recuperation, offered again. He wanted to help me enjoy life and be happy again. He compared pot to the fun of drinking and the feeling of being happy. Buddy called it being high. High was better because it didn't have alcohol's bad effects of slurred speech or stumbling. "It's a cleaner liftoff to achieve a buzz like laughing and being happy," he said. "The only way to know if you like it is to try it."

It made sense to me. If it didn't work, then I could just drink. If it did get me high, then I could do both. But pot was illegal, and my fear of getting arrested was intimidating. However, I finally gave in and said I'd try smoking it. But I didn't like cigarette smoke and was embarrassed about possibly choking on it. I said if he gave me some, I'd try it alone. Buddy wanted to make sure I got high the first time and said he'd look for something good.

The first thing I tried was some black THC resin balls from some far away place. I used the leftover cardboard roll from the toilet paper as a pipe. A small hole covered with tin foil held the gooey tar. With one hand covering the end, I lit the THC and inhaled. After gagging on the pure white smoke and repeated inhales with red-faced hacking, I got high. I was real high and very happy. Being high was like being someone else inside of me. It was like letting loose a prisoner who was locked in a cell without windows. I was free to see the trees and the sun and feel the grass as if it were my first time. When the high wore off, I got high again. Then I saw the difference between pot and alcohol. Pot was more manageable and allowed me to be high but not clumsy-drunk.

Once more my life changed in a radical direction. Along with the drug came a new set of friends, new experiences, and a new life. All my roots in radio rock-and-roll music soared with discovering albums and bands playing cool music. Henceforth, whether it was for the good or the bad, a change in life happened. Dyslexic alternatives, latchkey freedom, off-the-treadmill searching, and now getting high were all on my path to somewhere. I was without a pattern and had no outside control, no supervision. Hope didn't want to try the drug. She felt foreign to it like I used to be. I felt like Buddy and wanted her to know how much fun it was. But she said no, and she would wait to see me until after I had my fun.

Drugs and booze and music reinvented me into another personality. Coming home from the last few months of school, I would crank up the family stereo and get high with friends. School was a complete nonissue, and basketball fun was traded for another motorcycle, a Triumph Bonneville 650cc road bike. My world was turned right side up when I discovered that there was another way of escaping what was wrong. The negative outlook on my young life was replaced with the pleasure of living for the moment. Drugs combined with alcohol were like an enormous set of unlocked doorways that led to friends, conversations, and different thoughts.

I graduated from high school in 1972 alone. It was a day to get behind me. Prior to the ceremony, I picked up my diploma at the school cafeteria. I saw the festivities, the caps and gowns, and my classmates. I brought the diploma home to my mother. She was very hurt that I didn't want to participate in what should have been a good memory, not a very disturbing day. I knew I would have to be getting a job, and making money didn't seem like a bad idea. My habits cost money.

I began working in the construction field as a mason helper doing heavy manual labor. The repetitive lifting of building blocks and pushing of hefty wheelbarrows of cement inflamed my injury. I tried working with carpenters, and I liked making money. But wood was heavy, and the heavy lifting didn't work for me. At last I learned that getting high helped ease the pain enough to hang in there. Damaged body parts didn't scream as loud after work surrounded with marijuana smoke and alcohol.

That June I had turned nineteen, and within weeks, the Selective Service Board contacted me by letter. It told me I was a prime candidate to be inducted 1A. I did not enlist. All summer I fought with the idea. I played along with the draft board saying I had a bad back, which contradicted my choice of work. I continued to play along by appearing at recruiting offices and talking to the army, and then the navy and the air force. I resisted being drafted due to medical reasons; I was stalling for time. I was worried. I considered going to Canada, which was only a few hundred miles away. The facts were clear. It was a difficult time for me, Ma, and Pa. There were no lengthy serious talks. The huge decision was at the highest and most important point of my life.

The hostile social climate brewed, with a war and the draft that nobody wanted. Hippies and drugs had worked their way into my shifting values. But the high court was still undecided about abortion, and I was thinking about what I would do if I got a girl pregnant. Life was life, and murder was murder. How could a law change for the worse? The Vietnam War had been ongoing to the point where the Selective Service needed more recruits. They initiated the lottery system. Of the 365 days in a year, birthdays were picked out of a hat. My lottery number was 032. The Selective Service Board called me for a hearing and wanted to see me. I went with X-rays from my doctor. That's all: just me, the X-rays, and Ma. After all was said and done, they thought it would be best if their doctors were to check me out. In order to be examined, I needed to be in the military service. They urged me strongly to make a selection according to law.

My hemming and hawing went on for a few more weeks or so, until we got a call from the sheriff's office. They urged me strongly to make a choice as to which branch of military service I wanted to go into. They called again a few weeks later. The officer on the phone said they would come out and arrest me. He said he knew it wasn't easy, but the law was the law. The pressure was tremendous. I really had nothing good going for me.

I was in love, but I had nothing to offer her. I was considering Canada, only 350 miles north. My father hated to see me go to war, but he also hated to see me become a draft dodger. His best advice was to do what I had to do.

One morning I heard my mother's voice, the voice of the happiest woman in the world. She had just read the newspaper headlines and was joyfully yelling. I'll never forget what my mom yelled upstairs to my bedroom that morning: "President Nixon declared the military voluntary. He put an end to the lottery system." *Hallelujah! My worries were over. From that day on, it was going to be only a volunteer military.* My mother kept saying it over and over as she made her way up the stairs to my bedroom with tears in her eyes and telling me *I was safe, I could stay home.*

After that, there was much celebration. The curse of dyslexia and failing third grade produced many life-changing effects. Being held back a year may have saved my life. After living through the idea of going to war or not, going to work in a factory seemed like a blessing. The pressure was off; the draft thing was over. I thought I did not have to make any more hard decisions. But I was young and foolish, and the ways of life are old and patient, like shadows at dusk tricking your eyes.

Chapter 4: Farewell, Love: Travel-Bound

Those high school days were gone. At nineteen years old in the autumn of 1972, I enjoyed life. My outlook after the draft issue was aimed at earning a regular paycheck. I lived with Ma and Pa. We all came from our jobs, ate, slept, and left. Once in a while we all sat together for a meal. Ken continued his education, climbing from two years of community college onto the third year at a state college. He and Carole were still in love. Her four-year college was two hundred miles away but was considering quitting. Ken drove himself hard in school and on the football field. A knee injury took any glory he hoped to garner on his field of dreams. With more time on his hands, his infatuation with Carole became idol worship in my eyes. Every chance he had, he drove the distance to be with her.

Being in love and loving life became parallel issues for me. Hope's passionate love for me never relented despite my growing absence. The way marijuana led my attitude toward speculating on what was beyond the next hill only helped grow my urge to travel. Hope never got high, and that gap remained as we still grew together for a while. Our differences didn't stop us from having fun. We drank wine in candlelight, and holding her next to me gave me a power I had never known. "I love you" were the only words that expressed the feeling within. She was still my sounding board. I gathered thoughts about the value of time and tossed them her way. She loved listening and carefully questioned my values and fondness for freedom. She also loved to wonder what would unfold in our lives.

Unlike me, Hope had a blueprint for her life. Her large family was steeped in tradition, and their treadmills were laced with hard work and financial reward. Her attraction to me was genuine, without pretense, as was mine to her. Part of her was drawn to my love for life. She wanted the excitement I felt. But mostly she wanted to be pushing a baby carriage. She was hoping, wishing, and gambling with her emotions that I would eventually fit in. Dinners out, going to nightclubs, and sitting close at the movies were beautiful times. We loved growing up together. Our values at first were comfortable together but didn't match over time.

Enjoying life was a growing belief system as I engaged in the workforce and negotiated with pain and problems. Smoking pot, loud music, and motorcycles rose in their importance as life became a bigger party. I found construction jobs and learned how to avoid repetitive movements when I could. Smoking pot helped me work on through the physical pain from my damaged sciatic nerve. Psychologically the pot helped my thoughts escape the limits of the truth that I faced a life of hard work. As I ached and soaked in the hot bathtub water, comfort was found with the thought of traveling. Hope's traditional ambitions saw us like her cousins and their kids. But they weren't mine yet. Her love saw what it wanted to see and didn't look for truth that only time would reveal. Even though love can blind out the truth, change is constant and people do change.

I never really gelled well on the job with reading the ruler in a consistent manner. Measurements somehow would move on me when they wanted to. A small line on the ruler to the right or a line to the left appeared or shifted. The measurement three quarters could somehow become three eights. If I was told to cut a board a foot and a half long, I would. But sometimes I'd cut it one foot five inches. It was the same mystery struggle as in school with words and numbers. My eyes or my thoughts or maybe it was a brief bit of memory that would move things around. I didn't know for sure what was wrong, just that something was going on inside of me. Stupid mistakes kept me away from tasks requiring accuracy that paid more money. I did grunt work instead.

I liked physical labor. The simplicity allowed free thoughts to gather. My hip and lower back screamed for rest, but were pacified with the marijuana. Pot was a self-prescribed mood enhancer that made life more fun and relaxing. Because I was stoned, I was less likely to complain. As far as impairing my judgments or coordination, yes, there was that too. Those were the side effects and chances I took. Pain was a condition I had to learn to live with. After work, some beer and more pot kept me in a stupor. Hot baths, exercise, and lying on thin foam mattresses on a floor rug were my therapy. The good repetitive motion of bringing my knees to my chest also brought introspection. There was no looking back. I had only me to blame and could only stare at the future. My self-analysis and sleeping on the floor became my normal nightly routine. The floor's firmness let my tense muscles spread out; its inflexibility had me wriggling for relief.

On paydays, I'd count my money and go see friends, or some would come by. Horseshoe games, ping pong, music in the garage, and deals made for pot were typical. Fun was what the money was for. Getting high had become the new norm. Watching girls go by in the early seventies evoked hoots and hilarious sexual outbursts. That was the way it was at that time. Some guys loved doing it, and a lot of girls really liked the vocal attention. Most girls did nothing, but others just gave you the finger. The basketball hoop attracted friends, and the more the merrier. When I got my first stereo, I chose music albums for their sounds and the messages in the lyrics. Savoy Brown, Cream, Ten Years After, and the Beatles' Sergeant Pepper fed me feelings and ideas. Alone with the records playing, deeper contemplations led to more curiosity about life.

✝

In the first snowfall of 1973, I found factory work at a large multinational company, General Electric. I was nineteen years old going on life and thinking of marriage. Money in my pocket and the security of weekly paychecks for several months in a row achieved a new status in my thinking. The money gave me options. I bought Hope nice gifts, and we did the boyfriend-girlfriend thing at restaurants, bars, and movies more often. Holding hands, we held life together. Her youth and mine spoke of a larger life union and the words of love forever. Looking at her face and eyes took away my thoughts of self-absorption. She had a beautiful laugh. When I flipped back her thick shining dark brown hair, her lip gloss shimmered invitingly. With her in my arms, the problems of getting from now to forever would be fun to discover and live out in unity. I was in love and thinking ahead, like an average guy would.

At first working in the factory was challenging. I labored at work—digging, picking, or fighting to hold onto a jack hammering. At times the pain in my hip was frightening and caused me to walk like I was lame, leaning to one side.

✝

MANUAL LABOR

Manual Labor is my name.
They call me hey you all the same.
They tell me do this and do that;
By the time you're done, I'll be back.

Manuel Labor first degree, I sentence my body,
For my mind to be free.
Manuel Labor makes me strong; for dreams I long,
Which I know can't be wrong

    The human backhoe is for hire
    Shoveling through the muck and mire.
    What can't be reached by a machine
    Manual digs it; he don't run on gasoline.

Laborers they come, and they go;
Hard to keep around, they're in the flow,
'Cause their mind is free from a trade,
They live for the choice that they made.

✝

I listened at lunchtimes to the old-timers' chronicles. They sucked on cigarettes, working the cancer stick pinched by lips or fingers. Blowing smoke seemed as natural as a baby shaking a rattle and laughing. Those eyes of tired men spoke. Wearing many wrinkles pressed together with great stories, they limped and leaned in and out of work. The blue-collar or the white-collar guy all said the same thing, "I was your age once and in love." Their cynical eyes looked into mine a few seconds. Their gaze flipped back a few decades. They articulated their love for their wives and children. But when they addressed the unforeseen college expenses or the second and third car, they rolled their eyes. Then came the lecturing words: "Watch out for what you ask for because you just might get it. When I started out, I didn't think I'd be here thirty years." At last they declared what they would do when they would get out.

For them, it was all about retirement, pensions, and a long-awaited rest. Florida away from the backbreaking snow shoveling was their dreamland. They were on the downside of their seesaw of life. Those veterans of time in the workforce were balanced with knowledge. Being with them gave me a glimpse of what the future might hold. What I saw wasn't appealing; it was a contradiction. It was a look of loss, with a wish to do it all differently, but they wouldn't if they could. Their knowledge came at the expense of living out their experience. But I was just beginning, and thirty years seemed so far away. I wasn't tied to anything yet, just testing the waters.

My factory time was at hand, working with a variety of trade mechanics. Electricians' one day, then millwrights, masons, carpenters, welders—it was a great experience. A few coworkers became good friends who were similar to me. We were young, got high, and partied a lot. That life of working eight or ten hours a day had all the trappings of financial security for an entire life. Young or middle-aged, single or married, most of the employees talked about what they would do with their money. For some younger newlyweds, it was new toys like boats, cars, homes, or another baby. For most of the older guys, it was about the remaining time. They just wanted to get out and have some time to themselves. They wanted to stop and get off the ride they were on. The men who worked every day on the same machines like robots were nicknamed "lifers." But it didn't matter if your spot was at a desk or moving around the plant. What mattered was living the life you accepted.

These guys, who worked twenty-five, thirty, thirty-five, forty years of their life in one job, or two or three, all seemed to be in a type of time prison. They confined their wills within walls that held them all there in time together. Hundreds of men invisibly chained to hundreds of machines. They were looking through bars of bought happiness in their marriages. The prison cell of debt still had bills after some were divorced. More bars of time, more bars to drink at all were keeping some families apart. Their self-imposed sentencing was exchanged for the security that money promised and that their retirement would bring. The married men jokingly blamed their wives, who sat home and spent the money and wanted more. Kids in college, cars, and more bills all meant working overtime. Everybody's kids were too good to work like they did—they had to go to college. Some single guys wanted more toys and faster cars, and loved gambling nobody had enough. A few or many dollars would be wagered every week in gaming pools. Laying bets on numbers or horses or sports games was exciting. That was their long-shot hope, their pleasure—to hit it big and retire early. Everybody gambled with time. So did I. But they gave up their youth and hoped for an old age of ease.

The old factories had very tall walls with brown stained glass that kept out the bright sunshine. Opening doors let in glaring sunbeams that always drew my eyes. The light called me. Outside was where the mystery was and where I wanted to be. There was nothing mysterious in the factory. Only the paycheck kept me there on the inside. I labored very hard for my pay. Factory work was where I found another kind of real camaraderie. The mixing of good times with coworkers was a great experience in learning about people. It was the party side of youth integrating with on-the-job dedication. I saw again the process of fitting in, similar scenario to fitting in at school. Fitting in was a repeating theme. Again it was about me being a square peg trying to fit into a round hole. Again conditions of life, the mallet of society, were trying to trim off my edges and make me fit. At the same time, I saw the tradeoffs others had made for love and family. The decades of everyday work and the workers' eyes were looking at me.

The process of trying to fit in took its toll on me. Those human molds of routine, those tediously positioned men at their machines, were somehow my distant reflection. As all who passed through the gate each morning and each evening, so was I. What could become of my life? I was indeed becoming extremely troubled and grew discouraged. Like anesthesia numbs pain, I needed my reality dulled. Getting high before work, again while at work at lunch with a beer, and especially after work with another beer.

Hope was still in love with the hope we once called love forever. But when I wasn't in her loving arms, the idea of forever began to feel like a ball and chain. I was asked to work overtime and liked the idea of earning more money. I saw Hope less and felt her absence more. The old parallels of loving her and loving life became unequal rails. My life had come to be about making adjustments. Hope was sandwiched in between staying and going. Eight hours of work a day was a third of my life. Eight hours of sleep was another third. At twenty years old, I found that I was not happy with the prospects. Only having a third of life for everything else was not enough. The sight of two thirds of my life gone for thirty years didn't look real. Where was being happy at what I do? Marriage and working in a factory job for most of my life crowded my mind. A choice had to be made. All I knew is what I did not want. I didn't know what I wanted. I felt more strongly toward exploring for what I might want.

✝

BOUND FREE

I've been eighteen for so long,
Grew a wild, funny face,
Rode a hundred shooting stars,
Wished for nothing but my space.

> Life sleeps, creeps, and sweeps to hit and fill in
> Among all the holes around me.
> I'm square. There's nowhere to fit and chill in
> Among all the holes around me.

> > I'm young and Bound Free.
> > I'm still young, I'm Bound Free.
> > Where am I bound to be Bound Free?

Watch and wonder, can't always stop
What I will and won't let in.
Planted wrinkles, harvest smiles,
Years of laughter in every grin.

Sheep graze, baa-baa-baa, mouse maze, Shangri-La,
Sunrays, cha-cha-cha, wolf plays, Ali Baba.

✝

I mentally walked off the treadmill of life. My mind was moving out, but I still had that one foot on the treadmill. Everything was about time, and time was exchanged for money. I chose to stroll around in the thoughts of experiencing more or less. I liked to contemplate that perhaps I could buy a twenty-foot recreational vehicle to live in and do some traveling. I entertained the idea of being a professional laborer traveling with the seasons. That idea worked for me, so I prepared for the event.

I bought a small vacant lot of land from my Aunt Lucy. It was across the street from my mom's house, where I could park my house on wheels. That was something worth working for, and I would shortly be out of debt. Aunt Lucy was cool; she let me pay the lot off over a few months. She was Granny's sister and lived three houses away. Sometimes she and I would have a brandy sitting on her front porch watching the cars go by. She was the kind of lady who knew a lot but didn't say much. She was a good listener. She was a widow without children. Aunt Lucy never mentioned her husband, nor did anyone in our family.

I needed to do more than what was expected. I wanted to create my own path of what was practical and do it at my own pace. I questioned how people valued things like expensive luxury vehicles and flamboyant clothing. I examined my desire for a lifestyle with an RV. My motives for a necessary living space and freedom to move seemed practical. The sizzling spark of frustration was lit. The fuse of restlessness and need for revolution was burning. The bomb of change blew up my fledgling identity. I did not want to be a lifer. I did not want to spend my whole life in one place. I was young, I had time on my side, and I was willing to take chances. Thoughts of where to go and what to do became a constant fuel for my thinking.

I was drawn like once before to TV. Another series of weekly shows throttled my interest in finding what it was I wanted. The show *Kung Fu* was about a misfit sojourner fighting for what was right and good. He denied himself more than what was necessary. He resisted the temptations of society. It appealed to my searching soul. By 1974 I still had not traveled; instead, I watched my friends travel while I was working. Seeds of discontent and disenchantment seemed to have been planted deep within me from time past. Long before my opportunities began to unfold, there was a design for me to live out. I knew nothing of my blueprint or purpose. I just knew I had to move on. My winter of dissatisfaction melted into my spring of transformation.

The last snows of complacency and the bad luck of injuries melted. A season of a fresh new direction had arrived and was forcing my growth. My emotions were tearing. I needed to be fair with Hope and cut our ties. I couldn't be what I was a few years ago or what she wanted me to be.

I still had a genuine true love for Hope; she was the first. Through her, my undiscovered territory of "being in love" happiness was recognized. Her love filled spaces I did not know were empty. The joy of having her love on my mind brought a happiness that was a great life pleasure. I poured out my captive emotions. Loving was an overwhelming and unstoppable power that found completion. Our faithfulness was perfect and relentless. We were running hot with high hopes, and our whole lives were ahead of us. I had the once-in-a-lifetime love that many people can only wish for. But I couldn't continue to falsely indulge in what was once a destiny of love. There was something over my head and over my heart telling me to let go.

Our love should have made the waiting for the rest of life to unfold a worthy goal. Our intertwined lives tried to work out differences born out of time and change. I wasn't comfortable with the idea of playing house or living for the expectations that were acceptable. I couldn't fit into the mold of designer love. I knew I'd relive a sense of regret from walking away from true love. Looking into Hope's eyes was like looking at a shattered mirror waving good-bye. Our hearts could not be any closer, but my mind grew far apart, separated by independence and curiosity. The split was made.

$$\dagger$$

CAN'T FRAME THE WIND

I got a pain in my back, and my truck don't run,
Load of worries on my mind, must weigh a ton,
But I still think of you, on top of it all,
Wondering what I really saw.

       Times are getting harder, each and every day.
       Can't help from thinking, will I find the way,
       Home, your loving arms, you're still on my mind.
       My troubles on my back keep me down the line.

The picture you painted, with your diamond ring, wasn't me.
You Can't Frame the Wind—it's meant to be free.
Your image of happy was good, but didn't look like me.
You Can't Frame the Wind—it's meant to be free.

       Your sweet loving arms once waited for me there.
       That's what made me go, I said it with a tear.
       Hurts me when I hear me tell how I feel.
       Truth cuts deep within, the damage is real.

Well, my back's okay, and my truck, it runs.
Don't have any worries, all I have is fun.
But I still think of you, on top of it all,
Wondering what I really saw.

Spring popped out with warmer sunrays on my face, as it does every welcome spring in the Northeast. Life starts coming up nonstop from under the melting snow. Exhilaration is one of the benefits from living in a distinct four-season climate. Grass, flowers, and tree buds were seen opening every changing day of the week. New life comes at you, surrounding you, looking at and grabbing you. Natural life-changing cycles demand attention. Post-winter factory hibernation caused my natural agitation to bubble within. I had a few thousand dollars in the bank and drove a good sturdy pickup truck. Driving with my windows down in the annual campaign of warming sun and fresh air, I giggled for more. A notion arrived, and it began spreading its wings.

If I didn't change the factory, the girlfriend, and my outlook, I'd be living the same life. I didn't want to live the same way anymore. The springtime vaulted my impulse to design a makeover blueprint. My family's unused summer home at Galway Lake was just sitting there. First I would get a puppy and raise that puppy to be the best dog. The idea was an opportunity to live out a childhood fantasy to raise my own dog. He'd be like Thunder, my old friend, always happy to see me, loving me unconditionally. I still brushed Thunder, and he still lay on the grass watching me shoot baskets. Thunder was liked by all my friends and would ride with Hope and me up to the lake. But the new puppy would be trained better. He'd be my best friend, a companion to travel with. Life would be a mobile adventure, not just a vacation with a friend returning to my hometown. I had the money to do it, I had the place, and I could take the time. Time was still on my side. That plan once conceived was like a burning fire on all my hay bales of restlessness.

The right day came. I saw an ad in the paper saying puppies were for sale out on a country farm. I was ready at twenty years old for a revolutionizing adjustment. One guy I worked with at the factory was in his fifties; he was a lifer. Another guy in his thirties was becoming a lifer. He had a young wife and a new baby. But he wasn't sure about sticking his feet in the cement of so-called security. He gave thought to starting his own business and living a little riskier life before old age. The older guy used to pick on him and say, "That's it; after your first kid, you're done, you're a lifer." I told the boys at work I was leaving and I might not come back. "I'm going to look at a puppy. If this dog is for me, I'll quit." They laughed and said, "We'll see you tomorrow."

I drove out of the factory with the rest of my life. I thought about the adventure and saw myself smiling in the rearview mirror. I headed straight for the puppies, about thirty miles northwest into beautiful farm country, Schoharie County. Brilliant warm sunshine landed on my left arm and the side of my face in the opened window. The fifty-mile-an-hour balmy breeze rushed past my arm and face, blowing my hair. Sincere cheerful ideas breathed adventure, and images of an early retirement lifestyle got fired up. The tape player played Marshal Tuckers "Can't You See?"

Turning off the highway and then off a secondary road to a dusty dirt road, I drove slowly past farm fields. The old leaning mailbox post showed the number of the lot where the rundown mobile home was parked. Young children's toys were scattered on the muddy driveway and grass. A woman came to the door clutching a baby perched on her hip. She said her mixed-breed female yellow Lab with vizsla was mated with a large pure yellow Lab. The local dogcatcher had caught the male at a chicken coop on a nearby farm. Making puppies to sell was their intention. The plan worked, and then the dogcatcher took the big Lab to the next county, where he thought it belonged.

I first saw his small bright yellow face and legs coming out of the woods. He was limping on one hind leg, leading his mother and the pack of three remaining yellow puppies. I knew he was for me, the one in the litter of a dozen. "Old Yeller" was the biggest in the litter, but he was left in the bunch. A few weeks prior, he was sleeping with the other puppies under a car near the tire. A small kid had pulled the parking brake off, and the car rolled over the pup's right rear leg. The local vet said he'd be okay, but since he was injured, people did not choose him. He was sturdy and very alert, and he tried so hard. I knew he had a great heart. I felt that a bad experience with a car was good for the pup to know. Dogs seldom get a second chance with a car. After paying the woman thirty-five dollars, I put the yellow Lab and vizsla mix in the back of my pickup truck. I tied him between the sides of the truck-bed box, placed my coat in the middle, pushed him down, and told him to hang on.

With a few hundred dollars in my pocket, we drove to the lake and moved into the family camp that same sunny day. We drove to the country store and used the pay phone early that evening. Ma was shocked to hear I quit my job. She couldn't understand how the frustration she heard me talk of in the past year had taken such a dramatic turn. I couldn't express accurately the force within me that pushed me into my actions. Her weighty words of concern needed to be comforted. Hearing myself explaining my spontaneous new situation, I felt the gravity of the decision. After I told her I'd be in town within a few days to tie up loose ends at work, she felt better. Her suggestion that I ask for my job back fell on deaf ears. I had the pup, I had a plan, and I was sticking to it. I was opening a new box of experience with this dog. I had an understanding of a dog's love from Thunder. Adding knowledge to love, the pup and I would begin to fill a fresh box of life's encounters with learning.

The pup and I began bonding by resting on the floor by his food and water bowls. Quietly together we sat while he ate and drank. We listened to the forest and talked with our eyes. Nobody moved; we stayed by the food and water. I carried him to the lake the next day. It was cold, with snow still lying behind the beach in the shade. The shoreline was clear, so I walked with him in the water. The cold buoyant lake was good for his injured leg to stretch out its tightness. Every day I carried him back to camp in a blanket next to my chest. Before I dried him off, I stood him in a pail of hot water and moved his leg, massaging it. I told him about me and how wonderful he would be. The pup grew strong and carried a "Grandpa McCoy" limp just on his first few steps. Then he skipped and ran with the wind. He was fast and could jump like a kangaroo. When we marched, we were an army of two; when I was at ease, he remained on duty. I raised him in the solitude of the country, enjoying twenty-four hours each wonder-filled day for six months. Obedience and learning were his proven strengths. He obeyed without getting a biscuit or reward. He did it for my love. He would work for my approving smile, kind words, and hugs.

For as long as I could remember, I wanted the chance to raise my own dog. Moved by reasons and seasons of rebellion, I found myself to be in that position of responsibility. How ironic—I wanted to be free, and I ended up being a parent. Unlike Thunder, who arrived when I was nine and received a kid's coaching, this pup would get my best. I did some reading up on dog training and came across the idea of the pack theory. That's where only one leader commands respect and leads the challenging follower. After much thought and with a little experience, I took on the task of training and providing for that chosen animal. The teacher-student relationship worked well.

The camp was going to be our home. I tore down interior walls, making a bigger arena to teach in. The visual space and comfort to train in one very large living room was to our advantage. We sat under a tree practicing to be still. Being still, taking in sounds of the birdcalls, crickets, and wind, was a satisfying way to build our partnership. Telling him to go see was the payoff for his patience. He loved to run and hunt and chase. He was never on a leash. Rain did not hold us inside; it found us under tree limbs watching how the water commanded the forest. I named him Piper. Pie and I were making our own rules in the elements as much as possible. To say I was unconventional would be an obvious understatement. I had no boundaries, no time constraints, and no responsibilities other than the Pie dog.

To get up in the middle of the night and sit in silence under the stars felt natural. We walked barefoot in the moonlight to the warm lake that summer for swims. At times in rain or shine, the Pie heard me thinking out loud. He caught my tone, my words of loss, abandoned love, and forsaken income. He listened to my anger toward the mystery alien within. He noticed the frustrating questions arising from the lack of peace. We lived without direction, off the treadmill of tradition.

When Hope drove up to see us, we hugged and had a party. Pie loved her attention. He twisted, spinning around her legs, and then bolting for a stick, proudly waving it clenched in his teeth. She rubbed his coat and spoke to him like he was a baby. They played like kids on vacation, free from any rules and regulations. He had seen other campers, but he never saw me hold and kiss one. Walking to the beach at sunset with her hand in mine, we were as sad as a solider leaving for war. After six years of our growing young love, I stood on new ground alone. Without her in my plans, I tried to explain what I didn't fully know myself. Just next to the old box of tradition, my feet were still not firmly fixed on the greener grass outside of it. Off of the customary treadmill of life, I was halted by the reality of my singleness. I paused in doubt. Her sacrificial love for me shone like a lighthouse beacon. Her reassuring words told me I would find what I needed to find. Hope was the heroin in our drama with her effort to let go. Night fell and fell and fell; I was so alone without her. Sitting next to my life's new empty box of post-love experience, I put a piece of sorrow in with one hand. I petted the Pie with the other, recalling the lifers' warning: "Watch out what you ask for because you just might get it."

✝

On June 16, 1974, my birthday, I was twenty-one years old. Everything was going my way except love. I tried going to the bars around the lake and the small towns looking for love. There was hollowness where there used to be the surety of Hope's love waiting for me. Bars were no longer fun. I couldn't find love again. I had the best love once and was unable to settle for less. I found jobs working on house repairs and doing some roofing with my carpenter friend Calvin. We kept working irregularly, and our partying remained the order of life. He often stayed at the camp throughout the summer.

One warm day during the middle of the week in July, we ate some hallucinogenic mushrooms. I locked Piper in the camp and closed the windows. Calvin and I made our way to the beach laughing hysterically, walking as best we could. At the water's edge, the idea of crossing the lake still seemed to be reasonable. We looked far into the distance over the calm glassy lake top and thought we found a landing spot. Our only plan was to start and not stop. All my years of swimming off the shoreline, I always had the intention of swimming across. That day the lake was an exciting thrill.

The water welcomed us with such a noticeable softness we both commented on our smooth effortless strokes. Talking and swimming didn't go well together. On our backs, we laughed at our stupidity and agreed not to talk. When we were halfway, we paused to look around. At that point we realized our vulnerability before plunging our arms in with more determination to reach shore. Hauling ourselves up onto the front lawn of somebody's property, we stretched out on the grass exhausted. Looking at the lake in reverse with a new view, it looked wider, like a bigger job to get back. The seriousness of our whimsical choice came after we rested and were at the water's edge again. Returning over the water started out okay, but became more of a chore at halfway again. Reaching the sandy shore on our hands and knees, we laid at the water's edge. Feeling like a million bucks with satisfaction, we were puffed up with pleasure. Walking back to the camp, we both agreed how stupid it was. The next day, Calvin left for his apartment and his girlfriend.

✝

A few weeks later, I found a job in a bakery as a food processor making bread. My predawn 4:00 a.m. job was lifting hundred-pound bags of flour into the bread mixer. I learned the painful surprise of just how damaging the Harley crash still was. The repetitive motion pinched my sciatic nerve, causing a spasm in my lower back. Leaning over heavily, I managed to drive and ever-so-painfully lay on the floor of the camp by 9:00 a.m. and slept. I woke at noon but couldn't get up. I was flat on the floor with a painful pinched nerve in need of total rest. Experience isn't always the best teacher. That time it taught me how I should think with caution and how not to repeat the pinch. In and out of part-time jobs as a short-order cook or laboring in construction, I discovered that by self-denial, a type of early retirement could be enjoyed fully. If I didn't need much, I worked less; and through financial prudence, I had more time. Working for money, true, that had to be done, but I'd rather work for less and have more time and natural fun. Only once would I be young.

Natural fun was enjoying the simple things, like living in and out of an all-day rainfall. Walking hearing the raindrops fall on my hood or letting the warm rain cover me with just shorts on. Pie and I ran in the woods with rain pouring down in our quest to be primordial with creation. I would sit at a window watching raindrops and sipping warm tea. And then there was being fully awake waiting for the sunrise. I was in control. Without a direction, my best plan was to see what came. I gave daily attention to raise my dog. The building blocks of learning could be taught only in those few months of puppyhood. Conversely I kept out the negative influences that caused distractions. Like the city and people and noise.

Accepting who the leader was and who the follower was allowed Pie to expand his personality more freely. He learned his role well and appreciated his free time. I always gave Pie his own time, and he took it. He knew when to stay close or how to find his way home. I hoped his obedience that was put in place early would remain. I had that yellow dog trained well. Our next goal was to travel. The advantageous thought of what-if that eventually lured me away from a young woman's love and a life of mediocrity blossomed. I wanted to find out what the world had to offer. The southern grass looked greener with coming winter.

Autumn was in the air with the smell of old leaves, and another change was coming soon. Once again, my plans for winter were to seek warmer weather, and my strategies were shaping up like once before. My rebellious antiestablishment style of living was different. My personal ingredients made my leap into adulthood harder. I had no skill, no trade, and no higher education. What I had was a busted back and an unexplainable way of making stupid mistakes. I still had a great desire to be free from the typical lifestyle of those on the treadmill. I discovered at the lake the worth that came from teaching. My investment of time rewarded me with a very unique animal.

One of the reasons I named him Piper was because he attracted life like the Pied Piper. People and other dogs loved my dog. Many, many times I was told how special he was. He was like the wind moving, smart and independent. He would chase a scent and always come back. I saw him kill a few woodchucks and rabbits; he wasn't afraid of blood. And he never backed down from the few fights there were. The Pie was protective of what was his and mine. He required low maintenance; it was one of his strengths. Just put the food and water out and he'd take care of everything else. My pickup truck was like his doghouse on wheels. By September I drifted in from the lake to my hometown with only the reality that we were going to travel soon, maybe by next spring.

Chapter 5: Brain Trauma

It happened one fantastic autumn afternoon, just after one more great time with twenty friends. The big party with a keg of beer and lots of pot to smoke was at my friend Buddy's farm. We played volleyball on the grass and rode our motorcycles while his huge stereo speakers blasted guitar solos over a hundred acres. Just before sunset, the party was winding down. It was time to load the trail bike up on the truck and put the Pie dog in. Without my helmet on, I rode my motorcycle for one more lap around the sun-filled upper hayfield. I felt the freedom with wind in my hair, the orange clouds hanging in the clear autumn sky. The last corner I took went wide, going fast into high waving grass. Hitting the unseen crumbled rock wall, I crashed and was pitched through the air. My most severe transformation in life came swiftly and suddenly. The near-death experience dove in and pinned me to the ground like a hawk clenching onto its prey and squeezing a slow death.

Later I was told I flew high enough to bring a tree branch down with me. Friends found the bike, the branch, and then my body. The Pie lay near me, curling his lip and giving a low growl. He saw me crash and was protecting me as friends approached. Death swooped in for a visit, but it wasn't allowed to stay. God spared my life again. Everything that was going my way left with the grim reaper. My body and breath were saved, but time and life continued to move slowly. Friends told me I was mumbling something incoherent, with blood coming out of one ear. The six months of gracious living at the lake training my pup crashed to a tragic end in the sundown of a summer day. Friends said the Pie acted strange and uneasy at my side. Cautiously they led him away and took me to the hospital.

X-rays showed I suffered a traumatic brain injury, along with a dislocated left shoulder. Waking up in the hospital room, for the first thirty seconds I didn't know my mother, who stood tearful at my side. She saw my opened eyes. I heard her assure me I would be okay. That's what I was told. But from what? My memory was gone. It was the first afternoon of what was to be an extreme life-altering event. The family doctor said time was needed to recover. There was no specialist, no training, or anyone who could help. No more, no less, just waiting for the moments to move on.

Recovery from my second major motorcycle accident meant more than lying flat and discovering how to think out of the box. This time there was no box of thinking to get out of, only time and space to be in. At age twenty-one, I was completely shut down, without any recall. No going back in my mind and wondering what I would have been like if I did not crash. God only knows.

The head concussion altered me for my remaining life. Without any memory at first and without any way back or any way forward, I was and I wasn't looking for me. When I found a piece of me in my memory, I did not know for sure if it was myself. I wasn't sure because there wasn't anything before or after the piece I recalled. It was just a piece. I wondered how I was acquainted with the thought, and then the thought vanished. I didn't know what to think.

Those few days in the strange hospital room must have been what Frankenstein felt like. A mix of old maybes and new moving pieces of who and what and where. When I did recall a portion of me, it was only for a short period of time. Most of my time was in the present, with wide eyes wondering about what was going on. I was alone in my thoughts, waiting for more pieces of me to show up. I needed a lot more than a part-time nurse; I needed a full-time granny. Ma and Pa and their yin and their yang, their sweet and sour, all got pushed to the side. My health was so important that my family finally crashed and split. Pa moved out of the house so Granny could move in.

The daily routines of forgetfulness were freakish. While eating, I would fork the food, but halfway along I'd pause in thought and forget to put the food in my mouth. Granny would say, "Go ahead, Mikey, eat the food on your fork." I sat at the table like a foreigner in a train station who can't read the signs. When I went into the bathroom, I'd forget why I went in. I would look into the mirror and look, look, look. I would turn and turn back to stare at my face for long periods of time. I would hear my grandmother calling me and prompting me to finish what I started. My internal fight to find me, be me, and grow was a tremendous setback for Ma. It broke my mother's heart and her mother's heart. Sitting in the quiet living room, Ma patted my head and wiped her tears. With a crack in her voice, she told of her love and wishes to make it all go away. My dad would come up and sit with me. His big hands would hold mine. He told me to go slow and everything would work out.

Those days were such a struggle, and I didn't even know that I was in a struggle. I was always tired and wanted to sleep. At first I could remember nothing more than the surroundings—like the shell of a person not knowing what was inside. When I did remember something like someone's face, that was all I remembered. There was no perceived emotion or love involved with their smile. The overall sense of being misplaced within me was one of the loneliest losses. I surrounded myself on the floor with my dogs, petting Thunder and Piper. I knew them; I knew their love. Their loyalty and love never escaped me. My only comfort was found on the floor with them. Hope came and sat with me and the dogs. They were happy to see each other, but then she choked up. She and Granny hugged each other weeping. We sat in the basement on the old couch. Her fingers brushed my hair, and the parts of my memory that remembered touched her long brown hair. Talking with her brought rapid images of our time together. The feelings of love were much stronger than the vague feeling of why I left her. She told me more about myself than all my family combined.

The memory section of my brain and time moved slowly, like the moon moves all month to be full. I didn't look like I was working at it—just sitting and staring. But I was. When I started asking simple questions, my tongue was awkward, slurring words. I was able to retain briefly some information given me. The swelling in my brain would not allow me to keep what I was told. I always wanted to know what happened to me. As many times as I was told, I would forget. Any glimpses of the past that were issued through my memory would flash and keep on going. My questioning attitude, which came with the recovery, was growing more intense. Not only did I ask my family members why this and why that, but I would also interrogate my friends down on Buddy's farm. Hearing some of them complain about low wages and say, "At least I'm not starving like the people in China," aroused my curiosity. Like a little kid, I kept asking why. My questions got bigger, like "Why are the people in China starving?" They did not have the answers or seem to care like I cared or see things like I saw things. I wanted to find answers to simple questions.

At that time, I first began to conjure up questionable thinking habitually and out loud. I wanted, needed, and gathered information to clarify and evaluate what was important to me. I began to engage in the debating side of a conversation. But I would forget. Later I remembered not remembering and that what I didn't remember was important. Those few seconds of recall and my awareness of not remembering became longer flashes, which grew and became more frequent during the late autumn of 1974.

One day I began to write. I jotted down questions like, "What will I do in life?" On small pieces of orange-colored notepaper, I wrote out the answer: "I have to wait; time will tell." I needed to write so I would not forget. My thoughts and feelings were like medicine. That practice of relating to a piece of paper with a pen became my outlet. I would not have to bother my friends and family with questions. But I always wanted to know when I would be better. How long would it take? It was answered by the doctor, who said, "When you stop asking." My first times of writing to myself were times of great need. Thoughts were mixed, and yet seemed to be concerned with friends, dogs, music, bands, and especially a longing to recover. The most powerful repeating feeling I wrote was of my desire to not just fit into a system of being on the treadmill of life. I didn't know what to be, only what not to be. At the same time I was asking myself what to do, I drew little pictures with the words. Small cabins with trees and a path leading to water; there were always trees and water. That initial writing outlet would lead into diary writing.

---

†

CIRCLES AND LINES

Music, Circles, and Lines.
Around and around it goes,
Keeping the people tapping their toes.

Music, Circles, and Lines.
Measures and measures of tones,
Stories of lovers in different poems.

Feelings, way deep inside,
Watching and waiting for love,
Hoping for someone I'm dreaming of.

Dreaming my life away,
Looking so lonesome and blue,
Waiting for a dream to come true.

Sorrow, there's no surprise.
Sadder and sadder I grieve.
No one to blame, still someone must leave.

Over without your love;
Never forever again
Will I tell myself it's just pretend.

People, Circles, and Lines.
Measures and measures of tones,
Stories of love in different poems.

— † —

I began my official scattered diary writing at age twenty-one early that winter of 1974 on medium-size white pieces of notepaper. I became more and more reliant on my dialogue with those notes. Thought writing became my closest friend. I not only looked forward to it, but would rely upon my fledgling routine for the peace that comes from bonding. To release my burden was to be able to talk to someone. It was a blank piece of paper, but it was a start of my new relationship with the new me. Some deep emotions that troubled me were let out in tiny glimpses to deal with. Times I hated sitting in summer school conflicted with my new friendship with writing. Feeling the distaste of school with feelings that liked the writing gave me a special sense of worth. My fears of making a commitment resurfaced. The ways I quit the factory job and discarded Hope's love were painful memories to relive. But with the pad and pen, I sat processing and felt more worth.

All my preparation with Pie and plans to live free traveling were crushed, and they crushed me again to grasp a little of that loss—like knocking on the door of a great room and seeing through a small crack the huge size of what I can't see. I sat searching for words, for my feelings, and felt good doing it. I had no other help or means to let lose my feelings. Thinking and writing were more than just passing time; they were remedies. Expressing my thoughts was the most writing I had ever done. The pad heard my written thoughts. The spaces between the words and lines spoke back to me. Reading what I wrote caused me to think more. I didn't care if the words were misspelled; what mattered was my thought. My thoughts weren't for a teacher; there was no test. I was free from trying to be correct.

My essential challenge in recovering the missing pieces was doing it alone. It was agitating at times. Seeing some of my past coming back in phases was an abstract impression. The reality of turning my back on the traditions of love, marriage, and the responsibilities of paying bills for thirty years was a lonely view. But discovering what I had done was like looking at my life from a different dimension, as if I were two people.

I kept questioning myself as I slowly lived out the road to recovery. It was like walking before running on my own one-way street. I saw other people around me like vehicles quickly moving on their known paths. But I walked slowly and surely, looking down. Assessing my private battle to regain whoever I was and seeing my resistance to tradition was a struggle. How to regain that noncompliant attitude was a mystery. There was no rock of stability I could identify myself with and cling to. All I had to guide me were the stereo, song lyrics, and music I used to associate with. They all helped build back and add to my new identity. A kind of rebirth, a type of redesigning of my mind, was undergone. Like the radio lyrics and music taught me as a youth, my albums were teaching me what was important, what to keep hold of, and what to let go of. The plastic LP recordings offered a variety of emotions for me to cling to and write about.

✝

Winter was upon me, bringing uncomfortable cabin fever with it. The public bus ran by every hour. Riding it became comfortable, familiar, and interesting. I liked the schedule and the known stops on the route. For the most part, bus-stop people don't say much; they just look. I fit right in. Just to get out of the house I'd walk around downtown looking into the store windows, exploring the city where I grew up. A lot of building blocks of memory were found here and there. Sitting in local cafés, I would watch people and write inconspicuous notes about the moment. My evaluation of people and situations was like trying to find a keyhole in the dark. The surroundings unlocked what I was okay with. The public library was good to get warm in. It, too, was a place where people looked and didn't say much, another comfort zone.

At the Schenectady Community College library, I found a book on philosophy and the religion called Taoism. It was what the guy on the TV show *Kung Fu* believed in, I thought. I used to date the librarian, so she liberated that reference material and brought it to me to keep. Reading the Tao's profound messages on life with the solo ways of the sage reshaped my outlook. Blending with nature and not accumulating possessions was its focus. I took very seriously the values taught. It spoke of self-denial, and those words rang true to my core. It answered the questions about people's greed with a satisfying direction of the harmony that comes from having enough. The sage was also off the treadmill. I wasn't alone in my thinking. I wasn't crazy for letting go of commitment to materialism and the routine behaviors offered in society.

When I began to recovery more fully, I essentially became someone new living with someone old. My new gods were the same as the old gods, things I could see and touch and didn't cost much. They were smoking pot, doing drugs, drinking booze with loud music, and chasing young women. My commitment to those things was okay.

I got back on a motorcycle and began riding with my friends again. Experiencing an increased vigor to live more fully in the reshaping of life, I once again felt complete. I almost died but lived, and I loved life more. I did what I had to do to maintain those gods with zeal. Those important aspects of my life would lead me onward in my misguided path for the next fifteen years. Living in the woods like the sage was not possible, so I tried new jobs in warehouses and remained unsatisfied with my attempts at finding work. Delivering early-morning newspaper bundles or short-order cooking kept me quitting jobs and uncommitted. I did like the idea and the practice of looking for something new, but nothing interested me enough to stay.

A kind of help-hurt was stifling my finding satisfaction. I was in some kind of atypical adolescent zone, unable to be serious enough to do what I didn't like. I hung onto the focused look at myself through the eyes of marijuana and telling only the diary. Parts of my personality wouldn't age. Or perhaps they never grew up well. I continued much further than I originally intended in my lack of commitment. Those focused days and looks, at me, through my searching eyes, were aiming at being an individual. Those years of me talking to myself in the diary were an ongoing type of friendship and job and medicine. Depending on where I was working, I often had some time or lots of time on my hands. Consequently I would daily write in the diary. Often I would pick up the diary three or four times a day and use it to talk myself into an ease of accepting myself. Those wire-spiral notebooks were my first diaries, and they were the continued evidence of my recovery. I liked the wire binding the pages. The wire was like a lock, locking in the pages and locking out any additions; nothing could be added. My thoughts were so valuable; tearing them out wasn't even an option.

Several months rolled by as I progressively evolved in my writing. At times the winter cold was deafening, and serene silence was perfect. Full moons froze my staring eyes open. A powerful lunar magnetic pull locked me up in long gazes of complete attention. My concentration was acute with insight; nothing went unnoticed. My mind's eye was a mix of intuitiveness and perception. It caused me to cock my head and ponder what all the writing was about. Effects from smoking pot and drinking were also more intense. My reaction to their influences brought a more radical, untamed change over me. My pad and pen took what I had to say and satisfied my need to tell others. My thoughts and writings were recycled and accumulated through all of 1975 into 1976.

✝

THE MAN IN THE MOON IS LAUGHING

I start smiling, like the Man in the Moon.
Listen to life play the same old tune.
Parties and barrooms, the usual sight
Over the town, a bright Friday night.

> The Man in the Moon Is Laughing, even though he's all alone.
> He takes his time when rising, moving up all on his own.
> The Man in the Moon Is Laughing, moving up all on his own.

Making some fun, couldn't get much higher.
A woman to hold can burn like a fire.
Wait for the one, keep searching for love.
Looks draw me close, like the moon above.

Late in the evening, with no one else there,
Up at the full moon, I stand still and stare,
Looking for someone to replace true love,
Finding no answers in the face up above.

✝

Some of the most powerful experiences those first years of my recovery were alone at night. I would routinely look for the timely phases of the full moon and write about the kinship I felt. Somehow the effect of the big friendly moon would greatly influence both my composure and agitation. The rising fluids in my brain or something mysterious would alter my thinking and attitude. Thoughts about my memory loss and gain were more intense. I drank more in the bars and howled louder with friends down on Buddy's farm. I wanted sex more and stayed out later looking for a friendly woman. After the frenzy, I came home calmer and wrote with more patience. I saw my contradictions more clearly and my chosen path to write more soberly.

I recall the gradual building of that friendship between the solar giant and my skyward anticipation. It was almost a type of celebration when I would prepare for the full moonrise. My sightings of a quarter, then a half, increased the lengths of my stares for the moon man's face. It would be a small get-together, just him and me and the dogs sitting under a pine tree in my backyard. It would be there that I would entertain myself with dreams of someday. Perhaps my writings would lead to a book someday—how wild that would be. I would see myself in the future with the ability to do well and be good. I'd be happy with making an income as a writer, able to finally settle down and in love again. All my dreams of someday took place near some mountains in the forest by a river or lake. I would absolutely be surrounded by God's creation.

Nightly peering diligently, my eyes would fasten on the moon's first rising crest. As it ever so slowly inched up, excitement forced me to stand and take in more of the globe. Wows and mutterings of amazement came forth in low weighty tones as I paced the yard in awe. Without taking my eyes off the moon and trying not to blink, my breaths were taken in deeper through a wide-open mouth. I felt the energizing power pump increasingly as the huge yellow sphere rose. Losing the golden hues to brilliant florescent white, the exceptional glow confirmed all my projections for a full revitalization. My willpower became a smiling dynamic to push out the joy. I laughed and paced, and the dogs paced with me, wagging their tails because I was happy.

I was amazed at my monthly love for the few minutes of unfolding full moon birth. The rise was complete and priceless. I wrote of my thrill but couldn't write fast enough. I began to carry a small mini-cassette tape player to record those moments before they were gone. From the distant stars in the dark to the closeness in the rising power, it was certainly all of God's doing. Even though the clarity that there is a God was obvious, I did nothing but acknowledge the fact.

A favorite experience was to glean from the muse a nugget of profound clarity like, "Patience is the handle on time." The large idea in a few words was a treasure to be captured; it was me in my recovery. Time alone putting pen to paper became my most sought-after objective. Writing was the new essential god in my new life. How I balanced and spent my nonessential time was still valuable time. The relaxed time writing was also a work of love, which helped me but also kept people out.

As a customer in my night drives from bar to bar, I'd shop for love. I walked about with a drink and a wish, expecting to settle for just sex. Glancing through a small crowd, I joined my hunting eyes with the other darting eyes in their survey. A prospect's up-close smile made my shyness break down. Laughter joined us as we listened for our likes and dislikes. A mutual zone of comfort was being weighed with appealing thoughts of closeness. Women's attractive shapes and slight touches were added to the scales of decision. The exciting live performance of discovery was moving beyond just window shopping. The fulfilled hunt became more than just an intimate thrill. At times I found some of the most satisfying moments sharing pillow talk with a woman in the darkness. Relaxing with warm feelings, a piece of friendship was found in my puzzle of missing love. However, within hours or days, the thrill was gone. I was left with a hollow, empty feeling most of the time. When the series of emotions was played out, I was still out of balance, longing for more than just the affair.

A week or a month later, after seeking and finding sex, the conquest was followed with morning disappointment. The daylight showed her shallowness and mine. The attraction of the hunt and the chase was born in the glitter of her advertisements in my view of lust. Before sex, the makeup drew me in. After sex, the makeup drove me away. A disdain developed for women who were obsessed with overindulging themselves in makeup. Behind a false face and into my sober or hung-over-opened eyes, the truth of genuine incompatibility advanced. The reality of seeing how she valued time by putting on her false looks was misplaced time in front of a mirror. Our values were too stark a contrast. I didn't have a compromising attitude toward how I valued time. My lust was fed, but my heart was cheated. With one last kiss and closing the door behind me, I'd shake my head. With conceded pride and self-disgust for my own weakness, like a dog in heat I seldom stayed around for more than a week. My real desire was for a simply dressed, down-to-earth woman who thought well. I idealized blondes in blue jeans. I looked for subtle beauty held by an interesting mind that could hold my interest. And yet I stopped myself from pursuing anyone who would take my time away from me. I was in a paradox. I was the doctor, designer, and destructive force of my own life. Again and again, driven just by lust, I looked for love and lost time.

†

The summer was fading fast. Seeing me doing yard work and hanging out in the garage were clear signs for friends to stop by. Ma's house was on a main road in suburbia. The hundred-foot driveway gave room for trucks, cars, and motorcycles to pull in. Sandwiched between shouting ping pong games and compliments on throwing horseshoes, we'd have a beer and smoke pot. Regardless of whether Mack, Ike, Fanny, Mattie, or Calvin and Laura came by, I felt more at ease once the casual talk crossed into deeper subjects. I listened to larger topics on government, politics, and taxes, but they weren't as interesting to me as employment, travel, and the future. But talking was tiring, and it was time to go to Buddy's. Very loud music pounded into my ears while huge breaths of marijuana were held to prime us before we hit the bars.

The fall of 1976, I celebrated my own private independence day. I declared myself a diarist. I continued to build a relationship, a partnership, with the pen and paper. That lofty goal of selling what I wrote was not just thinking in my new box; I was creating my own box. I had always daydreamed a lot from grade school on. Writing my thoughts put a handle on my imagination; it gave me a purpose for drifting off. As my thinking traveled down my arm, I found some flaws in my sentence construction. More than the obvious misspelled words, my thoughts were backward. Reading them I saw they were written out of place or somehow jumped around. Maybe that was part of the still undiscovered alien dyslexia within, which led me to checking and rechecking my logic.

Similarly, exchanging viewpoints with friends would lead me to ask more probing questions, which revealed what was really valued. Consequently over time, my conversations with others were tainted with me pointing out our potentials, strengths, flaws, or negativity. Not everybody liked that unless it helped them. But I enjoyed it. My examination of their reasoning helped me evaluate and justify my values as a writer. Inside my thoughts rode an escalator upward, looking for those missing concussion times and spaces of confidence I needed going forward.

Within the diary writing, I captured many memories and feelings relived, and those lived anew. Pitching horseshoes with my dad, sharing the competition, and hearing the clanging of a ringer on the peg. Seeing my mom making Christmas cookies and smelling the house filled with goodness. Laughing at the way my brother practiced his Spanish lessons. The inner voice was piping up with musings of past feelings. The need to express myself was an increasing hunger, which wanted more time to think. I was filling the void of the concussion with no regard for counting the cost; I was without direction. I earned money and paid my expenses, but kept going from job to job. My love pursuits were just scoring and sinking, without lasting activity in a relationship. A few women came close to my heart.

Coleen was the one who might have been perfect. Blonde with blue eyes, witty and beautiful, she was calm and loved to smoke pot. She liked to walk her dog Friendly and wore her blue jeans every day. She was a perfect fit for the classic expression "the right woman but the wrong time." I was twenty-three. I had a desire to express myself with words, but how does a person share that? Dwelling on who I was and what I might be caused deep unrest in trying to explain myself. My selfish path of one was still a young naive path I wanted to follow alone. But Coleen was different. I had to force myself not to want to see more of her. She might have had the love I couldn't walk away from. My turbulence within was being played out in bars with drugs, loose women, and no lasting victory; I was no winner. Contained and lurking about in my wandering were expressions of longing that needed identifying, and they found their way to the surface one snowy night.

Chapter 6: The Lyric Muse

Much more came with the drink on that snowy night in the winter of 1976. The Town Pub was a favorite to many of the locals in Rotterdam, New York. It used to be called Harvey's, and that guy who ran the old bar had a tattoo on his forearm, The Bull. Some say the bar's history went back to the Great Depression, but what mattered to me was the snow that night.

The creamy, dark and light, starless, snowy sky dropped millions of pieces. Outside of the bar, fast-falling flakes wowed me and then lowered my jaw and those of others as surprised eyes took in the invasion. The fluffy, layered, frozen crystals heaped up; they did not compress. The invading softness of snow was a cause of joy. Snowflakes played and played hour after hour. White frosty butterflies landed with a plan to mount up and debilitate the town's roads. Acquiring their rightful space during the night, they would try to conquer driveways, roofs, and parking lots. Soon the mass of silence rendered the suburban streets useless.

Looking out the window, I could see easy fun sliding in the streets around corners. Exciting, yet the potential to drown my vehicle was also there. The calm, silent, weightless chaos laid its deception as the old watering well accommodated its patrons. For some inside the pub, it was a quiet time as they dropped their heads, lost in thought and memories. The jukebox songs and voices were loud and then soft. Even with the speakers ringing out the guitar solos, some people sat unemotionally. Hurt on their faces looked down into their drinks, while inner thoughts wrestled an emotional quiet riot. Others let the noisy alcohol speak through wild eyes and thunderous drunken slurs. I saw mind games of noise and no noise.

Flesh seekers like submarines searched slowly for the arousing warmth of someone's arm to be wrapped in. Singles or married cheaters buzzed for the fleshy sexual arousal of another barfly or someone with more. Crossing paths with flirting royalty was only a chance, but a chance just the same. Finding somebody who had money or did something important was good fortune, but could be a disaster. Some tables were lit near dark walls and corners with quiet talk, face-to-face finding out if there were treasures of some kind to be had.

On stools of laughter amid all the activity of to and fro swayed the crazed drug- and alcohol-driven flesh seekers. There among all the fastest mouths and the quickest smiles were the watchful pairs of eyes.

Her head was tilted, her hair was flipped, and her shapely body positioned itself to give off more appeal. Six pairs of James Dean eyes deep in concern peered and focused on their target with need. Shifting, she tossed her hair back. Motionless cool stares scanned her moves. One went closer. Successful smiles first touched and began cutting into the framework operation of giving and taking. Her reach unlocking inhibitions came in a flurry of slight touches onto his arm. Fingers and feelings were turning combinations within. Hopefully the shy and cautious cravings would open up.

✝

JUMP-START MY HEART

Early in the winter of seventy-six,
Life was cold and lonely I needed a fix.
I was weak and weary, slow on the start,
Standing, waiting for love to Jump-Start My Heart.

> If you got the time, I know love will start.
> Will you take the time to Jump-Start My Heart?

I used to run around, but never ran cold.
A love kept me warm then, but love got old.
I started looking inside, took things apart,
Now I'm aching for love to Jump-Start My Heart.

> If you got the time, I know love will start.
> Will you take the time to Jump-Start My Heart?

I hope you're the spark. Many pass by,
Slow down to look, they drive on by.
I know I got fire, if you got the spark,
Will you take the time to Jump-Start My Heart?

If you got the time, I know love will start.
Will you take the time to Jump-Start My Heart?

Lost on hope's highway, no help in sight,
Her eyes flashed me, once then twice.
A bright smile came in close to touch.
She was more than a spark, I loved her so much.

If you got the time, I know love will start.
Will you take the time to Jump-Start My Heart?
You took the time to Jump-Start My Heart!

———————— † ————————

"Closing time!" The bartender's loud declaration sang out as white ceiling lights were turned on. Moans were heard through the dense chatter of one of winter's favorite indoor sports. Last call for alcohol! A general sense of need or want came over the patrons. Closing time at 4:00 a.m. helped distinguish the choices between bad and worse. Outside the white flakes kept sliding down, surrounding everything out in the open. Streets were not closed, but they should have been. Some took a chance driving through the twelve inch powder. Intoxicated others walked to someone's nearby parlor to continue their party. Amazingly enough, I chose to walk the distance home. I tanked up generously with libation and walked away from my pickup truck.

Dressed for the conditions, I started out through the natural white barricades covering the streets. The middle of the road was my course, plowing my knees, lifting high my face into the flakes. Inebriated in the uniqueness of the situation, I was isolated, enjoying the great amounts of powered snow. I laughed and sang Frank Zappa's lyrics aloud. During my trek across frozen cotton fields, I heard the inner voice. A tone of thought to mull over, it spoke softly at first, just enough to be considered. Minutes later, I was exhausted after numerous falls in the fourteen inches of deep white. I looked up, still amazed at the size and the amount of the flakes as I flopped back lying in the snow. Swimming, rolling, and scrambling up, I laughed out loud.

In my cheeriness, I started to say what I was hearing inside. My words came out in rhyme. Repeating it and adding words to rhyme was fun. It made sense; saying it over and over was surprisingly cool. They were my very first rhyming words in sentences. It was like striking gold within. Speaking out loud, I entertained the inward process, giving more words to my thoughts. Those flowing big-idea moments had always been accompanied by the pad and pen. Now my new treasures of thoughts were coming out loud, clearly but without a tape record. The short series of clever lines in rhymes stood there with me. Speaking in poems was amusing; it felt a lot like singing. Yes, I was singing my own words with rhymes. I whistled my thoughts like music, and there was feeling with the words. I found music to my words. In front of the jewelry store, lifting my feet and legs high, I began running with my golden desire. Running and falling, I repeated over and over my whistling with those words.

--------------- † ---------------

When it rains, it pours; when it's dry, it's a drought.
When it snows, it's cold. I sigh and I think about,
Love I need. I want that first kiss,
Love again, a woman's love I miss.

--------------- † ---------------

I needed to file a claim on a gold mine of words with my feelings. The streets were empty except for the rising fifteen inches of snow, with more falling. There was no traffic; there was no noise, just me rhyming out loud. Running, falling, laughing, whistling to reach my driveway, and I did. Once through the door, I found pen and paper to chain down my thoughts. I looked at them on paper, my first lyric. I sat amazed at the leap I had made from diary to poetry, or was it lyric writing? I recalled my days as a latchkey kid alone in the morning listening to the radio. Those early sixties' lyrics shaped my youth. Suddenly I was like the albums that I would listen to. Amazingly I was in the same company as my favorite bands. Lyrics of the James Gang, the Who, and Elvis singing "Hound Dog" were all with me. This was an enormous recognition of my past, present, and future feelings; they were yelling inside, "Surprise, welcome to the party!" I was a diarist and a lyricist. That snowy night, creative writing had been explored and added to my life.

—————————— † ——————————

Miss her more, when I do reminisce.
Snowflakes bring all the ways I do miss.
Can't complain about the weather;
Snow will stay. How could I forget her?

—————————— † ——————————

Writing the diary became tasty thoughts of sweet medicine. With pen in hand sitting near a window flipping through thoughts, I'd write and watch for what moved me. Building lyrics was a carousel ride of reaching for a prize. Grabbing a thought like it was a tool that needed sharpening, my stare would glaze over, cutting off what was most disagreeable. Pulling apart words in my mind and seeing the roots of ideas, my thinking made options. When a shaft of light came bursting in exposing a story, creativity's thrill fostered more. Ideas were pouring out of my head onto the paper faster than I could write.

—————————— † ——————————

Love makes the world go around, but still,
My mountain, my desert, is empty to fill.
The sunrise sets, whether it rains or snows.
The day brings regrets, and nobody knows.

—————————— † ——————————

A relationship took time away from writing, but a relationship was what I really wanted. Trying to put off the need for emotional connection just wasn't right. I always found myself wanting to be in love. I still sought to replace Hope's true love I had discarded. For me, there was genuine passion in my plays for the temporary type of love I sought in bars. Through the turbulence of living out my being as an unattached artist, I fought against my most basic need to be loved. So I wrote about it. In one night or a month, the words added up to finally become a lyric.

——————————— † ———————————

WHETHER TO LOVE

Love I need, I want that first kiss.
Love again, a woman's love I miss.
If love makes the world go around, I'm still.
My mountain, my desert, stand empty to fill.
When love comes, just maybe it will.

    Whether to Love, Whether to Love.
    When it rains, it pours; when it's dry, it's a drought.
    When it snows, it's cold. I sigh and I think about
    Whether to Love, Whether to Love.

The sunrise will set, whether it rains or snows.
The day brings regret, and it stays till I doze.
A choice is a choice only time knows.
Love I need, I want that first kiss.
Love again, a woman's love I miss.

    Miss her more, when I do reminisce.
    Snowflakes show all the ways I do miss.
    Can't complain about the weather
    Snow covers, but I can't forget her.

Whether to Love, Whether to Love.
When it rains, it pours; when it's dry, it's a drought.
When it snows, it's cold. I sigh and I think about
Whether to Love, Whether to Love.

$$\dagger$$

My general lack of ambition and direction that was missing before and after the head concussion was finally found. Lyric writing was what ignited my interest, moved my heart, and prompted dedication in my life. Big ideas were captured, swirled, distilled, and dropped from the funnel of my mind, to spread before my eyes. Writing about politics, money, employment, and especially love was what I loved. That one snowy night changed me for the rest of my life. Christmas came with a confirming desire, and the diary was capturing what had grown from within and was going somewhere.

I came alive again along with the 1977 new year. The idea of a goal appeared. Like those lyrics I heard on the radio helped me when I was young and home alone, perhaps my lyrics could help someone else. I actually began writing my own rhyming dictionary before I found one in a bookstore. I also found magazines for musicians and songwriters. I mailed in the subscription form for *American Songwriter* magazine. The book of rhymes was like seeing color TV for the first time. Alternative ideas flew about like birds to a full feeder of special seed. My work without pay became a labor of love. Books became my new friends and teachers. A dictionary, a thesaurus, synonyms with antonyms, and a small book on the elements of poetry would talk to me. I still maintained my square-peg status. My art did not fit into the round holes offered on the pegboard of life. At last I had a great reason, a crutch to hold up my rebellion not to conform. How long could I continue to rebel off the treadmill? I was blessed with the love of my mother and grandmother who watched me recover and supported me every way they could.

In the diary of 1978, I had an average grasp of evil in the world. I had noticed the evil in government, in money, and in excess materialism.

Watching people keep up with the proverbial Joneses bothered me. I was also bothered by the weakness of the greater mass of people not practicing self-denial. A growing distaste for TV commercials that fed materialism increased. Every fifteen minutes, voices and pictures telling me I needed this and I deserved that were a brainwashing I didn't put up with. Commercials breeding discontent hoping to get my money were as wrong as a politician saying one thing and doing another. Something was still very wrong after all the best election promises our leaders made election after election.

I had a completely wrong outlook on the good in the world. What I thought was good was me. Being an individual and not participating in anything was good to me. I made myself in control. I was aware of God but not in His true capacity as Sovereign Lord over all. I only thought of me.

But my writing was taking me to bigger ideas. I came to the conclusion that the answer beyond all questions was God. I wrote several times that God was the only answer that would put a conclusion to my circling thoughts. To look at nature was to see what God had done. Creation was no accident; I was no accident. I was only aware of God in a general sense, not in tune like in a guiding relationship. To write my thoughts was my purpose, but I wasn't 100 percent sure of it. I was sure 100 percent sure that my life was no mistake or accident. Life wasn't from a pool of slime, and I wasn't living by some freak chance. I was aware of my conscience, but not its purpose to function as a moral compass. I had no idea where my conscience came from, only that it was a working mechanism on the inside. It was alive and elusive; it came and left whenever it wanted to.

My values were very basic. In fact, when it came to collecting things or having more than I needed, I was boring. My distaste for the sport of shopping, and for those who enjoyed it, came with a double-edged sword, cutting me over and over. I was always looking for a woman with values like mine. But I lived in a generation of self-absorption. I found that the prettier women were, the more they spent on maintenance. Shampoo, conditioner, fingernail polish, wardrobes, shoes, and time to go shopping topped their list of things to do. My grandmother always said, "When you don't have money, love flies out the window." Granny's words made sense, so I would only visit with pretty women and not stay very long. A relationship took time away from my narcissist ways; writing took priority. Taking love out of the equation, I settled for just the pleasure of sex. Lusting for women as sex objects was fun at first. My skewed view was more common to a worldwide outlook toward the wrong motives for intercourse.

As a walking contradiction I did not seek a woman's love, but sometimes it happened. Meeting someone new, I would speak with sincere interest; I unlocked my honest desires. Diary stories of love that came close but was held back and good women lost were too often too real. Country rock music was perfect for my fast-moving foot-stomping feet. Dancing was a lot of fun and a way to meet women. When I put my coordinated feet on a dance floor, I found a new playground. Loud bars, laughing women, parking lots with rocking vans, or one-night motel rooms were all fast fun at first. There were those situations where I knew I was used as a replacement love. A few glances, a smile, and I was caught. Sometimes I knew I was just a pawn to make a man jealous because a woman told me so. The emptiness that comes from being used hurt and helped me see better how I was using them.

✝

THE SUBSTITUTE

She was lovely, longing for affection,
Her eyes cloudy, looking out in question.
In a gesture, I was leaning her way,
Body motions slowly put on display.

With a whisper, the guilt was on her face.
She had feelings she wanted to replace.
In a moment, she described her despair.
I can help you, you need someone who cares.

I'll be The Substitute, in place of what's real,
Emotional substitute, who gives what he feels.
After the confusion of a pair torn apart,
I'll create the illusion of mending a heart.

She was only turning from rejection
When I found her, asking for direction.
It's my pleasure, I'll show you all the way.
Maybe you'll be going, maybe you'll stay.

---

†

I was very selfish with my time, and I guarded my emotions. My kind of artist's life kept me walking away from good women as well as bad girls. Sometimes my diary heard some truth that was more serious. Once when I got lucky in the parking lot of a nightclub with one chick, two hours later another chick brought me back to her house. I was led through a dark home holding her hand, being told to creep quietly so as not to wake her baby and the sitter. That put me off at first. I saw her a few more times. When she started showing up at my house, she didn't say how she knew where I lived. She kept coming back without an invitation and at any time. The affair was getting beyond my control and creepy. It was difficult to get rid of her. I wished I'd never met her. The only fix I saw that might work was to get another girl to be with. It worked, but I could see the hazards of tampering with people's emotions, especially mine. Like emotional boomerangs, I saw the hurt I was doing and felt the hurt I brought to myself again and again.

I was filling up with new captured memories alongside the repeated themes of my desire to leave town. Thoughts began to form into ideas of how I could get my lyrics with music. I made a few failed attempts to find local musicians. My efforts to save money and travel to Nashville always seemed to fall short. Another injury to my body, a vehicle mishap, getting laid off, or quitting jobs for lack of interest all halted plans to leave. Filing for unemployment was a sweet-and-sour way of life, with more time to write but less income. At the same time, I couldn't stop looking for work. My sense of responsibility kept me hunting. When I found a job, I only enjoyed the variety of people and temporary work situations. Once the newness wore off, I got bored and quit. I could not improve my lack of interest for any type of work. My experience at assembly lines in a plastic parts plant or baking Italian bread at 4:00 a.m. didn't do it for me. Cutting pieces of steel at a band saw in an ironworks warehouse was just a way to put money in my pocket. The frustration from feeling held back from traveling was vented in the diary. I developed a strong sense of perseverance in job searching, as well as for my writing. I wanted to see the goal of my words helping someone come true. But for my dream to go through the door of opportunity, I first needed to get to the door and knock.

Over time, I learned to read people and developed a kind of chameleon persona. I blended my genuineness in with what the employer or someone else wanted to hear until I got the job or what I needed. My mother used to tell me I was "kissing the Blarney Stone." I spent many, many evenings long into the night alone writing. I deliberately made choices to stay away from having girlfriends, expensive toys, vacations, luxuries of all kinds in exchange for time. Time was needed to take the fuel of experience and reshape it into words.

✝

THE DEVIL LIVES IN AMERICA

The Devil Lives in the United States of America.
He has two jobs to try and pay for another car.
He doesn't have to worry when the going gets tough;
There's a credit union to be sure he has enough.

Enough to buy what makes him high, he can't take when he dies;
More you have, might think you win, misspent money is your sin.

You see how your time on earth has eternal worth
For an endless life in heaven or in hell.
The Devil Lives in America, and it's lies that he sells.
The Devil Lives in America, and it's lies that he sells.

You're working hard, still run around, but you can't behave.
It's the Devil's work; he's gonna get you in the early grave.
The more you want, the more you work, and never got enough.
Get another job, spoil the kids, and collect all that stuff.

Heard it all before. Listen now before you finally know.
Life's not a wheel, but up or down, death is friend or foe.
It's never too late. God is always there day and night.
The Son of God is the only path; ask Jesus for His light.

✝

This continued narcissistic way of life became a style that lasted for a decade unchallenged. Youth was on my side, and I enjoyed watching life go by. I daily took pleasure in surveying my life as I went walking the big Pie dog. Some of his nicknames were the Duke, Squeaker, and the Pie Lapper—he was famous for giving kisses. Walking was one of the best exercises I could do and needed to do it routinely. Stretching my legs and keeping my back strong were imperative. Walking the dog was a great exercise for life. Piper loved to cruise through the neighborhood like Thunder. Pie was a chip off the old block; when he caught a scent, he was gone. I gave him his own time, and he took it. Sometimes I wanted to walk with him, but the dog was already gone. He knew when to stay close and how to find his way home. He learned his role well from Thunder dog and appreciated his free time tramping about. Thunder was getting old and waited with me for Pie's return.

✝

DOG GONE

He may be just a dog with a bone.
The animal has a mind of his own.
He's the best friend I've ever known,
But the dog's gotta roam, the dog's gotta roam.

Yes, there's times when he's my livelihood.
When he wants to be, the dog is good,
And then there's times, it's understood,
He's cruising the neighborhood, cruising the neighborhood.

Dog Gone … the dog's gone … Dog Gone … the dog's gone …

My dog's got a different point of view.
Well, I wish some of you only knew,
Dog's gotta do what he's gotta do,
Strolling down the avenue, down the avenue.

Dog Gone … the dog's gone … Dog Gone … the dog's gone …
Dog Gone … the dog's gone … Dog Gone … the dog's gone …

It was necessary to maintain a healthy daily routine that worked best for me. Walking the dogs, writing, and staying off the treadmill of tradition worked best for me. The path of choices was really becoming the way I was getting on my own treadmill. No one I knew was living like I was. Daily and nightly walking, thinking, and writing at twenty-five years of age was a bit uncommon, but it worked for me in 1978.

Chapter 7: Optimism Found

By 1979, I stopped asking the doctor how long it would take before I would get better. After five years of writing through my recovery from the concussion, I was past realizing the effects of the damage. I was me. Confidently I read the *American Songwriter* magazine and thought of someday finding musicians who could put music to my words. I began to consider ways to sell my lyrics or potential songs and had thoughts of searching out the music industry. When some local friends started up a band, my imagination soared. I was asked to be the light man for the band on a handful of occasions. The yellow window van I drove was used to haul band equipment. Once again I identified with a different group of individuals. Hanging out with so-called artists, I felt the association to be more than gratifying. Again, I got more confidence being off the mass treadmill of normal and on my own artist treadmill. I built a wide bunk bed in the yellow van with secure locks to hide stuff. With all the windows, it was dubbed the Canary Cage.

At a bar during the Lake George Winter Festival, I was christened into the band as lucky number seven by Sam, the lead singer. His beer bottle slipped out of his hand as I was being toasted. We all watched it drop, and the bottle bottom landed upright, flatly hitting the floor. The ejecting fountain of foam shot six feet high into the clinking bottles, signifying the induction. I was toasted as the electric light man. Not being on stage, I stood with the light boards and spotlight among the crowd. Pushing levers controlling the lights, I changed the moods to fit the music.

†

ELECTRIC LIGHT MAN

He don't sing or play guitar,
By no means a rock-and-roll star,
Works with the band, drinks all night,
Creates moods with electric lights.

He listens how lyrics tell time,
Paints a picture using rhyme,
Flips a switch, drinks more wine,
Adds more color with every line.

> Electric Light Man now with a country band,
> Bunch of good boys having fun.
> Electric Light Man let love slip out of hand,
> Hardest thing he's ever done.

Hear the story, how it's told,
He misses her heart of gold.
See it unfold, amber red,
When he left her, the words he said.

Sometimes when they play his song,
Starts out right, ends up wrong,
He shows it with shades of blue,
Lets it fade with thoughts of two.

> Electric Light Man now with a country band,
> Bunch of good boys having fun.
> Electric Light Man let love slip out of hand,
> Hardest thing he's ever done.

Times are happy more than sad.
Life is good when life is bad.
Puzzles of love, one of a kind,
Feelings don't fit, time unwinds.

Colors of love, which one's best,
Love's not easy to invest.
Waiting now, hoping time
Paints love's picture using rhyme.

✝

Progress was going after what I loved. It wasn't for the money or the fame. I just wanted to earn a living at what I liked to do with time. I was unbelievably high on life and felt that I was destined to be making progress. Girls came after me! The notoriety or exposure of being in a band changes the way some girls perceive you; it was amazing. The tables turned, and the foxes chased this dog. They gave me their phone numbers without me asking for them and bought me drinks. They stopped by and took me out. I found more pleasure than the guys in the band. I'm not going to dwell on this. To say the least, I was like a raccoon in a henhouse.

But I wanted to do more than just go from bar to bar. I wanted music with my words, and the guys in the band were players, not songwriters. Sometimes unforeseen bad things happen and turn out good. Just after purchasing a Super Trouper spotlight for $1,000, I ended up using the light at only one show, and then the band broke up. All good things come to an end here on earth. Fortunately I got my investment back. The kind man who ran the stage lighting company knew how musicians and bands were unsteady. I had borrowed the cash from my Aunt Lucile, whom I was very close with. For years she and I shared small glasses of bourbon and talked mostly about small stuff sitting on her porch watching the cars go by. She knew my aspirations of becoming a writer. Her brother, my Uncle Oakley, was similar with his creativity and traveled about. Aunt Lucy told me to hold off paying back the money. I sat on that money, thinking from springtime into the early summer.

My dad had been doing better with making my mom happy. He was helping me around the house, and they would go to dinner every week. Pa and I often worked on Aunt Lucy's fence before having a few beers at a bar. It was hard for him to talk about his drinking, but he did say he was going to AA meetings. One day he brought me a plaque to nail on the garage wall. It was a serenity prayer from the Alcoholics Anonymous twelve-step program. He also gave me a book by Jack London called *White Fang*. It was the first book I ever read. He said I should read *Call of the Wild*, saying I'd like it because of Piper.

I got closer to him for the next year or so. I'd visit at his apartment, and we'd get some food and have a beer, like buddies. I was old enough to want to like him and love him more. When I drove him around, we talked. There is something free that happens, and thoughts flow better when you drive. A vehicle kind of opens your thinking. For some reason, he told me he wanted a toast at his grave someday and the empty beer cans stuffed in the dirt. He said, "The funeral thing is no big deal; get it over with and get on with your life." His most frequent comment I heard growing up was, "You gotta make a mark," which meant doing something significant. Making an accomplishment was what he always wanted. It didn't make sense hearing him talk about death and graves, but we were just shooting the breeze.

At that time, I was intimate with a lovely woman; I even considered it to be beginning love. While in the throes of soul-searching, pursuing my creative writing, and wondering what to do with Marylyn, we parted our ways. She left town for Pennsylvania. It was always a struggle for me to consider commitment without a real income. After the band fell apart, I made plans to live in Bar Harbor, Maine, for the summer. I really wanted to drive away in that old van and clear my mind. When I talked with my aunt about traveling and what I owed her, she gave me her blessing, saying, "Keep it, it's a gift. Go for it, Michael."

✝

Driving out of town a week after the Memorial Day traffic with cash in my pocket, I felt like a gambler who had won. Like the summer at Galway Lake, I once more experienced early retirement. It was great to feel the luxury of a full twenty-four hours to fill any way I wanted. I did not have to feel the irritation of exchanging my hours working for money. Again, time was free, and all of mine was with the Duke that summer. Duke was my favorite nickname for Piper. His faithful yellow eyes watched me as he sat copiloting in the passenger's seat, hanging his head out the window. The liberation of rolling down the highway helped my struggle within. The view of open fields brought calm as I thought of how to be an artist. But I still had Marylyn on my mind, so I didn't head east to Bar Harbor; I headed west to Pennsylvania. She touched my heart, and that was good; I wanted more.

The farther I got, the clearer I saw things. The guys in the band were just players. With just my lyrics, I hoped to work with a serious collaborator somewhere. A woman who could sing and play guitar would have been a beautiful combination. As difficult as it was leaving the women I cared for, it was the price I was learning to pay for solitude. Being in love meant sharing time. As unfulfilling as being alone was, my love for writing was worth it. I made no compromise; I had nothing to offer any women. My attitude of "just looking, only shopping, but not buying" affairs left me empty. Every chick who got to know me could see that. In a way, I was dealing myself a risky hand in the game of opportunity hoped for. No shared sacrifice with a woman; no complications. No pair in love, to bet on for that someday jackpot. I gambled with my time alone. I was one card in the game, just me, the lonely Jack of Hearts.

Crossing the border out of New York State into Pennsylvania, I ran into the national gas-rationing crunch. I could only buy gas every other day. America did not plan well, or something went wrong again with politics. I thought of paying taxes and the responsibility of the politicians who called themselves leaders. There was trouble in the economy, but it didn't concern me. There was always one kind of trouble or another. Waiting for my day at the pump, I drove on, thinking. I wondered about God. I always knew there was something big and powerful going on. I saw in nature that only God could be so big as to make it happen. I saw all the churches that so many people went to.

But God was always a big mystery. I only looked a little from a distance from time to time.

Marylyn had no idea I was driving to her location on a Christmas tree farm outside of Lancaster, Pennsylvania. I finally found the dirt road to her friends' beautiful farm. These people made knish and drove into Philadelphia and New York City to sell them. Marylyn was so kind to me; we lingered a few days. She took me to meet a lovely elderly matriarchal lady living in a country home near a beautiful pond. The old woman was dear to that family. I felt privileged to have had the opportunity to be in her presence. There was a special quality talking with Marylyn, whom I couldn't seem to let go of. But for the second time, I did. She too gave me encouraging words to go with, like Hope had done telling me I would find what I was looking for. Heading toward southern New York and crossing into Connecticut, I aimed northeast for Hartford.

Traveling onward to Bar Harbor, Maine, I was so glad at last to be out of hometown Schenectady. Somewhere near Hartford, I stopped near the home of Mark Twain and looked the museum over from a distance. I never read his books; I hated reading. The only exception was the book my dad gave me, *White Fang*. Pa said I'd like it and to stick to reading it. He said it was about a wolf. I did stick to it, and he was right; I liked the story of the Indian puppy growing up. I saw how I missed out on reading by having trouble with words in school. I saw the mistakes I still made in writing in my diary. But fixing the mistakes in lyric writing was a work of concentration I loved. Just plain reading was just too much work that wasn't worth it. Those thoughts of missed opportunity always left me feeling like I was an unfinished puzzle, with spaces to fill and life had different puzzles to look at.

Those odd-even days to buy gas allowed me to slow down and appreciate the small towns on the way. I'd stop and walk the Duke in Anytown, USA. Under a tree or by a lake, our minutes were rich with ease in the comfort that comes from no pressure of a routine. I realized once again that time wasn't partial. The richest and the poorest were equal, each with twenty-four hours per day. I was passing through my minutes making my own adventure. I was beyond my boundaries. The calm, still, fresh moments at dawn were best. The prowling, wondering, moonlight roaming's were being put to rest. Or so I thought. I met some guys in a bar who invited me to a condo party that night. It was there that I was used as a tool by a lovely woman. She cunningly intended to exercise her scorned love and make someone jealous. To me it was another lucky night in a soft bed. However, the next morning I found one of my tires punctured. Pie was okay. While I changed tires, unbeknown to me the women called the police reporting the incident. The cops gave me a little hassle but never searched for pot. Luck is hard to figure out. Getting on the road again after that episode sure felt good.

I continued driving past antiques-for-sale signs, with cluttered yards and little kids in cribs. Nightlights shining in distant farmhouses captured me imagining the lives of those who plowed in the fields I passed. Dark rooms, hearing a kid cry in the night, footsteps, and the creaky rhythm from a worn-out rocking chair. Lives were so much the same in so many different places. But time was always the same, moving on its path. I ate McDonalds' takeout food, with Pie getting a treat of six hamburger patties, and we walked some quiet streets before sleeping in a warehouse parking lot. Stopping several times along the way to walk with Pie, I saw over and over the simple settings of small towns. A few days before arriving, I ate a steak and lobster meal at a fine restaurant. Sitting in an overstuffed easy chair at the window of the plush lounge, I sipped brandy toasting Aunt Lucy, casting thoughts onto lines of blank diary pages. Anonymous, with no idea what a mile down the road or the next hour would bring, I thoroughly enjoyed wondering about it. Each night I slept on the wide plywood bench seat covered with a rug in a sleeping bag. If I couldn't find a rest stop, I'd pull up in a small town. Driving around just looking was always a pleasure. I knew I'd most likely never be back, so going slow was okay.

On and on in no hurry, at last I could smell the sea salt at the precipice of the New England coastline. Standing on nature's cliff top, I peered over sharp edgy muscles of rock, flexing their strength.

Below, frothing ocean waves swelled and surged, wrenching continuous assaults against the cliff's tower of strength. I was a casual spectator of the power that both natural wrestlers displayed. I and the solid strength of the tranquil rock faced earth, glaring down on the wet challenger's force slapping and smacking relentlessly. Endless foaming liquid was jumping over and over again in the pursuit to wear down the rock. Only time and God could be the eyewitnesses of these millennial combatants. One of the greatest events in God's creation and design was found. I was a witness held in awe of nature's perseverance. Taking time out that summer, I firmly established that I was beyond putting the lost pieces of my past puzzle together. My journey had joined me to the present; my path of perseverance loved living in the newness of life.

Whether I hit the big-time with a song on the radio or not wasn't as important as moving on in my effort. The big-time was just a platform to gain attention so people would listen. I wanted to help people, and before I could do that, I had to help myself. It wasn't the destination as much as the ride. To endeavor through discovery was what mattered most. Getting out of my hometown and heading for the music industry was a sight yet to focus on. I was sure a dedicated composer who could sing and collaborate with me was out there somewhere. I was confident in my writing and hopeful in the American Song Festival entry. My confidence to keep going in the direction I was going came from self -denial and being unattached. In those years, I felt love for a woman here and there, but continually abandoned the luxury of sharing time. I also rejected the luxury of steady work opportunities. Any distractions from my writing on the course of hopefully becoming published were eliminated. In my tunnel vision, I was teaching myself harmful narcissistic ways of living. Without knowing I was doing it, I had begun growing into a vain recluse. Only time would tell what the harvest would be. Would I reap what I sowed?

I got to Bar Harbor and drove around Acadia National Park. Seeing the open-space hilltop beauty and isolated homes, I felt so thankful to have arrived. Driving down from those small round-topped mountains on the curvy roads close to the ocean, I felt a connection. Pulling over in a rest stop, I walked to the water's edge. The cold ocean water linked my journey with contentment. My rite of passage as an artist was realized; the match between my life and writing was made.

The local paper led me to a room to rent. I lived in town and worked in an oceanside family-run restaurant, the Fisherman's Landing. Just being out of New York was the real payoff. I would sit in the center of town at the park watching hundreds of people who were having fun with their families. I was shy, hoping that the end—getting a record deal—would justify the means, living my solitary life. Few people could relate, or so I thought. Sitting at the water's edge, I looked over the ocean away from the vacationers' cheerful laughter. I somehow wanted and yet didn't want to be alone. There I was alone on my chosen path, realizing again it was for better or for worse. I was different. Maybe the way I was wandering was the way of an author. Maybe I would write a book someday. Maybe I'd love again after all my running and find another great love. For one reason or another, life was not going be normal. The Pie and I swam in the cold fifty-eight-degree ocean water. I stared at the waves, and the waves waved back.

✝

One of the more unusual Bar Harbor sightings carved into my memory was that of an old dilapidated mansion. It was so overgrown and hidden by weeds, wild plants, and bushes that very few may have known of the fallen giant. Hiking the local hills, Pie and I discovered the crumbling manor of decades past—from a time when decadence was king, perhaps before those rip-roaring twenties ushered in the Great Depression. The crumbled foundation of someone's rewards in this life died there. Conceivably built in the industrial age of 1850, money couldn't hold up that house of affluence. A puritan would have died of a broken heart if he'd spread his eyes on the elaborate inground pool.

The secretive cement rectangle was surrounded with a walled-in walkway. The hallways allowed peering eyes to look in on swimmers through glass portholes. These passages also led to large underground stoves for the heating of the pool's water. Looking at the disintegrating structure of American progress, I heard a cry for help. Chains of money locked the hands and feet of the skeletons named Progress. However, they weren't calls of distress or pleading words of enough. The one word repeated over and over with a greedy voice wept, "More, more, more." The edifice surely was huge at one time; now the ruins were roommates with weeds. The results of overindulgence and carefree ways that only money could allow raised both a desire and a note of caution in me. It seemed appropriate to question my motives again for pursuing the rewards of success. Yes, the financial gain was up front in my thinking, but that was to sustain the leisure to write. Or so I told myself.

The diaries were in mind, with the desire to help the world with words of warning. Look out for materialism and debt! Find enough, find peace with time, and avoid the pain of greed. How naïve I was in those innocent days and months of regaining my memory. I used to ask, "Why are the Chinese people starving?" It was because of greed and political mismanagement. Communist China had rulers, dictators, and many who ate well, with millions of poor people to feed. And I thought of America, having freedom and elections with politicians, and there still was corruption and people without work going hungry. The only peace in my life was a lonesome satisfaction that came from writing.

I was, however, a greedy ruler with my time. I thought about time and how quickly good times pass and hard times seep in. I thought some more about America. How did materialism and greed become popular? Like that former palace and its disintegrating stones, our country is crumbling with aging infrastructure. The pouting twins More and More still lie screaming for attention and get taller buildings. Larger high-speed racetracks are built. Millions and millions of dollars are paid to professional sports players to carry, hit, or throw a ball. A massive amount of money is spent on Hollywood productions. And the races, the games, and the movies come and go. Meanwhile, time is running. The once-rich castle of fun crumbled and looked like a carcass. The poison of self-indulgence was all around me on the hill. I saw the fever of discontent rising still higher in our society.

I turned my view from that hilltop toward the ocean. The waves kept persevering to reach the shore. My appreciation for the natural outdoors seemed to unite with that experience and with God, who created it. Seeing those porcupine islands, where the tide rises and lowers twice a day, held a mysterious aura as the fog rolled in. Locals spoke of smugglers and thieves lurking around under the cover of the quiet gray mist. I was secure in my self-denial, as twisted as it was. I walked back asking myself if I really knew the value of Enough and his brother Enough.

Mornings, working at the restaurant near the end of July, I boiled and shelled lobsters for their meat. Afternoons the tourists came in and ordered lobster rolls covered in butter. I helped haul up lobster traps off the boat onto the dock using a winch. One day while I was guiding and setting down dripping wet traps, someone called my name. I turned and looked, and it was Ma standing with Granny, with Uncle Shawn and Aunt Susie up from Florida. My surprise so startled me, I hugged Ma and lifted her off her feet. Their summer wasn't the same without me, so Uncle Shawn drove them all up to make Ma happy.

As vacation time in Bar Harbor was ending with Labor Day, the shops, streets, and bars were filled with happy people. The tourists were leaving, and I needed to get off the island. The summer resort town was going to close up, so I left first. My intentions were to see more of New England and make some money before returning to home. I drove north to Bangor and considered working in the nearby blueberry fields for their harvest. But I turned south to Portland, and once there, relaxed in the city park. Piper met a girl with a guitar sitting under a tree. His good nature drew people to him, and we sat with her. In thirty minutes of casual friendship, she heard my story and I heard hers. The old acoustic guitar she strummed was left by a guy who had loved her and moved on. Even though I couldn't play, she said it was best that I should have the instrument and gave it to me. We walked away, and both of us were better off.

I settled in a small town just outside of Portland in a second-floor rented room on the main street. In a few days, I found work hanging aluminum siding. The job begot another job, involving heavy lifting for a new roof on a huge three-story house. I hurt myself slowly, working too hard, climbing the ladder over and over. The high wages shaded my once-learned common sense regarding my damaged sciatica. Greed silenced my conscience, pushing me past safety. Suddenly on top of the roof, the slow-forming lower-back spasm pinched my sciatic nerve like once before. I gritted my teeth in silent fear as my nerve was screaming for me to stop. I was sixty feet off the ground, almost touching the sky. I slid my body's mixture of pain and fear to the roof's edge. My crawl onto the ladder was hidden from the boss. Like a crab on a hot rock, I winced with a quick prayer, asking God for help. My frozen limbs opened and closed on each rung of the ladder. I inched my way to the ground, and then I quit. I limped out of Maine sitting sideways, tilted to the right leaning halfway over into the passenger seat. The Pie lay in the back on my bunk bed half-asleep, with one eye open. He heard my pain and got used to it; I did not. I returned to the garage at my Ma's house on her birthday, September 5.

✝

SEPTEMBER FIFTH

> Time slips with our family yearly,
> Taking birthdays we share dearly.
> September Fifth, oh, September Fifth.

Change is in the air.
Sweeter in the morning,
Slowly you seem aware
Summer was so warming.

> School bus stops and goes on,
> Flashing of times gone by,
> Missing what has been gone.
> Older, so you just sigh.

Notice in just your way
Your look of joy and cheer.
Mother was born today,
Goes back for fifty-one years.

Happy, I wish for you
Birthdays, many more to come.
Mama, what we've been through,
Michael, your loving son.

Time slips with our family yearly,
Taking birthdays we share dearly.
September Fifth, oh, September Fifth.

✝

Before I drove to Bar Harbor, another *American Songwriter* magazine came, with an entry form for a lyric contest. I entered the American Song Festival, the Sixth Annual Lyric Competition, with my best poem, called "Torn Threads." I was looking for some kind of recognition or critique on my writing. Shortly after my mom's birthday, I received a certificate of honorable mention from the American Song Festival. That shot of hope came out of nowhere; it was the boost I needed.

✝

TORN THREADS

When I don't know enough and go out on the town,
Living like a king, wearing freedom's crown,
Hear me late at night get drunk and sing,
Have to find a woman, without any strings.

Too many barroom scenes, scripts of sweet talk,
Let me buy you a drink, will you go for a walk?
After all the strings that were never there,
I find myself in knots, and nobody cares.

> Like old clothes that have been worn,
> Strings start to hang, show where they're torn,
> Through my years, in my head,
> Really appreciate a few Torn Threads.

> Through my years, in my head,
> Really appreciate a few Torn Threads.

I've known love and its many different shades.
Some people living it like a masquerade,
Wear their disguise, two-faced at times,
All they perform is a pantomime.

Come over from behind, stop your pretend,
Show you have a heart you're willing to extend.
Let your strings hang out, show how they fray,
The clothes will show the life you portray.

> Rags to riches is only skin deep.
> The simple things in life always keep
> Our hearts warm with love.

I sold the Canary Cage window van to some guy, who was leaving for
Florida for the winter. I bought a pickup truck, hoping to do more
traveling with the idea of going to Nashville or California.

Chapter 8: Old Thunder

In the fall of 1979, my grandmother was selling our summer home at Galway Lake, and she wanted one of us boys to buy it. We didn't, so she sold it. The camp was more than a memory; it was a great life. It was also a luxury. Losing it made me realize how much I had become dedicated to my writing. What was a lofty dream became a pursuit for identity, worth, and livelihood. I told my diary about my loss. I reflected on how my new treadmill of self-denial seemed to be a seesaw of good and bad times. Making the choice to continue in my radical, non-normal participation off the common treadmill of life was not easy. Life away from what the greater masses of people were doing was more appealing, but still a treadmill. The good times with the band were gone, and my pinched nerve was smarting; then losing the family camp was a hurt deep inside. Just a year earlier, I was riding high, having the time of my life with wine, women, and song. I had lived a vigorous Doctor Jekyll life of happiness and went about expressing joy in every breath. Alternatives needed exploring. I traveled, and I returned fully restored—that's where I was at the time. Surely Mr. Hyde would surface someday, and he did.

✝

Throughout the year of 1979, the three of us—Thunder, Piper, and I—would go for walks. Piper was my second-generation best friend, who was raised in the country. Thunder taught the Pie all the tricks of suburban life. The old dog was a master of going and coming. Thunder cruised inconspicuously in the neighborhood at will. But over time, he slowed and became an early-evening carouser. He would drag it in before sunset, eat well, and sleep more. Before the summer was over, both animals were out running on the town. Eventually the Pie dog also became a master to carry on the tradition of running nights and sleeping days. With coffee grounds on his face, Piper would come home at sunrise, happy and full of triumph. I took him to work with me on construction sites, and he'd sleep under my truck on the cool grass.

The summer growth provided in abundance several shades of greenery. The sun in its cycle of seasons was slower and further along. That year, God's love lavishly showed more autumn color than expected. Old and young trees alike were flush with His painted leaves. The full, undeniable splendor was seen by all. Foliage and seeds softly fell with a gentle swish, dropping silently to the floor of creation. Strange how not all seeds live; only some pass through time, allowing another tree to grow. The leaves were leaving their purpose of staying up; life was completed. That autumn view would serve my memory often and hang suspended in my mind. Reappearing as sweet and sorrowful stages of life, those memories are to be lived again with laughter or tears. In the passing away, the loss of things and sights I loved, the old makes way for the new. Such are the ways of life and death on a dying planet. It is said that earth is a great graveyard. I could see that no one and nothing got out alive; earth was indeed a graveyard. Winter's gray hollowness of cold days was coming. The memory of the trees repeating beauty would satisfy me again.

✝

On a crisp morning in October 1979, brilliant blue skies and sunshine bit my eyes as my mother's cries penetrated the garage walls of the room where I slept. Her upsetting words said that Thunder had fallen and his tries to get up were not enough. I rolled off the foam bed on the garage floor, picking up my body to answer the alarm. My mom walked with me and wept. My arm was around her shoulders as she told me of Thunder's cries for help. On the living room floor at his side, I could see that his back legs had given out. His fearful yelps were telling me of his panic and pain. We huddled on the same floor where we played in the mornings as the two-man riot before school. There was a flood of emotions when reality cleared away the confusion. His inability to stand after I picked him up was shocking. He was crippled, perhaps with a stroke. His bowels had let loose from fear, and not being able to get himself outside confused him. I braced him up in my lap. He was seventeen years old, and I was twenty-six. Carrying him to the backyard, I sat with my old friend of over a hundred dog years of love. Resting with him on the grass, I spoke my soft words of adoration. His effort to stand again caused the fearful panic to overwhelm him and me.

Our cries together with my arms wrapped all around Thunder brought Piper near. My tearful eyes looked into the eyes of Thunder. His eyes cloudy with cataracts, my old true friend saw Piper and still wanted to play. Thunder meant more to me than to anyone else. He was there for me way back when it was just him and me every latchkey morning before school and every afternoon. He was mine, and the way I saw it, the choices were clear. I could either take him to the vet or I could take him into the woods with a gun. That was the time of the end, and that was the time to decide. Remembering Old Yeller and the boy's last walk with his dog, I made my choice.

I packed up the pickup truck with a rifle, bullets, some water for the dogs, and a shovel. Piper jumped in the back, and I carried Thunder, who rode up front with me. The summer home was the best place in my memory, and that was where I would do the deed. His head was on my lap as I drove. I petted him and talked to him and cried my memories driving down the highway. It was the same road our family would travel together every year to our summer home through all four seasons. Past the old barns and antique shops and the cornfields we drove. Back to where I raised the Pie pup and began my diary roots. Back to furrow a place to plant my memories with my old friend.

There was no hurry past the familiar farms, past the milk and bread store, and through the six-second town. We rolled past the grown-up trees, with and without leaves. Different seasons popped into my memory; they had cornfields or they had snow. Right then it was autumn, a beautiful time of year, but I did not feel the beauty. I felt the sorrow, the deep, deep loss of death that was coming. It was the first time. No one close in my family had died before. My old hero was scared and confused, but laid faithfully at my side, with no glimpses, no view of death. Yet I knew within the hour, he would be belowground. Time and distance went by; again I questioned my kind of sanity and reason. I stopped along the way for some beer. Once I started again, I didn't stop; I cleared the tears from my eyes and kept on driving. With his head on my lap, I rubbed his ears and told him I loved him a million times. I parked my pickup truck on the land that had just been sold with the camp building out of our family.

That time of year, nobody was around. I let Piper run free to hunt through his property, his training grounds. I carried Thunder and set him on his old familiar territory where we were kids and puppies together. I wept as the memories raced past my eyes. The fireplace that my father built, with me and my brother helping him, was crumbling. The picnic table Pa built and we all painted was rotting. The tall pine trees that we used to climb were losing their needles, which covered the rich soil. I looked at the land that we lived on playing games, being a family, and just knelt still in the silence. The land was untouched. No one had raked up the leaves and pine needles like we did every fall and spring for twenty years. I looked at the trees Granny and I planted. They looked back. It was a beautiful picture up there like it always was, but that day it was a misplaced puzzle. I slowly got some composure and carried my pack along with the rifle slung over my shoulder, the shovel in one hand; and I bent over and picked up Thunder in my arms. Those two dogs did not know where we were going, and neither did I. We just started walking into the woods.

We found a spot, and Thunder and I lay down there for a while, talking things over, drinking beer. It was time for getting high. We were down at Turtle Cove. The three of us sat and watched the water lick the shoreline and gazed at the waves way, way out. I drank a few beers and rolled up a joint with tears running down my face. A tear dropped on the pot as the waves crawled gently on shore. Thunder ran in those woods and swam in that lake for seventeen years, and now was motionless at my side. Except for his eyes; he kept blinking his eyes and cocked his head toward mine. He could feel my torment. His eyes, glazed over from cataracts, still looked out, and he lay beside me concerned, content, and trusting.

The power in me that pushed me to that point of commitment was waning. How could I put a bullet in my dog's head? What kind of person was I to do such a thing to someone I love? Doubt and awe filled my purpose. Piper was worried about my crying. He had seen my tears before and knew something was wrong. Thunder could not hear me and could barely see me, but that old friend knew how I felt and licked my fingers. He knew me; we were friends since I was nine years old. He was there when I was all alone; his love was always strong, always there, unconditional and unending.

There near the water's edge, I backed up into the woods. There were no camps, no paths or trails, no roads, no place where no one walked. Just the trees where the animals lived, and that was where I led my two dogs. There in the woods I sat on a log with Thunder lying before me and Piper hunting all around us. There was the place that would become the moment in time. I dug a grave in the earthy soil smelling of rotten stumps and fallen trees that lay for many years. I made up the soft, fertile grave. It gave off the aroma of being in the center of the earth, in the core of nature. Everything was in place; all that was needed was for the deed to be done. All that remained was pulling the trigger.

I was a screaming, crying madman forcing myself to go against everything in me. I was telling myself I had to kill what I loved, that I had to do what I said I would do, and that it was for the best. Those thoughts were answered with cries of resistance from the good Dr. Jekyll, and then no resistance as Mr. Hyde came into his place. Dropping the rifle and hugging Thunder was love. Kissing him good-bye and picking up the rifle was also love. The shot rang out. The deed was done in love.

But the moment stayed; it swelled within the sound of the blast. With closed eyes, I leaned back my head. Mad with sorrow, whatever pain I felt before became a hundred times worse. With open eyes, I saw what was not done. I saw a second bullet was needed. I saw my old friend hurt, shot but not dead. Ripped in two, I wanted to help, but said

I was sorry and pulled the trigger again. I tossed the gun aside. Holding my loving friend in my arms, I cried for forgiveness and begged him to understand. I rubbed his ears, telling him I loved him a million times. Slowly my friend saw the night in my hands, and he breathed no more. I touched his eyes with my fingers. I felt his heart. He was gone, and I was left with the deed of death.

The earth laid ready to take the execution, the just cause, all because of my pride. I always told myself I would do it. Because I said I would do it, I did it. Piper was both in high alert and ready for action because of the gunshots. He was intensely aware that I was in great trouble. I cried and screamed in pain as if I had taken the bullet. His confusion on top of my grief made me feel bad for him. I called him over and spoke of my love. I showed him his old friend's dead body to have him smell death. I told him that I would never do that to him.

I laid Thunder in his grave and saw him for the last time before I covered him up and cried good-bye. I carried myself out of death row stumbling, blind with watery eyes, leaning on trees, howling in painful drunken hysteria. As I walked out of the woods, I was stunned and in shock over my capacity to do such a horrible thing. I recalled how at the house my decision was made not to go to the vet's as I sat with him. Thunder was seventeen and crippled. He was mine, and I could not let someone else kill my dog. I could not just leave him on a table and walk away. But now those choices weren't as clear. Here I was alone, walking away from what I had done. I saw how the movie *Old Yeller* had influenced me for years. Doing the deed myself was always held deep in my thoughts and mulled over from time to time. Thinking I would be able to respond to what I had pictured in my mind was an idea whose time had finally come. Doing it was a miserable tragedy.

I looked back at the grave and turned toward Piper, who waited on the dirt road animated with excitement. He had already moved on. I followed him, shaking my head, still wondering where the strength came from to do what I did. Remembering how I walked off the factory job and walked away from Hope's love stopped me in my tracks. I leaned against a tree, catching my breath and seeing my self-determination.

Where does willpower come from? What kind of man am I? The question questioned my sanity. Without an answer, I felt alienated and out of place. Walking to the truck through the woods carrying the rifle and shovel, I passed the empty camp buildings. I felt like I was a visitor walking out of a dream. Why was I living the way I lived, and where was God? The idea of God was abstract, and yet the idea removed some of my isolation. God could see me; He knew the real me. Something as far away as God seemed to be a comfort.

At the truck, I loaded up and sat there thinking. I drank a few more beers, smoked another joint, and thought about time and its value. I questioned my purpose for life, my reason for the direction I was going, and I searched for validity to live it. I searched for acceptance in my lifestyle of striving to be alone and having more time to create. I found solace in the fact that I did what I said I would do. I completed the deed of death, which was a horrible thing to do. A warped sense of satisfaction came over me as I knew that someday that event would be a story to tell. My deed was just one more link in a chain of events for the diary. Watch out what you ask for because you just might get it.

On the way back, Piper rode up front with me with his head on my lap, and I rubbed his ears, telling him I loved him a million times.

---

                                                        †

A BREED

Going on the road, only just begun,
Trade a heavy load, following the sun,
Looking for a sign, hope to find some gold.
Farther down the line, life slips from my hold.

> A Breed, A Breed, searching who has a need.
> A Breed, A Breed, searching, where will it lead?

A Breed of man who tells what he feels,
Tumbleweed a man, steering his own wheel,
A Breed of man, the sun lights his stage,
In his eyes, you see, each day turns a page.

To him the road has been a pre-destiny,
Loves it like a friend, together they'll be free,
Moving like the wind, in and out of town,
Never to be pinned until he wears a crown.

A Breed, A Breed, searching who has a need.
A Breed, A Breed, searching, where will it lead?

A Breed of man, who tells what he feels,
Tumbleweed a man, steering his own wheel,
A Breed of man, the sun lights his stage,
In his eyes, you see, each day turns a page.

Chapter 9: Texas Tenacity

That winter of 1979 to 1980, I had odd jobs. Sweeping and vacuuming offices wasn't difficult, but polishing linoleum floors with an electric high-speed circular buffer was. Finding the consistency of movement for the rotating brush took more care than I could give. Next, at a nearby soda factory, the line work consisted of extracting plastic bottles jamming up the assembly. I wore earplugs with eyeprotection and watched the machine filling the explosive carbonated soda bottles. The sticky liquid was pumped down into the upright plastic. Foamy suds caused issues before the next stage, where the cap was screwed on. Bottles dropped into cases, which were stacked on pallets and then removed by a fork truck. Bursting sizzling bubbly bottles exploded at any time in the operation. Those rinky-dink night jobs didn't last. I kept looking for something of interest, but they all just put money in my pocket.

Driving home early morning in the great Northeast winter, the freezing cold really makes you wonder why you're there. However, once I reached my small warm garage room, I really appreciated the quiet stillness. Lyric writing in those predawn hours became more and more consistent. I picked up half-done efforts to finish and started new ones about love or ideas on traveling or attitudes about myself in general with a growing dedication. Finished poems I called lyrics. They were written with a repeated metered cadence that rhymed. When reading them melodically, I wondered how music would sound. Writing after work was like having a job I loved but without pay.

For a short time, I worked as night watchman at a very old historical site. The Ingersoll old men's home might have been a hospital or at one point a hotel. High ceilings collected the heat, and tall windows allowed a way for cooler air to gather on the floors. Making the rounds walking in the dimly lit halls, my black rubber-soled shoes squished and squeaked from end to end. After circling in eighty-five-degree heat through both floors and climbing down the stairs, I'd relax. With perfect quiet all around, I took off my shoes, sighed, and slumped into position. Lounging in big overstuffed soft chairs placed about the lobby parlor, I'd try to write. But I would always fall asleep. The heat and the comfort would wrap me like a yawning baby. I looked forward to spring's fresh air and being outside on another job. Jobs would come, and they would also leave. I could not find satisfaction for wages, but I didn't mind looking for work. My dad always said to keep your best foot forward. That winter was cold. The old pickup truck's engine's freeze-out plugs were so rusty they didn't pop out when the water in the radiator froze. That truck died.

On April 1, 1980, it was Granny's eighty-second birthday. She made her own cake because she did it the best. It was a four-layer vanilla cake with pudding between the layers and chocolate frosting. It was Piper's birthday also; the Big Squeaker was six; he was the Champion, the Duke. The Duke and I again considered leaving on that southern trip sooner or later. I figured songwriters were in New York City, Nashville, or Los Angeles. A guy from Texas who was renting across the street was selling the idea of making money in the oil fields on the Gulf of Mexico. On those dark spring nights, I began hatching plans to leave town. Memorial Day was nearing; it would mark one year after leaving on the Bar Harbor trip. I set my sights on California. Heading west seemed a likely course to travel and live some of my life.

✝

In May 1980, I came home early one evening while my mother was still at work. I checked into the garage, opening some of the doors, and wrestled with Piper before going into the house. Granny was eighty-two and going about her evening routine preparing for bed. We got along great; she would always talk with me as I would come and go through the house. This one evening, she was not her normal self. My concern was elevated with her mumbling, and instead of calling 911emergency, I made the mistake of asking her if I should call 911. She insisted that her tired condition was temporary and would pass by morning. She was wrong, and I was wrong to wait. She had suffered a stroke. When Ma came home, she too was very concerned, but none of us had any experience with such a matter. Granny insisted she was okay.

The next day on my mom's insistence, we took Granny to the hospital. Tests showed and doctors determined that she did suffer a stroke. It's a difficult transition to accept when a close family member is forced to live with a limiting condition. I saw how fragile a flower life is. In a wisp of time, age dances through years and time's petals fall to earth. Granny still got around, but she was much slower and very tired. I helped her all I could while a primary plan was being developed. Aides needed to come in and be with my grandmother during the day. These were women of various youthful ages and ethnic backgrounds from a local agency to help those in need. Trained and willing to meet the needs of the needy was what we hoped for. My grandmother had worked hard her whole life as a top cook. She ran the kitchen and crew in a big restaurant in California. Granny earned her way into a male-dominated environment. She was not ready to settle for just anybody to hang around all day watching TV and smoking cigarettes.

The agency would send them up, and Granny would try them out; most of them were sent away. When a stranger is sitting around or working around your home, privacy is gone. I had to learn to tolerate the intrusion of strangers as much as Granny did. She and I would talk about the strangers and whether we were happy with their presence. That summer left quietly, as did that autumn. Winter dropped its cold and snow. Without a vehicle, I was fortunate to have the option of a city bus. I got a job as a dishwasher at Union College and became more comfortable with living out my dedication to write.

Over the frozen months, I got to know a few of the aides more intimately. One young beautiful blonde whom my grandmother liked related well with Granny and worked out the best. Her name was Roxy. It was a pleasure to see them talking as girlfriends do. Roxy and I became friends as well. We had mutual friends and went to some of the same nightspots. Instead of my taking the bus home after work, Granny sent her to pick me up. I enjoyed the ride in the cold months and looked forward to her company. I had a variety of fifty-five different lyrics written by the end of winter. My primary focus was on creating what was viable to sell commercially, and that meant lyrics about love.

By springtime there wasn't much I could do for my grandmother, though we still talked and laughed. The beautiful blonde left that job, and an older, more-professional lady came in. Granny liked her because she couldn't sit still so she kept cleaning the house. I was earning money working with a mason swinging a sledgehammer, busting concrete. Saving up for another pickup, I was planning for Texas. My dad and mom were getting along real good. Pa came up to help with the house and yard work prior to my travels. I thought maybe my exit would help my mom and dad get along better. This was going to be a big important push to get to California. But I first needed to stop in Texas to earn high wages. My thoughts about Texas ran together and came up with a lyric before I even crossed the New York state line.

EVERYTHING IN TEXAS

I've never been to Texas, but I hear that it's okay;
Got the word from a Texan, who had drifted far away.
He spoke with easy feelings, with a sparkle in his eye,
When he told me of Texas, how the sun sets in the sky.

I didn't want to bug him for his reasons why he left;
I could see he had his pride and was living with regret.
But I just had to ask him, of all the stories I heard,
He said, "Son, no stories, you can believe every word.

"Everything in Texas is so much bigger than life,
The air so humid, you can cut it with a knife.
Highways go straight, and there ain't a tree in sight.
You don't ask questions in the middle of the night.
Everything in Texas is so much bigger than life.

"The music in Texas will make you cry in your beer;
They don't have Top 40, you hear the same songs all year.
The people are crazy, they always think they're right;
Better mind your manners, 'cause the cowboys love to fight."

It didn't sound like heaven; it was more the tone of hell.
The Texan kept on talking, he was as clear as a bell.
Then he popped a grin, sure enough, he cracked a smile.
He burst out laughing, and said, "It's been awhile.

"It was so good to tell someone who has never seen the state
Of all the natural beauty, the things that make it great.
You can stop all the rumors, just tell your friends the facts,
You heard it from a Texan, whose heart is aching to go back.

"Everything in Texas is so much bigger than life,
The air so humid, you can cut it with a knife.
Highways go straight, and there ain't a tree in sight.
You don't ask questions in the middle of the night.
Everything in Texas is so much bigger than life.

"The music in Texas will make you cry in your beer;
They don't have Top 40, you hear the same songs all year.
The people are crazy, they always think they're right;
Better mind your manners, 'cause the cowboys love to fight."

At first I thought the reason he left was for his health.
Then I started thinking that I should go there myself.
I wasn't born yesterday, oh, I learned from my youth,
The way to keep a secret is by stretching the truth.

The Texan told me stories so I would stay away,
Gave me the wrong idea to make me glad to stay.
He gave away the secret when he remembered with a sigh
He couldn't hide his feelings or the sparkle in his eye.

✝

Once again, all the possibilities and potentialities came alive for me. Adventure fueled the fire of my determination. I entered the American Song Festival for a second time. I didn't realize the enormity of what I was attempting when I said to my dad, "I want to hear my words put to music and on the radio." He wished me good luck. I did know what was in store when I said, "I'll try my best." A year after Bar Harbor, I was ready to go to Texas.

Two days before leaving, I worked with Pa. He helped me finish up with my homemade camper shell for the back of my "new" used pickup truck. He mentioned that he was trying to go to Alcoholics Anonymous meetings again. He read the black cast iron plate with a prayer called the Serenity Prayer on it. Pa nailed it up near the workbench a year earlier.

He wasn't his casual self when he did that, but the moment passed. We worked in Ma's yard and put another gate on Aunt Lucy's fence. Pa was sweating a lot and looked pale. He said it was no big deal. We sat in the garage and talked small talk as the summer wind blew through the big windows. We hugged each other, and I shook his big hand. He told me to keep my guard up and that the Pie would protect me. I drove him to his apartment, we had a beer, and we said our good-byes. I shook his big hand again, we hugged, and we exchanged our love for each other.

I drove out of town on Memorial Day headed for Freeport, Texas. On the road again with the Champion, the Big Pie, for the second time, it was another beautiful feeling of early retirement. To have time and money in my pocket was a wonderful thing. To have that and living out a dream was a great thing. A dream was something more than thoughts. My life came alive with the truth that I wasn't talking about going; I was living in the freedom to do it. The last six frustrating years of recuperating and deliberately not participating in gainful steady employment was my choice. Dedication was proof that my hope was real. Driving put my choice and hopes into action. Was self-denial a worthy venture?

This was my repeated thought driving in a southern direction across the New York border into Pennsylvania once again. I thought of Marylyn. I saw my lifestyle and the women I'd known since her. Content and willing to extend the gamble with my time, I never looked back. Fifteen hundred dollars was in my pocket. I never gambled, but I suppose you could say I was gambling to find fulfillment with my time on earth. I was investing the time in my life. Driving over the Mississippi River, I thought of Mark Twain and his house in Hartford. The names of Tom Sawyer and Huck Finn were just names to me; I never knew what they did. I never read the books, but I wished I had. I drove on stopping here and there in rest stops to let Piper run. The tractor trailer big rigs seemed to occupy most of the highways. The farther south I got, I saw fewer trees and flatter land and felt more heat. My continued adventure thrived and brought more thoughts of doing the uncommon, more of the ends justifying the means.

Texas was hot. I maneuvered through Houston's massive raised concrete rivers of traffic. Broad, thick, horizontal cement thoroughfares hurled my rusty pickup. I'd never seen such a collection of highways. I was impressed and rocketed through the midst of other high-speed motoring metal. We all rolled along in lines like ants to their magnets of responsibilities, like an army of indebted motorists. Searching for road signs to get out of a sea of transportation, my eyes bounced to a road map and back before pulling off for lunch.

✝

CROWDED

Discordant yawns, alarmed radios,
Traffic attack peak-hour city waves,
Houston roars of freeway thunder.

Shifts of people pouring on and off roads,
Pedestrians dance the heat-rising pavement,
Seeking in-room, cool central air, of course.

The truth rings, doors slam, forms appear,
Consecutive confrontation, attention spans
Stretch, patience thin, rubber-band man.

Pulled to adjust, expand the Houston control,
Think but be still, movement gets growls,
Search, snap, where is the balance? I'm so Crowded.

✝

The city's incinerating heat pushed me out of the chaos and then nonstop to the Gulf of Mexico. Driving through unfamiliar streets and highways without air-conditioning gave me thoughts of abandoning that fiery stepping-stone to California. Determination drove me like a needle on a compass searching for opportunity to earn a living. It was a difficult hunt, because it was an election year and jobs were tight all over. Being from the north and inexperienced in the Texas southern heat made my life tougher to fit in. My plans to stay with friends in Freeport fell through. I stayed with friends of a friend; Jessie and Peggy were very gracious and honorable people. After two weeks of travel and searching, the Pie and I had a temporary roof to stay under. I was surprised when I got an envelope in the mail a few days later. My dad sent me a birthday card with twenty bucks and his love. It blew me away. His card came like he was looking out for me.

The experience I had gathered from job searching over several years paid off after the tenth or twelfth application was filed. An international construction outfit hired me to frame footings for concrete pillars, right on the Gulf of Mexico coastline. The job was one of two major objectives to be conquered. I still needed a fort. As an army of two, the Duke and I quickly eliminated possible apartment rentals. Nobody wanted a dog, and I really couldn't blame them. However, in a neighborhood of opposing ethnic groups, standards were lower for whatever reasons.

That barrio of tension consisted of small, single-unit apartments maybe four feet apart. All were ground level, separated by a maze of narrow alleyways. The Duke and I ponied up seven hundred and fifty dollars for rent and deposits. That left me about five hundred until my first paycheck. After bombing the place for cockroaches and fleas one night, I returned the next evening to scour the kitchen stove and sinks. After the hot construction job and hard sweaty work and a shower, Duke and I returned and lay on the linoleum floor with the air-conditioning blasting. Eight days after we landed and first swam in the Gulf, we were in our fort; the goals were met. We rested in the dark of the Lilliputian castle we called home. Like two Yankee candles nearly melted out of existence, we both lay there breathing a sigh of relief. We heard gunshots in the near distance and voices outside our walls. We were locked in. We had successfully engaged the enemies against progress and established a beachhead to advance our California-bound battle.

But once again, there was a wild card. My mother and I hooked up on the phone, and I received the news of my father's sickness and hospital care. My mother could not tell me anything more other than that the doctors would operate to investigate his stomach pain. Forty-eight hours later, my brother called and told me Pa was dead. The operation exposed cancer, which spread rapidly, taking his life. My presence in New York was needed immediately. I had to move fast. I bought a one-way ticket for me and Duke with the last of my money. Hours later, we left all we had and were on a jet returning for Pa's funeral.

Ken met us at the airport. We bonded like only brothers can. Our dad was gone, but our love for Pa removed any space between my brother and I. He gave me the details of Pa's last two very painful days in the hospital. The surgery was the only option. Before Ma could bring him home to care for him, he died. I left my truck, my bicycle, and my tool chest in Texas. Things would be sold for me, and they were. But I brought home confidence. That leg of my journey was cut short, but that cut sharpened my perseverance. I was back in New York after five weeks of hectic life. But life didn't fit; it never did unless I was moving toward my dream. I wanted to be in California more than ever.

A few hours after my dad's burial, I sat alone outside at the picnic table near the driveway. The jet lag, the sorrow of my dad's death, and the loss of giving up my momentum to reach California were all beating me up. Just as I was looking down trying to make sense of it all, I saw feet approaching. Clark stood there with a brown bag telling me how sorry he was for my loss. He used to be in the band, and at one point we tried to write a lyric together. We used to play chess, drinking and smoking joints as we plotted our moves. Since I hadn't seen him for a while, it took me by surprise when Clark said, "How about a drink?" He pulled out a dark green half-gallon bottle of Tanqueray gin. We both smiled, and if the Devil were there, he smiled too. Like old times, we drank and shared stories; the gin went down as if it were water. My mood went up, and plans spilled out to forge ahead to California no matter what. We finished the bottle, and the real trouble began when I remembered my Pa's wishes. I told Clark how Pa wanted a toast at his grave and empty beer cans pushed into the fresh dirt. Clark's eyes got as big as a kid seeing circus lights. Against my mother's wishes, I drove off with her car.

On our way to the bar for a drink and a six-pack, I recklessly drove up on the front lawn of someone's suburban home. Stopping short of hitting a tree, I put the Chevy Caprice in reverse and left quickly. At the grave, we sat drinking our last can and shoved the sixth one into the dirt. Aunt Lucy's long 1962 Cadillac convertible pulled up slowly with her and Ma inside. Ma called to Clark and me, and we slowly crawled to the Eldorado. They took me and Clark away, assuring the cemetery caretaker we were family and asking him to please understand.

At Ma's house, I was in a far worse condition with the alcohol mixing with my emotions and jet lag. Just minutes later, the local police arrived. Not only did I scar the front lawn of the home with my irresponsible driving, but I nearly drove over a child. The mother of the child watched in horror as the few seconds of my foolishness unfolded. I was told to come to the station the next day. The police severely scolded me and laid out the demands of the family. After apologizing in person, I needed to repair the front lawn. I thanked the people and the police for their leniency.

A few days later I met with my dad's sister Aunt Jean, who still lived in the Rourke family home. My aunt showed me Pa's room, where he stayed at times. We packed his army discharge papers and the few things he had: a bottle of Old Spice, an empty pack of L&M cigarettes on the table, and a few pieces of small paper with poetry written in pencil. We sat on the front porch talking about the neighborhood she and my dad grew up in on Schenectady Street with their brothers and sister. I told her of my stupidity drinking and driving and my foolish emotional acts. Having a beer is okay, she said, but you need to stop after one or two. Explaining how I should have been arrested, she said, "God works in mysterious ways." When I showed Ma Pa's things, she cried smelling the Old Spice and remembered how he liked to dabble with poetry. I was so surprised and couldn't understand why his fondness for poetry was never mentioned to me before.

For the rest of summer into autumn and over the winter, I felt like a wounded bird grounded with one wing. Suddenly having all my California momentum ripped away and racing backward to the starting point was a major bummer. Granny had a wonderful mature aide who came every day, so the house was uncomfortable for me but good for Ma and Granny. All the cold months I looked but found no work. Most of the day and night, I put together the pieces of my shattered determination. Without a vehicle, job, or cash, I walked a lot with Piper. Many days the Pie and I visited with Buddy's mom down on the farm. At night it was walking the suburban streets under street lights the cold was comfortable. Friends stopped by, we partied, and I rode with them to bars. I had little control but was learning more patience.

When spring of 1981 came, I became more hopeful construction would be starting. Looking in the newspaper for jobs and asking around was what I could do. It was tough without wheels; few jobs were close. Ma and Granny wanted to buy me some, but I couldn't take more of their generosity. I was in a cycle and knew I was learning a new phase of perseverance. I didn't like it, but knew it was a cycle.

✝

Another Monday morning, I looked in the Schenectady *Gazette* newspaper for a job. Without wheels, my likelihood of finding something close was slim. However, Pa always said put your best foot forward, and I did. One of the radio stations in our area had an ad for help wanted at WMHT. They played the very best classical music, with interesting comments on the great composers, and were also a public-access TV station. The radio station had received funding that was used to enhance the lives of disadvantaged youths. Summer maintenance and construction jobs were supposed to expose city kids to how the station operated. The building was in the town of Rotterdam, less than a mile away. I walked over, filled out an application, and waited in the lobby to be interviewed. A thin man with a quick step, older-looking with light red hair pushed back flat on his head, came for me and showed me into his office. I sat near his desk, watching him read my application. He introduced himself as Bob Golden. He was the carpenter for the building and made TV props for the sets on stage and took all around care of the building and grounds.

Bob asked about my work in Texas. I told him about working in a crew on the Gulf framing forms for concrete. He sat quietly thinking. When he spoke, he asked why I was back in New York and why I came home so suddenly after just getting the job there. I told him the story of my journey to California, the Texas detour, and my dad's death. Bob said with surprise in his voice, "It sounds like you're determined to get to California. Not many people would have left what they had to come back." With emotion in my voice, I said, "I came home to bury my dad." He hired me and told me to start work the next morning.

One August afternoon, Bob and our small summer maintenance crew were working outside at the radio tower in Altamont. He and I worked alone, quietly spreading and raking gravel on the road away from the others. Bob spoke up and said, *"I knew your dad. We spent time together growing up. I know your Aunt Jean, your Aunt Ellen, and Uncle Will. I knew your dad's whole family and your Uncle Joe before he died."* Thinking I was over my dad's death, I stood there choking up again. We talked about what Bob knew. "After your grandfather died, your Uncle Joe was the oldest son, and then he got married. Your dad quit school and he and Joe started working to help your grandmother, their younger brother Will, and your Aunts Jean and Ellen. When the produce truck drove by, he'd climb up and throw me cabbages and carrots while I ran—oh, we had fun. Times were rough; it was in the Depression. Then the war broke out, and he enlisted."

Bob was like an uncle. He and I were closer after that day. I watched him more, and his sense of humor shone more. Maybe I saw my dad a little in him. Bob was a master carpenter and the treasurer for the local carpenters' union at one point. Bob also showed me the proper ways around tools and safety precautions. Bob gave me a little more attention and allowed me to be the leader on a few of our excursions. Every day I rode a bicycle to work, rain or shine. Work would only last until the snow fell, so I saved my money.

†

By September 1981, I took care of the land of both Ma's and Aunt Lucile's properties. Aunt Lucile was always a good listener, and one day while I raked pine needles, she had something to say. Aunt Lucy told me of her friend in California who was a TV producer. She was going to tell me when I got there, but Pa's death rerouted me. Having some kind of contact in any part of the movie or music business surely must be better than having no contact. Or so I thought. The news of a potential California contact helped the cold months go by. Being so focused on writing lyrics, thoughts of acting were foreign to me. I expanded my repertoire writing about politics, the social condition of America, my dog, and more love songs. I had eighty-five lyrics.

In my November diary of 1981, I wrote a long section about my booking a flight to California for January 1982. I was sitting in my room in the garage by candlelight listening to classical music alone. I had been writing then for seven years. Thoughts of Christmas and then leaving town put me in the shopping mood. In December, I walked in Schenectady with my diary like I had after my concussion eight years earlier. Before standing at a bus stop, I sat in coffee shops freely writing openly and aggressively and shopped with the joy of giving. It was a bitter cold but sunny day, with high winds squeezing my eyes nearly shut looking for the bus. Turning quickly to shield my face and put my back to the wind, I stood face-to-face with my Uncle Will, Pa's brother. He loved to walk; I had often seen him crossing the Gateway Bridge over the Mohawk. He stood there like a boulder; he lifted weights when he was younger the cold didn't deter his walking at all. Sometimes he would stay at the Rourke house with Aunt Jean and Pa. We talked about growing up and how all us kids were cousins and would play running up the spiral stairs at his house. I told him I was leaving town, and he just stared. His wife and kids left him several years earlier. The bus came, and we hugged wishing Merry Christmas, shook hands, and parted.

I worked at the radio station up till Christmas. Bob gave me a great letter of recommendation to take with me; and had Connie the best looking lady in the station take me to lunch. He said to call him if he could help me somehow get a job. He was a great influence and source of confidence. Before leaving the station, I had yellow T-shirts made for all of our summer crew and Bob. Above a picture of a clumsy carpenter with his saw and hammer were the words "Uncle Bob's Misfits." I saw Aunt Jean before leaving, and she said Bob's nickname was Red because of his red hair. She knew him well and knew of his friendship with my dad. She was so surprised and just said, "Red Golden, God works in mysterious ways."

With great anticipation of flying to California, I mushroomed with motivation. It would be just me and the Pie and two suitcases leaving New York. My preparations into the winter culminated in the first week of 1982. My day of departure came January 7, 5:00 a.m., upstate New York, Albany Airport. Freezing rain in the early morning hours held the plane in blackness on the runway. The small commuter prop plane with its motors idling, being loaded with baggage, might not be allowed to take off. As speculation and doubt rose, our Philadelphia connection for the big jet seemed further away.

Those were tense moments for me in many ways. My dog, my best friend Piper, was in the cargo compartment freezing. He was a seven-year-old beautiful intelligent male, a yellow Lab-vizsla mix that would die for me. His faithful yellow eyes were never off of me. I knew he was looking for me. His eyes of faith always told me that he would be by my side no matter how beautiful or ugly life got. The bitter cold predawn escape was to be our second plane ride. The memory of Texas and Pa's funeral were more proof that struggling was part of my life. That bitter pill of truth didn't make me comfortable; it made the trip even more urgent. Time wasn't flying by that morning, and neither was I as I watched the clock.

Standing at the window, I tasted the lost love of my father with fear in my throat. I wasn't afraid of falling from the sky but fearful of the repeated failure to leave my hometown. Pressing my face against the cold glass of the terminal, I saw how fragile life was. Bouncing raindrops forced my eyes to blink like the slow rhythm of the yellow caution light on the runway. Rain hitting the glass tapped out memories as my eyes tried to focus on the plane. Flashes of hospital-bed recoveries and painful recuperations were some of the worst recalls. The defeats, setbacks, a chosen lifestyle of a rebellious artist swirled faster and faster in my early morning funnel of hope. I was still swallowing the lost love of my father with the too-familiar fear of things gone badly.

In the icy glass reflection of the raindrops was the wheelchair where Granny sat weeping. Her stroke-twisted face let the tears loose. I knelt next to her, and we hugged and wept. We both knew that would be our last time together. We spent many long hours together as she nursed me through the years of recovery from some serious accidents. Without her, my life would have been much worse. Likewise my mother, who bore the worries of the world once again, had concern for her second son. Ma had seen me live through my hard times. Ma and Granny were my nurses and benefactors, who lovingly cared for me through the years of my near-broken back and the head concussion. They watched how I could not stop my dreaming, and we all watched how time tore me up. There Ma stood, seeing me leaving her and her mother dying slowly. A year and a half earlier, she was at my dad's side in the hospital before his death. She lost him to drink and finally cancer, but never stopped loving him. I took after my dad. I was the black sheep of the family, whom she loved and cared for beyond measure.

Ken paced with me, eyeing the clock and the frozen rain hitting the glass as we considered the weather conditions. His suggestion that I could always wait and book another flight fell on deaf ears. He had no idea what my life was about; we never had heart-to-heart talks. He never asked questions or had any interest in my writing. He could not understand my artistic drive or necessity to leave. How could he? We were on the fringes of each other's lives. We each had our own worlds to live in. Without a steady job, wife, and baby, I was invisible to him. We were related bone of bone, blood of blood, but we didn't relate well. He was patient with me and we loved at a distance and as deeply as only brothers can.

On the one hand, my life was a lonely searchlight of laughter, booze, women, drugs, and songs, looking with hope. On the other hand, living was at times extreme pain and not so much fun for me. I felt like I had lived two long lives with all my body aches. I spent thousands of nights sitting alone, writing my dreams in a diary, my emotions forming lyrics. Remembering the past and recording the present was like a medicine that worked wonders for me.

— † —

SONGWRITER

Songwriter, I've got a lot to say
About the world's position or just the time of day.
It doesn't really matter who, what, or why,
Laugh, live, or cry; what matters is how hard I try.

I write some words and sing them in a tune.
Some people call me crazy, like snow in June,
For writing those words and speaking of a change.
Isn't it ironic what people think is strange?

Songwriter, listen to me speak,
Try to make a rhyme, if it takes all week,
Doesn't really matter if it rhymes or not.
With a pen and paper, I can't say I forgot.

Writing those words in the afternoon,
Or if it suits me better, do it with the moon.
Just write those words, then put them in a pile,
Sit back in the muse, and crack a smile.

Songwriter, ideas in hand,
How American castles are turning to sand,
Doesn't really matter, I write to be free,
Writing what I feel, whatever it may be.

Writing those words, chasing dark with light,
Stand firm in the Lord, in the power of His might,
Just sing those words, while I have breath.
Life is a gift, and the Lord decides death.

Then the good news came, and the doors were opened. People shuffled around hugging and kissing, saying good-bye, waving farewell as the boarding began. Holding my family with hugs and kisses was so important to me. I was emotional, and I knew I was leaving a source of strength. Looking into Granny's eyes for the last time broke me. I turned and walked out the door with tears into the windy freezing rain. I welcomed the ice on my face as I looked up into the dark sky leaning into the wind. I knew I would miss that Northeast weather I loved. I was fortunate in that I loved and was loved.

I sat on the plane surrounded by freezing darkness, stiffly relaxing under the dim lights. The pilot said the small plane would be going into a very strong wind for Philadelphia. We would be shaking and bumping, but once we were flying high enough, we would smooth out. Being on the plane and rolling down the runway made me the happiest guy in New York. Seeing green lights, rocketing past caution, I sat in the seat of opportunity, aiming to cross a continent of hope. Closing my eyes, I rested and smiled like a little kid. Within me, a surprise came like opening a gift. At last I was leaving the collected mess of mistakes and dues paid. I held my diary and closed my eyes for a small thank you prayer thinking of Aunt Jean's words: "God works in mysterious ways."

✝

IF

How does a man stop, being a boy,
How can I live a life to enjoy?
If there is a miff, will I stand still?
Should I lash out and know the thrill?

If is in the middle of a serious riddle called l-if-e,
If is before me, If is what will be.
Will I know for sure what will be?
If is in the middle of a serious riddle called l-if-e.

Lost in choices of bad and good,
Climbing a ladder, I should and could.
If there is a cliff, will life hang on?
Will Mighty God, send me beyond?

If is in the middle of a serious riddle called l-if-e,
If is before me, If is what will be.
Will I know for sure what will be?
If is in the middle of a serious riddle called l-if-e.

Take the If out of life, you still have to guess.
Put the If in your life, will it spell more or less?
Take the If out of life, will you have happiness?

Life could be a breeze, slow before fast,
Sun on a lake, then it's overcast.
If there is a riff, will I fall and die?
Who but Lord Jesus, can justify?

If is in the middle of a serious riddle called l-if-e,
If is before me, If is what will be.
Will I know for sure what will be?
If is in the middle of a serious riddle called l-if-e.

Part II

California—The Goals, Grinds, and Joys

Chapter 10: West Coast Flight of Perseverance

January 7, 1982, touchdown came after a seven-hour flight into one-hundred-mile-an-hour turbulent headwinds. John Wayne Airport in Orange County, California, was like an oasis. The shocking climate difference was very satisfying at first. Walking into the sunlight was like a giant step through seasons. Standing outside of the airport terminal, my body agreed with my eyes. Peering into the calm brilliance, I smiled wide into the clear blue skies. I was indeed initiating another life. Overwhelmed at first, I was taken away by the warm fragrant aroma.

A cousin on my mom's side was gracious, along with her husband, to allow me access into their home for our adventure to begin. She picked us up at the airport. The Pie, loose from his crate and happily out from the icy plane's bottom, christened a hibiscus. Two suitcases stood between my feet, which Pie was circling. Excitement lifted me.

Riding from the airport on what looked like all new suburban streets, I questioned the purpose for the cement walls. Solid six-foot-high concrete walls were everywhere between homes and businesses and along streets. They were like border hedges, almost as if they grew, but they had that prison look. I was told they were for privacy. Apparently that modern high-tech state had a high demand for its citizens' views to be walled in or out. The Duke and I were driven through avenues of mini stockades of West Coast life. The cleanliness and the newness were most impressive at first, along with the palm trees and lush vegetation.

The Pie and I walked in a local park. We were overpowered by the scent of eucalyptus trees. Slowly we strolled on manicured lawns that must have landed there out of a travel magazine. That life was normal for those living there, and yet I was finding all the strange aspects. It's interesting that I looked like I belonged; I did not, and yet I did. I was living out ambitions that were coming true, away from New York and in a discovery zone. Sitting with my best friend, relaxing from jet lag, it was a powerful time to reflect in the diary. With joy and trepidation, pinching my thoughts to see if it was real, I wrote. Landing in another time zone and climate was good, but being closer to achieving my goal was better.

Two days later, I began looking for work in the newspaper ads and making phone calls. I was lent the cousin's extra car for going about my business. I appreciated the very old automobile; we became friends quickly. Its well-kept rust-free looks represented a clean, simple time gone by. The old piece of equipment and I found the unemployment office. In my limited travels within the first week, that comfortable time machine drove me to a local bar in the afternoon to see what I could see. That bar had the basics, but the prettiness was too new, too bright, and too young for my liking. There was no character, no personality; it was unmanly—it could have been a delicatessen or used for travel agents. While playing a game of pool, a Californian dude offered me a general tour of the area. His long hair and beard seemed out of place when he spoke of his love for surfing. We had one for the road and headed out.

He described the setting of twenty years ago during the hippie love-in days as I drove. Stories of smoking pot openly and walking guitar players having clashes with police and drug busts were plentiful. It was ironic to be hearing the twenty-year-old news of peace, love, and crime while driving in the timeworn wagon. All was well until we reached the summit of a community park, where bands once played to thousands. I pulled in and parked next to several modern cars. That local dude quickly jumped out and began checking for unlocked doors on the cars until he found one open. He began searching a woman's pocketbook, all within thirty seconds. My disbelief had barely registered alongside the nostalgic thoughts of the 1962 events missed. When panic began to set in, I put the car in reverse. The thief hurried back with some items before I put the car in drive and jumped into my borrowed getaway car.

I was shocked to be a part of something like that and even more shocked to be so naive. Thank God we got out of there without difficulty and returned to the city streets. The stranger hopped out at a streetlight and went on his way without a word. Meanwhile I was left in the escape vehicle with someone else's cassette case. My vulnerability stripped away any self-reliant confidence I arrived with. Praying to God for help came naturally with that trouble. My entire surge across the country, all my work and hope, were suddenly at great risk. Who else could fix something like that but God? I thought of Aunt Jean saying, "God works in mysterious ways." In the past, the diary heard my questions about who God was, but my interest was short. That day's trouble brought my interest front and center for a while.

There weren't any repercussions from that afternoon's heist. No jobs were found; no cop cars were in the driveway. I became much more aware of my vulnerability with first impressions and very skeptical of what seemed to be friendly situations. I made my initial phone calls to my Aunt Lucy's lost friend in Hollywood. I was glad to leave a message with the answering service in Beverly Hills. Knowing that there was a wild card like a movie producer who might be a friend or just lend a hand made my pilgrimage more of a thrill.

The diary was capturing those moments of my first ten days in southern California with great enthusiasm. I got hold of the producer on the phone, and we talked about me coming over to meet at her office and have lunch. With much map preparation and car inspection, I started out for the first time on the freeways for Beverly Hills. It was a fast and furious drive. The thrill ride was like lighting the fuse of a sky rocket and feeling the sparks. The vintage automobile and I drove eighty-five miles to turn onto Rodeo Boulevard, Beverly Hills. My eyes saw the money stores, cars, and people shopping. There were palm trees and flowers; everything was pristine and in place along the immaculate fairy-tale boulevards. I was shocked to see Mexican men using large air blowers to clean the dust from spotless sidewalks and storefronts.

After I climbed the stairs to the producer's small office, I stood before the door that could unlock my future. A woman answered the door. She looked at me and exclaimed, "Joey!" I apparently looked a lot like her brother-in-law from Florida. It was a strange first impression. Not recognizing the titles of the movies she helped produce, I felt naïve.

"They were just investments," she said. Shortly after I got there, she went out to meet someone important. She left me alone and told me to make myself comfortable. I thought that was also strange, but then again, I was seeing lots of strange things. The producer had a small gym in the corner; she even had a heavy bag hanging ready to be punched. She must have had a need to fight, being afraid of something. I had never seen that done before. The place looked like a mess, but comfortable; I liked it. I lay on the couch with my feet up looking at the place of a movie producer. I didn't know what being a famous producer meant. Just living in Beverly Hills seemed like it would qualify as some kind of famous.

She returned, and we left for some upscale restaurant nearby. People were coming over to our table congratulating her on her charity work. I was not familiar with the movie business or concerned with acting. The food was great, and yet the lunch was awkward. Her suggestions for health food and no alcohol sounded weird coming from a stranger. I got the sense that she was changing colors to fit in with those who saw her. I did try the recommended sand dabs, some fish dish that was very good. She had plans for going to Europe and spoke of how busy she was, and then asked if I had ever considered acting. I expressed little interest in acting, but a great love for writing lyrics. She had no suggestions or advice for me, only said she knew a few musicians. We only talked a little about my family, Aunt Lucy, and her days in Schenectady, New York.

When we returned to her street, I left some of my non-copyrighted lyrics with her. She said she would try to do something to help me. I trusted her. We agreed to stay in touch, and I drove away feeling like a million bucks. Even though her preoccupation with work and travel was on another level, it resembled mine except for the punching bag. My goal was on target, and my progress felt good. Like notches on the gun of achievement, my reality was carved into my quest toward creative recognition. A sense of worth bubbled up, and I could not resist finding more excitement before leaving the area.

I drove to the corner of Hollywood and Vine to see what I could see. Hollywood Boulevard was packed with people and stuffed with traffic. Intersections were jammed with a world of people. Young rebels with multicolored hair and chains with rings hanging from faces clad in clothing like rags. Body-pierced and tattooed carnival sideshow freaks walked arm-in-arm next to three-piece suits. High-heeled fashion shows sashayed between dull, obscure, moving shadows. I was watching their normal. My lack of tolerance for the wide variety of expression surfaced from within. I quickly saw how far I was removed from popular culture, and I was glad. I was confirming what I had always sensed: that I was never politically correct. I assumed those whom I saw were tolerant of the variety of differences and wondered how they got so broad-minded. Did they just put up with each other and keep their dislikes hidden? I didn't know if time would change me. I hoped not.

I drove on, past aging store signs and buildings signaling much-needed repair. And people, so many people. Quickly I forced my eyes back and forth, like a weird ping-pong match. I craned my neck to see the famous stars on the concrete sidewalks. Advancing through the heavy traffic past thousands of street walkers, I turned around and parked. I wanted to see more and to walk the streets. I had a beer with some locals in a bar. Bars don't look alike, but the content is all the same: just hangouts hanging on. I liked the inside darkness, the mystery. People's faces held stories in their wrinkles.

With a bit of an attitude adjustment, I walked within the street confusion. The amount of foreigners filling the famous footpaths was impressive. The real sights were unlike those seen on TV. I imagined something more prestigious after decades of hearing about the famous Hollywood Boulevard. I saw a number of Chinese driving Mercedes-Benz cars and thought of my 1974 comment: "Why are so many Chinese starving?" I found some that weren't. I wondered about the rest. Seeing their exterior wealth sparked the idea of those who found opportunity and went for it. There I was among those who had broken out of their hometowns. It was my turn. The buildings were dirty, and the streets looked crummy in the daylight. I wondered how it would look at night, recalling the famous nickname Tinseltown. It was not the American center of attraction I thought it would have been. I got another dose of the expression; all that glitters is not gold.

My first sight of the Pacific Ocean was magnificent! Far, far the water went out, and wide was the shore of waves pushing in. Santa Monica's long sandy beach was almost empty of tourists and swimmers. Small rolling waves supported a few slow surfers slipping sideways, rocking inward. From out on the pier, the coast was looking good for being in the month of January. I drove the Pacific Coast Highway (PCH) through a million of everything. Cars stuck in traffic, stores sticking signs in faces to force your thoughts to buy, and no space to rest a pair of eyes. Then I reached Venice Beach. The power displayed by the largest and warmest body of water I had ever seen, with its continual motion, drew me to the touch. My barefooted wet feet and sandy toes made good my official christening on the West Coast.

Before heading back, I stopped at a beachside restaurant and patio bar for a beer. Inside, fishing nets, surfboards, and Mexican sombreros hung on the walls. The surroundings were real, provoking imagination. I was nameless, an unknown traveler with a gold miner's secret identity. I liked it. In my obscurity, I realized I was not inhibited by anybody's judgment of any kind. I sat as king of my own world, free from answering to traditions or expectations. In rapid fire, one new event after the other was logged into the diary. Newness was all around me, except for my clothes, my rag friends that came with me. Like my dog, these clothes were my only friends, my old traveling "Torn Threads." I liked those few pieces of me; they were me.

Witnessing the new land, lifestyles, and attitudes as potential mold breakers, I sat comfortably. No ideas or drifty ways from my normal me and my tunnel vision called for any new patterns to be made. With my flaws tucked into my hidden baggage, I was me, take it or leave it. I still felt strong, keeping the pot and beer as a relatively cheap means to stimulate my thoughts and have fun. Yet at the same time repeated subtle urgings within wanted to get those monkeys off my back. I didn't like the command those drugs had over me. I couldn't help myself. The drug was illegal, and the drink didn't go well with driving. The baggage always brought risks. They were tolerated risks. No amount of self-will could change me for more than a few days. Similar to the question I often asked myself after the concussion, "When will I be better?" another question was getting louder: "When will I be free of the drugs and see the real me?"

In the diary writing, I would ask myself the largest of questions from time to time. Who, what, why, and where am I in the big round picture of earth? Where is God in the vertical view? Where is hell? Is my life right or wrong? Am I okay, even if just a little illegal, on my horizontal plane? I didn't get an answer; I always kept guessing. Looking back at my life was helpful. I knew that years from now, I'd be looking back again and knowing more. After years of living a lot of alone time, I seemed to sense the presence of God. Being alone seemed to enhance my overall awareness, but I only acknowledged the big picture. Often I'd recall the nights waiting for the moonrise and the display of God's power in the stars. The sky and trees also made God's existence more real, but only in a vague sense.

When my meal came, I asked to sit on the patio. The Venice Beach foot traffic passed my table, and I could hear the tourists talking. The kids wanted to swim, the parents wanted to keep moving, and I wanted to look between them to see the ocean. The beach waves were small, constantly pushing and pulling. Eating the plate of refried beans, rice, and stewed pork smothered in hot sauce, I pulled on another bottle of beer.

Writing out the internal investigative questions that I asked myself helped me to think and look back with a refocusing query within. My mind's eye, my internal viewpoint that saw words as pictures, also saw in three dimensions. My perception rose up, way up over the beach and buildings. As if I were sitting in a big tall tree house, I saw the Pacific Ocean, the Venice Beach storefronts, and the city behind. My eyes could pass through the roof of the restaurant and see where I was sitting at the table and then on the patio. I was alone in the big place looking about, and then looking out at the water thinking. Maybe God was watching, maybe not.

Dear Diary was always on the top left of the first page of every new entry. Hundreds of people passed me just sitting, eating, drinking, and writing. My shooting at life from the hip wasn't always a good confident feeling. Ironically I realized again that I ran from the treadmill of obligation and security into my adventure-seeking security. I wanted to live life my way, but at what cost?

The sun was still hanging well above the water. After paying the pretty woman dressed in a senorita's white blouse and floral skirt with a flower in her hair, I walked to the water. Massive was the water stretching out and out to meet the sky. The beauty came by being near and with the water. The sunset would have to wait for a little while. Wondering about how the moon would look aroused my curiosity. Turning to the boardwalk, I saw where men with muscles were lifting weights. It was just another view among the many for interested sightseers. Reluctantly I left the water's edge for the long drive back to Orange County.

✝

The approach I was living of being the captain of my own ship was in many ways a contest like the proverbial salmon swimming upstream. The inner struggle with confidence and fortitude got more intense with emotions. I had to keep climbing up the ladder of self-centeredness. My certainty in approaching life may blossom into guesswork the closer I got to success or ruin. Time would tell how my search for identity would evolve from a medicinal diary to an unfolding mystery.

✝

Through the unemployment office, I obtained a job interview for a painter at a large hotel in Buena Park with five floors. Just down from Knott's Berry Farm, it was one of several hotels in the area. A recent change in managers and the maintenance department left the hotel understaffed. I knew a little bit about painting, and nothing at all about wallpaper. Once again I was able to talk my way in. To my surprise, the woman who interviewed me called Bob "Red" Golden. Uncle Bob verified my skills and spoke highly of me. The interviewer was a fiery redhead named Tina, from New York City. She sounded like the city and had toughness about her, but I think she had a soft spot for New Yorkers. That became my first job. I was hired specifically as a painter and wallpaper hanger. The money was real good, and the job came with health benefits after a trial period.

A few weeks after touchdown, searching the local paper for a place to live, I answered an ad for a room to rent in a house. Two younger guys who just got out of the army rented the four-bedroom house from their boss. The property had just stood in Garden Grove as a neglected investment. They each had a big dog. I think the owner was a vet who helped the young vets and didn't charge them rent. They were told the house was soon to be torn down or resold, but it never was. At the end of a cul-de-sac, the old house and garage was almost in the shadow of the 22 Freeway, the Garden Grove.

I rented a bedroom in that real rundown four-bedroom fixer-upper house. Pie and I moved from my cousin's home, thanking her and her husband for their temporary hospitality. My space became home for me and the Duke for a mere one hundred dollars a month, with utilities included. The cheap rent was almost next to nothing. I was right where I had to be to get established. It was a godsend. I lived seven miles from Huntington Beach and about five miles from work. Going to the beach was a big bonus, a priceless experience. The warm water I swam in and the relaxing waves massaging the clean comfortable beach sand were beautiful. I fixed my eyes on one calm evening's dinner-plate Pacific Ocean view serving up the enormous moon.

A glorious sight made for a grand reunion with my old friend. That old man in the moon's face smiled and lifted my travel fatigue up like a crutch to lean on. He grinned at me and the Duke sitting on the Huntington Beach shoreline. I couldn't comprehend the moon's massive beauty. The scope of God's creation was far too full to conceive. I was locked in the moon's power, and yet I had no fertile thoughts of God, just small musings bouncing back. I had no depth, no reason to search for more understanding. Like the waves, my thoughts swished in and out. My life, my struggles were all about me. Things were looking up after eight years of diary dreaming and lyric writing. Hollywood was eighty miles north, but here is where I began my journey to get closer to the music industry. The value of my initial landing was important. Once established, I would build my plans in that direction. I was near the arena to compete for the prize of a song on the radio. More dedicated, I was definitely in the fight.

My temporary wheels that were on loan were abruptly taken away. Fortunately I lived a half-mile walk from the bus line. I was no longer able to ride about with the Pie, so he was confined to the room. Without wheels, I was unable to do simple errands or use my time efficiently. My main concern was for my dog's safety while I was at work all day. So far the battle to get established looked better than my times in Texas—so far. Amazingly the rent in the rundown house stayed at the astounding twenty-five dollars a week total, including electric. The old house was a mess, but my pup and I had a cheap place to live on that almost quiet cul-de-sac. I could throw a stone and hit the 22 freeway. After the morning and evening traffic rush hours, the noise became normal during most of the day. Late night, however, some freeway traffic with spurts of tractor-trailer noise made me use earplugs to avoid wakening. I learned that nights were the hours when the big rigs serviced cities most efficiently and effectively.

At the hotel, my exclusivity as a specialist in painting and wallpaper was, of course, all fabricated. I was faking it eight to ten hours a day on my feet painting and fixing holes in walls. At times I needed to repair a full section of the room wall or hallway. The industrial-sized vinyl wall covering was forty-eight inches wide. With the wall covering heavy with paste and often five to seven feet in length, I was overwhelmed at times. Difficult to work with it alone, my learning curve was steep. My skill was outmatched by the needed repairs, but desperation pushed me into each task. Each day I learned more on the job and by asking questions of the other painters at the supply store. Standing and working the long hours was taking its toll on my lower back, though.

Twice-daily walks and tiring forty-minute bus rides became the next obstacles I needed to overcome. Winter rains didn't just fall; they pounded like hammers and nails. Streets were flooded by the torrential rains. My half-mile bus-stop walks often made me feel like a third-world resident. Under my raincoat hood, looking down at how I was avoiding puddles brought my dad's words to mind: "Put your best foot forward." I was, and it was soaked. The old Harley crash still caused pain in my lower back and right leg. Sciatic pain crept in, limiting me after work each day. The house had two bathrooms, one with a large tub. Baths every night and rest on my plywood-with-foam bed was what being on my feet so much was getting me. I got a good cheap spot to rent for my West Coast launch, but it was not good enough for a clean start with a car. The two army guys did what I did; we all smoked pot and drank beer, but mine was for pain also. Sometimes we were all home at the same time, and the three of us and three dogs all sat in the living room. We had fun sharing stories. One was stationed in Germany and told me of the bars and women; he had the largest bedroom. The other guy was here in the states and told me the same; his room was medium-large. I had a 10x12 room looking out at the front lawn. The fourth bedroom was very small and used for storage.

Long about this time, my boomeranging dark calamitous shadow of misfortune came to cloud up my life. Being accident-prone came in all shapes and sizes for me. One day when we were all at work, there was a dogfight. Piper got the better of the other two dogs. Pie had his ear torn, but a Doberman received a gaping wound on his front shoulder. The Dobe's wound looked like an expensive fix at the vet's office. I had always treated Piper's wounds and even put stitches in him at times. So I did it again and fixed his ear. Being poor, a person learns to make do. However, my compassion for the younger Dobe tilted my thinking.

I began dressing his wound also, to help his owner save money. That was my mistake. He was a strange dog who used to guard a liquor store for a Chinese man who couldn't speak English. While I shaved the small black hairs around the open puncture, the Dobe freaked out and bit my right wrist. I yelled in pain, and the Pie jumped in. Teeth were flying, and yelping growls snarled between snaps and bites. I had to beat that Doberman dog down and tear Pie off of him. Man, it was a crazy thirty seconds—talk about pumped-up adrenalin. Unfortunately the injury to my right wrist happened when I was without my own medical insurance. My employer was still trying me out for a month or so pending permanent employment, so all benefits were on hold. I was hurting bad. Brushing my teeth and pulling up my zipper were painful.

In just a few seconds, my life took a different course, and dedication became desperation. Desperate people do desperate things in desperate situations. I lied. I went against my conscience and forced myself to tell my boss the injury happened at work. My right wrist hurt a lot, and I received the medical attention it needed. I was gladly put on light duty and was scheduled to see a doctor. But my sciatic pain was still worrisome. I didn't like the way my California struggle was turning into a slow tragedy. I felt as if the ends were not going to justify the means. The cloud of adversity began to feel heavy, like a menacing, bullying kite pulling on me. Hardship was roughing me up and clinging to me somehow, trying again with weighty blows to take down my climb in life.

In late February I got a letter from my Aunt Jean. She was the only one to ever give confidence to me. Her reinforcing words to go follow my dream rang true again, and she sent five dollars for a beer. I pictured us back east sitting on her front porch down in the city having a beer. It was a lot like sitting with Aunt Lucy sipping on bourbon. But Aunt Jean's eyes saw life differently, and her ways were more like my dad's and mine. I thought she was real special and enjoyed being with her. It felt like she was the only one to see the difference in me. I believed her encouragement, smiling as I toasted a drink to her. In March before embarking on my search for collaborators, I decided to copyright all my 110 lyrics I had written up to that point. Except for my Aunt Lucy's friend the producer, I didn't trust strangers. I called my book of lyrics *Lyrics by Rourke, Volume 1*.

In April I began dating West Coast women. At the local bar within walking distance of my house, I briefly got involved with a woman named Rosa. She said her accent was Hungarian, which I didn't question; I wasn't interested in her accent. A few times we went to nightclubs, where I saw the same activities of dancing and drinking as on the East Coast. She liked going to those places, and I didn't. We were new for each other, so after the newness wore off, we stopped seeing each other.

Working in and traveling through the hotel, I saw some of the most beautiful women I had ever seen. The expensive surroundings and vacationland attitude among visitors and staff gave a more sensual fun atmosphere. Beautiful women worked as department heads, sales representatives, bartenders, and waitress and restaurant staff. In my all-white painter's pants and shirt, I was easily seen throughout the five floors as well as banquet rooms and poolside. Meeting women employees ranging from eighteen to sixty, I enjoyed talking with them all.

There was a variety of local and transient personalities, all with different stories at that point in their lives. A twenty-five-year-old woman named Lu from the Midwest was a dancer in Japan. Her long tan hair and long legs returned with hopes for Hollywood's big-time arena but landed in that hotel dating the shuttle driver. Cayce worked in the kitchen delivering trays of food to the rooms. An eighteen-year-old native of southern California, Cayce's brilliant blue eyes dutifully earned money in her first job after high school. She was a modest flirt, learning how to be sexy. Even in her unbecoming uniform, her potential to be a model secured her many compliments.

In the business wing of the hotel was where the stable of beautiful fillies had their desks as sales representatives. These women in their low to mid-thirties, with track records of success, were veterans of the fast lane. Looking for high rollers with big money, their fast romances kept them dealing men in and out of their lives quickly. Visiting the back offices, I felt like a judge at the Miss Universe Contest. So much charm, so many smiles, their advantages to sell were so obvious. They were selling space in the hotel banquet rooms. Looking for money, they were in the market to make a deal. I met blondes and brunettes, saw lipstick and jewelry, smelled perfume, and could almost feel the well-chosen fabrics, which added accent to my imagination. I stood unarmed, unacquainted with the ways of a harem. My East Coast anonymity, along with my struggling artist syndrome, was as appealing to these women as blood is to a shark. I had a purpose, a direction, and a goal, but nothing to see was really what I had. We were all looking for happiness. One of the pretties saw I had the potential to be a long shot.

She smiled, with sharp blue eyes drawing back like hooks holding bait luring a fish closer. Tall, taller in her red pumps with matching red lips. Blonde, with one curled bounce placed above her shoulders. Gina put out her hand, and our beaming smiles met. We laughed from the start, enjoying each other's sense of humor. I found mesmerizing experiences in the fast lane under the tutelage of that most gorgeous of those foxes. I got romantically involved with this beautiful woman Gina, and she came with an appetite like mine.

Divorced with two children, she was at last fulfilling her lust for freedom. After fifteen years of motherhood, she fought for more than what looked like a regular life in the suburbs. Her flare for adventure was stronger than the need for security. She fell out of love with her husband, who provided well but traveled a lot. She wanted her chance to shine before the wrinkles took away her sparkle, and she got it. They split the children, and she got the teenage daughter named Samantha.

Gina and I had a craving for each other like a drug, which grew into love with an addiction. Wanting pleasure more and more and not seeing the harm in it was the cause of my blinding fever. Seeing that beautiful woman drive up in her sexy car and sexy clothing and walk her sexy walk into my crummy bachelor pad was baffling at first. My two younger roommates were spellbound. For them and me and the neighbors, it just didn't add up. She was a dreamer of sorts and liked hanging onto my dream with me. She paid for our dating. Like the greater mass of people, she loved to spend money and complained she never had enough. I never had any more money than was necessary to spend. What I had was a lot of enthusiasm and commitment; it was something she was drawn to. When Gina read my lyrics, her eyes expanded, and her emotional sighs and her giggles were real. Sharing life was good. She was a California native who loved the beach, and we walked holding hands, barefoot, laughing and hugging.

When we weren't eating at a Mexican restaurant and drinking margaritas, we were at her condominium eating popcorn. Gina was a mom who enjoyed cooking and was very good at it. I, on the other hand, was learning what it was like to share the small family atmosphere with her daughter. I helped prepare supper, setting the table and dicing the tomatoes. Samantha came out of her room and shredded lettuce while talking with her mom about boys. I felt like an outsider, but also like it was okay to be there. We ate Gina's tacos because that was the meal her daughter liked. Samantha missed her brother, and when Gina spoke of her son, Stewart, her love showed. She loved her kids, no matter how crazy things got. Gina felt bad about the divorce but not bad enough to stay in the marriage for the kids' sake. The teenage girl liked the privacy of her room listening to cassettes and the radio.

After cleaning up the mess from dinner, Gina and I sat together on the couch. With my shoes off and feet up, I felt good. In Gina's search for identity, she loved conversing with me and comparing our values and lifestyles. She was a wild child who came from a broken home. Then there was a home for troubled girls and running off to Hollywood. The thought of a wedding brought the picture of a new life, so she married. But her wildness was only delayed. As the picture of love changed, the couple's belief in God was what helped to hold them together. She spoke of reading the Bible and mentioned her thoughts of how important it was to her. "If you are God's, no matter how far you stray, you can come back," she would say. Gina's eyes clouded over when she saw how she ripped apart the family she loved. She wanted something more from this world but didn't really know what it was. Her unhappy marriage continued and fostered a desire to make up for lost time and opportunity. Girlfriends of hers were in like scenarios and also felt trapped, without finding their fulfillment. Now she was living with both a little regret and a lot of desire.

Five years older than me, at thirty-four, Gina was accumulating the thrills of being single. She had the beauty to get whatever she wanted, and I was one of the things she wanted. I told her how we were alike, how I walked out on love, and how I wanted something more. My goal and direction with my lyrics brought me to California to live out a dream. That was more than what she usually found in the men she was dating. She didn't have a cause or a dream or even a plan, but at that time, we had each other.

The fact that everything was new affected all of my life. The climate, the land, my quest, my lust, all brought a love for living. It's amazing how true dedication can unintentionally but not so innocently get twisted and replaced by lust. The pride of life, the pride of self, commanded my self-denial into negotiations. My youthful ideas of togetherness and situations of love that I fought off in the past were then compromised. My emotions journeyed onward with hers to new regions in love. I shared my wandering heart, my valued time, my genuine ambition with Gina. And like a conquering solider, I lusted for the pillage and spoils I found on my way to victory. I was free to indulge with what I wanted, but I was captured by her natural beauty.

In the morning I watched her move about her room toward the mirror. She was born to beauty. The high cheekbones, an elegant nose, full lips, and smooth skin—all rested on her slender neck. We talked as she got ready for work. I wondered at what age she started her routine of masquerading with makeup. Like most plain, pretty, or beautiful women, she had a fascination about her looks. Perhaps it was an inward complaint or lack of confidence from which a desire manifested outwardly, creating a mask. How vain, how sad, that she was not content with natural beauty. Perhaps she learned the tradition from her mother. She was on the treadmill of pride and couldn't resist altering her attractiveness for more. Makeup, make-believe, pretend, acting, trickery—all of her exterior choices were driven from within. I witnessed how her enhanced features illumined the mirror. Her hand moved like an artist with a brush, a stroke, a pause to look. There was the salesmanship of selling the outward lie; the Devil was in the details of her imagination. From within she said, "I don't give a crap about this job. If I didn't need the money, I'd quit today." She looked at me in the mirror and laughed. "Men don't have to do this crap," she said and laughed again.

Behind the façade of her corporate image of glamour, there was a down-to-earth girl, a mom, a woman torn between two worlds. Overgrown with household complacency, she wanted to grow in her search for happiness. But the real challenge and fun for me was to know what was behind the captivating eyes motivating her charismatic charm. We were two people torn away from lives we couldn't wear and attracted to each other. When she glanced in the mirror toward me, she'd say, "Don't look—you're making me blush." Sarcasm rolled off my tongue, and realism broke down her public image. "You're using your beauty to gain access to men who will be swayed by your sexy charms. You're like an illusionist, with one hand holding a sparkling diamond and with the other hand picking their pocket. Their minds are in the bedroom, and yours is in their wallet." Gina laughed and said, "That's right. They can look and think all they want, but as long as I leave with a check in my hands, I'm doing my job." Our humor overlooked our differences, and we laughed in harmony. Once we were out the door on our separate paths, I collided with myself, feeling awkward with neglect toward my cause. I was in the audience of her illusion; I was in her bedroom charm, and she was my filly riding in my dream. Betting on a long shot like me to win her a Mercedes-Benz, we both rode in the race to win.

I struggled with keeping focus on my search and goal of working with a collaborator. In the area, there were local collages I visited and advertised on message boards for a musician to work with. Meanwhile, I was sliding into a laidback, more casual beach life, continually living for the moment. Gina was fun, beautiful, and exciting. Lying with her on warm sand, the Huntington Beach ocean breeze fanned our talks. We heard our feelings while listening to the waves roll in. At night, her condo pool sat motionless before I swam in its dimly lit water. Life's luxuries surrounded me. The hot Jacuzzi we sat sipping wine in was fun. My commitment for a song on the radio was softening even more. We each loved life, and together we loved. My conscience contended with the pleasure that comes from filling wineglasses. The strength to snap me back into being dedicated was fading fast.

But my sense of right and wrong was only pacified; it didn't sleep, and it wasn't dead. Splitting my attention didn't feel right and good; there was an ache deep within. I knew I was wasting time. Along with the spoils of pleasure came excesses and emotional trials. Too many restaurants and too much lack of concern for money led life far too far into vacationland. Besides all the fun, there was still my time alone to think. The diary always heard the truth, and it heard my disgust. The mesmerizing experiences of the fast lane soon wore off and wore into disenchantment.

I followed up with the few students I met from the ads I posted and even spoke to a music teacher for any recommendations. I gave some lyrics to a few guitar players with an interest to write songs. I called the potential songwriters and stayed in touch over the next few months. Even though I met players in clubs and partied with them, they never struck me as being serious writers, just more players.

Moreover, my mind drifted into guilt and doubt. I was on a mission, not on a holiday. My biases, presuppositions, and expectations conflicted with that woman's fast-lane type of love. Not only was I floating away from my anchor of commitment, but I was in her flow of involvement. I was conveniently there when she was ready. Trying on the feeling of being used was new to me and uncomfortable. Even though it wasn't said, I was in an open relationship. I was being used like I had used women, but this time I was not in control. Even though I found love for her, I also found that I wasn't as callous as I thought my feelings were or could be. The lesson in an open relationship is better to hear about than to live through. We had different meanings for the word *love*. One woman to love was enough for me. When I accepted the fact that Gina was a player on the field of love and sex was a game, I had enough. Learning about the fast lane by experience was hurting me. We had something very real, but we were a mismatch. She was a dedicated player; I was a participating performer.

That woman consumed much of my diary during the affair and

after. The clarity of hindsight was explained on the pages. Whatever she and I had first was physical, secondly it was love, but thirdly I just felt empty inside. Since neither of us was able to make a commitment, what I got was sex; it was like a drug, it was fun. But it came with the potential to do damage. I was always quarreling with the romantic within, who needed real love, true love, not just sex. My conflict was really a fear to let go of the goal and first love of writing. Unable to compromise, I repeatedly chose women who I knew wouldn't last one way or another. I absorbed her bold affection, only to turn away. The falseness on the exterior behind her skin-deep beauty had to go. So did my greed to have it all. I found I could only go in one direction at a time. Being off the path wasn't a waste of time; it just took a while to get back on the path again.

My affair with Gina then became very distant, an occasional sweet-and-sour, on-and-off event. The rush of it all was over. We never regained the once-felt love of being in love. The open relationship closed. I was able to refocus on my goal. My roots of self-denial were nearly drowned in desire. But at last, abstinence surfaced like a damaged submarine. When we did talk about the beach, the rolling ocean waves, holding hands, the moments of our love, and time past, we were still able to laugh.

———————— ✝ ————————

THE PLAYER

Cover charge, the Player, hunting for jewels,
Among all, the standard, alcohol, set of rules,
Three to one in favor, looking for Lady Luck,
Bourbon talk, barstool lies, pass up the ugly duck.

> A whirlwind-like romance, a vision, could come true.
> The Player is patience, just waiting for his queue.
> The Player is patience, just waiting for his queue.

Plays don't last; they linger. Only time will tell
If she had a magic, love will cast a spell.
Odds against the Player, he'll meet his match,
Love will turn the tables, he will be the catch.

    A whirlwind-like romance, a vision, could come true.
    The Player is patience, just waiting for his queue.
    The Player is patience, just waiting for his queue.

 We're a people of desire, burning with pride beyond our need,
 The nation drowns on fire, heaven shake us from our greed.

A frisky, young filly, who also plays the part,
Spoke her mind, made her play, put the chase back in my heart.

    A whirlwind-like romance, a vision, could come true.
    The Player is patience, just waiting for his queue.
    The Player is patience, just waiting for his queue.

---

 †

My progress toward collaboration in writing songs once again became dominant. Before leaving New York, I communicated with the American Guild of Authors and Composers (AGAC) in Hollywood. I followed through with registering at the guild as a member. I learned again that there is no market for lyrics alone. I searched the music magazines for collaborators in my area. I kept in touch with local colleges for musicians, but nothing fruitful grew. I needed music with my lyrics to make songs to sell. Finding a collaborator was why I was there. I needed to deal with what was real. After six months, I still did not have transportation except for the city bus. I needed to be in Hollywood.

Chapter 11: Still Not Thirty

Six months after leaping westward, my June 16, 1982 birthday felt good and happy. Just to go walking simply for the enjoyment of ambling along in thought brought me to normal again. The Barbie Doll game was over. I just wanted to scuff the soles of my shoes strolling with the Pie. Slowing down, I caught my breath standing on the sidewalk mulling over the basics. There was no consistent place to go where there was no one else. We were among a few million people in that area of Southern California. Once again, we went to the local school yard, like several times before. The open fields were good to cast my eyes over. Seeing the Pie race across the green turf, digging in his claws for traction chasing flocks of birds, was good. Only after all the school kids were out could I bring the big dog and be comfortable about it. A short window of time before sundown was the only daily opportunity if we could make it. If not, we waited for the streetlights to go on to walk the quiet suburban streets. Once it got dark, the city street traffic slowed, and there were fewer cars on the freeway as well.

That night we migrated through the broken fence at the end of the cul-de-sac seventy-five feet from the window of my rented room. Through the messy waist-high brush, I groped to the underpass as Pie moved cautiously. We climbed the cement embankment and ended up only a hundred yards from my house. The Duke and I sat high up under the 22 Freeway along Garden Grove Boulevard. I drank a beer to celebrate my twenty-ninth birthday. Traffic noise above us from the higher-speed vehicles and especially the trucks was disturbing at first. After a few beers and a joint, it was easier to deal with. As the darkness grew, the bothersome bright car lights turned my head away. Between the traffic racket and the mixing shadows and lights, I saw some street people come out from the taller brush. Even though Orange County did not seem to have many during the day, they showed up at night. Human silhouettes walked in the roadside glare of the passing cars' lights. The dark figures vanished once the car drove by. Seeing nothing in the dark and then a rising shape and profile in another car light made me uneasy.

Not far from us, a man appeared from the bushes slowly heading our way. Piper's ears went up, and a low growl oozed out. The nightwalker was disheveled, wearing rags, and very intimidating to watch coming toward us. He stopped short when the Pie stood up and added more voice to his warning. Fifteen feet of distance was close enough. The man spoke, but the passing cars drowned out his words. With his next step forward, I put my hand on Piper's collar as the big dog pushed forward. "Stop!" My one loud word stopped them both. In the lull between stretches of cars, we spoke. He asked for spare change. I asked if he liked dogs. He was quiet. In the edginess, I felt threatened, cautious. "I'm going to let my dog loose; don't freak out," I said. The Pie walked forward, and the street person spoke to him. I heard in his voice a tone of reassuring alliance. The man advanced with my approval. I tossed him a beer. We drank, and he sat a dog's length away. I held the Pie at my side and told the stranger, named Tom, it was my birthday, and we lifted our cans.

Passing lights shone on the dark hair of the white man's unshaven face. His worn clothing was far from being rags. He spoke calmly, sandwiching words between the flows of traffic noise. We swapped stories about the twists and turns of life. His apparent lowly station in life made him seem more likable, as if he were the first real person I could relate to in six months. Unlike the nice and pretty landscape, homes, people, cars, and modern community, he was an original. At twenty-nine, we were the same age, with some of the same and some of the opposite past stories. Tom lost his job after ten years when the company downsized and moved out of Ohio. His car accident happened without insurance. The crash caused him to lose his home and then his family. Injuries forced radical changes he could not overcome. Rather than staying where he wasn't wanted, he walked away from disaster and humiliation. We were both glad to share the best and the worst. I wondered about what he wasn't telling me.

I left him in the shadows with the few dollars in my pocket and walked back through the brush following the Duke. As we looked through the chain link fence, the street was quiet and almost dark, except for the glow of one light pole. My old house, with its threat of being torn down and its plain dry front lawn, smoldered under the yellowish night-lights' glare. There was my window; a room behind it was mine, and a door with a lock. Bending over, passing back through the hole in the fence, I stood on the other side of having less. I didn't have a lot, but in just a few steps, a world of difference filled me with gratitude. I realized how close I came with my wrist injury to suffering a loss like Tom, the underpass castaway, had. His dream for a good life had crumbled, and mine was teetering on a desperate lie. But for a few hundred dollars, a few different situations, I could be on the other side of the fence. My steps were slow; I felt the pressure from trying to survive and balance like a tightrope walker.

✝

A HOME

Lately I've been thinking about painting the walls.
Wonder why I'm thinking about painting at all.
It seems it's time to put on my walking shoes,
Leave it all behind me, miss it, and sing the blues.

Until I find a reason, I'll be changing every season.

A Home is for a man
With a wife and little kids,
A Home to make a stand,
Show the love you once hid.

Until I find a reason, I'll be changing every season.

The road never looked as good as it does now.
No more dillydallying, no more wondering how.
Bought a pair of new shoes, gonna drive that old van,
When it runs out of gas, I'll be a walking man.

--------------------- † ---------------------

The cul-de-sac was quiet except for the nighttime freeway big-rig traffic. Duke and I sat under a streetlight on the narrow round curb, stunned from meeting the drifter. I recapped in my mind the six recent months of California life and the previous ten years to get there. In 1972, I just barely graduated at nineteen years old. All I had was $700 in the bank, and I was riding a bus. After ten years, all I had was one great dog and two paychecks in the bank. Racked up in pain, I added another serious injury. Adding to my accident-prone life, I was living an impulsive lie. I was still looking for love in all the wrong places and settling for pleasure without the permanent relationship. How could I ever think of a serious connection when I had nothing? Relationships have always been stepping-stones that seemed to be a short pattern to nowhere. I was closer and stepping on prettier stones to achieve my goal. But I was so very near ending up like that old troll under the bridge. Was God watching?

That night the diary heard of my fears from being on the road I was traveling. What would extended drug and alcohol abuse bring me? What about the free sex and no commitment—how would that come to haunt me? Everybody was talking about the AIDS epidemic and not shaking hands. The TV showed people just tapping elbows instead of touching. And this business of dream chasing—how long, how far, and how much compromising would I do? One hundred yards away, the broken spirit of a lost man was more than real. He very well could have been a glimpse of a path not chosen or a look into my future. I was so much on the edge, surely God was with me.

In July, Piper broke through and out of my screened bedroom window one night. I had my earplugs in. He decided to roam the neighborhood for a few hours. He was up to his old tricks, dog gone. And like the saying goes, you can't teach an old dog new tricks. I could only suspect that there was a female dog in heat and her scent was in the wind. Pie also had the first of a series of three broken blood vessels in the ear, from scratching fleas. The cheap house came with dozens of little extras. Those veterinarian visits cost $150 each.

My wrist was in pain from working a job I needed. The doctor gave me a splint to wear, but it didn't help. I also needed wheels, but couldn't afford a car and pay for insurance. My right leg sciatic nerve was smarting enough to push me to an unsafe decision. Each day, I'd walk to and from the bus stop passing a local motorcycle dealership. Enough playing it safe was enough. I bought my first used California vehicle, a 370 cc Suzuki. That was crazy because I used my wrist even more to turn the throttle. I hoped the exercise would give me strength. At least I cut down a lot of the daily walking and standing at the bus stop. I knew it was a risk to get on a motorcycle again and especially dealing with the freeways with such a small machine. Desperate people do desperate things in desperate situations. During the torrential downpours of coastal rain, it was a challenge to stay up on the road. It didn't rain; it poured sticks and stones. But all in all, things were looking okay after I got the two wheels. I was off my feet more, and my back was less stressed and coming back strong with more time to rest.

By the middle of July, I was out of work and receiving worker's compensation. The wrist injury was causing too much pain and kept me out of work and under the doctor's care for several months. The doctor was talking about an operation. Worker's compensation checks in the mail allowed me to focus on my goals more easily. Once again, it was a type of early retirement. Out of necessity, I began learning to print left-handed before the upcoming wrist operation.

†

On August 5, my mother called me and told me my grandmother had died. Once again I needed to return to New York for a funeral. There were differences this time that allowed me to buy a round-trip ticket with my savings from the low rent. I put Piper in a kennel, chained my motorcycle to a wall in the garage, and locked up my one rented room. I was coming back. I called my only friend, Gina, who drove me to the Los Angeles airport and would pick me up. I felt my good fortune with her friendship.

My poor mom lived through the loss of her husband, the only man she ever loved. Then as fate would have it, she lost sight of me. Granny's health had slowly faded since her stroke. All the burden of her care fell on Ma, who still worked hard on her job. A charming people person able to make friends easily at her job, Ma took good care of Granny. The home health aides came during the day until the end and were a great help. Now Ma lost her mother seven months after I left. The house was now empty for Ma to come home to. My brother Ken's family came to visit her on holidays. It was only a ten-minute drive between houses, but Ma was left out of the closer loop she hoped for. Ma used to say that some families don't even have that. Not having a warmer bond hurt her, but Ma had the resource within to always forgive and rebound in joy. It seemed like my mom got shortchanged in life. But she never complained and was always there when someone needed her. Ma had the ability to accept how possessive I was with my time. She could accept how possessive Ken and Carole were with their kids. Her arms were wide enough to embrace the love she received and to also accept her own longing for more. She knew that the only thing she could change was her attitude.

I was so glad to be there with Ma so she wasn't alone after the funeral. The pain we both felt was shared. But Ma lost her mother, her best friend, and they were real close their whole lives. They helped each other through the worst of times. Granny was my caregiver and my nurse; her love was the medicine money couldn't buy. I can't imagine what would have become of me without her help. We all shared some great moments with Granny, but mostly it was Ma. So often they were like sisters and best friends, laughing, cooking, and cleaning house together.

My New York stay was short-term, but it reenergized my mom to see me. She was occupied with thoughts of me. We talked a lot about her selling the house since she was alone versus keeping it. It was too big for one, but she loved it and all the good memories it held. As we had seen my California ambition take me away, we also spoke of my desire to return to New York when I had had enough. At some point, someday, who knows when it would happen, but we knew I would return. In the meantime, she bubbled when talking about Ken's baby girl, named Cindy. Ma and Granny always wished they could see the baby more often, but they both said, "We'll take what we can get." Ma always said, "As long as your brothers happy, that's what matters."

I always wanted to do more for Ma. But I wasn't the family-man type, so she never got little grandkids from me. After growing up with my brother those last few latchkey years with him in the morning, we drifted apart. His life was lived by fitting into the same expectations as his peers. The college years, his wife, his job, and now his baby seemed to have met all his needs. I was happy for him. After he graduated high school in June 1970 until now, we didn't spend five minutes together. We couldn't relate with like values in the present, but we had our childhood in common and we had a brother's love.

I felt the limitations from being home compared to California. The sights and people's attitudes became more obvious. The West Coast was all new and unencumbered. There was a closeness I felt from the old neighborhood that I knew. Living in both arenas had the advantage of seeing the differences and how I had changed. When I left my mother she was grief-stricken. I felt her sorrow, but it acted like encouragement of my ambition to be a writer, to get the job done that needed to get done. I always wanted to bring some financial relief back to her, along with success of some kind.

✝

Once I returned to California, I searched out a few more local musicians and collaborators in the local colleges. I gave my lyrics to them to see what would happen. Nothing positive happened with them or the earlier students I met with. The Songwriters Guild in Hollywood was still in my thoughts, but the distance demanded more resources than I currently had. I needed better transportation, or better still, to live in that area. Then more bad news came my way.

My Aunt Susie in Florida died. She was Granny's and Aunt Lucy's sister and Uncle Shawn's wife. My poverty kept me in California. I could not and did not make that funeral trip. Granny always said that death happened in threes. I wondered who would be next.

Within a few months, my Uncle Will died. Again, I couldn't leave. I remembered seeing Uncle Will on that bitter cold day before Christmas. He was so healthy looking and smiled when we talked about growing up with his kids. My Uncle Will's three kids were my first cousins, and they arrived in New York and all stayed at my mom's house. She wanted to help the family in time of need.

The three deaths caused deep thoughts about my time on earth. Life was so obviously short, and I was one third through it. My thoughts were many and varied in my time without accountability. I waned in questioning my ambition and the pressure I put on myself. My dedication paused, and laziness sprouted. After cashing my worker's compensation checks, I'd drink too much beer and eat in restaurants more. It was easy to slip out of my motivating drive and into what I could see and touch. I was losing sight of my goal, which used to be my struggle, my life. Now I was in a medical health system. I was becoming alarmed about my lethargic fat-boy appearance. From too much waiting, I put on too much weight.

Gina boomeranged, from time to time dropping in to visit. My sedentary lifestyle often had me sitting in a chair in the front yard leaning up against the house near my window. Seeing her black sports car, hearing the loud music, and then watching her blonde hair blow in the wind was always a treat. When she placed her legs out of the car and stood, her walk induced my catcalls. Her blazing red lips broke forth her perfect smile, and she sheepishly wore her embarrassment, giggling as she closed the distance. Beneath her hard body and her cover-girl looks, she was still a mom and not used to the overt attention.

On one occasion, she introduced me to the idea of fasting to lose weight. I listened to her explain how she almost tried not eating for health reasons to cleanse herself. Her tall, slim, fit figure was an asset she took pride in from her youth. During the happy years of marriage, raising her kids, and reading the Bible, she also read about the miracle of cleansing the body through starvation. But she never tried it. As radical as the concept sounded to me, there was a truth that surfaced with that strange view of health. I described to Gina how I saw on many occasions, my dogs' behavior when they were sick. Dogs didn't eat when they were sick. Somehow their denial of food helped fix what was wrong on the inside. The idea of not eating food for the main purpose of cleansing made sense. While my weight loss was to be a secondary goal, I seriously considered her concern for cleansing. I bought a book to follow the guidelines it explained regarding the method to starve one's self. The point was made clear that it was very serious to starve yourself.

I hoped to rise to the challenge in time. But Ma's Christmas box came full of treats and presents. Just me and the Duke, the two of us, ate the cookies and bread, sharing with Gina when she popped in. The Pie dog and I celebrated Christmas alone. We talked about looking into the fasting thing next year.

†

The two younger roommates had a wild time for their 1983 New Year's Eve party at my rented house. Drugs, booze, women, fights, and sure enough, the police showed up. The cul-de-sac was less full of vehicles when I returned with Gina from our dinner. We missed the quick exit of excited people and then the arrival of police after the fight. Before leaving me, she wanted to come in and see the scene where the brawl took place. Her teenage enthusiasm for stimulation mixed with her life experience in relationships was a part of her that I saw in myself. Gina possessed a kid's attitude as she looked about and turned to me saying,

"It couldn't have been too bad; I don't see any blood." I let the Pie out of my bedroom, and he acted just like her—going all around sniffing and looking for what he missed seeing but heard.

I had lived there a year, but wanted to get out and move north, closer to the music business. But I was stuck in circumstances and situations once again. And now I was about to become very vulnerable. On January 7, 1983, one year exactly after I landed in California, Gina came to my house early in the morning. She took me to the hospital for my right wrist operation. I woke up by midafternoon in a hospital bed. My wrist was in a cast. The sun shone brightly, and I heard the voices of Gina and my surgeon. The only two people I had confidence in were happy to see my eyes open. I was glad they had a chance to meet.

My surgeon, who I shared a lot of my aspirations with, was a cool doctor. He was young, a family man with a great practice and a good life ahead of him. When he said, "You didn't tell me how beautiful your girlfriend was," I swelled with pride. I looked at Gina with my head still swimming in anesthesia. I asked her, "Are you my girlfriend?" With the wisdom of a sage, she replied, "I'm your friend, and that's better than a girlfriend." That being said, the doctor knew I was in good hands and left. In my follow-up visit, we looked at the X-rays. He told me that a surgeon could fix the X-ray, but not necessarily the patient. It seemed like a simple expression, but the weightiness of it was not clear to me.

Two days after surgery, I wrote left-handed in the diary and was extremely glad to have taken the time to practice. During my recovery, a few of the girls, including Cayce and then Lu, from work stopped by to take care of me and help with shopping. My usual walk to the food market was partly through grassy fields filled with power lines. The Pie and I liked walking there, but both my arms were sore carrying the bags home. Now I needed to make more trips with just one arm to use. It meant more fun for Piper.

I told my diary of the repeated struggles I had in quitting the smoking of pot and drinking of beer. They were both drugs I could not completely leave behind as bad baggage. Several afternoons while leaning back in the chair against the house on the front lawn, I'd complain to the diary pages. Two days of abstention had all the right motive, but not one good reason to keep away from the drugs. I was able to turn from the bag of pot, but I had nowhere to turn to. There was nothing to replace the love for the high from either drug. I still thought of them as justifiable means to reach the end of my goal. But in honesty, I knew they would hang on and probably with more gravity pull me down. The end of their use was nowhere in sight. Nor was the strength needed to cut them out of my life.

Gina was supposed to have been gone, but became more of a friend and then a periodic compulsion, but nonetheless a repeated obsession. I really hated the burden of carrying what I didn't want. The weighty addictions were all monkeys on my back. They were clearly a splitting thing, my Gemini thing, a schizophrenic thing. I knew nothing about astrology, physiology, or psychology, but I used those terms in the diary because they sounded good. I loved my addictions, and yet I hated them. What I really hated was my weakness and how I defended my addictions to myself.

A few diary pages heard of the trouble with roommates over power struggles. Space and control issues were coming to a head in the rundown house after the fourth bedroom was rented. My rented room was being drawn into the fray simply because I was there and I had the only phone.

Within two weeks, with one workers' comp check, I bought a cheap, large, old, red Chevy Impala station wagon from a part-time fireman. After a year, I finally got four wheels and more safety and peace of mind before the big rains came. The fireman said it used to belong to the fire chief of Long Beach. It had a strong 327 motor, and it made sense to invest in it because it had been taken care of. I sold the motorcycle and was laying plans to move. The Pie and I were able to travel about again. We were reunited on the road and could walk in parks, go shopping, or just drive and hang our heads out the windows.

One spectacular event we witnessed was the Pacific coast storm that took down the end of the Huntington Beach pier. Enormous waves crushed and pounded and drove into the eroding beach, roads, and storefronts. It was thrilling to be in the violence. Seeing that natural alarming event heightened my awareness. Time was passing without me advancing toward my goal. The business end of the music business was not materializing in Orange County for me. Like the deaths in my family, seeing the pier's unstoppable damage impacted the seriousness of my decision to live my California experience. I felt like I was on a ride and couldn't get off. I had created the self-made challenge, and I needed to do more to win or lose.

With a cast on my arm, I drove eighty-five miles to Hollywood's Songwriters Guild. I signed up for a songwriting class with an instructor named Jack Segal. The weekly class would run for twelve weeks, but the next class didn't start until sometime in May. Segal's other class was for lyric writing only; it was starting soon and met at Northridge University, also on a weekly basis. Northridge was farther, but I valued the songwriting class more, with hopes to meet a composer. The lyric class was on hold. It would cost more money.

$$†$$

In April, the doctor released me from his care. My job at the hotel had long been filled. I once again continued to look for employment. Searching for a way to make a living kept my mind on both the realities of life and of my dream chasing. It was refreshing to be actively looking for work. I was no longer sitting drinking beer waiting for the mailman to bring my check.

One interview was in Beverly Hills at an old neglected mansion. I was to work with others there and go about my duties in a live test of my painting skills. Refurbishing the huge home and grounds was greatly needed. My mind kept going back to the old movies showing the grand life of the rich and famous. There were far more movies in my memory emphasizing success and living large than there were about ruined lives and decayed structures. My mind brought up thoughts of the old crumbled mansion I found in the hills of Bar Harbor. I walked about in awe. I curiously looked at the patterns of deterioration and thought how time destroys everything from empires to people. The relentless process of time always brings death—and then what? I was again without an answer, as I always was when I asked myself that question of questions.

I went on a few job tryouts painting walls and doors and failed those as well for whatever reasons. However, the tryouts did cause pain. I was told I might receive occupational rehabilitation since I could no longer be a painter. But I never was a painter. I had to continue to reconcile myself with the lie I started and keep rolling with it. I was always justifying the means with hope for a good ending. I always felt guilty.

That was a challenging period to make ends meet and save up some money to move. I didn't want to receive job retraining in Orange County; I needed to move north. Piper was jumping out my window at night and jumping in come morning. There were too many loose ends, just like there were too many fleas in that house. I was dating three younger women just because I could, and that also left a hollow ill-at-ease feeling.

Gina stopped by to tell me she had found a rich man. That hurt. I knew it was a hurt that was coming, but when it came, it wounded me. The Mercedes-Benz parked out front was what she wanted. Even though I tried to end our relationship, she kept coming. I knew she was playing the field, and so was I. What hurt more were her words telling me she burned all my loving notes and the writings I gave her. She said the rich guy made her burn them to prove her love. That was that. All my loving cards and letters went up in smoke. She was as clear as mud from the beginning. Now it was another guy, or was he one more of many? Gina took her bets off me and placed her affection on a new horse in the race to win.

✝

In May 1983, I was put on disability, and there was less money delivered in the mail. The once enjoyable song of free time was adding on tones of distress. Goals were lingering as distractions became more apparent. My lack of discipline and laziness were both tripping me up. All the while, I added more pounds to my waistline drinking, smoking, eating too much, and not working. Enough was enough!

I started my first fast that late spring. I did a test pre-fast and just ate fruit and vegetables for two days. Then I followed that up by not eating anything for two days; I just drank juice. I wanted to see if the claims were for real. It went well. I waited a week, and then went for the recommended total fast for a week. I ate nothing, and only drank water and juice for the full seven days and nights. I bought fruit juice and diluted it with water. I boiled down a large pot of cleaned and cut vegetables for broth. Each morning I cleansed myself properly, with an enema aiding my body in its elimination process. After seven days of letting the body clean out the inside, there were still small stool feces with an enema. I lived. I lost twenty pounds. I weighed in at 180 and never felt better in all my life.

I broke away from the daily tradition of eating. My body and mind worked together and were told to stay away from food. Gina's description was accurate. Fasting was a miracle. I discovered a supernatural power. Or did it discover me? The first three days were mind and body breakthroughs off of the focus of food. The fourth, fifth, sixth, and seventh days were slices from the peaceful cake of heavenly newness. Once the body and mind broke the food tie, my feet were off the ground, and I glided with pure energy. I was so free and away from the energy-burning tiredness of digestion and the process of elimination.

My eyes had the clearest ability to join my surroundings with my inner comprehension moment to moment. Both distance and closeness were unity. I didn't move through a room; the room and I were partnering. I'd sit outside, and the fullness of the air, moving leaves, and sunlight happened with me. Colors were more vivid with an increased perception. My thinking and reasoning became much more enhanced. Preciseness was adding to the subtle clarity of the obvious. I had an inner mind strength I never had before. Through discovery, I knew I could live without food. That was a unique revelation of freedom. I was given new knowledge and understanding on that proverbial concept that less is more. It was another fact that was in the opposite direction from the greater mass of people. I found another freedom like being off the treadmill of materialism. Again I went off that popular path called normal. I completely abstained from food and was liberated.

After having made the acquaintance of something rare on earth, heavenly fasting, I went back to eating. My fasting was for cleansing, not a new way of life. But life was different after it. Like a jailer who has lost his whip, the notion to eat food no longer kept lashing at my back. I was okay to eat less or not eat and drink water. I kept half the weight off. Weight loss was temporary, like everything else on earth is. After a few months, my injury disability case was reevaluated, and I was put back on worker's compensation. More money came in the mail.

By mid-May the songwriting class began at the Songwriters Guild on Sunset Boulevard. The lyric class also had a sufficient number of students and started at Northridge as well. I had saved enough money and signed up for both. Those first weeks of night classes, I would sleep in the back of the station wagon with Pie in a small park off the 170 Hollywood Freeway. I checked out the San Fernando Valley neighborhoods during the day using a room renter's advertisement guide. The classwork involved studying the power of words in communication and structure. I needed structure with my ideas. Writing the weekly assignments was helpful and brought accountability into the design and picture of my expression.

✝

In July 1983 in my Southern California cul-de-sac neighborhood, there were what seemed to be thousands of people. Just a few short blocks away, wave after wave of traffic raced from red light to red light. If there were an announcer in the sky a thousand feet up, he would have seen the chessboard movements flow and jerk from square to square. There were blocks of vehicles: east opposing west and north opposing south. With hundreds and hundreds of cars passing me as I walked my dog, I felt like I would never get used to the congestion.

Right across from my house on the small street with a circle on the end was the house of an old Italian man named Dom. He used to live back east. We got along great. Dom loved to cook pasta and share his meal with me. Just me, not the two guys out of the army. Probably because of his pretty granddaughter, he kept them at a distance. That old Italian would have me over for macaroni dinner and homemade sauce once a month or more. Dom's kids or grandkids couldn't relate with him about back east, so we talked. I would leave Piper positioned in his Spinks pose in my front yard across the street; it was no big deal. The Pie lay there and stayed where I told him, with his eyes on Dom's front door. The dog loved his privacy, and he was content with his surveillance waiting for me to return. He loved watching the birds fly and sunsets drop.

As fate would have it, the neighbor's little kid wandered over to pet my obedient dog. I'm sure Pie growled first to warn the young boy. He always growled at puppies who were a nuisance. But what's a kid know? Pie snapped at him and drew blood from his face. A very small, thin, red line appeared. It was a warning shot like he gave to puppies. There wasn't a bad bone in that dog; he just had to have his space. I spoke with the parents. It was demanded of me and I did prove Pie had his rabies shot before the parents took the boy to the emergency room. But the law was the law, and they tested Pie for rabies anyway. During the test time, I had to quarantine him in my room for ten days.

Amazingly enough, the boy's parents just wanted me to pay for the emergency room expenses at first, and I did. The price tag came to about $250, which included a few stitches. Those people were Christians. Our loud music, profane language, the smell of burning pot, and parties with fights drawing the police, loud cars, motorcycles, women, and girls made us bad role models. We were everything they were teaching their children not to be, and we lived right next door.

Within a week or so, they sued me for $3,000.00. I paused and thought, *if it were my kid, I'd try for $20,000.00, so $3,000.00 isn't so bad.* My world went upside down. I told the folks the truth. I was on a mission living a dream, and I was poor and on worker's compensation. I was so thankful to them for dropping the suit and not having my future income garnished. Thank God they were forgiving people.

One month later, Pie and I walked to the market for food. We sat outside the large grocery store before I went in, like many times before. I told Pie to sit and wait for me, which he always did. A small kid came over to pet him, and that time the kid fell over Pie's feet and the little boy cut his lip. The butcher saw the whole thing while he was having a smoke. Regardless of Pie's innocence, it was another incident treated as a dog bite, and it alarmed the dogcatcher. I was notified again of the infraction. Piper was put under quarantine for ten days again until the tests for rabies were confirmed negative.

I was told that if Pie bit someone or it was reported he did a third time, the law said the dog would have to be put down. Who would have thought that the same thing would happen twice? But then again, I thought and realized I did name him after the Pied Piper. Everyone loved to pet him, even kids. That news set a fire under my feet, and I began planning to leave Orange County immediately. I was living in an emergency like many other stories within the Orange County diaries. Like when one roommate was growing pot in the backyard, which did not sit well with me at all. We were all saving money on the cheap rent, so why invite trouble? Or the truck driver who rented the fourth room and left his promiscuous girlfriend there while he traveled. What a nightmare that was before they left. The next fourth renter, who ripped my phone line out of the wall because he wanted it in his room, was just plain mean.

But there were also many quiet times of peace written about within the O. C. diaries. Like when Piper and I would walk up to the school yard, where he could run in the grassy fields and I would watch him hunt for critters in the amazing orange sunsets. There was a peaceful, still quiet in the large open field, and no motion from traffic or city noises. As I lay on the grass the Pie's silhouette passed to and fro within the giant orange ball dropping behind him. It was so good to find that space for a few minutes amid the mass of millions of hectic people, places, and things. Other times we would be at the beach hiding because there was never any room for tolerating dogs on the beach. So we would sneak down at night and swim and run on the beach in and out of the waves. We tried to avoid the mass of people as much as possible, and we did find a spot here and there. He lived out his standard fashion of running at night, albeit less frequently, and slept days.

Naturally appreciating life's subtle moments to stop and smell the roses I stood still enjoying the muse of living one second at a time. I didn't get all consumed by the tasks at hand and stopped often to smell the roses. But life has alarming ways. For instance, on the other side of the quiet scale, there was the time Pie caught a twelve-inch rat. At three in the morning, I was asleep in my bedroom when he frantically chased and tore through things until he had the rat in his jaws. Talk about a wakeup call! Then there was my first desperate move northward to Korea Town to get out of Orange County. I chose to live near the Wilshire district of Los Angeles, moving into a guesthouse behind a mansion. My car was parked out in the street. The first night, my battery was stolen. The next day my worker's compensation checks shifted back to disability. The surprising news came in the mail without notice. My budget shrank, drying up my finances which had enabled me to move out of Orange County. Less money forced my retreat back into the cul-de-sac all in one weekend. But I still needed to get the Pie and me out of Orange County.

In my urgent plans to migrate north in July, I advertised in the Hollywood *Drama-Logue* magazine for a composer to work with. A guy answered my ad. He was a composer looking for a lyricist. That is how I met my collaborator. For this book, I'll call him Chance. He lived in North Hollywood with his wife and young boy. We understood each other's songwriting desires. Our indulgence with word syllables, cadence, and rhyming were mutual. But he first started with music and then worked a little with words. Most of the friends he played with didn't write words. I mentioned my classwork with other writers and my weekly trip to Hollywood. We agreed to meet and show each other our efforts.

I found his condo near a cool, shady group of trees. I could hear the sounds of guitars and drums. The Pie ran about as I sat with excitement.

I met a few of the musicians leaving and locked up the Pie. Chance came from Wisconsin with his lovely wife a year earlier and had a baby boy. His talent hit the ceiling of his hometown and drove him west, like mine did to me. He had made some progress as a backup vocalist with some studio work singing with Rick Springfield and Kim Carnes. Or so he said. He was twenty-six, five-foot-ten, thin, with dark hair and a baby face, and played bass and rhythm guitars. We looked at my lyrics first and the many variations of the rewrites involved. He liked the amount of effort that went into my work. I explained the process of eliminating ideas and the crafting of thoughts.

As he listened, his young son, just able to walk, came in the room and wanted to see his dad. I saw how the interruption couldn't be helped, but also saw the inconvenience on Chance's face. The boy must have waited for the musicians to leave and now came through the open door. Chance picked up the boy, and we laughed when the child said, "Bye, guys." After the boy mimicked his dad, Chance put the boy aside.

Chance played guitar and showed me how he was hoping to fill empty spots with words, where he now mouthed in grunts and simply mumbled some syllables. I'd never seen how a song got started with music and a vocalist spouting feelings without words. I liked seeing the music played and hearing the surroundings of where the words might fit. We found agreement in identifying within his rough music the missing sections of verses and chorus. I asked him to isolate a section of his playing, and we improved his nonsense words to identify the cadence. Interestingly it was then that I found out that he didn't know what the song was about; he just had feelings.

Once we entered the realm of marrying the feeling of the music with the color of the words, we knew we had our work cut out for us. I made the leap and worked with a collaborator. It was a real good first meeting. Chance's wife came in and asked him to play with their son. I left with some of his music sounds and groining's on a cassette. We agreed to talk on the phone in a week and see what would happen.

Amazingly enough he lived in the North Hollywood neighborhood I passed through on the 170 Freeway going to my writing class. On those collaborative meeting days, I slept nights in the car near the local mall on the edge of a park. It always felt weird and vulnerable, but I knew the Pie dog would be on watch. Chance and I would meet the next day and work on our rock-and-roll songs at his condo. I could see then that his wife and kid were in a kind of second place. His family was in the background of his dedication to write. Collaboration continued on the phone during the week. I became very busy with writing lyrics. The crossover into writing lyrics with Chance's rock-and-roll music was work I loved doing. I took pride in what I wrote, which were words that could fit many kinds of music. I knew nothing about current music, top forty charts, and the public's appetite for new sounds. My interest was in songwriting, not how the sounds of music were produced.

On August 8, I started my second seven-day fast. After the success of the first fast, I returned to the old ways of eating and gained some weight back. I began my fasting in Orange County and took it with me for the next thirty years. I'm so glad I learned that dual lesson of denying food and cleansing my insides. Keeping away from some of the things that consumed the rest of the people came naturally for me. However, some of my vices rode me like an annoying saddle at times.

I lost another twenty-two pounds from that fast. I shrank to 168 pounds. I knew the weight would come back, but I also could see the cleansing take place again. My facial skin was noticeably cleaner, smoother, and younger. My senses were clearer and more acute. I was made younger inside and out. But there was an inexpressible something else that came with the fast. There was no mistake about the presence of a kind of special peace. Perhaps I was touching on a spiritual part of life. If fasting was like knocking on the door of something religious, I was intrigued by it. Perhaps the miracle of fasting was part of another system, something supernatural and divine.

Chapter 12:
The Business, the Bible, and the Bust

In October 1983, twenty-one months after landing on the West Coast, after all the struggles, all my ducks were lined up in a row. The urgency to get Pie out of Orange County before another incident with the law and the dogcatcher pushed me. My next move north came. I again rented a room in a house because it was the cheapest way to go. Renting rooms is also the easiest way to get in and the fastest way to get out with a dog. I moved with the Pie dog for a new start to North Hollywood near the corner of Laurel Canyon Boulevard and Burbank Boulevard. I rented from the owner/landlord named Emile, who lived there with his cat, El Gato. Even though he was a brainy type a few years younger than me, he was a man with many interests. He liked to smoke pot, and we had lots of good discussions. Interacting with his higher level of educated expression I loved to first notice the challenge to communicate and then see and hear my choice of words rising to have my views understood. We each enjoyed our almost-opposite upbringings and viewpoints. His Jewish heritage often found a way into our considerations, and he'd explain aspects of life I'd never before thought of. His dad had died and left him the house, with its wall of books and eight-foot pool table. Emile seemed to know which book to pull out to show me the source of his opinion. While he had intelligence and education, Emile lacked that certain savoir faire or charm women appreciate. He introduced me to Courvoisier brandy and fine South American cigars. Gina and I stayed in touch on the phone. Apparently her latest affair with the guy with wealth and the Mercedes-Benz came with a plan to have her work for his business. She was still a sales rep and only used the car in her work travels. The first time Gina came up to visit me, Emile melted under her smile. From then on, he was sure he could learn something from me.

I was at last out of Orange County. After living there in what felt like lifetime from A to Z, I was happy. The friend I left behind was Dom; I missed the wisdom that came with his age. His frank sit-down talks about the good ways it used to be with families were good for my ears. His comparison of the values found in the families of yesteryear to the newer computer-age selfishness of politicians and people was something we agreed on. He had a genuine gut feeling that things weren't going right for America. He worried about his kids and grandkids. He had the privilege of hindsight and saw the wrong path American leaders were taking. I saw in him how he recognized the speed of time and damage done.

I was in a position to start my postsurgical rehabilitation. It came with an increased steady income. I enjoyed the new climate and time to walk the new streets. At that point, I was only a few blocks away from my collaborator Chance and his family. It was also good to make a connection with his father and his musician friends. Visiting his wife and kid helped put a normal face on my nomadic movements. Going to see the young family in a real home had an honest quality. Chance was an accomplished studio vocalist, energetic and working with recording artists, or so he said. He was very inspiring and talented, but most of all, we worked well expressing together my words and his music. My neighborhood bordered Mulholland Drive and the Hollywood Hills. I was actually living among famous people and ten thousand other hopeful wannabes searching for fame and fortune.

The San Fernando Valley life was another provoking challenge, some kind of dare like a salmon swimming up against the rapids, to conquer. Piper was eager to explore the streets with me. He was always there for me, and he was mostly there, if he wasn't chasing some smell in the wind. He would run the streets some nights. I kept him close most nights; the Valley was an older, more dangerous place. Gang activity made the news at times, and carloads of young men could be seen at night. Almost daily we walked to North Hollywood Park and would occasionally drive west to the beach at night to run in the waves near Malibu.

In the many years walking in the suburbs, I found again and again that very few people walked after dark. Coast to coast, I was alone with the Duke in the suburban streets 95 percent of the time. The park was a favorite daytime spot for Piper to run, and so near our house we walked there during the early evening times.

The day people who were drawn to the park played tennis or walked fast during their lunch. They were the sunlight people, common on the outside to the average eye sitting under a tree reading. The Valley was a lot older than Orange County and had more places to hide the street people. I drove at night to see what I could see and who would come out after sunset and roam in the various shadows.

The few times we strolled late at night, we saw grocery carts pushed by men mostly and some women, some of whom even had dogs. Wheeling their world to and fro, that invisible army of day marched openly at night. The park was like a magnet, with true opposite polarity. Nighttime drew the uncommon. Those who gathered were seen and largely ignored. They were like a set of old clothing once used often, but then put away. Only a very few times did I venture out in the dark for a walk in that direction. Driving by at night wasn't the same realism as being shoulder-to-shoulder with the nightwalkers.

The caravan of the uncommon came every twenty-four hours. I saw the reverse of the daylight people. Passing by hookers pivoting on corners waving at cars, I saw some scary people reciting mantras. It felt like I walked into the frames of a noir film. They rolled the rocking carts and themselves over sidewalk cracks through the avenues of dark. Streetlights hung over the shadowy theater of despair. Those ghostly hours carried both confusion and chance to the doorstep of vulnerability.

Shadow people existed like quiet vampires obeying the law. Survival was king over its subjects of stealth. They shared a basic garden of nocturnal life before the breaking sun broke their nightly pass to overtly engage. The predawn gray signaled retreat off the street. Light drove in the recognized daily affairs of normal and drove out the valley silhouettes of society's shame.

Another day another dollar came and left for most, but for others their life hinged on counting pennies in the absence of light. Nevertheless, the motion of survival continued twenty-four hours for them and me and you. When the routine sundown's and stars of cool dimness appeared, so did the rivers of the night's street natives. Returning once more, I witnessed the emergence of the underground and shared what I could share, coffee and donuts.

—————————— † ——————————

SHADOW PEOPLE

Shadow People, Shadow People,
First they choose they will, then choose they won't,
Doing solitary dos and don'ts.

Shadow People, Shadow People,
Hazy daisy in and out of sight,
Layered rags walk away from light.

Shadows, shadows, all outsiders with the same place to go.
Shadows, shadows, all followers with the same place to go.

Shadow People run to the steeple,
Shadow People find the love they need,
Shadow People under this steeple,
Shadow People faith is their seed.

Public seldom seen and hardly heard,
Unsealed, underprivileged, unknown world,
Shadow People, night's black pearls.

Confinement, verses, come what may with a tie,
Corners of their eyes slide side to side,
Shadow People, they're worldwide.

—————————— † ——————————

My every-so-often reoccurring awareness that quick-changing events needed to be dealt with accurately again caused me to be still. I paused on that page in my diary and thought of the old troll under the freeway bridge celebrating my birthday with me. In my pausing, I saw the necessity to be adaptable. I was only a few dollars away from living in my vehicle. Growth in flexibility was becoming like a type of relative I became more aware of as time stretched out. Mixed in with give–and-take were my steady unchanging ways. Still rooted in me and accompanying my priorities were the habits I loved.

Remaining a nonconformist, I still felt strongly about my addiction to smoking pot. Albeit illegal, it was a means, a vehicle, a cheap way to have fun. At the same time, I grew more in wanting to get that twelve-year-old monkey off my back. The irritating tear of uneasiness was causing wishful moans of surrender. The dueling Gemini continued to reign in my two districts of good and evil. I could sense the old Dr. Jekyll-Mr. Hyde routine lurking in the shadows of my heart and mind—a warning, a notice, a silent alarm! Was it just me, or did that happen to everybody in general? An inside nudge.

My financial income was on a seesaw of worker's compensation and disability. One check paid more than the other, but either way, it was all a lie. My dream was being funded by a lie due to another injury in a life of being accident-prone. I thought of the old troll under the bridge. If I had told the truth, would I be like him? Would I be pushing a cart to the park at night? Will I be?

I was told in a letter that the insurance company would be testing me and sending me back to work at some point. In-between times were tough. The income level would change and have lag periods between checks. There were weeks of no money. I was in a lower system trying to break into another, higher system. The systems were there, and I was like meat going through a grinder. The grinders were always there. Treadmills were grinders; rich or poor were all in a grinder of one sort or another. Who was turning the handle of the grinder?

Evolving out of my New York ways and adding on some California ways was ongoing work. I became more tolerant of other cultures, but did not always like the foreign languages in my ear. What I didn't know didn't hurt me. And I didn't know what they were talking about, so I lost interest. When I lost interest, I lost a degree of caring about them. There's something distracting, however, about being left out of a conversation. It's bothersome not to know what's being said because it all sounds like noise. It's very irritating to not know what is being said and not be able to turn it off or tune it out. It's like being stuck near someone having a one-sided phone conversation.

On the other hand of culture change, there was real Mexican food. From a small local corner burrito stand, I would get great food and meet some wonderful people. I loved the Mexican and Latino people. I enjoyed those hardworking folks and endeavored to enhance my Spanish lessons from high school. Often I would think of my brother, who shared Spanish class with me, and laugh out loud at his awkward Spanish-speaking skills. Even though our bonds didn't grow with time, my brother could still make me laugh thousands of miles away.

Likewise the Chinese restaurant workers and gardeners also worked hard. Walking past the local groundskeepers in front of condos doing their work was a reason to smile. A few times I'd ask how to say, "water or drink," but I never got the understanding. Once I brought those men down the street a soda—man, oh man alive, they were so happy. They were just a few of the millions of people all around me. I was in a sea of strangers, the general public with their popular opinions and social statements.

My own grinder turned. I basically kept a low profile, plowing ahead in my own field of dreams. I could see some results. Living my days near the music industry made my journey west real and worthwhile. I was an established "wannabe." My pilgrimage toward recognition had wandered in the direction of Hollywood. I was doing both the dreaming and meeting of life head-on, by hook or by crook. To travel and to try my best in life was becoming the dream come true. Much of my time was full of original lyric writing. I used what I was doing correctly and learned how to enhance the art of rewriting thanks to Jack Segal.

His night class at Northridge University and the Hollywood songwriting class were challenging and produced better material. Chance and I created our own songs and put together dozens of three-song demo packages. We read articles in past and current trade magazines in the library, gathering the names and addresses of executives in the industry. While Chance rehearsed with musicians at his place, I operated the phone communications, calling the music industry from my rented room. I learned fast how to phone schmooze! My youthful energetic radio announcer's voice asked for names, applied humor, and finally got to the decision maker. The major record labels' A&R (Artist and Repertoire) department heads were reached. Producers, managers, and the independent record labels were all contacted. We became completely occupied and dedicated with soliciting our original material to the so-called inaccessible music industry.

Without a budget for postage, we literally were driving to Hollywood and Studio City, as well as corporate buildings on Wilshire Boulevard. A lot of legwork pounded concrete. We would actually go to the offices of music executives and meet their secretaries. While we were there, we got more contact names from those listed in lobbies and stopped in offices for the phone numbers. We made our own book of contact information. I began additional calling to new decision makers for permission to send our demo promotion kits and got dozens of favorable approvals. We were in the rock-and-roll business. A few months later, we assembled the second recorded cassette of three different original songs. Straight-ahead rock was our sound, mixing flavors of the Stones and REM. We chose a variety of contacts from our research that favored the kind of songs we wrote. The hand deliveries included lyrics, Chance's bio, and photos, as we hoped for a record deal. Each time the packages were given out, we enjoyed what gamblers enjoy—the thrill of maybe winning.

†

HANG ON, HURRICANE

Going full speed, east to west,
He's a hurricane on a quest,
Writing songs of life coast to coast,
Skies carry dreams for the most.

 Living a long shot without worry,
 He's taking time and in no hurry,
 Occasionally touching down
 Pick up some love heading uptown.

Hang On, Hurricane, hang on for the breeze to put you at ease.
Hang On, Hurricane, hang on, day to day, change coming your way.

Around and around, flying higher,
Hopeful emotions drive desire,
Cross divides, roll over hills,
Exploring life, never fulfilled.

He felt the breeze of one woman,
Her circle kept on, hanging in.
Spinning, shining, without anger,
Hurricane, hang on; you finally met her.

✝

My collaborative work with Chance was first talked out and then put on
paper. He began singing rough mixes of lyrics and short pieces of music
on cassettes. I'd build on what I heard and wrote a variety of verses.
Every week I'd meet at Chance's place to review our rewrites. One day
I came early to hear the so-called band rehearse in his garage. I could
hear the familiar tune as I drove up to the big closed garage door. I sat
in the shade on the concrete, listening to them work out arrangements.
Chance had a good voice, it seemed, but I was no expert. Hearing
my lyrics being sung for the first time with original music by a garage

band was the greatest of all highs—as if a large rubber stamp with the one word *Approved* was pressed against me. I felt the exhilaration rush through and through. With a childlike joy, I realized that the struggle of writing over nine years seemed to have been compressed within like a piece of coal to produce a diamond.

The big overhead garage door opened, and the sunshine filled the rehearsal space. My beaming smile saw the players' squinting eyes as they moved out like mice and greetings were passed. The makeshift band was made up of Chance's friends, who were also in the music industry to one degree or another. They played together and arranged the songs' music, changing this, adding that. Hearing their comments about guitars and keyboards while the equipment was packed made the dream real. To be on the ground floor, engaging my own destiny, was more than the ultimate gambler's thrill. My work was paying off. Those first days of launching the packages of originals were extremely electrifying. We were overdosing on hope. The atmosphere all around me was one of immense anticipation.

By October, Chance and I agreed to a 50/50 partnership in songwriting and signed some papers at a lawyer's office. By night, I kept active driving to and from classes a few times a week. I loved learning and exercising my imagination. I'd stop at diners, bars, and Mexican food stands—they all were spots for enticing the muse. I was playing at being an artist. Watching people live while my thoughts eliminated words and chose others was my private party. Walking Piper in the streets to the park and easing into the diary also helped root out times for the muse to appear. When I refer to the muse at that time in my life, which was late 1983, I am referring to something very unique to myself. I was very familiar with the aura of the muse since I first began writing my diary. As I practiced to develop a method, the time I spent musing increased and became more intense. Sometimes the processes of gathering similar and contrasting ideas were like building a recipe of thoughts to bake. Other times, obscure notions popped up that led to different, unexpected views. Continually returning to the work of thinking is what mattered as I mixed the ingredients. Locations like diners, under trees, and so on, with or without distractions, at all times of day or night, all fostered good work zones.

†

THE BIG MUSE

Out the door through the mist,
To socially enlist,
You're quite sure nothing will be missed.

Cars snaking red to green,
Sipping on hot caffeine,
Watching your drive-in movie screen.

    The Big Muse starts with the small news,
    Crossed and confused, burning a fuse.

    The Big Muse, like an avenue,
    Driving tattoos, sheep in canoes.

    Sunset Boulevard, corner of Vine,
    Into the Big Muse, Hollywood Big Muse,
    Into the Big Muse, Hollywood Big Muse.

Unlock the old anchor,
My will, what will occur?
Drifting in the muse, for sure.

†

My disability checks gave me the free time to write, which was a luxury of the rich and famous. Of course, it's always magic when a unique idea comes out of the blue. Jack Segal called it lighting in a bottle. Chance and I came up with a method to capture his original intent of feeling in the music. Recording synonyms with his grunts and ideas in free verse worked well. I used the tape player and headphones to listen and got the feeling of the first versions of the originals. I'd walk around the house, yard, and streets singing the "doodahs," getting myself into the feeling or emotion of the music. After I consumed the feeling of Chance's original, I could carry it, whistled it, and then sat down with the whistling and the feeling and wrote lyrics. I used a corresponding tape player to record my thoughts as I listened to our rewrites. The songs often came out with some of the exact words that were chosen in the beginning.

†

LOVE IN THE ZODIAC

I was waiting for a sign in my favor,
Hesitating when I should have been braver,
Undercover, looking for the missing clue,
Found a lover, wearing her red rose tattoo.

We kept looking.... We got closer....

I got high hopes for the one I'm thinking of.
My horoscope's telling me I'm in love,
A Gemini, who admits he don't know
Can't deny his love for Scorpio.

We kept looking.... We got closer....

By compromising our hopes held high,
The new moon's rising, love filled the sky,
We go to the limit of our Zodiac,
Love every minute, Love in the Zodiac,
Zodiac bounces back, Love in the Zodiac.

Sight to behold, oh so, so far above
The pot of gold, those colors of love,
A rainbow ride, the best love we can find.
When we slide, our love is one of a kind.

✝

One fine day in January 1984, I walked. Often my two- or three-hour walks to both sides of North Hollywood Park included going through the tunnel under the 170 Freeway. The tunnel was a semi-scary, dark, echoey place linking two halves of the park's brilliance and beauty. Exercising was one of the highlights of my day; there's nothing wrong with walking. The Duke was like having a personal trainer to prompt me into getting up, out, and on the move. Those giant eucalyptus trees must have gotten their starts from the Mexican land barons from many decades past. Spacious green grounds for a person's eyes to relax away from the chaos of wheel and foot traffic were found daily in my piece of peace. I'd get a coffee at the 7-Eleven store and sit under a tall tree, casually hoping for the muse to visit. In the background of my thinking, I'd hear a mixture of subtle freeway traffic roaring.

One day I stood in line at the 7-Eleven store with a donut and heard someone tell of a beautiful city called San Jose. Someone else mentioned that water was being pumped in from the Colorado River for the sprinkler systems along the California freeways. When cities were spoken of, I did not know where they were. How little I knew of California or where all those cars and trucks on the highways went. Piper and I calmly strolled through the park's grassland, thinking about those places and freeways.

Another day during our walk, the Duke was off his leash like always, and we heard someone yelling far off. As we circled about the squirrel-filled trees, we both spotted a small dark dog running frantically toward us in the distance. Again and again, we heard the desperate cry to halt. "Gypsy! Gypsy!" Screaming the name did nothing to stop the furry four-legged black bowling ball. The dog was coming straight on like a ground-hovering torpedo. I looked toward where the voice had shrieked out its distressed plea and saw a very pretty blonde-haired woman. I told Piper to "go see," and he raced to intercept the tail-wagging, blunted, low-level, overweight projectile.

The dogs instantly became friends. Gypsy was a girl. Approaching the blonde, it seemed appropriate to ask her the first thing that popped into my head. I asked her, "Do you know the way to San Jose?" She began singing the song and broke out in a beautiful smile, laughing. She had gorgeous white teeth and snickered like a veteran who had years of good times behind her. We both roared in laughter, and within a few seconds, the woman and I were sitting and smiling like old friends. Gypsy and Pie were bumping into us as happy as we were. That was the initiation to what became a beautiful, sometimes scary and crazy relationship.

Her name was Melissa. Experience rolled within her blue eyes and contrasted with what appeared like silly immaturity. There was something more than unique about her. Her down-to-earth, easygoing ways were most appealing.

On our first date, I picked her up in my old red station wagon. Unfortunately, the night before I'd gotten drunk at a pub called Ireland 32 throwing darts and threw up on the floor driving home. Even though I cleaned the mess and smothered the stain with Old English cologne, I couldn't hide the truth. Melissa got in and didn't say anything. We went to the movie *Scarface*. After the show, we came back to my rented house and sat on the living room couch. I found out she was a recovering heroin and cocaine addict, alcoholic, ex-barroom stripper and a little more, as well as a mother of a teenage girl. Her smile seemed to bubble like champagne, but behind her eyes there was insightful, irreplaceable know-how, like a sage.

As soon as my ears heard her words "stripper and a little more," thoughts of sex pushed Devil's horns out of my head. A mischievous smile slowly gathered itself from ear to ear. Eyeing the pretty crumpet with a lustful craving, I tried necking with her, but she firmly resisted. She explained how she was in a specially arranged court-ordered recovery program. Melissa had been separated from her daughter and had recently been reunited with her. The program insisted that no relationships were to be started up for eighteen months. She said she'd love to be friends, thought I was her type of nuts, and wanted to hear my dirt. She said everybody has some dirt to tell.

I began telling her about my drinking in the streets of suburbia, poor grades, and summer school. Then onto the motorcycle crash, painkillers, booze, and my shift to marijuana. I mentioned other drugs. She loved my enthusiasm partying with my friends on the farm. My quitting the factory, walking out on love and responsibility, registered well with her. Her eyes drew into mine with my story of the second crash and discovery for my love of writing. When I told about the Bar Harbor trip, she wanted to go east and see a Cadillac Mountain sunrise. The first attempt of going to California via the Texas oil fields and returning to New York for my dad's funeral stopped her attention. She told me about her real dad and her mysteriously wealthy-recluse second dad, who was friends with Howard Hughes. Holding back the details of her relationship with her mother, she rolled her eyes and groaned but treasured telling me of her grandma.

We were both surprised at each other's craziness. I asked her if she'd like a beer, and she gritted her teeth, kicked me, and said, "I told you I'm clean and sober." I told her I was sorry and that it was all new to me; I never knew anybody our age who tried to be sober. We laughed at each other, saying simultaneously, "We both should be dead by now, but we're not!" Laughing even more, I instinctively tried to kiss her again, and she laughed, pushing me away saying, "You nut! Can't you remember anything?" We both realized the comedy of my concussion and the dilemma of caressing with my animated libido. The mutual insight brought on even more hysterical laughter. We were having so much fun and not doing anything to alter what came naturally for old friends.

I thought she was nice and very attractive in a dizzy blonde way, with a touch of larceny in her looks, and told her so. She said, "There's always a little nasty with nice," and laughed like a pirate. She lived in

Toluca Lake, about four blocks from Bob Hope's estate. That's where she grew up next to the houses of the very famous, adjacent to the Burbank Studios. She was shacking up in the back of her grandmother's manor occupying her father's former dentist-office bungalow on the estate. Having a dentist in the family explained her gorgeous teeth. The two-stall garage now housed her enigmatic stepdad's twin antique Cadillac's hidden under huge car covers. The five of them—Grandma, Melissa, her daughter Kiya, Gypsy dog, and three-legged cat named Peg—enjoyed security and seclusion.

Melissa grew up there in Toluca Lake and hung out in the San Fernando Valley. She was an original 1960s hippie chick. As a wild teenager, she grew wilder with drugs and with the man who fathered her child. She never stopped her craziness until she was forcibly stopped by the law. By then, she was far out of control. Her little girl was taken from her. The shock of their separation devastated Melissa, and her will became compliant. Her penance was to live in Hawaii among other troubled women in an exclusive forest colony. By intention, it was a small secluded jungle-setting society of desperate females. Daily they all studied a course from a collection of books on miracles. She said those books were special and nobody gets to see them unless they're really screwed up. I wanted to see those books and wondered if I'd ever get that screwed up.

Grandma's house was the place to continue her recuperation united with her daughter. She said she was doing well, although she was agitated by the movie scenes of Al Pacino smothering himself in cocaine. Again we laughed so easily together. We liked each other's different styles of living. We both lived our "out of being normal" lifestyles. We were both misfits not adjusting well into the pegboard of life. The mallet of society didn't pound her edges off either. She liked my "off the treadmill" analogy pitting typical American culture against any counterculture artistic ways. We became great friends, sharing stories about how we resisted the conforming mallet of society.

✝

One morning I was walking the Pie down Chandler Boulevard to enter the park through the north end. Almost past the tennis courts and picnic tables where the street people met at night, I suddenly stopped at the last table. On top of the green painted boards at the far end, I found three walnut half shells. A thin, small, two-inch-square red paper-covered Bible was next to them. I sat down at the table and found nothing under the half shells. I opened up the tiny Bible. It had surprisingly large print. I began reading a few of the names, numbers, and words, and then saw the name Jesus. Mark 1:1 read "The beginning of the gospel of Jesus Christ, the Son of God." That was the first time I ever opened up a book called *The Bible*. I left the shells and felt good keeping the small book.

Across the street from the 7-Eleven store, I bought a better cup of coffee and a wonderful Danish at Sitton's restaurant. Crossing the traffic, I continued into the park under a tree where I could sit and write. I read some more from the tiny book. "For God so loved the world He gave His only begotten Son, that whoever believes in Him should not perish but have everlasting life" (John 3:16). *Perish* had to be hell, and *everlasting life* had to be heaven. Believing in God's Son, Jesus, kept *whoever* out of hell and got *whoever believes* into heaven. I never before realized the significance attached to the name Jesus.

I told the diary of the impact those Bible words and the name Jesus had on me. The name was special, like opening a door and finding more than what was expected. A sense of surprise and intrigue seized me. I knew I was seeing and holding something much bigger than two-inch-square pieces of paper bound together. The words *everlasting life* wouldn't let go of me. The idea was foreign to me; I never gave much thought to the real meaning of forever. I never saw the name Jesus printed out, except around Christmastime on cards that came in the mail. I wondered about the pull on my interest and the meanings of those words. As for me coming up with an answer, I had none. But the magnetic impact stayed. Like many times before, I wrote in my diary, "Only time will tell."

A month later, one late afternoon I was sitting with Melissa outside her bungalow. Her progress with the court system was going well. Grandma's daily afternoon highball provoked Melissa into inching away from her progress. She began drinking beer, and we each had one. Beyond the fence and below the embankment, the Hollywood Freeway traffic tried to roar but was blocked by the high ridge of trees. We were getting high waiting for sundown, to walk and buy some peppermint schnapps. To Melissa, getting high on pot and a few swigs of sweet liquor was almost insignificant. Hearing how she used to live, I understood better her comment, "This stuff is like nothing compared to the way I used to be."

I showed Melissa the small two-inch Bible and read from it. I made some mistakes in my reading, and she stopped me. She abruptly said she wanted to buy me a good cigar and some brandy, so we walked to the nearby 7-Eleven. The back wall held a large sliding-glass-door humidor case with imported brands of fine cigars, and I chose the Portages 525. I recently smoked my first one with Emile. It felt good to know what I liked. It was a pricy seven-dollar smoke, so we skipped the brandy and just got the schnapps.

We stood in a slow line at the busy location watching people hurrying in and out. Melissa asked me to read the smut newspapers near the register. I read aloud and made mistakes even though the words were in larger print. I didn't notice anything wrong. She held the paper, pointed to the words, and explained how I made my mistakes. She read what was printed and then repeated what I said, and I saw the difference. I nodded my head up and down saying, "Yeah, I've been doing that my whole life." Melissa turned to me with a big, beautiful smile and gleefully announced, "You're dyslexic too!" I looked at her in confusion; I didn't know what she was talking about. She repeated the words with more enthusiasm in her eyes and voice, "You're dyslexic," as if that meant something. I looked around and saw people looking at us and felt out of place. I was thirty years old and had never heard that word *dyslexic* before.

She was still smiling and real happy. I asked her what she was talking about. She explained to me that I had the condition known as dyslexia and that she knew I had it because she had dyslexia also. She made it sound like a disease, and whatever it was didn't feel so bad anymore because she had it too. The line moved up one person closer to the register. I leaned down, and I asked her in a low voice, "So we both got what?" She laughed and said, "Don't worry. It's nothing bad; you'll live. I'll tell you outside." Walking back to Grandma's house just after sunset, she told me all about the way my eyes switch around what I read. I was beyond myself in awe. With exciting joy and thrilling relief, I was so happy I laughed out loud, and she laughed with me. She knew all about what I went through in school because she went through the same stuff.

After thirty years of living with the slippery backstabbing thief of my learning, I finally caught it. She ripped off the hood of ignorance and revealed the bittersweet look at truth. I was learning-disabled. We sat on her porch next to each other on the lounge in the dim yellow light coming through her parlor window. Sipping schnapps, I smoked my expensive cigar, and she smoked a cigarette. The red glowing ends burned, and puffs of smoke rose up past the roof. Again we connected in harmony and felt satisfied, like astronauts landing on the moon. My long journey with the unknown alien within was over, and she helped me get there. We celebrated and shared stories of stupidity and perseverance, laughing and shaking our heads at the times we lived.

However, she had no interest in the words found in the two-inch Bible. She said the Bible wasn't for her. I asked her about the difference between the books on miracles she had studied from and the Bible. She said both books were like medicine, but she said the Bible was way more intense and it wasn't for her. She said she knew some people who were taken by the Bible's words and never came back. They gave up on partying and changed. She didn't want to talk anymore about it. But I liked carrying that small small Bible in my pocket. I liked the idea of it being big medicine. I read the words often; they sounded good, so maybe it was for me.

The next morning, the realization about Melissa's diagnosis of my learning problem was first on my mind. My conflict was solved. I couldn't wait to tell Ma. I phoned my mom with excitement and said too much too fast about my failing third grade, poor high school grades, and years of successive summer schools. When I told her the good news that I wasn't stupid but I was dyslexic, it made no sense to her. Like me, my mom had never heard of the word and didn't know how to spell it or anything about it. For her to hear how my eyes could rearrange the words or numbers on a piece of paper was unbelievable. She couldn't understand the concept and couldn't share my newfound happiness. She didn't know who Melissa was and doubted her because someone was saying I wasn't good enough. Ma told me instead that I was her son and not to let anyone call me stupid. I could do anything as well as anybody else and I shouldn't let anyone tell me otherwise. We talked about her job, her health, my brother's family, and others things before saying good-bye.

That's my mom, and I love her. Even though I was thirty five hundred miles away from her, I had more than her voice and her words telling me she loved me. I felt her love, which would stop at nothing to defend me or make right what was wrong in my life. I was her son, and Ma would love me no matter what. Maybe initially hearing about how my eyes and brain processed information incorrectly was more than she could handle. My new discovery, my victory in my private war, was my own. I finally had a name and face to put to the elusive thief of my mystery struggle, my alien within. The menacing troublemaker in my mind became a pair of eyes on a wanted poster I could shoot at.

Little changes took place at first that helped me, like Melissa said they would. Repeating phone numbers and directions out loud so I could see where I was making mistakes helped. I still made mistakes, but the truth became real in catching and seeing the mistakes. The difference was in the relief in knowing the cause for my carelessness. I had a reason for blunders, and I could watch for it. I did no research, made no doctors' appointments, just looked for mistakes and saw how they were made. To at last know the truth made all the difference.

†

Oftentimes blessings or troubles will begin with something as small as one word or a seed. That is exactly what caused positive and negative complications in my life. Emile heard me tell stories of how I or my friends in New York would buy and sell pot. He was a tight-fisted man with money, and he understood the business of business. For him to get a small amount of pot to smoke for little or no cost, he'd have to sell to others. He began practicing the art of buying and selling pot for the first time. That really did not sit well with me. It was one of the things that made me uncomfortable in Orange County. Why invite trouble? Then he took it into the next step of greed by planting some quality seeds and growing marijuana plants in his backyard. My living situation took on the exact same risks and more.

It was February, and my worker's compensation case manager was demanding that I become a working unit again in society. His letter said I was approved for the next phase, and I would receive written notice. But I was leery of the compensation system and its delays and methods after what happened to me in Korea Town. I couldn't afford a mistake like that again. Not knowing about the decrease in the amount of money I would receive from the state almost ruined me once.

On March 3, 1984, the letter came. I read it out loud a few times and walked around with the paper informing me that I had secured rehabilitation training. The decision also brought the assurance of the future cash settlement. That big news prompted me to quickly reach out for help so I could move out of what had become a small-time illegal drugstore. I sensed my own measure of desperation and hated the feeling of impending trouble. Another inside nudge quickened my awareness. My intuition, experience, or conscience was telling me to move, but I had no financial means to even consider a search. I didn't want to alarm my mom of my need for advance money or my need to move again so soon because of drug use. That was the truth, and I always told my mom the truth. So I asked an uncle who lived fifty miles away for a small loan that would help me to move and establish renting somewhere else. I only had the worker's compensation letter for rehab and the cash settlement as collateral. I gave my word toward my obligation to pay him back. He said no. He was also a businessman who understood the business of business. I really can't blame him; he didn't know me or know that I would keep my word. So I regrettably stayed where I was.

In April, I desperately decided to save up money for my move. I suggested paying less rent by living in Emile's truck camper, which was off his truck and rested on stilts. Emile was then able to rent my room. He liked the idea of collecting more rent. The camper in the backyard was small and stood near the garage, but still made a good target for the sun. Summer life was beginning to heat up in general, and there was no coolness during the day under the hot California sunshine. Piper and I went in and out of the house for the air-conditioning. I was still writing lyrics with Chance, who was still trying to form a band to showcase originals in Hollywood nightclubs. His experience using an eight-track recorder mixing musical instruments and vocals made good demos. We had sent out another three-song promo package to several specific people in the music industry.

Amazingly MCA Records called Chance and wanted to start talks about a deal for a song Chance wrote with someone else when rehearsing in his garage. That phone call was what was supposed to happen. Making an impression on the music industry was the objective and the reason why I came to the West Coast. But Chance put that option on hold to think about it. I was in shock. A week later, Chance told the producer, Mike Curb, no deal. He wanted a band deal, not just the sale of one song. I was stunned, naïve, and stupidly jolted from my bottom to the top and back to the bottom. But Chance got his advice from others in the industry and went with it.

I had crazy mixed thoughts on passing up the opportunity since we didn't even have a band playing in clubs. I didn't understand the logic or the politics of the music industry, but I saw how one phone call could change a person's life. Moved by the confusion, I began writing a lyric called "Almost Is Addicting," still a work in progress. It was a title that held a lot of my feelings for sticking with my dream. Working with talented people in the business encouraged my eagerness to remain near them.

Life went on, and I was still being tested for future employment. Dating Melissa, who was doing some waitress work in very nice restaurants, continued as we became better friends. Piper began running more at night, and that was not good in that area. But when that dog picked up a scent, he was gone. Pie was ten years old and in top shape. He was with me, but both our hearts were back at the lake in upstate New York. I started my annual spring fast for my second year. The fasting was a bit more familiar and every bit a miracle blessing again. Fasting was nothing to take lightly. The shock of starvation was less. The reality that the quality of my life was illuminated came again.

✝

By May 1984, the urgency I felt to move had subsided. Without money to move, I reasoned that I was stuck, but my conscience knew better. I was lulled into accepting it more easily by enjoying the homegrown pot from Emile's backyard. I sold none of it; in fact, I had to buy it. One afternoon while sitting in the backyard shade of Emile's camper with Piper, life changed fast. Like an unforeseen devastating lighting strike, the backyard and house were invaded by a SWAT team. Police armed with rifles and handguns were clad in helmets and bulletproof vests. They came like a storm from all directions. With guns pointed at me from behind fences of the back and adjacent yards, I was being screamed at to put up my hands. Since I was sitting there getting high anyway and drinking a beer, I was cool, shocked, and dumbfounded.

Piper, on the other hand, was in full alert and raged in his anger against anyone in a uniform. He was especially alarmed about seeing the guns. He curled his lips and growled and barked. I was commanded to subdue the animal, or they would shoot him. I held back the dog in my arms. I led my canine friend inside the camper, with the small cab window opened up for him to exit into the yard later. I told him to stay, and he did.

I was put in handcuffs. Emile, the new renter, and I were all taken to the station for fingerprinting. To make a long story short, I sat in jail a few hours. I was scared because I was guilty, alone, and poor. Forced into a system shackled with handcuffs, I was on my own. The beauty of life was taken; I had nothing but loss to consider. I needed something. I remembered that small Bible and regretted not having it in my pocket. We were all released on our own reconnaissance. Since I had given up my room and lived outside the building in the camper, my residency was questionable. The new renter, on the other hand, claimed he knew nothing even though he did. So the prosecutor was less aggressive with us but more so with Emile. Emile's expensive lawyer wanted to cut a deal with the prosecutor's office. I obtained a public defender, who sold me out months later. The new renter just got a warning. I ended up taking some of Emile's heat. Money talks! I was in the legal system for eighteen months on probation.

My conscience and those inner urgings or nudges were clearly warnings of importance. I should have moved when it made sense to move. But I was caught in my own web of poverty and illusions. Of course, some of the illegal activity was as much my fault as anybody's. I'd been getting away with that illegal crap for twelve years. I got what I deserved. Every sin has its consequences. I continued living in the camper. I was getting more desperate, and could only hope that somehow my stay at Emile's would end soon.

✝

Then, exactly then, I received notice of the insurance company's objection to my receiving training. I was to have an impartial physical exam on my wrist. The outcome of the doctor's findings would determine if I qualified for vocational rehabilitation. Without rehabilitation,

I'd remain injured, with a diminished wrist and without a job. The upcoming examination was far more critical than I had expected. I was scheduled to see a different type of doctor for an exam, and his impartial words would carry great weight. I reported to the doctor's office in Long Beach.

Looking around his very impressive elegant furniture with its polished carvings gave me confidence in his concern. During the preliminary questioning, I mentioned to the doctor when and how my wrist pain began in the morning. I told him of my concussion and the diary writings' help and how pain arrived when I would first sit down to write. The doctor took a particular interest in my diary writing and asked me how long I had been doing it. I told him I began after my head concussion at age twenty-one, about eight years earlier. My mentioning to him that writing was a great relief that enabled me to express my thoughts and not forget them interested him. This doctor was fascinated with my dedication toward diary writing. Explaining further, I conveyed my love for creating lyrics and my pilgrimage west. Even though I felt exposed telling a stranger of my love, I felt reassured. As he sat behind a huge wooden desk of undoubtedly great value, his involvement in listening so intently came with a genuine look of fatherly concern.

He began telling me the story of how he was a military physician in a MASH unit during World War II. I liked hearing him tell of the chaos and rough conditions of the hospital field unit. He spoke of a shell-shock concussion patient who was brought to him. As part of that man's healing, the doctor advised him to write down his thoughts. His professional status made his therapeutic words carry power. Surprise filled my eyes and a smile began as I recognized my own therapy of diary writing. The shell-shocked man did write his thoughts, and he shared them with the doctor. That unbiased doctor told me the man's name was Rod Serling, who later became the author of *The Twilight Zone* TV series. My eyebrows rose when I realized how intimate our discussion really was. The dark shining wood of his ornate office surroundings seemed more silent. The painting on the wall behind me seemed more special than my first good impression. Bringing my eyes back around to meet his, I caught his stare into mine. The condition of my wrist and the implications of using it to write with had far more meaning than I expected. He encouraged me to continue my writing of whatever I thought about. I assured him of my dedication. He called for his nurse, who led me into a dressing room to remove my shirt.

My physical involved being hooked up to a machine that would test my nerves and the electricity in my arm. The doctor began to administer his exam and held my wrist. His nurse was befuddled when the machine would not work since it was working properly the day before. Without the electronic equipment, which was unexplainably broken, the doctor began to perform my physical by testing me himself. By the end of our meeting, he told me that his findings would be reported. He wished me the best in my writing career. I thanked him and left his office.

Standing in the plain, boring, unattractive hallway, I wondered about what had just happened. We talked about the past experience; it was real. The surreal patterns of head trauma recovery due to writing down thoughts were eerie. I thought with regard to the test, the power failure was not real. Whatever the conclusions of the test would be, I knew they were under control from far, far away. The broken fifty-thousand-dollar machine was spooky. Such an important decision was to be based on a physical exam by a doctor who, by a twist of fate, saw some kind of déjà vu in me. How did I get into such a mess? Each form I filled out, each time I told the story of the lie that took place, the lie got bigger. The truth wasn't being drowned out; it was being amplified in my conscience.

Outside his building, I found myself surrounded in the waters of rising truth. After I ended up living with a Doberman that used to guard a Chinese-owned liquor store, he bit me on my wrist. Compelled by desperation, I lied. The continuing rippling effects of the lie increased. I thought the catalyst that forced my desperation was the fear of being in pain without medical insurance for a doctor's care. But I now was able to admit the real stimulus that drove my thinking to create the lie was my own distressed thoughts of how another accident might be the cause forcing me to abandon my dream. And now I had lost whatever control I had in determining my own fate. That doctor's report would determine if I would continue receiving my disability checks. More importantly, it would determine if I would be physically rehabilitated and learn a new occupation. The news was going to be big, either way it went. A few weeks after the exam, the doctor's evaluation was fully in my favor. The worker's compensation process would continue.

I began vocational rehabilitation in Burbank. The first phase was to evaluate my manual dexterity. I didn't do well with putting together the small components of a pocket watch. I was also given a series of written tests to assess my academic level. My cavalier artist attitude and tunnel vision into my dream were hard for those people to break through. I participated, but I did not engage with the dedication they were looking for. Test scores showed I had a two-and-a-half-year college education. Through life's experiences, I apparently got smarter. Go figure.

By mid-1984, my only collaborator Chance and I were doing our best marketing our originals, hoping to be discovered by the music industry. The hope of success was felt as progress was being made. Our efforts in marketing the originals were accompanied by a kind of electric buzz among musicians we were working with. By word of mouth, some really good players with a lot of talent got involved. I learned about the transient nature of musicians who found work with famous singers or groups on the road. When their gigs in and out of town ended, they became available to plug into a circuit of searching talent. There was so much talent in Tinseltown, you could scrape it off the street with large spatulas. Our band was just for recording and had some monster players, whose talent was immeasurable. Chance told me of the connections of the drummer, bass player, and the keyboard player. It was a thrill to hear the reputations of who worked with whom in their music world. The significance of being part of the pool of talent that was finding work brought more realism to my invented life. Sharing the news with Emile, I could see how the excitement was transferable.

I had been writing several more lyrics and also managing the office end of our own music business. My steady phone calls to the music industry soliciting for our newest music package were received well. I was thankful for the telemarketing skills that first blossomed by helping out my lyric class instructor Jack Segal. From time to time, I called his students for upcoming classes, and in return, I received class attendance for free. Jack was a great inspiration and a businessman who knew the business of business. He had several decades of experience distilling the gems of creative lyric writing, teaching classes, and associating with the Songwriters Guild.

In December 1985, I got a card from Aunt Jean with five dollars, and she told me to never lose my faith, that someday things would get better. When Christmas came, I got my care package from my mother full of presents. There was underwear and socks and lots of good home-baked things, like bread and cookies and cakes. Pie dog and I would share them with Emile as I would then sip on his brandy and coffee while writing in the diary. There was always time to write in the diary to reflect my thoughts and consider life. My mother always sent me something for Christmas, and I loved her love. She had tremendous love to give. I missed her greatly and wished I could be there just to help her.

That Christmas Day, Piper and I walked to the North Hollywood High School football field so he could run and run on some real good grass. We ran and tumbled on the grass and played like two puppies. There was a very light rain, but we didn't care. He growled and pulled on my old clothes and tore the sleeves like he used to do in the snow, and I didn't care. I told him he was the best dog in the world and I loved him. We sat in the quiet, cloudy, gray mist panting from our jousting about and shared cookies from New York. All we cared about was spending quality time with each other.

Chapter 13: Garage Life

The state of California wanted to train me in the spring of 1986 to use a micrometer and be a quality control person. They wanted to plug me back into society as a working unit inspecting things I had no interest in. At thirty-three years of age, I could have been a "this or a that," but wanted to be myself more than anything. Not wanting to disrupt the music project by going to training and then working an eight-hour shift someplace, I turned down the vocational opportunity. I ended up with a three-piece suit from the state and a state-sponsored job going door-to-door for a local computer company passing out flyers.

Burbank was the target, and all the businesses on Burbank Boulevard were where I pounded pavement. Cold-calling was an art I likened to my days as a paperboy. Once a week, I'd have to collect the money owed me, and then I paid the Schenectady *Gazette* for all the papers. Knocking on doors this time around brought back those lessons in greeting others face-to-face. Going through the front door of restaurants, appliance dealers, and a few dozen other establishments was fun. Getting off the hot street in March and April and into air-conditioning was my real goal. Maybe meeting a nice chick was my second goal. My introductions to clerks and owners were what I thought acting must have been like. I pretended to be enthusiastic, concerned for their enhanced welfare, and glad to gather and leave information. My third goal, was to leave a flyer it was the least I could do.

Once the six-week sponsorship was over, I was back to relying on myself. I was so far out and away from any kind of normal that I refused all the good opportunities that were offered. How foolish. How immature. How narrow-minded. One good thing that came with the end was that I no longer had to live the lie. The lie bought me time, but the time came and left as well. I continued to try my best and got a telemarketing job. In April 1986, the worker's compensation case completely ended. By my own doings, I was left without a conventional job that I liked or any kind of steady income.

My old North Hollywood rented room was more than I could afford. The backyard camper I lived in was sold, leaving me without a place to rest my head. Emile and I agreed I could sleep on the floor of his computer room. That didn't work out; the dog's hair was getting into his equipment. I finally ended up with the Pie dog outside in Emile's one-stall garage. I still paid a small rent and needed to work off the cost by doing yard work and odd jobs. But it did give me access to the bathroom, refrigerator, and the AC in the house for the Duke. It was fair. Renting garage space to live in was a unique situation in the dream-chasing experience. I'm glad Sara, our good neighbor, was cooperative. She was an elderly woman who missed cooking and chatting with her deceased husband. We became friends, and she invited me for supper several times.

Garage life was a desperate option but very appealing. It was reminiscent of my mom's garage in New York, but one sixth the size. I morphed once again in my transient pilgrimage, this time into a small, overcrowded one fourth of a one-stall garage. Emile's dad had collected tools, and Emile had ham-radio transmitters in there as well. The building was not connected to the house and not used regularly; I loved it. With just one small door to pass through, I moved into the dark windowless building. Glad to get out of the fray of televisions and gossip and telephones, I sat in the shadows watching a spider cast its web. My best friend, Piper, loved it as well; we both found some peace and quiet. This was another gift, one of a million blessings in my life. That garage existence was placed on the list of my choices of how to live. My family's lake home, the Bar Harbor van ride and rented room, the camper-shell ride to Texas, the Garden Grove rented room, and now the garage were the least appealing to most people and the most engaging to me. Away from the herd of distractions and able to be mentally quiet was so very much the kind of stuff the Pie and I enjoyed. We were in an atmosphere of cheap, semi-comfortable stillness alone with time. I felt bad for Pie in the outside heat. It was cooler if we kept the door closed. Sitting outside under the night sky, I realized how much I had missed by being in the house. I saw more clearly why I valued my night walks with Pie. Looking up at the stars, I wondered if how I lived was by accident or by choice. I felt the night's comfort like I felt at sunset in the school fields of Garden Grove. The beauty of creation's star-filled sky brought peace.

It was in June's summer that Pie and I really missed the steady air-conditioning. Emile's renter objected to paying full rent for a two-bedroom house and having three people use it. Emile lowered his rent, and I needed to be outside more often. Outside in the San Fernando Valley, heat temperatures ranged daily from 85 or 95 to 102. However, that quiet setting changed when my collaborator needed a place to stay. Chance split from his wife and kid; she wanted a more traditional life without the long shots of dream chasing. She was in need of more than second place. His wife finally had enough of waiting for the big record deal and decided to move on. He seemed more upset about losing his garage for putting together a band, rehearsing songs, and songwriting. Their marriage's demise gave me a glimpse of what I would have perhaps lived through if I had gotten married. The force within me was a selfish force, like Chance's. His devotion to walk two paths didn't leave much room for him to practice life's alternatives in his twenty-nine years. In many ways, he had been sheltered from the ways of the world that add flavor from a variety of relationships balanced with solitary meditation. He kept himself naïve by being obsessed with songwriting and became very prolific in his work. It was because of his dedication to songwriting that I chose him as a collaborator. My dream was hooked to his. Unfortunately when he lost his garage space, that project got blown up temporarily. So I offered a small space in "my" garage. But first Emile had to be baited for this arrangement. He would have to again work it out with the renter.

Emile was very similar to his cat El Gato; both were shut inside the house before I got there. Emile got out occasionally, but his cat never did until I couldn't bear the cat's whining meows to get out. Like Emile, who learned to live a fuller life with some lessons that hurt, so lived El

Gato. The cat was cool, got along with Pie, fought with other cats, came home tired and hungry, and slept. When I talked with Emile about Chance moving into the garage, it was like watching El Gato stalking a bird. Emile got buzzed. It was the same buzz as when he first learned about my songwriting pursuits. It was the same as the look in his eyes when he saw Gina and realized what came with me if he let me rent a piece of his world. Of course, Emile would need to clean the garage, but having a rock-and-roll band hang out on his property was a big score. It had potential for nightclubs, women, parties, and more women. Emile said, "Yes, just temporarily," and Chance had to pay him some money.

Chance slept on a piece of wood like a bunk bed. I slept near Piper on the cooler floor, just off the cement. The only comfort we had was a phone line extension from the house. I was still working at two telemarketing jobs. Four years had passed, and I was both better and worse off than when I started. I sold the old red station wagon and bought a brown window van to perhaps travel in. I quit one of the phone jobs and was doing yard work in the neighborhood. Emile got me a job up near Mulholland Drive, where I worked on a fence for some Japanese people. Each day I looked across the quiet road at the house where Frank Zappa lived. Stuff like that would pop up to always keep the aura of Hollywood alive.

Chance was working in nightclubs making good money playing bass and singing in a top-forty band. At four or five o'clock in the morning, I could hear Piper's tail start banging against the door. Chance walked from the street down the driveway. He always started playing with the Pie. There was no more sleeping after that racket. The cool morning air was inviting and prompted talks with coffee about our project. His heart, like mine, wanted to selfishly keep the cool of the day to write. I worked in yards while he slept. Then one day he was tricked with a phone call; it woke him up telling him he had won a prize. He gave out the house address and went back to sleep. That night he got ready for work and found out his car had gotten repossessed. Money concerns got mixed up when he split with his wife and couldn't work it out. He lost any hope of keeping his nightclub job. He went from being a friend needing help to being my dependent. He began working with me cleaning yards and doing small odd jobs and house maintenance. We talked a lot more, and ideas were flowing like they hadn't done before. Once he was stranded, he began to deal with his divorce more seriously. His wife got a lawyer. Recognizing his need to provide for his son's well-being, Chance saw more clearly his need to become successful.

We were one bad break away from living in my van. We were stuck in a backyard with nothing to lose but dreams. In July, we figured out a bold plan to approach Emile with. With his permission, we would advertise in the *Drama-Logue* magazine. Our goal was to audition players and form a band to write and perform with. Chance could have tryouts and rehearsals in the garage. The goal was to play original songs in nightclubs and showcase our songs for the music industry. Emile could think of himself as a producer, or at least a quasi-financial backer. The thought of wine, women, and song would surely be more than enough incentive to put up with the people traffic and noise.

Chance was thrilled with his own morphing, thinking that he was going to start a real garage band. Conjuring up the image of his huge pool table surrounded with girls and him pouring drinks at his bar, Emile was hooked. To be a bigger part of any kind of entertainment gig was something he hoped for. I helped Emile rearrange a lot of his dad's old tools and the stuff he had collected in the garage to make room. The community right there in North Hollywood and areas surrounding it was riddled with industry personalities. When the actual process of finding band members was underway, Chance held tryouts and rehearsals in the garage and called the band Mischief.

Our neighbor Sara was a sweetheart and needed to know more. She only invited me for a meal never Emile. Eating her southern cooking, I'd tell her of all the news from next door. She liked the security of a man on the property and so near to call on if there was trouble. She and Emile got along great, and she said she'd be willing to let the band rehearse on a trial basis. Emile didn't know the other neighbors, but if the noise bothered them, we would find out.

✝

In August, my mom's arrival for a relative's wedding was something very good for us both. After the motor in the van blew up, I was driving a cheap $400 1966 GMC pickup, and we had a lot of fun rattling around in that old truck. I picked her up at her brother's house in Glendora. He had a beautiful sprawling corner estate that overlooked the golf course, and my mom loved it. We drove around slowly at first. I showed her typical neighborhoods, pointing out differences from the East. At my place, I showed her the garage and the band operation. She was so glad to see the Pie. The big dog loved my mom and was so happy to be with her again. It was good for our family of three. She was a bit put out that I was living in a garage again, but she knew my determination.

I drove her through Hollywood to see the landmark spots, and that was special. Like me, all she knew was from watching TV; unlike me, she loved the hustle and bustle. She was fifty-eight, in good shape, and wanted to walk on the famous sidewalk stars. Ma was both her worrisome self and funny in the crowd. She wanted to hold my hand so she wouldn't lose me. We drove south to Huntington Beach. With sun, sand, and water on our feet, we talked and watched waves roll in. A stranger took our picture. On the rebuilt pier, I told the story about the huge waves breaking it apart. In my favorite beachside café, we ate baklava. I showed her Newport and Laguna and went up to Malibu. She especially liked going through Malibu and returning through Topanga Canyon. Ma couldn't get over the cliffs' heights and the winding, narrow roads so close to the ocean. That evening we ate Mexican food and bought souvenirs at Olvera Street in downtown Los Angeles. Before heading back, I wanted her to see the Hollywood Hills. She was thrilled to drive up Laurel Canyon onto Mulholland Drive and pass by the big homes all lit up. High on Mulholland looking north into the San Fernando Valley, we saw millions of lights and lit streets. On the Los Angeles side down below looking toward Santa Monica, we saw miles and miles of lights and lit buildings. Down Laurel Canyon, we drove through Hollywood at night before returning from our tour. We got out at Grauman's Chinese Theater and walked about. Again, she was so impressed with the flow of people. I drove her to the wedding, and I talked with her daily on the phone before she left. Her loving concern for my safety strengthened my resolve to follow through with my plans. I missed her. I was glad she had fun and glad we took pictures.

✝

In mid-August, I finally got to know my other North Hollywood neighbor, the Big Guy. Piper would see his dog through the thorn branches of the overgrown lemon trees at Emil's fence. But the man always stood away at a distance. He looked like a short bowling pin, with a firm, large, round belly. His hair was short, and he wore creased work pants like my dad wore. They were permanent-press, wide-legged, with cuffs resting on his black work shoes.

One day the shy, quiet man was in a bit of turmoil, with the fire department standing at his front door. He was not taking care of his tall, dry, uncut front lawn, which had become an obvious fire hazard. Shortly after the fire department left, I knocked on the front door, and his big dog barked loudly and sounded very angry. Inside a man's voice spoke calmly to the dog, named Rex, quieting him. The door slowly opened about six inches, and a gray-haired man with a round face, still young-looking, stood inside. I introduced myself, offering my services to help clean up his yard. Monumental meetings like that seem to have popped up from time to time and helped me. My words and intentions were clear, but he stood in the door struggling within to force out a few words. I felt compassion immediately. His emotions seemed to be tagged onto the few words he stuttered, and then they all jumped out at once. "The the the ffffire dedepartmmment gave me a wwawarning." He was just able to get a few words out and looked at me with even bigger eyes, waiting for my reaction. I spoke up, calmly carrying the conversation. I explained that my concern was for his well-being and to help him avoid trouble with the city. I was a bit startled at his apparent dependence, and wondered if he were capable of living on his own. We agreed on a price for my time and labor. Turning away, I thought how fortunate he was to have a friend like his big dog at his side.

I earned a few dollars, as well as helped him maintain his property by meeting the deadline he was given. It turned out to be where I believed I had to be and where I wanted to be at the same time. It may have been a great gift from God. I believe that house right next door was where God's intensions placed me. A few years later, I would find out that God is in control of all things and there are no accidents.

Prior to that day, the man never said two words to me. I saw him come and go over several months, and we had several sightings of each other. He shuffled in and out of his house quickly and never lingered out front. As I began the yard cleanup, I got to know the guy more and his dog Rex, a big German shepherd. We slowly became friends at his front door. He watched me work, moving from window to window and pushing a corner of the curtain to the side. Shortly after our acquaintance, Rex died. It had been just the two of them. I expanded my work to include the pruning of his overgrown shrubs in the front and back yards. The fenced-in backyard and long stone wall made it easy for the Pie and me to be together with him as we worked. He loved to sit in a lawn chair outside and watch and pet the Pie and tell him he was a good boy. I'd never seen him outside so much; maybe he now felt secure. My dog and I began to fill the void in his lonely life.

The Big Guy was about forty-seven or so from what I could tell. He definitely had some kind of speech impediment and trouble expressing his feelings. I felt embarrassed for him and found myself being very patient with him. Judging from the way the place looked; he had been ignored by his family and left on his own. He seemed to be a kind and gentle person, quietly coming and going to work. But he was more than met the eye. He showed himself to be a genuinely great person. I did not have any experience with people who had disabilities or mental challenges up until then except me. I knew how I lived and struggled for thirty years not knowing I had dyslexia. And I knew how good I felt when I was able to help myself.

One day he walked up to where I was working in the back, sweating, hacking down his overgrown vines. He just stood there. I knew he liked to watch, so I kept working. When I stood up for a breather, I saw the Jewish yarmulke. He came out wearing a beanie on his head! Quietly he stood there. I took a few deep breaths and said, "You're Jewish." He said, "Yep, bbbboth my parents were Jewish; they drove to California from BBBBrooklyn." I told him that Emile was Jewish, but he already knew that. I told him I wasn't much of anything and that I stopped going to Catholic Church when I was a kid. I pointed to the synagogue on the corner and asked if he went there. He said, "Sometimes."

Our friendship began to blossom quickly, which I believe with all my heart was a true gift of the Lord. In September, I talked with the Big Guy on a daily basis. He liked the nickname I gave to Chance, so I tagged him with the Big Guy. He liked it, but preferred to be called Big Guy. He was a little overweight. You might say he didn't exercise a lot. Or you might notice that he liked to eat. But with his subtle sense of humor, he gave as well as he took. He didn't say much at first, but at times, what he said was weighty. It wasn't as if he just stood and watched; it was as if he had X-ray vision. His comments would often stop my thoughts abruptly. I needed to do a double take.

I sat in his chair drinking a beer resting my wrist on another hot day when I was cleaning his jungle of a backyard. Big Guy came out of his house cool as a cucumber wearing his long pants; he never wore shorts. We said our acknowledgements, and I stared at the mound of work ahead of me. I expressed my concern for not taking the state job. I would have been working in an air-conditioned factory carrying a micrometer, I told him. He chuckled and said, "You ssshould have taken it." I mentioned that I hated the idea of working in the same place for thirty years. He said, "You get used to it." I knew he worked in a factory but not what he did exactly, so I asked him. He said, "Work with a micrometer." On several occasions, Chance and I found it hard to believe him, because we could never verify his claim. What he actually did with a micrometer wasn't clear. But on far more occasions, he was never mistaken so it seemed. I told him he was way ahead of me and asked how long he worked there. "Over twenty years," he said. I believed him. Then he said softly, "I wish I traveled with Rex like you did with

Piper. Time flies." I rewound the last few sentences, as I often did in situations with him, and paused to reassess them. His comments would then shine, as I could then see them as not just adequate, but profound. The still waters of his quiet demeanor ran deep. He was a good listener, like my aunts.

Chance got to know him better as we were both pruning trees and regularly cutting and watering his grass. I was able to help him fix his old Ford Granada and tend to many tasks at first and then just a few neglected house-maintenance things. The inside of his house was like walking through years of time. Everything was the way it was when his parents decorated it fifty years earlier. They died some time back; his mom was real sick, and he still had the hospital bed in one room. Big Guy not only liked to watch; he would pitch in and interact with us. He loved hearing us speak of the music project and live out our ambition. He took Chance and me and Pie by total surprise when he suggested we clean out his garage. When it was all cleaned out, out of nowhere, he offered it to us—to move into his two-stall garage. His garage space was four times larger and completely empty, and the building stood forty feet from his back door. The Pie, Chance, and I mushroomed slowly from one property to the next.

✝

THE GARAGE

The Garage is a haven, without strife,
The day's remote serenity to ponder the love of life.

The Garage is out back.
The mirage is a shack,
Far away from knickknacks,
No driveway or Cadillacs.

The inside is all black; the doorway has a crack.

The Garage, to lose track,
I move in my backpack,
No things to unpack.
It gives me what I lack.

The inside is all black; the doorway has a crack.

The Garage is a haven, without strife,
The night's habitat of gladness to ponder the love of life.

———————————————— † ————————————————

There was an old frail wooden gate between the properties smothered by
thorny lemon-tree branches. Millions of ants covered the brittle twigs
holding the sweet-smelling but rotting fruit. Emile allowed us to prune
through the overgrown, spiky barbs. We opened a never-used pathway
and had access to join both estates. Once Big Guy's garage was cleared
of crap, we arrived at the ground floor and launched Mischief, our
unique band project.

I began to insulate very heavily the floors, walls, and ceiling. Next
were the rugs, to hang on the walls and smother the cement floor.
Finding the right rugs that were good and clean enough was a bit
like being a prospector of a different sort. It was in the streets on the
sidewalks in front of new or remodeled apartment houses that we found
the best rugs and stuff. Those scavenger hunts were the first times we
went hunting on garbage night. Our best finds were the torn-up carpet
lying on the sidewalks outside refurbished condos. My truck sat in the
street as we unrolled the leftovers to be sure it was good stuff. Clean
and new Berber rug was rolled up and thrown in as we drove around
to dumpsters behind rug outlets. We felt like bandits robbing the rich
as Chance and I went dumpster-diving, passing our finds to Big Guy.
As we spread out our spontaneous original band, songwriting, and
production house, we grew in expectations.

When we needed a piece of furniture or this or that to supply
our needs, we joined the street searchers. Trash nights are like a free

garage sale for poor people and those who seek treasure. The new headquarters was more than enough space for us to live in, and it was rent-free. Our plywood bunk beds and leftover home furnishings gave our command center the look of a home office—a look you might find in a post-nuclear blast futuristic film. Chance's handpicked band, members of Mischief, began their rehearsals stomping about in the large center area. The four walls quickly became stuffed with stuff— broken guitar strings, drumsticks, cracked maracas, old cymbals, and microphones.

Big Guy, Chance, and I shopped at both the Salvation Army and Goodwill stores on Laurel Canyon Boulevard and in Van Nuys. Those indoor locations were another source of mining for gold. I found excellent Beverly Hills tailor-made sport coats for five bucks. We shopped at the Farmers Market in Los Angeles and bought in bulk to save more money. That new nerve center for our assault on the music industry became a more intense situation as time went on. Because of the value that comes from helping each other, we three shared a bond of friendship. Work for money and work for dreams was done in and out of Big Guy's house. We treated his property with respect and helped one another. Chance and I helped Big Guy by being examples and showing him how to maneuver more efficiently with the matters of life on a daily basis.

Big Guy was no longer alone; he made friends. We were a family related by our needs. The new improved garage life gave us not only larger living quarters, but also a writer's quiet secret workshop and rehearsal studio. Best of all, it was cheap, with just the shared utilities. We checked into renting a rehearsal space in some warehouses where other bands were going. We found that they were charged like $250.00 a night. I suppose the best—and I mean the very best—thing that could have happened was that Big Guy picked up three trusting friends, including Piper. Likewise, we three found a friend, benefactor, and brother. He helped all he could and loved to take care of Pie when we played in clubs. From that point onward, our project had a home base, with lots of amenities that were beyond our financial and practical means. Our friendships were developed, and we built a belief and hope for growing success among us. Once again, the hand of providence led the way in our expansion and then continued to shape our path.

Big Guy lived in the three-bedroom house, which was quite beautiful at one time, but decades of neglect had taken their toll. His living room was piled high, floor to ceiling on every wall, with old newspapers. Chance, Melissa, and I began to evacuate the clutter, with Big Guy joining in. It was sad to digest the fact that his own blood relatives could just leave him totally on his own. After the cleanup, we hung up newer, leftover Goodwill curtains. The place looked pretty good. Once again, Big Guy saw we needed help and invited us to share the house. With his joyful approval, we morphed, migrated, and slowly moved into part of his house in the back. Chance kept bunking in the garage, and I had a back bedroom with a private entrance and bathroom. Soon we had the complete run of the house.

The TV's glow flickered against the curtains in the front yard. Standing on the porch, I heard Big Guy snoring. A commercial selling a paint job for cars was booming. I looked west at the orange sunset with confidence that came from standing on the other side of adversity. Another rung on the ladder toward success had been climbed. The Pie and I returned to the backyard down the driveway and through the large swinging plywood gate. Some band members were carting in their equipment and smoked outside the garage door. Again we shared the story of the great gift of space to rehearse with band members. "Unbelievable" was the repeated comment. In the dark, I sat listening to the muffled sounds of drums and guitars warming up, check, check, 1, 2, then silence. Pie lay stretched out on the cool concrete of the patio. I lifted a beer bottle to my lips and sipped. The fading, dark blue sky held wisps of darker orange before stars appeared. The drum sticks click, click, click, click, *pow,* the first song began playing. and then Chance's voice rang out singing my lyrics. Like a Fourth of July fireworks explosion, my pride swelled as I sat there laughing before I began pacing. I sang my lyrics softly to myself, and played the air guitar walking around the yard grinning.

———————— ✝ ————————

Opening my eyes the next morning, bright sunshine and birds chirping filled my senses. Lying in an old, single-size hospital bed, I woke to more good fortune all around me. Hardwood floors and vintage wood planks stained dark circled the walls. I stepped out of my room onto the patio and sat under the avocado tree. The size of the houses unused rooms plus the big double-wide yard with the recessed garage was a slice of heaven. The garage saved us thousands of dollars in rehearsal rental space and travel time. Chance came out of the garage, and we sat in disbelief. We concurred that we were living in a miracle of some sort, and we planned to make the most of it while we could.

Big Guy was very fond of watching TV in his front room. He instinctively loved answering the phone and opening the front door for friends and band members coming and going. He was the watchman, the usher, and everybody's friend. His stuttering and fear of others was overcome with interaction. He was quiet, yet comical. To celebrate our hard work and smooth transition rehearsing in our new studio put together with unwanted material, we ate at Denny's Restaurant. Big Guy really found his stride when he gave the waitress all three of our meal orders. He read the menu like a TV character, a high roller, a millionaire full of prestige and dignity. It was awesome to see him in action. Like a family, we sat there waiting for our food, smiling as life blessed us, toasting with our raised orange juice glasses.

After answering the house phone, Big Guy delivered messages to the garage with delight. He trekked back and forth and loved to stand around with the guys talking up the music business. When the band and groupie chicks showed up unscheduled, the atmosphere in his living room filled with chatter taking on the tone of cherished chaos. But not Big Guy—he was as steady as a rock. He printed a list of names and slowly walked it out to the quiet garage. Through the door, he made his casual Alfred Hitchcock entrance. As always, he first said, "Hey, Buddy." Chance and I were both called Buddy. Then he announced in his best butler's voice the names of the group in waiting. His subtle, unassuming manner never let on to the hysteria in the house. We looked at him and asked if all those people were in the front room. Big Guy stood thinking. Then all at once, he said. "Yeah, they kept knocking on the door."

On one occasion, the message from the front room for Chance was awkward to say the least. Like a snickering schoolboy, Big Guy announced the names of two young ladies who were waiting to see Chance in the living room. The three of us looked stunned before I laughed hilariously. Big Guy started cackling, laughing hard, and his jelly belly bouncing. Chance led the way. I was jumping up and down exaggerating the situation, drooling to see a catfight. Our messenger followed quickly, moving faster than ever before. Chance went around the kitchen corner, and I held back in case something was thrown. Chance spoke in a happy voice of surprise but said little. The tenseness was already worked out by the girls.

I recognized Janine's voice and came out to say hi. The other girl, with the looks of a runway model, was very pleasant, but left after giving Chance her new number. I toyed with the soft-spoken Janine, pointing out that her quaint smile and earthy brown hair were far more attractive than glitzy gaudiness. She just looked up with her beautiful smile and said, "When you got it, you got it." I liked her; she would have been good for Chance, had she stayed. She reminded me of a girl back East named Punky, who was a friend. I heard she married a guy with a helicopter near a snowy mountain who gave rides to the top for people with skis. That picture in my mind was always fun to imagine.

The property was more than a space of creative freedom; it was where lives were lived within the richness and rewards of unity. Big Guy was a big guy, and he came with a big heart. He was kind and concerned about helping others, and he liked gadgets. Big Guy surprised everybody one day when he came home with a set of intercoms. He loved to call us from the house to announce who came by or to tell us the world news, with a few of his own thoughts that would help our project or the world. He was the best—one in a million.

<hr />

✝

I continued evolving as a writer and became a booking agent also. It was a new experience, and not a pleasurable one at that. Phoning nightclubs trying to book a new band called Mischief wasn't easy; in fact, it was impossible. We had no track record to offer club managers, so they couldn't count on selling drinks and making money. Some clubs wanted money up front for ticket sales. At one Hollywood club, the Whiskey A Go Go, we found how hard it was to play in a pay-to-play town. We were poor, but with help from musicians, groupies, and friends, we did it. Four hundred dollars were coughed up just for a chance to play in that bigger club on Hollywood Boulevard. We advertised with flyers, but had only a handful of friends to invite.

Loading my truck with equipment was like fueling a jet that would soar high. Driving through the shiny night traffic of Tinseltown, we taxied to the runway of excitement. Pulling into the dark parking lot of the club and hauling in the equipment began a slow rumbling thunder within my expectations. Hearing the first amplifier spark kicked off more anticipation; when the guitar was plugged in, electricity surged with a pop. The bass guitar and drum set boomed. Walking in the small rooms backstage, then to the side, and then at the bar, I felt the countdown as the tune-up stopped. Chance's brief hello to a near-empty house sounded loud and hollow. Still, the escalating rapture of live music from Mischief playing in Hollywood brought ecstasy. What a buzz it was for me to hear my lyrics being sung on Hollywood Boulevard. I was a step closer on a path that was really just a one-way street I walked for ten years.

✝

WHEN GOD CALLS YOU

Be a superstar, shooting fast and far,
    Driving wherever it takes,

'Cause curves in the road lighten up your load
    as you learn from your mistakes.

It's a one-way street with only one seat,
    dreams shine a light to see.

On a course straight to hell, there's a higher parallel:
    When God Calls You, you'll be free.
    When God Calls You, you'll be free.

Can you hear? Can you see? When God Calls You, you'll be free.
Can you hear? Can you see? When God Calls You, you'll be free.

—————————————— † ——————————————

The Whisky A Go Go was nearly empty mid-week. Janine and her few friends sat faithfully. It was comically embarrassing hearing them clap. The fact that we had to come up with a sum of money for presale tickets was good for the club. We got burned and figured other bands did as well. It was the wrong club to launch a new band. We had no following or money to back our straight-ahead rock-and-roll band. At that time, punk rock was the in sound. After the Whiskey showcase bombed with nobody and no fizzle, the band paused and learned. We lost a little pride at that chance to be publicly popular. Smaller nightclubs were found at the beaches and in the valley, and that's where we played. However, we did learn more clearly the power of the demo packages we had been sending out. The industry wasn't looking; they were listening. On one occasion at the Troubadour on Santa Monica Boulevard, a dozen listeners came off the street to hear our songs. The group stayed because they could sit with their drinks and talk. In smaller clubs, I sat alone, surrounded by dozens of empty tables and chairs before a few locals strolled in. A few times, it was just me and the bartender.

—————————————— † ——————————————

In November, the furnace broke, and there was no big cash to fix it. We froze in the thirty-degree cold desert nights. We all got electric blankets and two for Big Guy so he would stay warm for sure. The days were fifteen degrees warmer but often rainy. In December, Chance and I took a catering job to make a few hundred bucks apiece. It was a huge event to honor Lou Wasserman, the head of a TV studio. It was his birthday party, and superstars met to celebrate his accomplishments. Hundreds of famous people joined together in an enormous film studio. I saw Lucille Ball, Jimmy Stewart, Henry Kissinger, and on and on. I was starstruck seeing so many well-known celebrities eating, drinking, and laughing away the time.

December brought a holiday newsletter from my mom and a card from my brother. Ma's care package brought her homemade cookies and bread. Twice a year, I got cards from my brother—birthday and Christmas. When and if we talked on the phone, we still didn't have much at all in common. He told me of his family, house and his career and I spoke of fellow artists, living in a garage and hearing my songs played in clubs. Each of us spoke with enthusiasm. Our lives were on two different paths. Without sharing things of interest, all we had to share was our childhood, our blood, our name, and our love. No one was at fault; there was no wrong; we were just different people. I sent Ma several letters through the years. I knew she would enjoy them as she sat alone in the evening.

Right at that time, Melissa needed help. She didn't want to stay at her grandma's and wouldn't elaborate on why. She was a nut about having her own space, so I let her move into my room temporarily. I was living in the garage hanging on by threads in the freezing cold with no heat. But I liked the quiet without the TV and the part-time solitude; so did the Pie. Chance found some day work helping his dad, a contractor who also drifted out from Wisconsin.

On Christmas Day, Pie dog and I went to the windy Malibu beach to watch the big waves roll in. Returning at sunset, we walked two blocks to North Hollywood High School. We took cookies to eat like we did last year. Those were lonely yet happy times for us to be together in solitude. Empty bleachers at the football field would have still been empty to us, even if they were full of people. We were different; we just didn't fit in with most people. Alone in the stadium and yet not alone, we sat together on a small rug I brought. We looked out over so much grass, thanking God for the peace and quiet. We talked to God and thanked Him for Ma, and I wondered out loud how it would all end. The Pie loved to hear my voice; he always did. He looked up and raised his paw once, twice, until I leaned over to hug him saying, "He's my boy, the good Pie."

✝

January 1987 we assembled our promo kits in the garage. Chance was working steadily with one guitar player named John. Whether it was the band's name or the songs or whatever, there was still no record deal. Chance and I quietly discussed our writing songs and the band Mischief. Chance and John wanted to change the name and try for a new sound. I didn't care; the music end of the business wasn't my expertise. They came up with the new band name of Tom Sawyer. Chance and I didn't change a thing; we still wrote our lyrics. As long as product was being churned out, we were in the arena fighting to be noticed.

The forty feet from the house seemed at times to be miles away. It was like camping out or a kind of running away. We were like Tom Sawyer and Huckleberry Finn adventuring after hidden treasure. The music industry was like a mysterious river of ever-changing opportunity. Working hard for no pay was our theme in life as we struggled along the waterway of expectations.

We prepared several dozen promo packages with new photos of Chance and John on the front. A new edge to the sounds of the music went out to the music industry on a regular basis at substantial cost. Handmade, hand-delivered, and we lived hand to mouth. Every sign on every street we drove in that Hollywood town all had the same name: Pay to Play. We needed something new and bigger, and we needed a breakthrough; we needed the touch of money or an open door. I always kept hope alive for my Aunt Lucy's producer friend to make contact or open a door of opportunity. I left phone messages with her agency but didn't hear from her. Success may not always be in who you know or to whom you may be related. It's a mystery.

✝

These were rapid times, times when anything was possible, times when clear thinking became cloudy. After Melissa left her daughter Kiya at Grandma's and moved in the house temporarily, she stayed. Big Guy and she got along in a special way, like he was her brother. So he let her live in the small bedroom next to mine. She became our first renter, and I got my room back. She was supposed to help the band project save money and cut costs by helping pay the shared house bills. She brought Gypsy, her dog, and Peg, her three-legged cat. And she brought her baggage—the good, the bad, and the ugly. We knew and saw the good; the rest was yet to be unpacked.

The three-song demos and a list of our upcoming club dates did what they were supposed to, and my follow-up phone calls created some interest from the music industry. I spoke with Mike Curb of MCA Records, Anita Bennet of Platinum Records, and Tom Wally of RCA Records. The best was Herb Cohen, a top personal manager. One of his producers called and spoke with Chance about how Chance was producing the music on a sixteen-track mixer. Getting that level of interest was a shot in the arm.

The players we were using in the clubs were excited to hear the news. Shortly after we broke the ice on that trail of industry names, it went cold. The one phrase that lingered in my thoughts was from a year earlier, my lyric start called "Almost Is Addicting." The idea of the "slow no" came from my follow-up phone calls to the A&R (Artist and Repertoire) people. Their slow no was the drug that always wanted more. They'd say, "The material was good, but not what I'm looking for; send me some more." I and thousands of other artists of one type or another were getting the life sucked out of us from the slow no.

My telemarketing jobs weren't enough for us to make ends meet. Chance found a job in a prop manufacturing factory. He fit in like a hand in a glove. The people there were artsy, and some were excellent painters. The creative minds seemed to stimulate Chance's. After a few weeks, he came home and announced he was going to change the band's name—again—and the playlist and he wanted to push out a different promo kit. It was as if by changing the name and the songs, he would find the trick to gain industry attention. But it was obviously too soon to effect such drastic measures, and he backed off. Instead, he was looking for a new image to express himself with new gimmicks. He brought home used props from the dumpster to use on stage and bought costumes at the Salvation Army.

After playing several clubs and establishing our reliability, setting dates for our original songs to be played in public became a thrilling dream come true for me. Playing nightclubs to get public exposure was our goal—as well as showcasing our songs to the industry if they came to hear and see Chance's live singing talent. Just for fun, Chance dressed like Charlie Chaplin once and placed small cardboard people and painted objects near the instruments while the band played. He danced and moved about in his act while singing. It was difficult to say whether his inconsistencies were helping or hurting. It was hard to pin down what elements of the lyric writing or the sounds of music or marketing were good or bad. It was part of the mystery of success. Because we were nobody, most places had but a few patrons and always a bartender. On the other hand, other clubs on Hollywood Boulevard were packed with people. Hollywood nightclubs and all that jazz were both exciting and nowhere at the same time. Very reminiscent of the New York band with the bar scenes, they were just more bars and babes to hang onto.

Bars don't look alike, but the content is all the same; they are just hangouts hanging on. We played at a bar on Hollywood Boulevard called the Central. We had a lot of fun with a young movie actress named Olivia, who sang on stage with Chance. The bar was popular and full of people, but no one cared about anybody's music as long as it was loud. After that and a dozen gigs or so, the thrill wasn't the same, and yet it was still a thrill. Every positive adventure was another joint and a beer. I moved forward through my gauntlet of goals with my little steps of painkiller. We were still shopping promo packages to the music industry and waiting for a break. The idea for Aunt Lucy's producer friend to somehow make contact was fading.

Out of nowhere, I got a call while sitting at my desk in the house one day from Anita Bennet of Platinum Records. Our current promo kit did reach her desk, and we talked about the many solicitations our band project was making to the industry. Her interest grew past the phone call, and she invited us to meet with her in her office. The hopeful shaft of light put me in a spin of enchantment. News like that burned in my mouth as I told Chance and Big Guy. I called back and we set a date to meet. The day came, and Chance and I sat in her office down in some old building near the railroad tracks in an industrial part of Hollywood. The meeting was short. I think she wanted to see Chance and have more understanding of what he was about on stage. We left without as much thrill as we went in with. Anything was possible, though, and we saw how the packages and phone calls were working.

The air was leaking out of the balloon holding up my dream. Nights were near freezing—several were at thirty-eight degrees—and days were only nice in the sunshine. The day's sun was a gift to take in, like a lizard on a rock warms itself. The group of us sat outside like sun worshipers receiving warmth. A picture of homeless people came to mind. They also faced the warm sun; I'd see their weary faces when I stopped at red lights.

Chance was working on new material in the February cold spell. The garage never warmed up. The old house wasn't holding the heat well, so I was warming up with some brandy. I got too fired up and ran across the front lawn of Emile's house and fractured my ankle in a hole he didn't fill. After he took me to the ER, I was on crutches.

I started thinking a lot about traveling like I did when I got the window van. I was no longer working at telemarketing; there was only so much of that I could tolerate before I quit. Sitting in narrow cubicles reciting a script was over for now. Those jobs were a dime a dozen. I was good at talking people into making appointments for home security systems or donating money for baby heart transplants. I was again considering leaving town and giving myself deadlines that didn't exist. I was hooked again then and there on the idea of staying; Hollywood was a one-time town of chance. The beauty and the mess of it all was what I created. Sticking it out here gave me ideas about other options.

At this time, I begin dabbling with script writing and forms of dialogue on the pages of my diary. Recording life's events was becoming more surreal. Aunt Jean always came through with sending me my only notes of encouragement. She would enclose five dollars for a beer, sometimes seven. More importantly, her valuable letter spoke specifically about sticking with it. I kept all her letters. Also at this time, I again started my seven-day fast. The fast was always a place to go to and get a rest from the normal craziness of what had become the treadmill of art. A lifestyle of long shots and no safety net became more of a way to exist. I lived a gambler's life, gambling time and energy. I used to tell Ma that on the phone, tell her of exciting times followed by waiting. But like my brother she was removed from sharing my goals. It's so hard to infuse a dream into someone who has your best interests at heart. Traditional happy was long gone.

One evening Herb Cohen came to our garage with his producer, to hear and see the band. After three years of knocking our heads against the mountain of establishment, a few rocks of opportunity fell off. Herb Cohen was known for his huge success with Frank Zappa, Tom Waits, Shawn Duke, Alice Copper, Linda Ronstadt, and many more. This was the biggest breakthrough so far as having the band looked at for a contract. His music producer wanted Chance to narrow down his writing and stick with one style. This time again, Chance said no. That was his second refusal, twice the music industry opened the door for him to play ball with them. We were getting the attention that we deserved and needed. True, there were many pokers in the fire. Chance's call to wait for a record deal was made again. Only time would tell if opportunity would allow us a third chance. Times were exciting with potential, and the thrills made our hopes alive with anticipation. Living hope was there for us to laugh with.

After four very cold desert months, spring rolled in, and change rolled around like a wheel bringing the peddler's wagon of unseen things. We were living in electrifying times; it felt as if something good or even great was going to happen at last. It was also no time to be making stupid mistakes by continuing to turn a blind eye away from what Melissa was doing. Weeks earlier, I could see she fell into her old heroin habit. All of our best talks of love and encouragement had reached a point of giving her an ultimatum. I had lived through one SWAT raid; I couldn't handle another. There were no bitter feelings. She had missed the mark and was told to move out of the house. She went back to her grandma's place. I still tried to see her a lot, but she went into the wind. She was gone, living her old life again somewhere—no one knew where. Grandma, Kiya, and I waited. Sometimes Pie and I played with Gypsy and Peg.

✝

Our backyard stone wall on Burbank Boulevard near the 170 Freeway kept the world out. But it was in question. It secluded our garage life, which may have been against code with the band project. The forty-foot-long bulwark staved off the street people, rush-hour traffic, and the eyes and noises of Los Angeles. The barrier stood like an infantry line ordered to stand at all cost against the enemy. But there were rumors of easement rights, public domain, and the coming city sidewalk. The potential for the wall's destruction caused more thinking.

I started a garden in the large sunny backyard between the orange tree and that stone wall. I connected a PVC tubing system to water lots of vegetables and sunflower plants. There was not a lot of repetitive motion to agitate the pain in my wrist, but I wore a brace. I loved that hard work with my hands and focusing my eyes and mind on something very different. By using my time differently I was also under-the-sun growing in creative thinking.

Lounging on a reclaimed plastic backyard sofa was also something new to do. I began reading some of Dylan Thomas's writings. Writing free verse, thoughts emerged. I found his rambling to be very refreshing, taking me out of structure. I recalled Mr. Inside and Mr. Outside, the theory Jack talked about. He'd say, "Go do something you don't normally do and watch your creativity flow." It did. Jack was always right. The rumor of the wall's demolition brought me outside more often. I sat closer to it, enjoying it while I could. I watched myself sitting there in my mind's eye. I liked it. I began thinking of how to replace the wall and stop the public from looking into our opened yard.

Chapter 14: Chance Went to Church

Around mid-April of 1987, Chance decided to go to church. He did this for a few Sundays in a row. It started with a mistaken motive. First, John the guitar player gave him his old Ford Fairlane to drive. Then Chance began doing his top-forty nightclub gigs again. That's where he met other musicians looking for a link to the music industry. They enlightened him to the music connections available at the charismatic churches. The first time he came back from church, I found myself talking with him about God. We sat underneath the avocado tree with Big Guy, who brought out his three-inch-thick Old Testament. We all piped up about what little we knew. I showed the guys my little thin two-inch-square Bible. Other than that, God was a completely undiscovered area in any of our lives. Talk of God got all our attention, with lots of questions and no answers. The topic of God was exciting, like finding a new restaurant but you don't know what to order because you don't know the food. Still, it sounded good and it looked like a good idea; we just needed answers.

By May, we got another renter; he was an electrician, and his mom came with him. A shortage of money forced them out of their apartment. While renting Melissa's old room and saving for another place, they both worked hard. They turned out to be okay people. From that point on, we always tried to keep that room rented.

The big Pie dog was limping on occasion. He may have had arthritis, but he still wanted to go for walks and we did. He was thirteen years old. It was a kind of bittersweet time for him and me. We both wanted to sit in the woods and relax by some water. But he was getting older faster than me, and I couldn't make things happen fast enough for us to break out of Los Angeles. He was sleeping a lot, but always kept an eye on me.

There were lots of fun times when the band would come over and everybody was pulling together. I set up a badminton court on the huge concrete patio behind the house. There was occasional talk about who knew who and where Chance went to church, God, and the Bible. A tall, thin composer friend of Chance's, named John, seemed more fired up about Jesus. I had no idea what he was talking about, but I saw his fervor. The keyboard player and new bass player were in contention about the Bible's authenticity. Out of nowhere came such strong feelings of expressions about sin and its consequences and death and hell and heaven.

At thirty-four, I heard grown adults talk about God for the first time. I witnessed how strangers changed their temperament instantly, as if they were in a car accident defending their right of way. I made a note in the diary that my conscience was a little louder. I knew parts of my life were illegal when it came to drug use, and really I just smoked pot with an occasional pill or line here and there. The drinking along with the women, romance, and fun—they weren't illegal. In fact, I always had what other guys wished for when it came to babes. Nobody could ever figure out how a poor guy like me had great-looking women. The women, drugs, and booze—they were just some of my stuff.

The following Sunday, when Chance came back from church, he brought new information that he shared with us as we sat under the avocado tree. Talks about infinity and how big God was and the Bible being written by God caused more questions. We had no answers to our questions about big and small sins. Big Guy, Chance, and I went next door to ask Emile about the Old and New Testaments. He only knew about the Old and suggested that the people at church would know about Jesus and the New. I realized that seeing Jesus on the cross at the Catholic Church was all I had retained from my youth.

Next I asked Gerry. He was Emile's new roommate, a transplant from Queens, New York. He was another Jewish guy, about forty, who told good basketball stories about playing in the streets. He seemed to think Jesus was a troublemaker. The Gospel message or Savior from sins was false if it meant Jesus was the Messiah. Emile and Gerry were still waiting for the Messiah. I had never heard of the gospel message of Jesus. If the priests in church talked about it when I was a kid, I never heard it. Ma and Pa never said anything about it, and we never owned a Bible. The following week I asked the band members about the Bible. They talked about the requirements in the Bible on how to live a life that would please God. I cut down on my so-called bad habits a little, but that was short-lived.

By the end of May, I began a job as a waiter in Toluca Lake near Melissa's grandmas. I'd stop at Grandma's house once a week and ask about Melissa. She said Melissa called asking if Kiya were okay and that was all. My truck was broke, so I rode a bicycle to work, which was too much on my sciatica. I had to quit. I took hot baths and rested a lot flat on my back with pillows under my knees. Again I lay thinking in the cool dark garage about my journey through time. I lay on the floor on the thick layers of used carpet next to the Pie. He stretched his long legs, allowing his claws to scrape the rug for a better stretch with a big breath in. He let it out as I rubbed his chest and hugged him. He was getting older faster. Melissa showed up at the end of the month back from her heroin relapse. She needed to be quiet and lay low in Grandma's bungalow with Kiya, Gypsy, and Peg.

June brought more engaging talks with Janine and one of her friends about God and Jesus and now the Holy Spirit. These girls were ten or twelve years younger than me. I was impressed with the amount of interest other people had about God. When I spoke to

Gina on the phone, she started talking about when she read the Bible. She felt guilty about leaving it behind, but still clung to the idea that she could get back to reading it. For a few months in the diaries, a kind of continual but sporadic spiritual introduction about God's Bible appeared. The idea of heaven and hell and death started to roll around in my head. Seeing the Pie walk about slower and sleep more was not pleasant to watch. I began asking the diary what was next, either with or without a record deal. What about options? What would I do with Pie?

In July, Chance decided to change the name of the band to the Fables, and we kept marketing new material—the same rock-and-roll genre with one more attempt. I had continuing sciatica problems throughout July, but we still delivered promo packages to the music industry. Big Guy drove us to big buildings where the potential for lots of money was to be found. Our music project needed any and all attention from record labels, producers, and managers. August was a warm month for the vegetable garden to grow and for barbecues and badminton games and for Big Guy to wear his short pants playing.

The band was rehearsing in the garage one afternoon. I was sitting at my desk smoking a cigar, looking out the many windows. Sipping on a beer, I lit a joint and gazed into the back yard. I was so completely relaxed, with my feet up listening to my lyrics being sung in rehearsal. I always found that so satisfying. The phone rang, and I said hello to Mike Curb of MCA Records. He wanted to talk about a song Chance wrote. It was a ballad, and he needed it "now" for a movie. Chance's song was to replace another song that wasn't working out in the film. He said the deal had to happen fast because the movie was in its final stages. I stopped the rehearsal and told Chance to take the phone call.

Outside the sun shone bright against the big overhead garage door. Through the smaller door came the squinty-eyed band. The drummer, bassist, and guitar player stood with me facing the warm sun. I told them the exciting news about the ballad, about who called, and about our golden opportunity. The four of us waited years for this moment to arrive. Each of us had our own story of struggle and dream. At last, to become professionals and leave the arena of amateurs! Pacing, standing, looking, smiling, we could scarcely take in the news. My agitation bubbled within, replaying Mike Curb's words. All of our eyes kept searching the ground with cautious anticipation.

We looked at Chance coming from the house as if he were a doctor from surgery approaching family members with hopeful eyes. His casual low-key manner stunned us. "How'd it go?" I said. Joylessly disconnected, he explained he did not want to be known as a ballad writer. Collectively we said, "Why not?" The tone of the hungry pack shifted. We four needed more; we wanted a meaty reason, not a wimpy excuse. Our suspended craving ambition listened for more. Chance's only explanation was that he wanted it all. He was still holding out for a big new-artist deal. It was his song, no apology, no regret. He stood there like Peter Pan refusing to grow up. However, we were not the lost boys. This was his third refusal to grow up.

I got more upset than I'd ever gotten. The weight of time and his negative response were the straw that broke this camel's back. My journey of patience ran out. Enough time had gone by with enough opportunities over four years. Part of me could understand his rejection because of the other pokers in the fire from the other major labels and their interest. But this one song was a sure thing with MCA Records. Clearly this was an opportunity for us to be counted with him as worthy talent. Earning a step up from working with him as amateurs to professionals was the goal for all of us. It was more than I could bear, and the guys in the band saw his blunder as well. Soon after that, the band walked out.

He and I had a serious talk about life and times. Earning money for our project lessened for me and began to increase for him. It was his time to keep playing top forty on a steady basis and earn some bigger money. Time became more balanced. More free time for me, less for him. It was the beginning of the end of our collaboration. It was a big hurdle to jump over.

September was the month that I flew solo with my creativity. I was no quitter in what I loved to do. I thought that changing any of it would be like changing horses in midstream. So Chance and I still worked on writing. However, promoting and distributing new material was done at a slower pace. I needed to go about achieving my goal differently and make the most of my time in California. Since I was gambling with the time in my life, I placed new bets on new games. I enrolled in the Hollywood Script Writing Institute, and at the same time I enrolled in Los Angeles Valley College, where Camille Bouchard taught the intermediate acting course. My working days as telemarketer to pay for music promotion packages were over. Chance's income paid the bills at the house like I used to. Time allowed me to pursue acting. I would search for collaborators. And maybe in the acting circles, I might connect with Aunt Lucy's friend, the movie producer. The distant-relative idea was always a hope. Long shots are always a possibility, but they seemed to prefer staying at a distance. I found out that the acting and the writing courses were too new and too much at one time for me. Acting was the thrilling choice I made. It turned out to be a lot of work and a huge challenge. To make any part of me or my personal ways of life public, I had to deal with my dyslexia in the open. I dropped the screenwriting class after I got the syllabus, but continued with writing larger ideas. I was intrigued by the formula used to develop big stories.

The acting class at college was a boon toward discovering another way of knowing me. A small stage in the classroom was where we performed our homework and class interactions. Camille's advice to wear the same shoes during rehearsal as you would in the performance made a big difference in staying with the character. I watched fellow students and saw myself forget lines or blocking and receive Camille's critique. She once made the comment, "I love watching stage actors think on their feet. Seeing an actor in trouble by forgetting lines and how they gracefully get out of it shows strength." She explained how not to panic and to work at the scene. Her class was most beneficial, but was only the first part of what became the acting project. That whole business ended up costing money, with photographs and then time and energy on auditions and trying to find an agent. And then there were the classes, which cost so much. It was all another aspect of Pay to Play in Tinseltown.

Chance was making good money doing a top-forty gig playing bass guitar but not singing. He couldn't wear his costumes, and he couldn't move around onstage; he just stood all night. It was his turn to pay some bills, and he did. He was also gone a lot at that point and hanging out in clubs, so the house had more peace. He finally got snagged by a groupie and started staying at her place. When he did bring her to Big Guy's house, they were like peanut butter and jelly stuck to each other. She was tall, with dirty blonde hair but without anything exceptional in her walk. Pretty, with a touch of country or small-town common appeal, she seemed to be quietly putting on airs. At his side, her questions were low and only directed to him. His direct attention was what she absorbed, and he willingly gave his thoughts to her. Chance pointed out how good a dancer she was. He was captivated. It was good to see him live through a change.

There was more than what met the eye with the one Chance thought he found. She was the first woman since his wife that he paid any real attention to. He surely must have told her of the potential that still lingered for a record deal. If she believed him, she may have thought he had more chances than a lottery ticket. I called her Miss Fortune. What a pair Chance and Miss Fortune made. I was glad for him to be able to do so much the opposite from his hibernation in the garage for a year. I wondered what good would come from it, though. Living the opposite of self-denial, with both Mr. Inside and then Mr. Outside, was good to stimulate creativity. Chance was certainly living life differently these days.

However, with him gone, I really appreciated the privacy to memorize lines and practice my playing at make-believe for acting class. It was so childish at first and so obviously just a matter of trying to pretend. The obvious undeniable motive was one of deception. Acting was intentionally a form of dishonesty. It was not real! It was about faking! Falseness! Acting brought to the exterior what was worked out of the interior emotions. Transference or shifting a past true moment was a method. I could enjoy both seeing acting and now acting myself. But I never questioned it until being in it. There was something going on with the intention for relocating truth. I continued the classwork of memorizing lines and blocking out body movements, timing and the staging of humor and drama. I had read the book on the Stanislavski theory of method acting as well as a book on acting by Uda Haugen. At the time, they seemed like very clever ways to tell a good lie. Drawing upon experiences to bring forth to the present obviously seemed to slow down going forward in life. I could only imagine that a well-accomplished actor kept himself or herself revolving in a cycle of reliving the past. It, too, was a treadmill of repetition, like a factory worker sitting at a machine grinding large pieces smaller. But the factory worker was doing honest work and was not engaged in the art of deception.

While I practiced the method of acting, the profound emotional impact that my old dog Thunder's death had on me came forth. I again cried remembering him, like I always did. But this time it didn't just come over me; I forced it to happen. It was a little scary to go back and drag up such strong hurt and pain. It was too real perhaps, too unnecessary. Memory recall had both a positive and negative outcome that lent itself temporarily toward the purpose of distraction—like a magician leads your eyes to one hand while the other hand tricks you. And for what purpose? What was acting's purpose? Perhaps acting was just a distraction, a vehicle with the intent to deceive, to lead people out of reality into fantasy. By pretending to be truthful the audience may connect with their own emotions. The message of the writer was designed by the director and they and the actor delivered more than one message. Messages that influenced and moved people's values, concepts and purposes in this short life were of great value. The value of the motive of the message was most important. Deception was being perpetrated and was perpetually accepted by society. So, in essence, deception was the normal way to influence and lead society.

In some ways, acting was very similar to what I had noticed in Gina putting on her makeup. Women choose to wear masks, a façade, or a false front for them and others. I asked myself, "Why intentionally mask the truth?" Why else but to move or influence opinions. Temporarily looking better is like feeling good by putting on better clothing. The outside aids the mind inside. But when the clothing and makeup come off, still there's always the truth to deal with. When the TV show ends and the picture goes black, there's truth to deal with. Perhaps the truth of reality doesn't satisfy. My confused attitude gave way to thoughts of the positive love I might meet someday.

CERTAIN DESIGN

She'll have rosebud cheeks, perfect big blue eyes,
A smile sugar-sweet, never says good-bye,
Sunlight in her hair to warm rainy skies,
Someone who can care and won't let it hide.

    Living a few years, turning in and out of time,
    Hooking up the pattern I made on my mind,
    My heart still calls a Certain Design,
    Looking for just one Certain Design.

        I've had my bitter, she would be my sweet.
        I'm not a quitter, I'm just incomplete.

She'll be fun and warm, with patience for me.
Calm before the storm, she'll rescue me.
A dream heroine, deliberately for me.
A love predestined, declared, and decreed,

Beginning in the autumn of 1987, acting influenced my next six circus-clown California years. With a grin or a frown, acting left me thin and still hanging around. My original intentions of struggling became more years of struggling. That new challenge was added to my list of already hard way of life at thirty-four years of age. My childhood survival techniques in dealing with the silent hidden dyslexic condition taught me well to seize alternative opportunities. An early learned mechanism to hide my low self-esteem came out as humor. Everybody likes a clown. Humor deflected the truth but gained an audience. Opting for the best way to overcome obstacles, I learned through experience the art of being flexible. My early adolescent teenage years as a latchkey kid ingrained the narcissistic self-seeking ways. The recovery from the head concussion at twenty-one exposed me to self-denial through the teachings of Taoism. The increased aloneness of living as a modern sage allowed me to be selective. Acting was another path still off the treadmill of popular lifestyles.

Now all my ingredients had evolved into my new chosen path of performing arts. I chose to engage with those memories or situations that served to enhance my acting. My unrealistic self-imposed burdens to find fulfillment were used. All of my life was about me living on the outside of the greater mass of conformity. As I followed through with the acting classes at college, I auditioned for a stage play. The challenge was one I took in stride; it seemed a natural fit to reveal my self-centeredness with my shyness. A Balley's health spa membership not only made my achy muscles relax; I also shrank off excess water weight.

I was chosen to play a father, Wayne Blossom Sr., in *Last Days at the Dixie Girl Café* by Robin Swicord. We rehearsed in a horseshoe-shaped theater, which was small and intimate with the audience. The first positive life-changing experience was my need to stop smoking marijuana so I could concentrate and memorize lines. For the first time in fifteen years, I had something more important to do than smoke pot. I was so glad to finally get that monkey off of my back and know my potential for ridding myself of that disease. I saw the years of addiction dragged off of my very own center stage and placed on the sidelines in a holding pattern. The priorities of my selfishness were restacked.

In October, I felt an earthquake that registered at 6.1, and it scared me completely. It was my first sort-of-big one. There was instability in the air. When I ran outside, I stood under the avocado tree and recalled our talks about God. Who but God could shake the earth? I recorded in the diary how powerful God is and how weak I am. The earthquake helped to sharpen my momentum to plow through my time living in North Hollywood.

In November and then December, the few months of play rehearsals went well, as did the performances. I wished there were more. Each night I learned more and became better while performing. The three-quarter-round horseshoe theater became a home I'd miss. I found my post-play life to be depressing. The letdown that came with not being in character and not performing was a surprise for me. The stage family of the crew and cast was gone. I stood alone in the middle between looking at Wayne Blossom Sr. in the play I was leaving and the normal me I was going to be again. Being in the middle seeing the fantasy and reality was a small shock; I did not anticipate that. It was like slipping on black ice: the surprise of being in the middle hurt. But losing the character was more pain than I expected; it was like a death. The pot and the booze came back with fervor, and that was ugly. I tried removing myself from my life in the role of Wayne Blossom Sr., a father. But the role didn't leave all at once. I needed to flush out the make-believe and be real again. I needed to calm down. I lay on the soft rug in the garage with Pie, but the floor was cold. I needed to help him up and walked with him in the yard to pee. He was so tired.

Pie was the only link to my past that was good and still with me. I was exhausted. I bought sleeping bags and heating pads for Pie and me and some extra pillows for him to lie on. We lay there in the quiet. The very basic stillness of breathing hour after hour brought sanity. I found out how to find my way back to the truth. Or at least what I thought was true. I also found out I liked acting and wanted more exposure. But I wasn't sold on the idea of living a lie and letting make-believe have so strong an effect on my present.

I learned about doing work as an extra and applied at some agencies. The people in movie and TV scenes other than the known actors, who are speaking, are working as actors without words to say. Their presence and movements are necessary, though silent for the most part. It was Christmas, and Ma sent another electric blanket with her goodies and her letter of what went on in New York. Piper and I shared our stash of cookies and bread with Big Guy. It was just the three of us now, with me and the Pie dog living in the garage. The alone time without noise from the TV was what I preferred. It felt good and tranquil at the end of the year. Our walk to North Hollywood High School was our tradition. The quality of the garage's complete quiet with the Pie was priceless. No words, but our eyes spoke.

In a way, the garage was similar to the family camp, where it was just me and the Pie. It was cold out there and got worse when it rained. Big Guy and I had hoarded all kinds of wood we found on garbage nights, and we began burning it in his fireplace. Old dressers, tables, broken chairs—they kept the house warm. He slept in his living room chair a lot watching TV. The Big Squeaker dog and I came inside for the last few weeks at the end of the year. Big Guy was so kind to us: he turned off the TV because he knew we liked it quiet. We were three adults camping out like kids watching the flames. The house was quiet; the fire crackled and snapped. He knew what was going on with me and Pie; it reminded him of his dog Rex. We camped on the living room floor in front of the fireplace. We watched the fire burn on and on for a week straight. I brought my dog his food and water so he wouldn't have to get up. Next to him in the tears of my eyes, I saw him as a pup on the floor of our summer camp those first days I got him.

I carried him outside when he needed to go and stayed with him twenty-four hours a day. I dried him off and brushed him, and we talked with our eyes. Side by side, the Duke and I lay on the blankets and sleeping bags on the living room floor. We stayed warm by the dancing flames, and memories got fired up. The shadows jumped top to bottom in our cave. We were hunters and gatherers. We laughed and cried, and I wailed in sorrow and pain in the near and coming death of life. We talked of going to Canada and finding another camp for Pie to start a litter of Pie pups. Staring at the fire, I saw the painful recoveries from my reckless crashes and injuries. I saw us running once again together, me and my puppy, at the summer home and swimming in the lake. I felt the fight of older life, the kicking for more room to move. And the thirteen-year-old Pie's eyes moved with me. I was thirty-four and had nothing to go back to—only the empty forward to look toward. When, when, when would enough show up? When would we get out of Los Angeles? Where was the end? The year closed, but time ticked on and things kept moving.

Chapter 15: The Bottom

January 1988 came without any hint of celebration. More and more, I was holding up Piper's hind legs for him so he could go outside to do his business. I was being called for auditions and hoped the madness of wearing my heart on my sleeve would pay off.

Every time Chance checked in alone to see what was happening at the house, we talked about God and Jesus and the Holy Bible. On the first week's visit, he stopped by to pet the Pie dog. He told me how hurt he and his brother were when they put down their family dog when they were younger. He gave me a small three-inch red pocket Bible to read. It was a real Bible and thicker. This small book with small black print had the words that were spoken by Jesus printed in red. Holding the Bible gift in my hands, I realized another link I had with Chance. Our collaboration grew, and now we were talking about God. I never would have imagined how my life turned out and where it was. The fact that this God thing was still happening, still unfolding, was a mystery.

On January 18, I took Pie to the vet's for some help with his legs, but I already knew the worst. Pie's vet visits had always caused him to keep his head low. He wanted to avoid the doctor if he could. The vet groped about feeling for injuries but found none. His advice was deadly. Pie's crippling old-age condition would only get worse. He recommended a lethal injection when I was ready to say good-bye to Pie. Back at the house, I couldn't live with what was so obviously the truth. The Duke just turned fourteen years old, hurting, and was going to have to go down. The inside of my mind swam in the tears of reality. My chest pushed up feelings filling my throat. Internal pressure pushed out the tears as my eyes looked at Pie's eyes. For three days we lay on the floor, ate together, cried, laughed, and hugged.

On the twenty-first, Big Guy cried saying good-bye to Pie. I loaded Piper into the old pickup truck. He stood with his head out of the window, ready to go with me. Fourteen years ago, we jumped off the treadmill of tradition together. His first ride in a truck was that day I quit the factory job. Nine years ago, we took Thunder for his last ride to the old camp. Pie walked out of the woods with me and rode up front with his head on my lap. I stroked his ears and said I loved him a million times. Only a few blocks away, we returned to the vet's parking lot. Lifting Pie onto the concrete, I watched his legs, looking for him to be better. The big dog teetered in the sunlight with both hind feet together for strength. A reason to turn around and go home wasn't there.

We checked in with the receptionist and waited a few minutes. I hoisted my comrade onto the metal table covered with white sheets. My best friend got his shot. With words of love, I held him and felt his breath go faint. I told him for the last time that he was the best dog and held his head, his eyes on my eyes. His trust was in my hands for the last "I love you." His eyes closed. I kissed him for the last time.

I don't remember going through the door out to the front desk. All I remember is turning to walk away. I don't think I paid any money; I don't remember paying any. I left without my friend. The sun-filled parking lot had only my truck waiting. The empty front seat filled my eyes with tears. I drove without him. But my heart and mind and eyes were still with him.

Home in my garage, I heard how quiet, how very quiet life really was. I turned on the classical music radio station and left it on for the next lifetime. I turned the volume up and wailed out the agony within. Alone, alone, alone in pain, I stared at dark emptiness. My knees went to the rug. Sobbing, gasping for air, I choked out sorrow. I was without responsibility; I had no one to take care of. Shocked by the hollowness of the truth, I had no one to tell of the hope I once told Pie. His loss weakened all my intentions in life. The revolving air vent in the ceiling spun slowly, casting its twisted shadows on the wall. I lay on the floor looking up, watching how the light turned. Big Guy came to the garage door and said, "Hey, buddy, are you okay?" He had lost Rex, and I had now lost Pie. With both our best friends gone, we were closer.

The box of all the dog experience, first with Thunder, now with Pie, was closed. I knew someday I'd have another dog. Someday I'd open up all my know-how and put it to good use. Knowledge is never wasted.

✝

The end of January, the motor in my truck blew up. Hard times found me sharing either Big Guy's or Chance's car, with no money and no offers to work. I was alone in the garage with cold nights in that desert. There was no staying warm—only a few fires; there was just massive surrounding emptiness. I caught a cold, I stayed under the covers. I cried from the loss of Pie over and over. I got what I wanted: I was alone amid millions of people. I was the Taoist sage. I was the lonely writer. I was the individual who never wanted to fit in. I was weeping and reaping what I had sowed. The drive that turned me away from the factory life and toward adventure was real. I had nothing but stories of life behind me. All I could do was wait and see what was ahead.

In February I wrote less and would only walk to the corner and sit at the burrito stand. I counted up my life in the diary in two columns. I listed the gains on one side and the losses on the other. The gain side was looking real slim. Life had paused in a void between just a few thoughts and far fewer thoughts. Any thought of getting another dog was immediately erased. To train a dog like I trained Pie would take commitment, time, and a forest to run in. Over the years, I lost values, time, and purpose. I had nothing to write or say. My words were useless to me. I sat in the backyard with nothing but a stare. I sat in the dark garage until I reached for help. I picked up the small Bible Chance had given me. It was brand-new. Looking into it, I found it to be just the New Testament Bible. I read some of the red words, and I liked reading it out loud. "Blessed are the poor in spirit, For theirs is the Kingdom of heaven. Blessed are those who mourn, For they shall be comforted" (Matt. 5:3–4).

Like the two-inch Bible, it was also a good thing, and the words were meaningful. I had time on my hands, so I held some of those new words in thought. I was poor in spirit and I was mourning and I did feel comfort. I had been telling the diary about reading the little Bible and mentioned that it was helping to fill the hole made after Pie died. I also wrote of noticing how I was drinking less beer and smoking less pot, but only in spurts. The mystery about God seemed to revolve around the words in the Bible. Because it was small, I misplaced it a lot, so I started to carry it. God's authority had weight to it; I liked it in my pocket.

I kept bumping around looking for work and going on a few jobs as an extra in the moviemaking business. But time was different. Somehow I was getting over the loss of Pie, and the hurt was set aside somehow. The Bible words weren't just thoughts; there was a small disturbance going on inside me. Not a clash with loud or fierce confrontations, but a rub, like breaking in new shoes. It was a different kind of motion or sound within. Amid all the screeching stops and running out of fuel on my inroads of life toward the city of worldly success, I detected something else. There was a shaping of a tiny groan, a small posture, a lightweight swaying within. Awkwardly I tried telling the diary, but I didn't know what to say to pinpoint the muse within. Staring at the page noticing myself doing a double take at the loss of words, I looked in the yard. Something was different. Then out of nowhere, I started getting calls for work as an extra.

I became very busy moving about Los Angeles, working on various films and TV shoots. The busyness was a new distraction. Extra work continued into March, increasing through the month. The driving to and fro kept my mind in thought, like driving always did. I would often bring my diary because there was a lot of sitting around on locations.

I met two young producers, Rick and Dick, on a movie set at night in Hollywood. Rick was also an actor; he invited me to work on their independent film hopefully going to the Cannes Film Festival. We did shoot some scenes out in the streets of Santa Monica one evening. They were like me, struggling to find a foothold. Writing of the new adventures in the land of movies aroused my satisfaction. Like adding an amusing arrow to my quiver of experience, I took in the unusual events. Still, there was that shrouded rubbing within, steadily repeating its subtle awareness, a kind of annoyance.

One bright blue sunny day, I was driving out through the Palmdale desert. Heading toward the Disney Ranch for some work on a movie set, I passed through some small bald-top mountains. I lost most of the radio reception and turned the dial in that old Ford I shared. I found only one channel, a Christian radio station, and listened. Impressed with the old man's southern twang, I leaned closer to the dashboard. His dedication in telling how Jesus was nailed to the cross and the picture of it in my mind were alarming. The nails that were used in his hands and feet, he said, were the sins of the world. Because of his sins and my sins, Jesus was punished horribly and died. He was really into getting his message across the airwaves. Not only did Christ die as a substitute for those who believe in what Jesus did, three days later he rose from the dead. The preacher said with passion, "Friends, Jesus Christ conquered death by coming back to life, and He is living still in heaven with His Father, God. Friends, He died for you and me; Jesus saves souls." That old man's intentions to teach the Bible were serious. The preacher read Proverbs 16:2–3: "All the ways of a man are pure in his own eyes, but the LORD weighs the spirits. Commit your works to the LORD, and your thoughts will be established." I felt both disturbed about not knowing enough about sins and a confirming connection to the rubbing annoyance within.

At the movie set, I sat around like everybody else did. The movie was called *Big Top Pee-wee*. Weird costumed people strolled about as circus members. Inside the big-top tent, bleachers were full of extras waiting to be told when to be a crowd happily watching the act. Between takes, crews of production people tried to reorganize the chaos of circus performers. The crowd of extras pretended to be happy. Seeing the organized crowd imitate cheery delightfulness on command had the opposite effect on me. I sat outside until I was used again. Pacing the grounds, I walked through a beautiful grove of trees, where perhaps other movies were made. The striking difference between truth and acting, real and make-believe, stayed on my mind.

Sitting nearer the buildings, I wrote about the preacher on the radio. I was getting shook up by what I could hardly perceive was a God thing. The strangeness in my head and around me in life was slowly becoming a supernatural awakening. The notion of God being so close caused me to stare with a blank face as I tried to rationalize the soft, unexplainable presence. Why was this happening to me?

Later that month, I made calls to the music industry to shop another batch of original songs and promo material. When Chance showed up, he and I talked more intelligently about the words in the Bible. We each had one and pointed to the words we had read. I had been thumbing through looking for explanation of sins. 1 Corinthians 5:9 said, "I wrote to you in my epistle not to keep company with sexually immoral people." Chance didn't have any kind of good answer when I asked him about him living with Miss Fortune at her place. In fact, he then asked me why I was a hypocrite drinking and smoking pot. He read onward in 5:11 ... "Do not keep company with a drunkard." I was in my own trap, guilty without a defense. We were both guilty of those sins, and we figured there were more so we agreed to keep reading till next time.

He took the Ford we shared, so I borrowed Big Guy's car after that. I auditioned for a part in another school play at Los Angeles Valley College (LAVC) that spring. I was writing less and stopped smoking pot again to memorize lines from certain plays and monologues for audition purposes. My time was filled with things to do. It took me ten weeks to fill the blank three-sectioned diary pages that used to take four weeks. Something was going on, but I could not put my finger on it. I started riding my used garage-sale bicycle to the park and through North Hollywood. I was glad for the exercise and glad to move about without the shared car. I missed the Pie, and I missed the daily diary writing. I was in transition out of my hollowness. Old ways were slipping by, and new avenues appeared slowly. The pain of losing Pie subsided for the most part.

✝

In April I was offered a part in another play at LAVC, *The Diviners*, by Jim Leonard Jr. Once more, I played the role of a father. Interestingly, my son in the play was mentally challenged. Once the play rehearsals started, they ate up all my time. Again the rehearsals and performances were in the three-quarter-round horseshoe theater. The stage was low again on the floor, and a small platform was up just a few steps. The audience was in the dark, and the closeness was appealing. Like before, the post-play withdrawals from the fictional life were mixed with the resurfacing nonfictional truth of life. During this second play, I realized more fully the conflict of living in the two worlds of truth and fiction. The zone between going from life into pretending and back to life was an uneasy space to be in. Going through the challenging zone was all in my mind. The problem was made manifest yet again through alcohol and marijuana. They acted like medicinal grease helping the slide from one zone to the other.

In May, Uncle Shawn, who was my godfather, came into town from Florida for a surprise visit, and he took me to lunch. He said he was visiting a friend. Twenty-one years later, I found out at his funeral that he was really visiting his son and family. That old sailor always kept his visits to his family secret. Ma and I never knew about his visiting them. How gracious for time to reveal the whole truth out of his hidden deception.

I earned $100 for work in an industrial film. I climbed up a ladder and climbed back down. What a way to make money! At least I made something back from the hundreds of dollars I invested in photo headshots, mailings, and classes.

In June, before the semester ended, Gina came with me to the college awards banquet for the theater department. I won best supporting actor for my work in the *Last Days of the Dixie Girl Café*. Gina was uncomfortable at forty years old being among the younger students. At thirty-five, I didn't care; you only live life once, and I was having fun. Once the good life of dedicating time to the arts was over, I went back to work as a telemarketer and kept up working as an extra.

In July I had an encounter with a mature Irish woman named Jackie. At fifty, she looked more like thirty. She possessed a stunning natural beauty, which drew me closer. We just happened to meet, and found each other interesting and attractive. In a way, she was reliving her youth as a model. Her daughter was beginning to break into show business, and Jackie couldn't let go of guiding her. Jackie's interest in me was another avenue of guidance, which gave me encouragement. Her generosity went as far as giving me a gift of a professional acting class in Studio City that summer. Our mismatch in age was indeed a mismatch, and we soon parted, and then reunited, and so on. The one outstanding appreciation I took from my good relationship with her family was with her son, Glenn. He had an enchanted way about him, like a leprechaun. Simply his magical presence could make me laugh. He was more fun than a barrel of monkeys, and one of the most interesting, creative masterminds I've ever met. When he showed up, imaginative powers blossomed. I think he was an undiscovered genius.

In August, we had a big surprise! When I came home and saw Big Guy, his face was fearful. He'd been home alone with the news, contemplating the potential fallout. Worry brought back his stuttering as he met me at the door with bulging eyes and a wrinkled forehead. He could barely say the words: "Hey, bbbuddy, my ssister wwas here." We were busted. His younger sister came out of nowhere. Apparently she was checking on him or something. Whatever had caused their distance ended at this point. It was a sore subject for Big Guy; he had only mentioned that they didn't get along. She found out we were renting her house (not his) out by the room, and she wanted her cut—three hundred dollars a month. We were floored. I quickly got another telemarketing job just to pay her. But the news also brought relief to me in knowing that Big Guy did have someone who could look out for him. Seeing his family still being family, like it or not, was good. Strange how things twist and turn. Whatever the hidden reason was for their separate ways remained hidden, and Big Guy calmed down. My thoughts went to New York and what it might be like when and if I returned. I was so removed from that world.

By August I was offered a lead role in my third school play as Elwood P. Dowd in *Harvey*. It was written by Mary Chase, who in 1945 won the Pulitzer Prize in drama for *Harvey*. This time the play at the valley college would be in the big theater, which sat about four hundred people. All three of my plays were directed by John Larsen. Halfway through my rehearsals, I made a choice of watching the movie *Harvey* with Jimmy Stewart. I wouldn't realize my mistake until years later. I would have brought a fresh, uninhibited, natural performance to the play. But by seeing Mr. Stewart's rendition, I was swayed in my choices to best present the writer's intent.

By working as an extra on films like *Midnight Run* and TV episodes of *Cheers*, I saw the business or the procedure of how a film was shot. Over and over again, on about two dozen other shoots, I watched. Sitting, walking, or standing as an extra, I knew my minuscule part was a great learning experience. Another audition allowed me to use what I had learned. A graduate film student of Northridge University named Reave chose me for the lead to represent his father in his directorial debut. I took the lead part in his independent film headed for the Cannes Film Festival. Reave was very determined to do his best. His dedication to tell his story using surreal techniques became a significant influence on me. Interpreting tough emotions by using film noir, Reave's visual techniques were on display. In clothing, makeup, obscure set design, and sounds, he allowed the camera to tell the story. Without a word of dialogue, his well-thought-out plans evolved in segments for the editor to weave the story.

✝

On August 28, I actually began to read the New Testament. I had skipped around in the small Bible enough, and I finally started at the beginning. It was so deep, yet some things were so clear, like in Matthew chapter four where the Devil tries to tempt Jesus to sin three times. In verse ten, Jesus says, "Away with you, Satan! For it is written, You shall worship the LORD your God, and Him only you shall serve." Satan was real. Jesus was more powerful than Satan. And in verse eleven, the devil took off, and then angels came to be with Jesus. I liked it, and I knew I would read more. I liked the fact that I was reading what I enjoyed.

Melissa came by driving a Volkswagen beetle, with Gypsy in the passenger's seat. I loved Gypsy; she reminded me of Thunder, all loving and happy. I sat on the back cement steps while she paced and smoked a cigarette. We talked about butterflies and the book called *Blue Birds* that she gave me. I read a lot and wrote a lot about the three plays during acting. I liked to try and analyze the Playwright's intentions and how they got there. Then I read three books Melissa gave me, but they were just okay stories. *Siddhartha*, *Blue Birds*, and *Out on a Limb* all were so-so and led me nowhere. Melissa said they were all a Buddha-type thing. She said they helped her with living. But the bad part of all that reincarnation stuff is you never get out of the cycle of living. "This life is tough enough; coming back to earth and living again just to die again, no thanks," she said. We laughed and agreed that once was enough, enough was enough on this earth. She was really a good friend, one of the top three in my life. I told her I was reading the New Testament. She rolled her eyes and said she knew something was going on with me. I picked up on her apparent disapproval in the tone of her voice and pressed her for a reason. I reminded her about the miracles books she read and asked her about the Bible.

Melissa said that a few other times in her life, her friends got Jesus. "Once they got hooked, they didn't want to party, no drugs, no booze, no sex, nothing," she said.

I was speechless for a moment, but then I asked her, "Then what happened?"

Melissa said, "I don't know. They started to go to church and read the Bible and sang hymns."

"Sang hymns?" I said. I wanted to know more and said, "Then what?"

She said with sarcastic resentment, "Then they die and go to heaven."

"Wow, that is awesome," I said. I asked her, "Why don't you do it?"

She said, "You don't do it; it happens to you, you nut." Melissa walked up close to the steps and reached out her arms. She wrapped my head in her loving arms and pressed it to her stomach. She stood and rocked gently while I held her legs.

I asked her in a muffled voice, "Will it happen to me?"

Her voice was small, and she said, "I don't know, maybe. You have to wait and see. Sometimes people say they're Christians, but I don't think they are."

"How do you tell?" I asked her.

Melissa gave a low pirate chuckle saying, "That's the tricky part."

I stood with her short frame in my arms, her head resting just below my chest. A few seconds of solitude pressed us tighter before she pulled away and wiped a tear. She called for Gypsy, and the short black cannonball ran to us. We looked at each other, and she saw the seriousness in my eyes. She said, "Don't worry, you nut. If it's real, you can't stop it; you just have to wait and see." She turned and left with Gypsy.

I stood on the inside of the backyard wall hearing her small car shifting away down Burbank Boulevard. The seriousness of her disclosure stayed with me. Whatever the aura of weightiness of the bibles words were, it stayed a mystery and intermittent. As soon as I thought of something else I should be doing, the God thoughts were gone.

---

†

Months earlier, I had read about the Stanislavski theory and also a book by Uda Haugen; I put some of it to use. I learned from acting class that it was common among actors to be prepared to give a classic and a contemporary monologue on auditions. I practiced Shakespeare's classic *Taming of a Shrew*. On my side of the stone wall in the backyard, the solid bulwark fought against the 5:00 p.m. traffic roaring down Burbank Boulevard. I glided about the smooth concrete badminton court in leather shoes, hitting my marks, whispering, and then yelling my lines. To contrast the body movements and vocal variations, I chose a calmer work as my contemporary piece. It was a Sam Shepard monologue from *Motel Chronicles*. Sitting still in the solid dark soundproof garage, I was among used props. Picturing a western Indian village and speaking slowly, pausing to see tepees, I rehearsed.

In September, I performed both monologues in my audition at the prestigious Beverly Hills High School Theatre 40. Nervously I waited in the hall pacing, sweating, sitting, and reviewing the words in my mind. Entering the small room with tables and people in chairs on three sides, I first introduced myself and my intentions. Prancing about with gestures and callings for Petruchio's imaginary Kate, I felt strong. My voice was sure with emotion. Arm gestures and quick feet paused and rolled on. Next I pulled a hardwood school chair to the center of the arena. Calmly I spoke of Shepard's beautiful Grand Tetons, crawling Indians, and a bloody buffalo lying in the desert. Then I was quiet.

Leaving the facility, I stood on the school steps breathing in the sunshine. That minute as I walked on, I noticed the escaping muse, the conversion back to real life. Amazed once more, I lived in the middle zone of life between fantasy and reality. I slowed to enjoy the transition. I saw my rehearsals in the yard. In my mind's eye, flashes of movements from the audition were replayed. Then looking down at my shadow on the sidewalk, the changeover dissipated as I walked. From behind the steering wheel, I put the key in the ignition considering the reflection. Driving off, I still felt the rush from acting.

✝

I understood the concept of reaching back into your past for an event that produced emotion, which could then be brought forth. Using the trick in a current performance was the whole idea. I tried that technique and it was hard work for me, but it did work. However, there was something shady going on. Calling it truth bothered me. The reality of an actor's truth was undeniably camouflaged like a half-truth. Anything but the whole truth was a lie.

I was young in the field of acting and had difficulty accepting that form of entertainment. I didn't know if I could feel honest enough to make a living as a liar/actor. Maybe that's why actors were paid a lot of money—to ease their conscience. What I thought I found was the inside story for myself to deal with. What was weird was my knowing that a lie was being sold, whether I had anything to do with it or not. The deception of actors was simply entertainment for sale. I knew there were beneficial emotions and feelings transferred to the audience. This pleasure was given and received, and that was a good thing. The business of selling a movie, live entertainment, or a sports event was in exchange for a person's money. Anyone could take it or leave it.

Watching a movie, TV show, play, or event pulled away a person's time as smoothly as silk through fingers—like a pickpocket would lift your wallet without you're knowing you were robbed. Once your time was gone, there was nothing to show for the brief escape from reality except the enjoyment of a fleeting feeling. Hopefully, time and money were invested well. Time was so valuable it was what most people gave up at their jobs in exchange for money. How I spent my time was always a choice I had to make. The great equalizer among people was the twenty-four hours in a day and night.

I saw the subtle exchange of TV's fiction for a person's real time as a slippery slope of losing more and more time. My youthful observation toward acting boiled down to a sense of right and wrong. Did I want to participate in taking people's time and give them make believe? Aside from how someone spent their time, it was the duplicity of acting, the deception, which irked me. I needed more time to figure out how to adjust my evaluation of acting into my world. It seemed like I couldn't get past my recent insight and was unable to accept acting as I found it. Perhaps it was my conscience. I saw my own hypocrisy and the lie I told about my wrist injury. I saw how truth was twisted, how deception was justified, and it equaled acting in my eyes. I couldn't balance the value of acting with the harms it might have caused.

Not telling the truth once had rippling effects in my life for years. I might no longer enjoy acting as innocently as I had. Finding the inside story showed me how enormous the business machine of making lies was. The massive amount of time, energy, and expense that went into avoiding the truth was staggering. Acting was universally accepted, and I once sat like others, watching it without thinking. That insight took the edge off of my enthusiasm toward being an actor. What I found behind the scenes was more than just turning on the TV and letting the make-believe capture my thoughts.

I could see the similarities of falseness with a politician's lies. Regardless of who the politician was, he or she was in the business of saying one thing and doing another. Elected officials and actors were in a performance business of compromising the truth. My intuition told me that some of the half-truth charades had some good in them. Obviously there was good and bad in all things. Acting was just a thing. It seemed like the choice to express fantasy had many variations. Music, writing, sculpting, dancing, and more were just some expressions.

The choices made by the public to be entertained were multiplied over decades of generations. As the world seemed to be moving along, it seemed like entertainment was a huge part turning it. My awareness about acting seemed profound and was short-lived in thought but captured in the diary. My eyes saw how the temptation to stretch the truth was like one rotten apple spoiling the barrel. The motives for the messages and images in what was portrayed could create more harm than good. Overall, I was better off to move forward with my new attitudes. I didn't always think like that; perhaps I would learn more as I changed.

✝

ONLY PRAYER

I sing about the world, I debate both right and wrong,
Keeping one good answer for a moral in a song.
A verse for politicians, who really pulls the strings,
They're puppets for the people; it's God who places Kings.

> Politicians are puppets that have lost their way.
> Politicians are running from God every day.

> The puppets for the people, only God places Kings.
> The puppets for the people, what will God bring?
> Only Prayer by the people can change anything.
> Only Prayer by the people can change anything.

The few who have the most, they often say the least.
Identity kept secret, there's a handful for the feast.
Politicians A or B, all eyes on their illusion,
Beneath their pride and greed, are words of pollution.

> Politicians are puppets that have lost their way.
> Politicians are running from God every day.

> The puppets for the people, only God places Kings.
> The puppets for the people, what will God bring?
> Only Prayer by the people can change anything.
> Only Prayer by the people can change anything.

✝

YOUR TIME

You're learning to look how to fill up your well.
Want runs like water, you forget how you fell.
The taste is cool and sweet, one more of each kind,
More leisure you drink, it clouds up your mind.

Relax so quietly in that make-believe spell,
Buying from the TV the values it sells.

> Count it wise, Your Time, against God is a sin.
> Confinement of time makes a good discipline.
> Spend it wise, Your Time, against God is a sin.
> Confinement of time makes a good discipline.

Keep buying your pretties or objects that shine.
You're a number that's counted, a toy that they wind,
TV has what you want, in exchange for your mind,
Movies sell views, drama keeps you blind.

> Relax so quietly in that make-believe spell,
> Buying from the TV the values that it sells.

> Count it wise, Your Time, against God is a sin.
> Confinement of time makes a good discipline.
> Spend it wise, Your Time, against God is a sin.
> Confinement of time makes a good discipline.

Chapter 16: The Dead Life Ends

A few weeks before Halloween in 1988, there was calm in the street traffic on Burbank Boulevard going by our house. Kids were in school, and vacation congestion had ended. The summer sun moved just enough to allow a little more coolness in the shadows of the trees. Two months would pass before the seven-year mark would arrive in my pilgrimage. As I saw my dream winding down, my tolerance for California waned.

Big Guy, who was a magnanimous person and very often quiet, was also observant. He created quite a stir one day by announcing he would buy a video camera. He said we could make music videos, and I could use the camera with my acting. Chance immediately did research at the library, reading trade journals to find the right camera for our needs. We all went to the stores together, trying out cameras and tripods and picking the brains of the salespeople. In the car, we spoke about the Bible, what we were reading, and how we thought the scriptures played on our lives. We rode to four different stores, looking until we found the right equipment. Big Guy placed his credit card down on the counter and bought the complete package. We were in the movie business. You just don't meet people like that every day. Like Aunt Jean's letters gave me encouragement, Big Guy also believed in what we were doing. He wanted to help and often spoke encouraging words when times were tough. Once again his actions spoke louder than his words.

November's play rehearsals for *Harvey* were ongoing. I practiced my monologue in front of the new camera. "Harvey and I would sit in the bars ..." Harvey was the play's imaginary six-foot rabbit. I filled the play with my happy memory of my best friend, Piper dog. The big theater's raised stage, its length and depth, was to me a basketball court, another friendship for me to enjoy rehearsing with others. My mystical friend and I enjoyed our time, knowing what would follow the last show. But after recovering from the depression of withdrawal from the performance, I had no idea what 1989 would bring.

✝

Chance came back to the house with Miss Fortune and began making music videos in the garage. He soaked up the new opportunity to explore the visual arts with his private and personal videographer. Like I found acting, video production for him was another and different avenue of expression. Just like he kept changing the music and song demos, he worked at different concepts of storytelling with pictures. He still worked part-time in a prop house and helped with the rent. He brought home weird prop cutouts from the trash bin at work. He was off to the races with his creativity. It was good that he had fun with his girlfriend. Seeing them laugh and work together brought a little sanity around my life, the house's atmosphere, and life in general.

The *Harvey* performances were preceded by the actors' eager anticipation. The cast was a mix of students and adults. The big curtain opened in front of three hundred people or more for two weekends. The proscenium stage was electrifying, with high bright lights. Each night I sat on stage alone in the set of the library, looking out at the dark auditorium, enjoying the fantasy. But not alone; I sat having a drink with my large white imaginary rabbit, my Pie dog. I owned the moment. I relished the love that occupied my mind. I recalled thousands of days sitting with Pie in parks, on ocean beaches, and near lakes, and thousands of nights with the moon rising. On cue, walking off the stage and then standing in the wing, I'd crash a little each night. The emotion I carried for the capricious rabbit was still a strong love for Pie. Its power threatened to usurp my zone of illusion. Finding the memory crossed too easily into recalling Piper's death. Slipping back too far brought great sorrow. It was then I realized I was spared a lot of lingering distress from the recent death of Pie. Somehow the compartment holding Pie's memory had been insulated in the years' time. I did not want to touch it or even go there. Loving him was breaking me down.

When I practiced with the emotion I felt and considered the full effect of his love on me, I could stop it. I found in my mind a very thin line between the positive and negative memories. But in the performance, I lacked the discipline or maturity to handle the thin line well. I couldn't maintain the ability not to cross over. Standing in the wing tearing up, I tried to fight off the negative emotion of loss as I listened for my cue. Wiping the tears, I tried to recall my lines for the upcoming scene. I was a one-man train wreck for a few minutes.

One night I heard my cue and walked out on stage. I began partnering in dialogue with the actor playing Dr. Sanderson. As we fed off each other's lines, I jumped ahead and gave a line out of sequence. The look in his eyes was fear. He saw his fear confirmed by the fear that had just arrived on my face. We stared at each other with bulging eyes. If the person in the wings reading the lines said anything, I didn't hear it. I realized I had jumped a line. Three hundred people watched, not knowing of the panic within us. I said another line, and the doctor followed in perfect sequence and we went rolling along. It was a moment Camille, my acting teacher, would have enjoyed. We were stage actors thinking on our feet, not panicking but finding our way out.

Before Christmas, the play ended. On its heels followed the loss and the holiday blues. One of the most depressing times of my life was after the play *Harvey*. I kept living the life of Elwood P. Dowd; he was hard to let go. I wanted the character, the world he lived in, and the muse that was so powerful with Pie to stay alive. Following the play's last performance, Janine brought me a baby rabbit. I named him Harvey. Watching the bunny hop around released a lot of pent-up sorrow from the loss of Pie dog. The loss of my character Elwood and the loss of Pie again were made worse by the holidays. With no family or the love of anyone close, my sorrow was magnified with alcohol.

Thank goodness Melissa and her daughter Kiya wanted to come with her teenage friends for Christmas dinner. Melissa helped me pull myself together; she was good at recovery. I cooked two full turkey dinners, and everything was great. Melissa kept checking on me. She told me I was a nut and said I would be okay. "Look at me. Look at what I've been through, and I'm still living. You're a lot stronger than me," she said. Big Guy sat in his chair feeding Gypsy by hand; he laughed as she licked the gravy off his fingers. The kids ate well, and they all left in the small Volkswagen shifting down Burbank Boulevard. Big Guy slept in his chair while I cleaned the kitchen. That year I hid Ma's Christmas cookies and homemade bread from others. It was just for me and Big Guy. There was no Pie dog to share with, no walking to the North Hollywood High School football field to run around on the perfect grass. I sat alone a lot, no walking.

Near the end of December, I again started working at telemarketing, I needed the money bad. A month later, a very strange thing happened. One day while I was coming home from a Hollywood audition, I got stuck in the 170 Freeway traffic and was low on gas. I got off in Burbank and made my way up past the studios into Toluca Lake. It was there and then that I ran out of gas just before a gas station. It was a hot day, and the closeness caused me to get out and walk without thinking. I did not bring my backpack with me. I kept the car in my sight as I slowly walked to the gas station. Returning with the gas can, I discovered that all of my books and my backpack were stolen, including my diary. That was the first and only diary I ever lost. It left me with a very bad feeling of loss. Since I had been writing less, I didn't quite know what having it taken away meant, but it was another loss in a series of losses.

That evening I looked around in my life and started a new diary. I sat in the backyard under the trees and recalled the summer home in upstate New York. That simple life was what I wanted. But I also wanted to try acting since I was in California. Perhaps it would somehow produce a substantial sum of money. I wasn't staying in Los Angeles because I loved acting. I knew time would bring change, and I didn't want to look back with regret of not trying all I could. And there was still hope for a long shot in the music project. After Christmas, the room renter moved out. I asked the diary, "How much of this can I take?" A few days later, Melissa wanted to move back in on the last day of 1988. She did not move in; it was not wise. The last diary pages of 1988 were covered with words without a compass directing them. The pieces of thought were there, but the force to pull it all together was gone. Loss was more than just pulling paper days off a calendar.

✝

TO MAKE A MARK

Clear patch of blue sky helps me on my way,
Searching the future, wish for peace someday.

> Carpenters are happy with nails and wood.
> Actors like their money playing Robin Hood.
> Baseball is all right with the winning team.
> I wonder what I'll be. Will life be just a dream?

To Make a Mark, find the reason why I am,
To Make a Mark, get beyond the diagram,
To Make a Mark, beyond shows at a museum,
To Make a Mark, find the reason why I am.

Highways I'm walking, chase away a home,
Road signs and slow talk, the choices I roam.

Carpenters are happy with nails and wood.
Actors like their money playing Robin Hood.
Baseball is all right with the winning team.
I wonder what I'll be. Will life be just a dream?

To Make a Mark, find the reason why I am,
To Make a Mark, get beyond the diagram,
To Make a Mark, beyond shows at a museum,
To Make a Mark, find the reason why I am,

✝

The house was beginning a new era that January 1989. My plan A was always simple in theory. It was all about trying my best to earn money writing song lyrics and see what comes of it. Plan B was simpler: I would fall in love, give myself away, and get a job. Plan B was going to be a time when I would get to be like the majority of the population. Going into my seventh year out west, I could see plan A was looking more than haggard. It looked like a limping soldier, with bloody bandages covering the wounds of battle. I questioned the war. My fatigue came with recognizing how far plan A had driven down a one-way street. There was damage behind me and on me, with the pain of my worn body at thirty-five. Seventeen years after the Harley crash, my hip still hurt. Lost emotions for true love were never replaced. Passion for life was bruised, lying still; all my feelings were hurt. But I had survived. I thought about plan B a year earlier with Pie, lying in front of the fires that burned for a week. I was tired of being full of experience. But I could always fall in love, share my life, and get a job. I still had to make the most of California.

The video camera brought all kinds of interesting twists and turns. Many times Chance and I worked together with the camera and would carry on two conversations. We talked a lot about images that represented the words in the lyrics. Our questions about Jesus, the Bible, and the size of life were less talk, but it always was heavy to think about. Chance took to making music videos like a whale takes to water, but he never came up for air. I liked looking through the viewfinder and holding the camera. The equipment seemed to generate more ideas, and more footage was taken. As much of a blessing as it was, the video camera was also a curse. Adding the editing was Chance's job. All total, it literally ate up hundreds of hours and accomplished nothing more than amateur work. But I didn't see life the same after that. I began seeing visual expressions of larger thoughts. Like at the Farmers Market, where there were picture stories of life in every aisle. Fish vendors spreading ice dropped it to the floor, and I kicked a piece to the produce section. Looking up at heads of lettuce with people's fingers pulling at it, I saw me and my brother picking apples as kids. Little stories were everywhere to see.

When Chance again started to work for bigger money doing a top-forty gig, he moved out of Big Guy's house again. I missed talking with him about the teachings in the Bible. I had found in Proverbs1:7, "The fear of the LORD is the beginning of knowledge, But fools despise wisdom and instruction." I wanted to talk to him about the fear of the Lord, but it would have to wait. With Miss Fortune, he held back his share of rent money and left Big Guy's camera. It was my turn to create motion pictures. But without an agenda, I was without direction. Then the wheels turned.

I thought of my friend Reave, the Northridge post-grad film student and his crew of helpers. His mission was to create a film, a story showcasing his directorial skills. All I had to work with was the mixed experience I had gained from movie sets. Another asset was a feeling that my time in California was a ticking clock running out.

A change was coming, and plan B was to be lived out sitting on a big front porch with a wife and kids, telling exciting stories of music and movies.

I began joining my experience on sets as an extra with my acting knowledge to design a music video. Creative ideas poured out of my mind onto sheets of paper. How would I produce my own project? Then a larger concept of working with the local public-access TV station popped into my mind. That idea came from remembering my Irish girlfriend Jackie's son, Glenn. He dabbled with radio broadcasting and often mentioned his desire to work in a TV studio. What intrigued him was the public-access TV station in Van Nuys. He said it was an untapped source of available TV exposure. However, getting familiar with pushing the camera's buttons and editing came first. A set of special effects buttons needed learning, as did the camera angles with distance, height, and close-ups.

As I looked through the viewfinder more and more, I developed a sense for what to look for that would express my feelings in the lyrics. Much time was eaten up in thought for listing shots, shooting, and downloading to a VCR, then watching the tape on a TV monitor. The camera had a force that was subtle at first, but it became a force that squeezed out other thoughts. My subconscious was working with the camera's viewfinder when I wasn't.

✝

The new roommate was a limo driver who stayed awhile. His elegant long shiny car stuck out of our front lawn like a diamond pinned to a worn-out rag. The extra cash helped pay the rent until the guy ended up lying to Big Guy, didn't pay, and left the same day, burning us. The typical ups-and-downs continued for me meeting women, looking for jobs, and having problems with Big Guy's, and then Chance's car. Still, the business of going on acting auditions was my hope for a break and a big paycheck. Meanwhile, I started another garden in the backyard, along with a plot of sunflower plants. Melissa was going crazy on a streak of drugs again and was in and out of touch between Newport Beach and Ventura. It was at this time that Glenn showed up with his whimsical ways. His elfish charm at twenty-four ignited like napalm when I mentioned maybe making a cable TV show. We talked about his mom Jackie, and the next thing I knew, I was back in the arms of that Irish woman.

Our relationship began to blossom more fully as her charisma and lifestyle lured me in closer to another caliber of life. Like many people trying to keep up with the Joneses, she had a very nice house, a vintage car, and a beautiful swimming pool. Jackie was fifteen years older than me. She and her kids emigrated from Belfast. She worked in real estate but was hoping for a Hollywood life via her daughter's success if it were to happen. Sitting poolside in the lush garden surroundings drinking tea was certainly relaxing. But going around the corner to the Ireland 32 pub and shooting darts with Glenn was much more fun than acting my age. She and I were getting along okay. Her trappings were nice to visit, even though she said she knew better than to be so materialistic. She thought of herself as a Buddhist, but was in conflict with herself by loving the things in life too much. Like me, like other people, she put herself into a trap of wanting more than enough. Somehow we all don't see the trap. All we see is the bait; we smell it and we want it. And then we are in the trap. Jackie and I talked a lot, and I learned more about the movie business from her. She tried to guide me with her attempts at reaching a higher spiritual power. Her idea of spiritual meant loftier thoughts in general, nothing specific. Our discussions about life primarily centered on achieving our personal goals. We shared time.

In March, I was talking with some musicians who had come over for rehearsals in the garage on and off for two years. Their enthusiasm for the Christian song market was more robust than it was for the Bible. I realized more fully that there is a large market for Christian songs. Then the idea of producing a cable TV show got mentioned. Some of the guys seemed interested in just the money aspect, the wide appeal to a world audience. Others spoke more about Jesus and the Bible and so-called praise lyrics. They all agreed that today's Christian music was far from the sounds of yesterday's old hymns.

Apparently selling Christian songs was a contemporary growing business, which blended rock or a softer sound of music for the radio. Joining God's ways with the show business of rock and roll didn't seem right to me. The Bible seemed to be a special and separate thing. Taking Bible teachings into a world of sounding just like all other songs weakened or diluted them. Or did they? Switching from the classical station, I found a Christian radio station and listened to both the music and the preachers. Some of the music sounded hard; some sounded soft. The idea of marketing Christ was too much to evaluate.

I didn't know why I was concerned, but that inner annoying rub was like a shadow world knocking against my head. It was another enigmatic moment, like hearing the old preacher on the car radio in the desert. Thoughts of God emerged with more credibility. Christian entertainment was a confusing dilemma. I first mentioned in the diary an idea for a Christian art cable show called *Heaven High*. I also talked about my uneasiness with the commerciality of Christianity. Again, one of those unknowable feelings came. But unlike the others, which were positive toward learning about God, a negative mood was bounced off me. A conflict within was noticed. Even though the cable show idea seemed marketable, I left it alone and moved on.

✝

When I started to talk to Jackie about my discussions with Chance and the band about Christian music, she expressed her strong dislike. She hated to hear me describe how Chance and I engaged in great talks of what the Bible spoke of. There were so many mysteries about why Jesus died, why He died for people who believed in Him, and why He took their sins onto Himself. We were only guessing about what Jesus was saying in Matthew 5:48: "Therefore you are to be perfect, just as your Father in heaven is perfect." Asking Jackie what that meant was like lighting a bomb. She did not like any talk about Jesus. She told me of how the Crusades was a war causing thousands of deaths because of Jesus. When I asked what that was all about, she screamed, "I don't want to talk about it." There was something about the Bible that didn't just irritate her; it drove her over the edge.

She then tried to enroll me in a class on Buddhism. I did not do well with a room full of granola-heads sitting on the floor with their legs folded. I went one time, and I even spoke to the priestess as Jackie had arranged. This lady tried to explain the benefit of empting my mind. She then left me alone to think about it. When I closed my eyes and tried erasing all thoughts, I found the foolishness of that theory. I was not the kind of individual who could close my eyes and think of nothing. The little rooms and the smell of incense burning caught my curiosity. I got up and poked my head around the corners of a few rooms. The creaky floors gave me away, and I returned to my private chair. The truth was obvious. The priestess asked for my thoughts. I told her my brain worked too well to be turned off. I thanked her and left. Walking to the front door, I passed the room where I started and saw the group still quietly sitting on the floor emptying their minds.

The diversion I was sent on was a short false path. It didn't last; the truth did. I'm glad to say the red words of Jesus in the three-inch Bible had my attention: "I am the light of the world. He who follows Me shall not walk in darkness, but have the light of life" (John 8:12). Standing outside the Buddhist temple in the sunlight, I grinned at the whole ordeal. I knew I knew more than nothing. The priestess was no more, and Jackie, that beautiful Irish woman, was soon gone out of my life. It wasn't due to my vast Bible knowledge because I had little or none. It was the power of Jesus's words that stayed. "I am the light of the world, follow Me."

✝

I spoke with Melissa's grandma; my friend was still on a heroin streak. I questioned how people could destroy themselves. Like I was any different—I just do it more slowly. I was glad she didn't move in because she got arrested. My thoughts of her in jail were mixed. I was glad she was alive; maybe the law stopped her before it was too late. But maybe now she'd lose Kiya.

✝

MELISSA

> To go get a bag, but a bust is what she bought instead,
> No peace, no peace, no peace for her head.
> Today she's in holding, holding regrets, no coffee, no
> cigarette. No peace, no peace, no peace for her head.

Life was still rolling, sunshine coming down, no thoughts of how,
Should have gone bowling, pass beer around, eat Hawaiian chow.
Sometime before it happened, she knew what she knows now.

> To go get a bag, but a bust is what she bought instead,
> No peace, no peace, no peace for her head.
> Today she's in holding, holding regrets, no coffee, no
> cigarette. No peace, no peace, no peace for her head.

Sitting in lockup, without her morning coffee, no morning cigarette,
Sitting and thinking she should have gone right, but she went left,
Thinking she should have her coffee and cigarettes.

✝

By April the city notified us they would remove the sidewall of our backyard, which kept out Burbank Boulevard. We then would be exposed to the world. They wanted to put in a sidewalk. That was not good news. They would not restore the empty spot with a fence; they would take legally but not give back justly.

A cold reading class in Studio City intrigued me enough to sign up. I was still hoping for some kind of big payday to bankroll my exit out of California. My heart was never into acting; it was just a means to the ends. The scripted words we studied in class were called sides. They were used in auditions, and class became more than interesting. In the script, words were deliberately placed to lead the listener's mind to think a certain way. Expressing these words correctly was the writer's intent.

It was similar to lyric writing, but with quite a bit more wily intent. Knowing the intention of the writer was the goal of the actor, who then could emphasize words accordingly. Again I saw the deliberate intentions of actors, and now with the writer's intent to help lead the audience into emotional avenues. I likened the concept to my search for images for the camera to tell a story. Leading the viewers was supposed to be for their pleasure. I also saw how mixed messages or even biased messages could be sent with words and images.

"I think God is with me!" Those words were written several times in the diary. The elusive mystery that hovered about for several months came in phases like that. "How big is God?" I wrote. My inquisitiveness started in April 1987, about two years earlier than that spring of 1989. When Chance first went to church, we sat and first talked about God and the Bible. My hearing the radio preacher in the car while riding to the Disney Ranch still lingered on my mind. Talking with musicians, first about God, then about Christian songs, was another segment. The neighbors and the roommates also had their opinions about God and the Bible. I found that some people, like Jackie, got very angry when the Bible was mentioned. But Emile, my good neighbor, enjoyed talking about almost anything. Our friendship had taken a backseat with my move into Big Guy's garage, but we were still friends. We agreed on a plan for me to use his word processor in the evenings to type the new lyrics I'd written since being in California. I bought more floppy disks to keep my work on, like the one he gave me to type my lyrics onto for Jack's class. My two index fingers were all I was able to type with. The keyboard was very challenging at first with my dyslexia. The faster I went, the more mistakes I made.

I got word in July from Ma that she was going into the hospital to fix her back problems. Aunt Lucy helped, and Uncle Shawn came from

Florida. My thoughts were with her. I didn't know how to help except by asking God to help her. I prayed that God would help my mom. I was reading Matthew chapter five, the beatitudes, but there was no one to explain them. I just sat and thought alone in the diary.

Aunt Lucy called that Ma had her back surgery and was okay; I thanked God. I also prayed for Chance to not sin openly with the woman I so aptly named Miss Fortune. He called himself a Christian, and yet he lived in what the Bible calls sin. I was confused about what a Christian was. I wondered what I was, because I sinned and I read the Bible. I thought about going to church where Chance went.

By August, the city tore down the seventy-five-foot stone wall. Our backyard was exposed to the world, and we felt very vulnerable. The worst thing was that now more people walked by, looked in, and saw me walking in and out of the garage. The scary part was at night when the street people came out.

I tried something new with Big Guy to earn money with the camera so we could afford to put up a fence. I had business cards made to carry with me; they read: Street Heart Productions, Videos to Go. Big Guy and I had a blast at Venice Beach. He wore a sandwich board sign and passed out fliers. We milled about echoing, "Videos to Go. Live- action videos show your friends back home where you were! Stand by the ocean, eat a meal, make your own movie now, and take it with you." The sign and flyers advertised live footage of the ocean, boardwalk shops, and cafés, plus live weightlifters at Muscle Beach. We offered to take ten-minute videos on the spot. I could show them the rewound playback at Venice Beach boardwalk for $10.00 to ensure the recording had been made. I even put a small piece of duct tape over the blinking red light. I knew people got nervous while the camera was recording. I thought it was a sure thing, but you can't predict people—it didn't work. Nada, nope, nothing happened. I concluded that people and tourists are far too camera-shy. But Big Guy had fun, and we ate at a great local taco stand before going back to the Valley.

I thought again about going to church. I wondered where Chance went. Big Guy and I talked about why I wanted to find the church, but

I didn't have a good reason. We drove around Van Nuys looking for that church and found it. It was a big building, and the empty parking lot showed us it must be a popular place on Sunday. The marquee read "Worship." The times were given, and 10:00 was the time that caught my eye. "Now we know where it is," I said before I drove away shaking my head.

✝

August 19, 1989, outside in the backyard under the huge eucalyptus tree, I wrote about my times. Over half the year was gone. The play *Harvey* had ended last December, but the memories remained. The music project was still lingering, and there was still hope a phone call from a record label could change everything. Our three song demo packages had been out there in the hands of the best A&R people, producers, and record label management for the last seven years. All my experience with songwriting and acting was piled in a box. Now there were no more walks to the park since my Pie dog died. Pie's life with me was like Thunder's life—more experience piled in a box. I sat in the open since there was no wall to hide behind. There was no driving the car because it was taken away when Chance left with Miss Fortune. I was just sitting there thinking. Maybe one of the acting auditions would break for the good. I sat waiting for the phone call that would keep me there. But that was where I didn't really want to be!

I was a thirty-six-year–old, part-time drunk, drug addict, and womanizing, skirt-chasing, lustful man living in North Hollywood, California. My last relationship ended six months earlier. Jackie was another love that didn't work out. I was alone and singlehandedly confused. I didn't used to be confused about women, work, or money. I worked diligently and pushed hard toward a goal—only to achieve the loss of time, all for the sake of being free. I was an artist. Looking back, I could see no material gain from all my efforts with writing lyrics. I only wanted enough. Instead, I got carried away by those two sisters More and More. The crumbled Bar Harbor mansion came to mind. That New England summer had seemed like a launching pad for dreamland. But that was nine years earlier. It was time to rethink where I was and where I was going.

I continued writing. I was trying to catch my breath under the trees, but thinking was only getting me agitated. My life felt boxed in and at the mercy of people who had money. That was not who I started out to be. How could I somehow have come here and spent all my time? Now I only hoped to be part of a shallow system of entertainment for money. Of course, I would be part of it—that was plan A. If it ever came true, I'd learn how to jump through hoops for biscuits, like a circus-clown dog. Seeing what I wrote about the business, with musicians and actors performing for the producers or directors, became so demeaning. Work in front or producing from behind the camera, it all still amounted to pounding nails into wood, just another job. I was jaded. I had to walk, I had to move.

The diary was getting more than an earful of truth. The diary had always been a medicine since its birth, after the motorcycle crash fifteen years earlier. I was being drawn into the most serious thinking since that traumatic brain injury at twenty-one. Now at thirty-six years old, I was unable to exist in an industry that I found to be completely phony. I was jaded by the hoax that I told myself I could deal with stuff as long as I tried my best. I always just wanted to earn a living, take the money, and run to a home near a lake. My heart was never in it for the success side of materialism. My heart endured the drift of aimless diary searching after the memory loss from the concussion. My heart was led by the discovery of my imagination into lyric writing. The dream chasing was manufactured at the end of dozens of attempts to fit in as a working unit in one type of job or another. What was the truth?

The change that started slowly and quietly rumbling somewhere inside several months earlier was doing something with the truth. The mysterious agitation had become an unlivable disturbance, which defied being ignored. What was unmistakable was the turmoil inside me as I recognized I no longer had a direction or a goal or a plan A. Plan A was a life. What was happening to my life? I always thought that my plan B would be fun to follow. Plan B was to find a good-looking woman who could appreciate being with someone like me and live happily ever after. The plan-B woman was out West somewhere. That's why I was blowing off the women in plan A for the last fifteen years. Women always wanted to know why I wasn't married. I told them I had a dream to follow and didn't want to be distracted. Plan B always seemed comical and practical, and it was always in the back of my mind. I kept on being happy-go-lucky. But in those summer days of 1989, the lifestyle of Happy and Lucky wasn't going anywhere with me.

Troubled days and nights became more and more intense. The seven years I dreamed under a tree in New York became seven more years under a tree in North Hollywood. In those fourteen years, the two More sisters had me beaten up and left me More lost and More confused. Now I was seeing another year, but it was different. A change had started slowly—like a real big season was turning—and quietly, like a marching army of silence. I had become an island of exhaustion in a sea of perpetual self-gratification. But then there was something else on the inside.

As evening approached, I found myself figuratively sitting in a boat without a dock or shore, drifting in a Southern California desert. There was something about those words I read in the Bible. "I am the light of the world. He who follows Me shall not walk in darkness, but have the light of life" (John 8:12). During the past few days, I knew of the growing void within me as if it were a noisier marching army of silence. It was in that void that I gravitated to the words I heard the radio preacher say. He read the same lines I read in the small Bible. "The fear of the LORD is the beginning of knowledge, But fools despise wisdom and instruction" (Prov. 1:7). It was a message. I stood up and turned into my yard, pacing. I walked back through the doorway into the dark windowless soundproof garage. I knelt by the door and wrote by fading skylight.

The Christian radio voice behind me was talking about earth being about six thousand years old, based on biblical history and the genealogy of the lives portrayed in it. How strange that sounded in contrast to the TV reporting the planet was millions of years old. Sitting in an insulated room away from distractions, wanting to listen to Christian radio preachers, was where I was in my life. Perhaps my dilemma started with the two-inch Bible I found in the park. My mind raced, trying to find the logic for all the talks and inputs about God. While I was looking for logic, I was beginning to come once more to thoughts of a different domain. What was slowly emerging as being real was a supernatural power. Those days were when the confusion became a louder volume. The subtleties of questioning life became obvious issues to contend with. I was in a room of thought and consideration, where I had no answers that would get me out. I was restless like a caged lion. I went and sat under the backyard eucalyptus tree again with the diary and the small Bible.

Sundown came, but I didn't move. I sat in the semi-twilight darkness talking to myself. I was sitting and then standing and then pacing again. In the dark garage again, I looked out of the one doorway at the beautiful orange sunset. I stepped out, walking all around the yard and back one more time. All the while, I was wondering why I was thinking about going to church. I had begun to consider the idea, but resisted it for a few weeks. Church was a place where there was no fun. Everybody always looked good and acted good, and I was so bad. Church was no place for a guy like me. Big Guy and I had circled the church I was looking for two weeks earlier. We got close enough and found the time to be there for the worship service. As we drove on, I was shaking my head. Looking at the sinking sunset, I was in confusion and unable to be grounded in any way.

When I thought about church, it overwhelmed me. It was too much change, too much against what I thought was right my whole life. Church was for families, and a place for kids to stay out of trouble. Sundays and special church days meant meals with relatives. Going to church was part of the treadmill life, where the good people go one day and then be normal the other six days. I put the church idea off for two weeks. But there was no getting around the observation of the thought. I could not understand how I got to that point. But there I was Saturday night with the idea of going to church the next morning. That was the last night I lived on earth alone. A big, slow revolution kept quietly advancing in the mass of silence. Heaven was closing in.

✝

TIME

I went to sleep on a cloudy night,
With discontent on either side,
Into a tunnel of no coexistence.

I hollered for an ear.
Diary heard me, who cares
Over and higher, all at my own expense.

Time was only a thought away, sunny days,
Time, out of despair, being there in yesterday.

Whatever was real was not in Time.
What could have changed things was not in Time.

I went back to a younger Time,
When I was bent on finding out.
Balance is equal to all the love you lost.

All extra, the experience,
Not just here but lived in Time,
And there's no going back, not at any cost.

Time was only a thought away, sunny days,
Time, out of despair, being there in yesterday.

Whatever was real was not in Time.
What could have changed things was not in Time.

When I wake up to a sunny day,
With content on every side,
I'll be beyond Time, in coexistence.

Chapter 17: Born Again

Sunday, August 20, 1989, dawned like any other day. But it grew into the fullest life-transforming unsurpassed date in my thirty-six-year history. I'll clarify that. On August 20, 1989, the most remarkable disorientation and foundational supernatural experience unfolded. That morning was like no other, and there will never be another. I say that with all of the critical alarming certainty a breath of life can take in and let out. Like a rocket on a launching pad, all of God's design for my life's preparation was in place. There was approximately a twenty-minute countdown from first opening my eyes to my first clear thought.

A coffee in hand, I was again sitting under the eucalyptus tree, watching the birds flittering about searching for food. We all began the day hungry. They knew just what to do and where to go. I was past sleep but still between yesterday and the moment. With pen and pad, I began to process. My thoughts in the diary were stirred from the night before. Last night's idea of church didn't go away. Last month's notions of going and a few very weak stabs to get to church were overridden by thoughts of giving up my sins. Church meant being good, being like others. I saw my failed partial attempts held in check by the chains of the sins I loved. But those thoughts of going returned with the rising sun wanting action.

I couldn't just sit there thinking. I didn't know what to write about the idea of going to church. I had no peace. The disorder from last night was to be continued because its bullying of me wasn't over. I was hounded from thought into deed. I got fired up to do something about it. I was once again standing and then pacing in and out of the garage and all around the yard. I wondered why I was wondering about going to church. There were no drugs; I was not hung-over. There was no excuse for my deep thoughts and curiosity. Was I going nuts?

My mind was so out of the ordinary, growing in confusion and unable to be grounded in any sense. I could not understand how I got to that point. I really thought I was losing it. Again I remembered the few Sundays attempting to go to church before that morning. I saw the pattern of unsettledness between my sin and the Bible's words. In Proverbs 1:7 says, "The fear of the LORD is the beginning of knowledge, but fools despise wisdom and instruction." I was in the middle; I knew a little and didn't want to be a fool. The periodic annoyance appeared again in my thoughts, with more authority. That rubbing feeling within was the emergence of truth. The words of Jesus, "I am the light of the world. He who follows Me shall not walk in darkness, but have the light of life" stood in believability, and my sin was the only obstacle holding me back from following Him.

I began my liftoff rumbling between the house and the garage, showering and shaving, speaking to myself out loud. I looked at myself in the mirror and saw my eyes wide-open and the wrinkles on my forehead. I relaxed my eyes and saw the deep, bloodless wrinkle lines on my forehead fill up. I realized I had been walking around with my eyes wide-open looking for something. I couldn't stay home mumbling to myself, and I couldn't believe I was going to church. I realized there was no hiding once I was out the back door; there was no more fence as I crossed the open yard. Motivated and driven by something other than myself, I was going to church. I knew that the power of sin was being confronted. Those monkeys on my back were all shook up. I realized my dedication to sin was being broken down. As I prepared to go and find out if following Jesus could rid me of my sins, I wondered about heaven and if I was going there. There were so many bizarre clouds in my head, I knew without a doubt that I was in a powerful time of adjustment.

At 9:20 a.m., August 20, 1989, I was cleaned up. I even put on my best poor man's clothing. I borrowed Big Guy's car, walked to the driveway, and in disbelief sat in his car. My concentration was being rearranged way out of the ordinary, and then I burst off through the traffic. My mind was the battleground; my body was the arena. The next round of the struggle was in deciding whether to keep on going or turn around. I lived the battle between the new persistent inner urgings of

Yes and the old resistant ways of No. I drove on, impaled on the railing of Maybe gliding along.

I turned on the radio. Like a roaring crowd of a thousand voices, the Christian radio preacher tore me up with the words of Jesus. The preacher read Mark 1:14–18: "Jesus came to Galilee, preaching the gospel of the kingdom of God, and saying, 'The time is fulfilled, and the kingdom of God is at hand. Repent, and believe in the gospel.' And as He walked by the sea of Galilee, He saw Simon and Andrew his brother casting a net into the sea; for they were fishermen. Then Jesus said to them, 'Follow Me, and I will make you become fishers of men.' They immediately left their nets and followed Him." How could those words in the Bible "and they followed Him" be perfectly timed and be tearing my insides up with truth?

Stopping for a red light, I was crying tearful breaths. I saw in the mirror my insecurity running through my mind. I was being shredded. Nothing made sense. With the green light, I continued because I could not stop; I could not turn away. Driving through Van Nuys, those minutes of emotional chaos were powerfully captivating.

I got near the church where Chance and his musician friends went. I looked for a place to park, driving slowly past faces of families smiling. Parents with children dressed like they were going to church were everywhere. I sat in the parked car with my mouth open, breathing deeply. Wiping my tear-spattered face dry, I glanced in the mirror. I was scared. My eyes cried for help. Desperately I scrutinized my surreal point of view. Close by, neatly dressed, happy people talked and laughed, walking by my open windows. A whole new world was there in my unexplainable outlook. Getting out, I stood as if I were searching on an overseas map in a lost exploration. The closest connection I could relate to was the bizarre recovery from the head concussion. And like then, in my groping thoughts of identity, I was led to the writing in my diary and saw myself in the backyard. Now I had somehow been captured and maneuvered to church. A parallel event was like seeing something in a snowstorm but you can't quite make it out. I fumbled about for a reason for all the mystery. I can still see myself moving toward the church, feeling very conspicuous and out of place with embarrassment. I looked at the other churchgoers. Everybody looked normal but me.

Approaching the massive hall in a huge structure, I was greeted warmly and invited in. I passed into the building and stood looking at so many friendly people chattering. I sat near the door, which happened to be right next to a nice little old lady. The singing put me off. I never sang in public. I was floundering and bumping along like a baby bird just dropped out of the nest. It must have been a sight to some and a delight to others. I listened, I watched, I wondered about the place, the pastor, and how I got there.

The pastor read words from the Bible in Luke 5:32: "I have not come to call the righteous, but sinners, to repentance." He must have said a lot, but all I heard was the part about broken lives because of sin. When he spoke of sin, I knew I was in the right place to hear answers to my questions about sin. Sin was anything that offended God, who was perfect. The words of Jesus spoke of love and healing help. "No one can come to Me unless the Father who sent me draws him" (John 6:44). Jesus gave His life so I could be made right with God. "I am the good shepherd. The good shepherd gives His life for the sheep" (John 10:11). Sin separated people from God. I knew then that I never knew just how much trouble I was in with God. Hearing how Christ died in my place registered like never before. I was broken down within, like a shattered mirror without identity. A sinner in trouble in a church for the first time in twenty-five years was what I was.

The rubble of confusion lay inside my thoughts. As I tried sifting all that had happened to me in the last year, the last twenty-four hours, and especially since I woke up this morning, it was hard to believe. There I was sitting in the church that I had resisted at thirty-six years of age. That much I knew. Considering the words in the Bible, I was doing nothing right; in fact, I was all wrong. I walked into that church like a zombie, and then I got destroyed by words. Another close connection I related to was when I repeated third grade because of words with pictures of their meanings, and those without pictures. The words that would tear me apart now was the truth in the Bible. I was a total wreck. My whole life was swirling around. How could I have been so blind? As if I had never heard any of the Bible's words before, I was bowled over. Like I had been ripped up in the car by the old preacher, I was ripped again and now tied up with truth at the same time. I was so confused.

At the end of the worship service, the pastor asked the audience to consider the power of Jesus to change lives. Only Jesus could turn you away from your sins today and give you a life to please God. I heard and held my head, swimming in confusion. I didn't know what I was supposed to do. A tear rolled out. The little old lady sitting next to me patted me on my knee. I looked at her with cloudy eyes. She smiled like a lighthouse and told me I would be all right. I needed and wanted help. Sitting there all shook up trying to digest the immense idea of it all, I paused with head in hand leaning forward. Peering through my fingers, my head was so small, and my thoughts were locked in my mind. I was looking inward at my thoughts swirling. Again I sketched a kind of twenty-four-hour look back. My restlessness, my pacing, the drive to church, the crying, the Bible words, and then my life got pushed into church. What was going on? I was aware of my inner fight, like it was in a suit of armor—a tin man with truth knocking on the inside, bound in a body of bad habits and the wrong ways of life.

And then it was over. People were singing, then talking and leaving. I stood. How could something so powerful just stop? Everybody was walking away happy, like that whole thing was normal. The little old lady pointed to a door and said I could be helped. Walking that way, I shuffled into the back room. I did want to talk to someone, but at the same time, I didn't know how or what to ask. No one spoke of salvation. I was told about a water baptism and given pamphlets to read. That was even more confusing. I stood there in shock and awe, and people were milling about like life was no big deal. I was so out of place. I was not comfortable and headed for the door I came in.

I stepped out of the building bewildered, not knowing what to do next. I wanted to be in my backyard. I had to think. Walking to the car, I relived the last two hours. I knew nothing about the supernatural, but that was all I could think of. Something super happened that was not natural. I got choked up again, like some lunatic in two worlds. I didn't know anything for sure; my head was spinning. There was nothing peculiar in my speech, just me saying, "What's happening?" There was no out-of-body experience, no vision. There was just my mind and emotions in chaos. I was not in control of my reason. I was with church people; I had always stayed the farthest away from them as I could. And I listened to exactly what was wrong with me and what would help change my life. And I liked hearing it. But how could I change? I saw the two opposing paths of sin and goodness, and I knew I was in the middle. I thought of all the incidences of God, the talks, the Bible, now church. If they were started by God, then He would continue to expose Himself.

I stood at my car watching people drive away. Parking lots and streets were being abandoned. Hundreds of people came and left. How could something so powerful and dynamic take place, and then everything just revert back to plain streets? I looked around at what was a normal neighborhood again. The temporary frenzy of activity turned out to be an empty beehive. But my head was not. What I could perceive buzzed like electric dots lighting up to be connected. Was God making me a Christian? What did that mean? Finally I drove away.

As I was driving, I was dazed, crying, and laughing. I parked along Burbank Boulevard and sat there watching normal people walking in and out of stores. But I was in some kind of abnormal, trying to look at the whole picture in retrospection. I could not get a handle on it. Something earthshaking had happened in the last twenty-four hours. There was no known reason or explanation. Thinking I knew a lot about my life, I realized I knew nothing for sure. There were no possibilities that came to my mind except God. Traffic went by my open driver's-side window. What I knew as normal was all around me and yet opposed by what was new in me. Again I saw myself in the middle of two forces. Questions about what was real circled in my thoughts. I had to write thoughts down and think things through until I could grasp the reality of it all.

As I drove the last mile to the house, my thoughts kept circling. I could see that part of the mystery started in the last month with wanting to go to church. But where did the desire come from? Then I could see the desire started before a month ago. The little Bibles, the car's Christian radio preacher, and talks about God were in a line. I saw the pattern I had seen in the backyard last night. Things pertaining to God kept revolving and going forward. The radio preacher, the small Bibles, and the talks about God—they had to be things of God. But I wasn't sure.

What else could it be? Those revolving events happened slowly over a two-year period. Today I went to church through some kind of mind-bending abnormal travel, and yet it was just a drive in the car. And then there was a weird, scary church experience; a message about my sins and the guilt; then the need and want for help—followed by what seemed to be wandering between two worlds before I went out the door. The lion's share of my confusion had started to roar and now continued its stalking. Most confusing of all were the questions: "Why me? What is it all about, and why me? Why now, and now what?"

For the next six hours, I was up and down pacing all around in the house, the garage, the yard. I told Big Guy what was going on, but he had no answers. There was no one to give any answers; no answers were found. Eeriness was in both my inner disorder and around my searching isolation walking under the trees. I was unable to penetrate any understanding as the idea of God kept circling. The questions were coming, but the comprehension was still not there. In the backyard writing of my supernatural experience that morning, I tumbled into that afternoon. Midday was waning, and I was wandering, asking out loud what it was all about. The morning was gone and the afternoon was about to roll somewhere past the evening sunset into the night. That was all I knew for sure about August 20 in that time of the diary. Knowing God was yet to be lived and nearly upon me.

Just before sunset, I paced more slowly and bent my head and shoulders down, leaning over like a question mark. In a state of self-examination, my eyes shifted to the ground and to the sides. I questioned my life's drive with past motives and my current lack of control. In deep thought, I tried hard to answer the question, "What next?" The next few minutes were the most wonderful, mind-boggling, clear-minded minutes in my life.

I slowed to a standstill next to the fireplace and looked up into the warm turquoise-orange dimming sky. I was standing with a blank stare, asking myself out loud what was what. The Bible, the church, the tears—what was beyond all that, what was next? It was all happening in just seconds. It was at that moment that the remedy came. God gave me the believable answer. It wasn't in words—there was no voice—but it was big and brand-new in my mind. Clarity arrived. The pure authoritative truth was the presence of God. He opened my eyes. "God is real" was the answer. The surprising, unquestionable gift from God at that moment was His truth, which He allowed me to believe. I was overrun by God's Holy Spirit; His presence was made alive within me. The authentic power of certainty was given to me. My confusion was dispelled.

God had always been there, but He chose then to make Himself known. He chose then to vigorously draw me to Himself and let me know He was real. In one moment of my looking up, He made me aware and took me to Himself. I lowered my eyes; I wasn't looking but seeing how the huge spellbound moment came flooding into my life. It brought happy, gentle, loving support. My misguided thinking began its crash downward. The clearing away of my confusion was far and wide. I was given peace with a force. Simple clarity carried thoughts to my lips. *It's all about God,* and that was followed with, *of course, God is beyond all I can see or imagine,* followed by *God is real, and He just now let me know it.* Lastly I said, "Oh God." The presence of God flooded all around me; the size was so vast, and it was so frightening standing there.

Those first few moments brought with piercing clarity profound implications of my inadequacy. Realizing that I had been led and taken into a whole other realm that I knew nothing about took my breath away. I stood there blank. I felt naked, empty, and full with beauty. I was given the privilege to believe in Him. I was suddenly so small and insignificant, standing before God so immense and beyond all comprehension. Yet I knew of the bigness of His presence. I rocked a half step to one side, leaning. My face flooded with joy and fear, with peace and quiet I did not comprehend. I stepped back to that spot and looked up. I stared into the sky again. I confirmed with a big smile what had just happened in those few seconds. I knew I was given the greatest answer to my confusion. God was real. He had me in the place He wanted me to be in; my searching was over. The closeness of God's exposure came like a silent erupting volcano. The gentleness with which God gave me His truth of being soothed me at that moment. No longer was I between two worlds. On God's path, I was at peace, knowing He was real and waited for whatever came next.

August 20, 1989, I was born again at sunset. That's the way it was. Did it start the night before with the pacing and thought of church? Was it a lifelong process of living before a moment of change? Could it have been each of those God incidents of the past twenty-four-month journey? Was it the Christian radio preacher on the only station in the desert while driving? Did listening to the talks with the guys in the band do it? The little two-inch Bible—was that the start of it all? Was it reading the beatitudes in the three-inch Bible Chance gave me? Or today in church hearing the pastor read the words of Jesus? Whatever it was, there at the fireplace at sundown in just that moment, those few seconds, is where God let me believe. Was all of it my new birth? I did know for sure that out of all that was still not clear, I was given the truth that God is.

What I did know was that I was changed. I had a peace within I couldn't explain. To have been given the truth that God is real, by God, was the greatest event in my life. I did not have the understanding, but I did want to know more in my confusion. Seconds seemed like minutes in that twilight of the sun going down. I was in the same backyard in the dusk, but I was all mixed up, different in the same yard. My mind was surrounded by mountains of new thought I could not climb. Minute to minute I slowly moved about, thinking on what had just happened to me minutes earlier. As the sun went down I talked with

God asking for help. An hour later and still later that evening, I could not comprehend what had happened to me or how my life would go forward.

In just a second or two, my whole life changed. As if the old me had been removed, and in its place was a new me, all in a most mysterious way. But I was always in the same body. I slowly reaccepted the awesome truth that there is a living God. The unbelievable truth was becoming believable. In fragmented perception, my steps of reasoning persisted to the point of truth and trepidation. I was actually beginning to believe by seeing the subtle preparation and loving direction that led me to that point. Realizing it, I again was thrown into a dumbfounded stare. It was real! I was lifted out of earthly thinking and brought into heavenly mindfulness. That's all I was able to make of what I went through.

Time had been dragging the sun down one way and hoisting the night up the other. Twilight had nudged my baby steps of belief into footsteps along a passage from where I was to where I was going. Out before the stars among the first parts of darkness, again I spoke a prayer for help. Unlike past casual prayers with words, I now prayed in my gift of truth. God was with me, but I wasn't in heaven. I was on earth, a person moved by God and given a glimpse of His eternal being. Within my disordered life of supposed truth and awareness in my thirty-six years of errors, real truth emerged victorious. The powerful truth of God came alive. How could that happen if it wasn't a miracle? I recalled how I wanted to talk with Chance about the fear of the Lord in Proverbs 1:7: "The fear of the Lord is the beginning of knowledge, but fools despise wisdom and instruction." I wanted to tell Chance of the powerful and frightful ride to church. He would have listened. I wanted him to have what I had.

That evening in the garage, the classical music station was switched off and eagerly changed to a Christian radio station. Preachers talking about the life, death, and resurrection of Jesus came alive. A message of God and heaven being perfect came with the problem of humankind not being perfect. "Therefore you shall be perfect, just as your Father in heaven is perfect" (Matt. 5:46). The preacher put it simply: "Therefore if you're not perfect you're not going to heaven. Only Christ is perfect; only with Him can you get to heaven. No perfect, no heaven." The penalty for my sins was for my eternal soul to live in eternal hell. It was the same message as I heard in church that morning. Hell was called a person's spiritual death, which is to live without God.

When I heard this news as a Catholic boy about sins being black marks on my soul, I never got the clarity about their removal. I was only told to confess my sins to a priest and he would forgive me. My penalty was to pray five Hail Mary's, maybe an Our Father or two, and ask God also for forgiveness. Then maybe between the priest and God, there might be forgiveness. Maybe I'd get a white soul again, and when I sinned again, I'd get more prayers to say again. At thirty-six, what I read in the Bible, heard being said, and now believed, is that Christ died once for all my sins. He paid my penalty and I was forgiven forever, because of Him and His sacrifice on the cross, where He said, *"It is finished"* (John 19:30).

I used to think casually about God and wonder a lot, but never knew beyond all doubt that He was real. Now my belief that God was real was a strong, powerful elevation of undeniable belief. My belief in Jesus was more of an understanding belief that what He did was, in fact, done. My belief seemed to be surrounded with gray and stretched out before me. I didn't know where to go or how to be more positive. It was all so new and so strange. I was me, but I wasn't. I was changed. I was thinking differently, but I could still think of whatever I wanted. I left the radio on and went outside to sit in the dark. I could slightly hear the radio. I could see in my mind's eye my day's actions in that sunset revolution when change had come. I recaptured the still-shocking movement from my unbelief to the gift to belief. I went back inside for more preaching messages on the radio.

The radio preacher said that as God, our Creator is perfect and just, He in His perfect heaven demands perfection. "No perfect, no heaven," the preacher said again. When God judges people, He will demand justice because He is perfectly righteous and holy. It's His right as God. He didn't have to create us. Life is a gift. Ignoring His Son,

Jesus, is the worst of all sins. For my soul to live in hell suffering forever without hope was going to be my ultimate punishment. But I never knew it. Jesus was born sinless and perfect. He was the perfect substitute sacrifice to fix humankind's problem of not being perfect. Jesus took my penalties for being a sinner onto Himself in His perfect death on the cross to satisfy God's perfect justice. When He rose three days later and walked out of the tomb as the King of life and life eternal, He had conquered death and death eternal. That certainly was good news.

The truth was that yesterday I didn't know I was going to hell. I didn't know that my sins were a huge problem with God until church that morning. I didn't know I was supposed to ask for Jesus to come into my life. He just came. And that day, I found out I was going to heaven. All of that was because Jesus Christ died on the cross for me nearly two thousand years ago and took my punishment. Because of Jesus, God had made me different. I was then living in the difference. That was a lot to believe all at once. The first night fell. I lay down; my head still wondering and sincerely asking God for help.

✝

Monday, August 21, the next morning's first full day of learning arrived. I woke up to a sliver of sunlight. Cutting through the crack in the garage door, a line of vertical light lay on the dark wall. The past twenty-four hours came in flashes filling my consciousness. I rose up and sat perched on the edge of the plywood bunk bed. I gazed at the straight line of light carved into my room floor to ceiling. Unable to recall any overt notice that my life would radically change, I lowered my eyes. As I diagnosed those gradual spiritual introductions by the Holy Spirit, His subtlety became more believable. The shock of communing with God in thought came back to me. The confirming truth that I wasn't alone but was with God was enormously incomprehensible. Yet it was true. Whatever changed was all preceded by the Spirit's overtures. They were facts in the diary, and it was with those facts that I began building my new day.

Tucked away with the Spirit's occasional discrete nuggets of knowledge was His kind, warm friendship. How else does one become friends but by spending time with each other? Thank God for the Spirit's measured ongoing acquaintance. His visits, those God incidences, were the only place for my mind to go and find a reasonable support. His visits were those covert rubbings of annoyance I underwent, and they always left considerable information and a twinge for more. If yesterday's all-day Sunday church experience had happened all at once without the Holy Spirit's previous two years' rhythm of installation, I would have gone round the bend. I repeatedly went over what was unclear but then became the facts of the many steady giving's by the Holy Spirit. God was with me. God could do anything. So why was He now overtly invading my mind and body? Why was He with me now? There was so much to understand all at once, and I needed help. I prayed.

Many times I have found experience to be the best teacher. I was sipping a coffee thinking. *A leopard can't change his spots, but God can*, I told myself. I took an overview of my life's experiences. My lyric-writing plan efforts led me far down a dead-end street. And then I was taken over by God. I sat in the garage looking at the truth I had just written in the diary. My life was never mine; it was always His. God knew right then that I was thinking of Him. God knew everything; He was God. He knew about my bad habits, dyslexia, head concussion, and my diary. I felt stifled. What was the purpose of writing? He knew it all already. I realized how my real life, my physical life, was merged with my new spiritual life and they were collected in my diary life. My diary was also born again, and recording my new life was its purpose.

My curiosity was by no means settled. Investigation went forth. I turned on the radio. Again glued to the radio preacher, my thoughts and eyes were following along in the small Bible in Colossians 1:26: "The mystery which has been hidden from ages and from generations, but now has been revealed to His saints. To them God willed to make known what are the riches of the glory of this mystery among the Gentiles." That was me—those words were talking about me! Again I saw the power of what words had done and were doing in my life. "The mystery which has been hidden from ages and from generations, but now has been revealed to His saints." I was let into the mystery of God; I became a saint. The part about the mystery being uncovered made a lot of sense. I was on one side of the mystery, not knowing God, and then I was brought to the other side by God to know Him. The part about being a saint threw me because I was no saint. I always thought saints were perfect. But I didn't feel like I was perfect and I knew I wasn't. Then I recalled it was Jesus; only He was the perfect one. I believed the news about Jesus, but I didn't know how to live a changed life. I sat in the Holy Spirit's classroom grappling with realizing the catastrophic and drastic change in me. I realized that I was not only notified by the Holy Spirit; my life indeed had changed, and the changes were going to continue. And I wondered about what changes would occur. But I knew I was being taken somewhere by God.

As I sat wondering, the patience of evil wore thin and made its presence known. My morning routine of getting high had been disrupted. Small commotions of sin's desire agitated my godly thoughts into a conflict with depravity. Sin wanted me. I, the self within, wanted sin; even though I knew I shouldn't want it. The protest of evil bubbled inside; it wasn't lived on the outside yet. The evil of sin's effect that I had lived with for thirty-six years was still very much alive. I reasoned that God knew what was happening. Mayhem and sin in my life could have been eradicated immediately if God wanted to take them out. But I knew He didn't because it was there. What I didn't know was how to deal with the turmoil.

My thoughts became the center of tension, similar to yesterday's dogfight in the car to stay on course going to church. In my infant status as a one-day-old baby Christian, I had to deal with eighteen years of smoking pot and its new sinful presence. In my mind, my reasoning was again the center of disorder. At that moment, my half-a-lifetime predisposition for marijuana outweighed my insight that God was with me. It wasn't a fair and even fight. Like a defective magnet, I yielded to sin almost instantly. As if I were a bystander watching the fight, I chose to watch myself light a match and smoke.

The debate had been short-lived. I comprehended that I was 99 percent sinful man and 1 percent armed with the Holy Spirit. My limited unlearned thinking collapsed in the first seconds of debate with sin. As I smoked, my treacherous willpower laid before my discouraged eyes. Just knowing the sin was wrong wasn't good enough or adequate to stop it. And then something new came. God's gracious Spirit brought nudges of condemnation. My conscience received guilt. In shocked weakness I saw how I was guilty of desire and failure, which led to my treason. I saw my new life in the arena of good and evil. The fight was on.

The sin that had been an unshakable monkey on my back was at last being attacked from a stronger power within. From being ignorantly happy with sin, I then, by God's grace, became irritated with sin. I was then made aware of sin's viselike power. The casual arena of sin's earthly pestering presence was elevated to a fight in the eternal amphitheater of God's glory. I was learning God's serious hatred for sin. My activity with my so-called bad habit was reclassified as sinful and never again thought of in the same old way. When it came time to decide what to do about a habit, I discovered sin's influence within my strong sinful desires. But within the dilemma of decision, my conscience spoke up out of nowhere. In not so ignorant weakness, I deliberately chose to turn my back on God and sinned. Why would I do that? When I chose to express the sin in me, I temporarily diminished the clean conscience. After sinning, I became sorry, like having hurt the feelings of a friend. And then out of nowhere, guilt rolled in making me sorry I sinned. When I didn't sin, I'd enjoy the benefit of God's harmonizing presence, so why did I have such strong urges to sin?

✝

From the radio lessons teaching the Bible, within my first several days I learned a lot of new concepts and listened to a lot of talk. I heard the words, beliefs, and facts that filled my mind. Creation of the planet is a gift of God. For His own reasons, He created Adam and Eve sinless. God did not have to create humankind, but He did for His own pleasure. That's what it is to be God. Eve was the first to sin or fall, and then Adam and together they passed on the weakness to sin. All humankind, the entire human race after that fall into sinfulness, are born with a sinful nature. Because people are born with sinful natures, they often choose to sin and can't be perfect. A sinful nature condemns a person to death. The penalty for sin, what sinning earns a person, is separation from God. This alienation from God deserves His righteous justice or lawful punishment. God's wrath sends sinners into pain and torment by unrestrained evil in hell.

Predestination meant that six thousand years ago, before God made the world, He chose to bestow His grace on some people, granting them eternity in heaven through faith in His Son. He did it because it pleased Him to do so. "Having predestined us to adoption as sons by Jesus Christ to Himself, according to the good pleasure of His will, to the praise of the glory of His grace" (Eph. 1:5–6). Others He did not choose. That was God's prerogative; He was God. At the same time, God loves all people and invites all people to come to Him. In John 3:16, God tells us that "whoever believes" in His Son Jesus "should not perish but have everlasting life." Because some of the attributes of God are visible and can be seen in His creation of people, earth, and the stars, humankind is held responsible to seek Him out. In a person's heart (Rom. 2:15) there is a God-given ability to know God's law written in their heart and in their conscience. God first draws people to Himself, as evidenced in nature and by sending His Son to die on the cross and be raised for us. Then it's up to people to respond to His invitation. Only God can explain how He chooses some and invites all. I may not understand it, but I do believe it. Some people respond well. But most people choose to deny God's plan of the cross by sending His Son as their Savior and Lord and all the evidence of His creation. Instead of living lives that please God and give His Son worship, people choose to live lives of sin, displeasing God. Living for God out of love for Jesus is humanity's purpose. If humankind chooses not to seek God and honor His Son, they will be held responsible. No cross no salvation. They will fairly receive God's holy justice. The penalty for the sinful life they choose to live is hell, and there's no second chance. Earth and obedience to Jesus is a one-time deal.

God gave His grace to His predestined; they are also called His elect or chosen. At His predetermined point in time, God regenerated, or restarted, my fallen, sinful nature into a new nature capable of believing His truth. He called me to Himself to hear the good news of the gospel, allowing me to accept His love. *Gospel* or *good news* means Jesus is the Savior of those who believe in Him. I became reconciled, or brought together with Him. "But now in Christ Jesus you who once were far off have been brought near by the blood of Christ" (Eph. 2:13). Only those who are God's chosen hear the gospel and begin a new, genuine spiritual life. Sins are forgiven, or atoned for, and washed away by the blood of Christ. Thus, I was born again and saved from hell in the new strength of the Holy Spirit's presence. Salvation is the elect being regenerated, believing, trusting, and obeying in faith. Faith is a gift. "For by grace you have been saved through Faith, and that not of yourselves; it is a gift of God, not of works, lest anyone should boast" (Eph. 2:8–9). The time for people to respond to God, knowing they are sinners, and asking God for His Son to save them is now. 2 Corinthians 6:2 "Behold, now is the accepted time; behold, now is the day of salvation." Repentance, or turning away from sin or darkness in faith, is guided by the Holy Spirit. Only by faith can obedient walking in submission to God be a work of God. Continued repentance is a constant goal and worked out in submission to God. There is no perfection in this lifetime except the sinless life of Jesus. Any repentance apart from regeneration is just human works.

Eradicating sin is a lifelong process called sanctification, or being made holy. *Lifelong* meant my fight with sin was here to stay. I was a hypocrite. Hypocrisy is knowing not to sin and still sinning; it is a huge issue. Sometimes sinning is because of our sinful nature and our weakness. Other times we could choose to stop but choose to sin instead. Either way, it's hypocrisy. My sanctification by the Holy Spirit would decrease my hypocrisy over time. Learning to love God was also a gift that came over time. The Holy Spirit did it all. Loving

God was key to opening a blessed life. Deuteronomy 6:5 "You shall love the Lord your God with all your heart, with all your soul, and with all your strength."

†

I saw the magnitude of my problem with sin more clearly. I saw the great need for Jesus as Savior and as Lord to follow. He was the only remedy to please God. I prayed for help in my salvation and for Jesus to always be with me. Jesus is the only way to heaven, and I was one of His on my way. A new life was growing within me, adding a new set of words to communicate new concepts and beliefs. My head filled up faster with facts than my heart did with love. Love needs time to grow. I was allowed to believe and now trust God to continue to clear away the gray areas. I wanted more elevations of strong, powerful, undeniable belief—more light to break me away from darkness.

Beside evil and sin, another enemy during those first days and months was my being alone. Over the years, I had learned how not to be attached, how not to stay in love, and I got good at it. Solitude was a learned friend. From my early latchkey days, I learned early how to be alone. Jumping off the treadmill, I continued to separate myself from the greater mass of traditional family life. Over the early years of lost memory from my concussion in my twenties, I was primarily alone and stayed that way. Now I was born again into a family of Christians. There was no one I knew who was Christian to talk to. I had my hands full with only the Bible and the radio preachers to help me seek out answers.

The only Christian I knew was Chance, and he was gone, off living with Miss Fortune. That part was very confusing. Was he a real Christian? Was I? But back in front of the radio with the preachers, I followed along in the Bible and gleaned some good news. On August 20, judgment came on the sin in my life. Sin's power over me was hanged to death. Christ killed sin's power in His resurrection from the grave. But the presence of sin in me was like having the silhouette of the sin's power. It still lurked about within me. Hiding underneath the gallows, waiting for the noose of time to destroy it completely, sin's presence fought for lost ground.

Oh so many, many times I have wished that the rope choking the life out of my sin's power would have been sharp and completely cut out its presence as well. Many times I thought of my rudderless thirty-six years of learning to sin and growing to love it. How many, many times I wished I had been raised in a Christian family, with godly parents to instruct me. I'd see families in church and wonder what it would be like. How would it be to live in this evil world with a family built on loving God? But the Bible teaches that God is the potter making man, His clay vessels, for whatever His plans and purposes are. "O man, who are you to reply against God? Will the thing formed say to him who formed it, 'Why have you made me like this?' Does not the potter have power over the clay, from the same lump to make one vessel for honor and another for dishonor?" (Rom. 9:20–21).

No matter how good I was at only allowing some love in my life, God's love was bigger and better. God loved me. I can never repay God. His love, grace, and mercy are a gift. I can only trust and obey in faith. I live in His plan in His time, and He let me love Him. August 20, 1989, came. It would be several months of crawling like a baby before I came to realize a little more fully the truth of my new Christian spiritual birth and earthly situation.

---

†

KING OF KINGS

Saw life shine, but never bought her,
Learning's hard on a self-taughter.
From rented rooms to captain's quarters,
Heaven only knows my raging waters.

Pushed a path, never found home,
Trapped in pain, lost love in poems,
Tinseltown, walked castle domes,
Heaven only knows where all life roams.

Then came the Mysterious, God took away the perilous,
Christ gave His righteous, now Emanuel is with us.

King of Kings saves souls. Lord Master, You provide.
King of Kings saves souls. Holy Spirit lives inside.

Believing God, perfect harmony,
Lifting the curse, in faith receive,
Putting Him first, following to see,
Heaven came down. Do you believe?

Then came the Mysterious, God took away the perilous,
Christ gave His righteous, now Emanuel is with us.

King of Kings saves souls. Lord Master, You provide.
King of Kings saves souls. Holy Spirit lives inside.

Chapter 18: Alone on the Range

After the August twenty-first evening class, I was tired with excitement. After several hours of listening to a few dozen radio preachers talk, I yawned. At the onset of my learning, I was taught two life-changing principles. I had been ignorantly in league with and committed to my evil sins, which offended God. And that which was good and was pleasing to God, I had unknowingly omitted. My omission was also an offense to God. Blindly in the dark I would have continued if not for God's grace to give me His light to see the truth. Now I could see and read the Bible to live accordingly. I now had to fight for good and fight against sin.

Well, since I was reading the Bible, I thought I got the good part right. But the Bible was huge, and the words were so small. I should also go to church, but that part was a problem. Because of my deliberate choices to not involve myself with society more than I had to, I was stuck. My admiration for the Taoist sage awkwardness with fitting in with others for more than thirty minutes was my problem. I had often found from meeting and talking with people a divide between our mutual interests. Emile lived alone; I was his first roommate. Big Guy was a quiet loner like me, and we got along. Chance was a loner lost in his art like me, and we got along. Now with his one failed marriage, he was trying again to let someone squeeze into his life. The verdict was still out on that. I only talked with the guys in the band and the actors I knew for twenty minutes at a time. They all had steady jobs or schooling, with families to support. After relating my life to them as a struggling artist and hearing about their "normal life," we didn't have much in common. My choices of dedication and seclusion were a positive helping me write, but were now turning negative. I didn't know anything about churches. I'd have to keep trying to adjust my attitude about going. Or maybe I could find another church. I should also pray regularly. That part of the good stuff that I could do I should do. I should do all that and more, and live a life in faith that was pleasing to God. The life-changing event was going to be just that, a life changer over time.

I learned that I was basically seized, snatched, abducted, and taken away from the Devil and hell. I was captured by God the Holy Spirit. The Holy Spirit would teach me and help me to shake off sin and put on the goodness that pleases God the Father and God the Son. All that and more had been planned out by God. God always was. He had no beginning, and He has no end. God does whatever He wants to do, and because it pleased Him to save me from hell, He saved me. He chose the time and the place. He knows about all the ingredients in my life—the good, the bad, and the ugly that make me, me. He's all powerful. He knows everything, and He will bring me to heaven when He is ready to. So I learned what God did, what He does, and what He will do.

I never previously thought about the unbelievable, but the truth was that most of it made sense. After all, He is God. But what I couldn't understand was why He chose me. I watched and lived through the event of God choosing me. And I was given more goodness and joy than I would ever be able to understand. The catastrophic life-changing event happened to me. It was like being in an air balloon up above the earth but tied to an anchor. I was lifted up off the earth and was looking up higher, wondering what way up there in heaven was like. And I was looking down at all my life between New York and California. In between heaven and earth was where I was. But still I asked, "Why me?"

That evening I turned on the peaceful classical music. Sitting in the sound-insulated, windowless garage, my eyes searched out the familiar props used in our music videos. We had collected swords, small people, a half-built cardboard house, signs, and surreal paintings of life and death. Some body parts were the skulls, arms, hands, or legs off mannequins we obtained from the garbage of a prop warehouse. Old and broken microphones, cables, and guitar strings hung on walls covered with slices of rugs from the living rooms of North Hollywood. An old globe hung on a very thin fishing line suspended from the rafters. It was half crushed in with dents and swayed over the menagerie. There I was with bits and pieces of advertising messages and copies of top-forty lyrics to study, all scattered about me. It was a strange, uniquely peculiar site.

Components, elements, and ingredients of this and that linked with memories all about my uncommon thirty-six years. I lived through violent swings of inconsistencies, bridging my path of existence into that rare garage setting and solitude. The past tragic motorcycle injuries literally altered my physical walk and redirected my thoughts and judgments even more. I had reckoned myself to a modern-day Taoist sage / Huckleberry Finn. Over three decades, I had separated more and more from society. In my reckoning, I was surprised by the sudden awareness that I was no longer anchored to those sin habits though I was still attached. That night my path of thinking was challenged and altered. I realized I was living in a huge dilemma. What was I going to do about sin? That's where my hypocrisy continued. That's where the fight in my mind between good and evil carried on into action. That's where I started to compromise in my baby Christianity.

I knew enough to know better, but I wasn't strong enough with spiritual muscle to do anything about it. How I lived at that point was something I would not want for any Christian to go through. I was alone and a loner. My vulnerable situation was in the Devil's workshop at his disposal. But I found myself with that small Bible reading it for some answers. I wasn't reading because I found out I was dyslexic and reading made me focus more. It wasn't because of some actor's cold reading class that I analyzed the words. The words I read in the Bible had life and power. Those words let me see the truth about the will of God. And those words also shone a condemning light on my sin. "Every good gift and every perfect gift is from above, and comes down from the Father of lights, with whom there is no variation or shadow of turning. Of His own will He brought us forth by the word of truth, that we might be a kind of firstfruits of His creatures" (James 1:17–18). I wasn't alone.

The battle between good and evil began that day and night for me and didn't stop. What had been was a life of ignorant, casual sinning. But once God pulled me on His side of the divide to see His truth and knowledge, sin as evil sin seemed to want to grow. Once again I turned to the diary and told as best I could and appraised as best I could my new and old values. Over and over again, I replayed in my mind those small events that led me out of my blindness. The two-inch Bible and three half walnut shells I found on the park bench. The only radio station received in the old car in the mountains had a preacher. Wow! In the first few days of confusion and seemingly directionless living, I began accepting the joyful, miraculous change in me more and more. And yet in those same days of confusion my bad habits were hunting me, stinging with sharp arrows, but were graciously followed by a guilty conscience. Amazing!

Any guilty conscience I had before was never a sustaining force. I was bothered more by the habit having control over me. My sins were livable as long as I did not hurt anyone or get myself arrested. Then I did get arrested. But that old guilt was short-lived. Strong guilt came alive when the Holy Spirit showed up. I told the diary my thoughts as my mind raced about in disorientation with what to do with sin. I was a bag of birds and worms, all shaken up together. Day in and day out sin was exposed and eaten up, or it crawled back in out of sight.

I thought about church and where Chance went and I followed. I knew I needed help. That next Sunday, I returned to church. I went a few times, but something was wrong there. I didn't know what it was at the time. I saw how that church placed a large emphasis on the weirdness called speaking in tongues. Something just did not feel right about the acting with what sounded like baby talk, so I didn't go back regularly. The idea of church was still so new, so foreign; I backed off the notion of looking for help there. Instead, I listened to the radio preachers in the garage, and I kept reading the Bible and writing my thoughts.

✝

Ten days after my supernatural rebirth, Christian lyrics were coming out naturally. As I mused about the spiritual revolution, I loved bringing it into the art of written expression. The new topics of grace, sin, salvation, and heaven revolved around my new union with God. But I got an ill feeling that I was commercializing my union with God. Secular topics were first written about with the intent to help others and earn a living at it. Over the years, I saw my motive for doing good change once I understood what sells and what the music-industry machine wants to market. In my new Christian birth, I could not justify a transition from my old secular motive to make money into thinking about marketing a Christian lyric for money. To take my personal involvement with the power and gift of salvation from God and exchange it for money was more than I could deal with. I tried to force my thoughts eventually into accepting the idea of writing Christian lyrics for money, but thinking that way never took off. I could not initially go through with the exchange, diminishing something so special for money. Because I knew

God was involved, the seriousness of my motives and then my intentions needed to be worked out. So I wrote with just the love of writing, like I had first written on that snowy night in New York.

I continued to write, walking in that direction with only the motive of goodness. I positively shook my head to a tune that kept me humming with the newness in knowing God. My old motives were like excess baggage I didn't want to come along. However, the irritating presence of persistent sin was lodged in me like a pebble in my shoe. Sin caused me to limp like that evil Mr. Hyde. I always prayed for God's forgiveness. The conviction of guilt was alarming. I walked more slowly, with good contemplative musings of Dr. Jekyll and new steps of Godly caution. As often as I stood still wondering about my complex planet-sized revolution within, life around me was rolling on.

------------------------------ † ------------------------------

A few short weeks after my August twentieth rebirth, in September the short independent film I starred in had a screening in Hollywood. It was a big deal for my friend Reave, the deep-pocketed grad student producer/director. The premiere showing was held at the Directors Guild. I took a girl named Gee because of her supposed business connections, beauty, and charm. The affair's outdoor low lighting hung from leads strung on fake trees in the large preshow chamber in what seemed to be a parking lot. Gathered together were would-be hopefuls and executives who pulled strings. My date shook free of me to rub her slender elbows against the arms of men who could possibly tug her career forward. Like a fish out of water, I munched on finger foods and drank wine alone, watching and waiting for the movie. Face-to-face schmoozing was not my cup of tea; I was much better at it on the phone.

Among the nicely dressed people happily mingling and conversing with charming smiles, my discomfort rose. I should have taken Melissa. With her brutal honesty, I would have had more fun ridiculing the pomp and circumstance. Following through with what I started, I put up with it. Somewhere between those hopeful puppets like myself and the puppeteers, I stood with and without them. I wanted the rewards, but not the socializing. Old and new motives crisscrossed in my zone of rebirth and mixed values.

Sitting among dozens of Hollywood industry-type viewers in darkness, Gee and I enjoyed the thrill. Reave's screening might launch his career. But it was me and my pride that rose as most important when the film was shown. I was thrilled to see myself on the big screen. I saw how important my part of the story was. The surreal film was based on a true story of a man whose life ended tragically. I was that man, and I committed a slow suicide for the camera. After the movie, I was recognized and given handshakes. Pride swelled even more, and Gee was then clinging to my side, wrapped in my arm. Everyone was happy, and congratulations were given to Reave along with good-byes.

The flick had begun shooting a year earlier. Within that time, I had been methodically dying inwardly as my California dream world collapsed around me slowly. Unbeknown to me, God had begun to surgically remove my old ideals, reasons, and purposes for being out West. In His plan with perfect timing, He utterly shattered the old me in preparation for His new me.

✝

I sat outside the door in my backyard the next morning after the movie premiere and thought in the diary. I found that the thrill of "Me" wasn't dead yet. It was just beginning to wear off. I was still very much full of me. The big screen of make-believe and the blah, blah, blah handshakes were pride pumping. The night before was a small sample of what I had hoped for. It was drastically obvious that I was living in two worlds. Those blasts of temporary compliments were in a huge man-made domain of temporary stuff. They could not compare to God's eternal truth. I had received something bigger than a mere earthly accomplishment on the silver screen. My head was in the clouds with thoughts of God. But my view kept splitting. Life between good and evil, between my spirit and body, between heaven and earth were forces on my mind to constantly be assessed.

Again and again, I objectively saw the subjective Dr. Jekyll's good view and the subjective Mr. Hyde's bad view both woven into me. As I wrote, I was sitting on cement steps. My thoughts were above, but gravity pulled me down to earth. I kept thinking of how invisible God from heaven became real in my mind. It was the same struggle I had in the car the first time I went to church. I was being torn in two directions. I wrote down both views and came to a conclusion. I was in trouble with my body and sin and the Devil. And I was getting help in the grace of God through His Son, Jesus, in faith. Without faith, I had no anchor to believe. Faith was all I had. Faith was invisible, but it was an undeniable gift from God and most necessary to go forward.

My diary was my only friend to hear all of what was happening. I was overwhelmed and consistently out of control. My thoughts caused a reaction in my body. My conscience couldn't stop me from doing the sinful deed. After the deed was done, my conscience screamed louder, and I believed I was worse off as a hypocrite. I was woefully inadequate to help myself and saw the great need for the Holy Spirit's teaching and power. I prayed for His help.

The newness of the immense, profound, startling awareness of what Jesus had done on the cross stayed on my mind. With the help of the Holy Spirit, I began to slowly replace those earthly things I had lost. The most important of those things was my best friend, the Pie dog. He was a good thing whose time had come and gone. It was the same with all my accomplishments and collaboration with Chance. He was the means to have my lyrics put to music and be heard and played in Hollywood, maybe on the radio—and he was gone. All the music-industry solicitation came very close, but no cigar. I thought about how I was thirty-six years old and once had nothing but that hope of a big payday.

I sat for two or three more cups of coffee and serious thinking. My past efforts to find an answer to my problem of putting one plus one together added up to calamity. I knew that if I had been fortunate enough to obtain some kind of financial success, I would have most likely gone further down the road of destruction. Even if I had found another great love and went that route growing old, it too would have eventually ended in death. What I had thought of as success or any success was for the first time in my life looking like a deficit, a graveyard, not an asset. So-called success on earth was false; it was a temporary lie, followed by a graveyard and then hell in eternity.

The list of fleeting lies was growing longer: film debuts, face recognition, cocktail parties with name dropping, and now some small success. They were all connected on an invisible rope of good intentions. My youthful thoughts as a diarist became hopeful life choices that were put into actions. Alcohol, pot, sexy women, and working with a band in Los Angeles were all fun. As I lived, I became more misguided and got crossed up with society's fleeting falsehoods of fame and fortune. My so-called fun had its teeth in me and shook the life out of me. Family, friends, and even strangers living lives like mine or not, we were all headed to the graveyard and hell. My good line of intentions was never informed with the truth of God until now.

I saw how people could have no eternal hope for heaven. I was once with them. Somehow their thinking took a subtle or deliberate misguided twist to ignore God and only produced earthly outcomes from their good intentions. Without the directions of God, as found in the Bible, people had become wayward. It seemed like most Americans were sealed in ungodly distractions. So-called common sense largely ignored discussions about God's truth and the reality of hell. There was hardly any mention of God in the news, on TV, or in the newspapers. If there was it was opinionated and not bible based or explained in context. Between the cradle and the grave were diversions of money, sex, and materialism. Jesus was the only hope for heaven, and He was only found in the Bible. "Jesus said to him, 'I am the way, the truth, and the life. No one comes to the Father except through Me'" (John 14:6). The truth was there, outside that circle of ignorance, but generations of people chose to ignore it. I thought of my ignorance.

As for my girlfriends for the last twenty years, well, what could I say? Sexual desire was natural and normal fun for me and the women. I know I got hurt along the way, and I was sorry if some of them got hurt as well. How could I have been so blind as to not see the obvious wrong path of just having sex and turning away from love? I had been wasting opportunities. Some of the more special ones would have been keepers. I didn't know why there were so many for me when I had so few things to offer. Some of the bad ones should have never happened. My lust had lived on a path that was tolerated by God for His unknowable purposes. God's plans allowed for my sin of fornication to persist until He shifted me into the awareness of His light. By knowing His good, I could identify my bad. The timing of it all was a mystery. Now was clearly a time for my faith in His plans.

What became clearer to see was the darkness of sin compared to the well-lit teachings in the Bible. Immorality wasn't innocent regardless of my libido. All sin was outside the will of God. Lust and sex outside of marriage were another lie I had lived in. According to what little I knew from reading the Bible and hearing the Bible taught on the radio, I was all wrong. However I never knowingly placed myself with a married woman. I always thought relationships were very difficult to maintain and respected that. With all the single women running around, I never knowingly had any ambition to interfere with a man and woman's ongoing relationship or marriage.

Thanks to the gift of God's grace, the Holy Spirit of God was present in me and on my mind, replacing those wrong thoughts and desires with His truth. Seeking God was bigger than any earthly desire. Lyrics, songwriting, acting, or any creative endeavor I could have ever hoped to reach all fell short. If my life or my affiliations were not honoring God in their content and results, then they were dishonoring Him. If what I did with my time had no good, truthful, eternal consequences, then my time was spent in lies. I was being allowed to see that I had been lost in a temporary world of lies. Out of nothing I did, it was God who first sought after me. Holy, sinless God opened our togetherness and lived in my heart. "I will give you a new heart and put a new spirit within you; I will take your heart of stone out of your flesh and give you a heart of flesh. I will put My Spirit within you and cause you to walk in My statutes, and you will keep My judgments and do them" (Ezek. 36:26–27).

The once vague idea of God was gone, and the real living truth of God was present. That new and largest reality I could never, ever have begun to consider having or earning came as a gift. Salvation from hell was a gift of love through Jesus from God. It blew me away every time I thought of how He chose when to give it and where. His gift caused me to seek after His Son and His teachings in the Bible. My purpose for my time on earth and for my way of life is all there in the Bible. "Jesus said to them, 'You shall love the LORD your God with all your heart, with all your soul, and with all your mind. This is the first and great commandment. And the second is like it: You shall love your neighbor as yourself'" (Matt. 22:37–38).

And in Ephesians 4:17–24, it says: "This I say, therefore, and testify in the Lord, that you should no longer walk as the rest of the Gentiles walk, in the futility of their mind, having their understanding darkened, being alienated from the life of God, because of the ignorance that is in them, because of the blindness of their heart; who, being past feeling, have given themselves over to lewdness, to work all uncleanness with greediness. But you have not so learned Christ, if indeed you have heard Him and have been taught by Him, as the truth is in Jesus: that you put off, concerning your former conduct, the old man which grows corrupt according to the deceitful lusts, and be renewed in the spirit of your mind, and that you put on the new man which was created according to God, in true righteousness and holiness."

I needed no more figuring out how and why and no more plotting a direction in life. God was all in all. I needed to follow the teachings of the Bible. The Bible was part of God's love, and examples of His love were built into it. Living out the teachings of Jesus in the Bible would please and honor God.

As one radio preacher pointed out; it was God's love for the nation of Israel that America should learn from. The Bible says in Deuteronomy 7:6, "The LORD your God has chosen you to be a people for Himself…"

God blessed nations and people, and He made promises to do so. God was in the business of saving people. God would direct my path also. In the Bible, in the book of Isaiah, chapter fifty-nine, I learned that His chosen nation Israel had gone astray. The LORD Himself figuratively armed Himself to do battle against evil. "For He put on righteousness as a breastplate, and a helmet of salvation for His head; He put on the garments of vengeance for clothing, and was clad with zeal as a cloak" (Isa. 59:17). Verse 21 says, "As for Me, says the LORD, this is my covenant with them: My Spirit who is upon you, My words which I have put in your mouth." God has always guided and led His chosen.

✝

LIVING IN HIS WAY

He just spoke up. I was dead and then made alive.
He just spoke up. By His Spirit I live and thrive,
All broke up, confused body and mind,
All broke up, I can see I was blind.

> Now I'm on the way, Living In His Way,
> With the words of Jesus, with a life in Him,
> On the way, yes, Living In His Way,
> In the words of Jesus, with a life in Him,
> Living In His Way. Living In His Way.

All choked up, His Spirit convicts my sin.
All choked up, I'm off the road to ruin.
I just woke up. His truth tore off my blindfold.
I just woke up. His Word broke sin's stronghold.

> Lord Jesus saved my soul,
> Christ's love has my soul,
> Holy Spirit guides my soul,
> Heaven is home for my soul.

Now I'm on the way, Living In His Way,
With the words of Jesus, with a life in Him,
On the way, yes, Living In His Way,
In the words of Jesus, with a life in Him,
Living In His Way. Living In His Way.

—————— † ——————

September 5, 1989, was Ma's birthday. I called her in New York. I told her of God's miracle in my life, of being born again. But Ma was a lifelong Catholic. Ma had no idea what the Bible taught or what it meant to be born again. She was in the dark, chained to man-made traditions. I spoke of struggling out of one world of sin and living in God's world of grace. But my story was confusing at best. I couldn't relate to her what was difficult for me to know. Only an act of God could explain the sudden, miraculous, powerful, redirectional, unforgettable, life-changing tangle of old and new. My words must have sounded crazy in Ma's ear. But I had something really mind-boggling, and I wanted to talk about it. I told her I was reading the Bible. She then grasped the intensity. She felt bad because she couldn't give me any advice. I assured her of my love for her and spoke of my joy in realizing the truth that God is real. She said she knew God was real. That may have been true, but I didn't see her live like God was real with a love for Jesus. Only God knew her heart.

I couldn't just sit there. I told my next door neighbors Emile and Gerry, but they didn't want to hear it. I told Big Guy every day; he liked hearing about the things of God. Of course, I told Melissa I was born again. Melissa rolled her eyes and said, "Different people handle it differently." She had heard all about God, salvation, and the Bible before and didn't want any part of it. Once I began explaining my bonding with Jesus as Lord and Savior and the Bible's teachings and feeling guilty from sinning, she groaned. I told her of the power of the Holy Spirit's forgiveness and comfort to reassure me of God's love. At that point, Melissa got upset and said I sounded obsessed with God, like a Jesus freak. She was right. She knew she had lost me. I saw the division between us had happened. I was passionate about Jesus. I had changed. And the change was on the inside and the outside. Even though we hugged and said at the same time, "See ya," we knew I was different. She walked away, then turned and said, "I'll be in Burbank if you need me, you nut, love you." She went around the corner of the house. I heard the small car start up and felt lonely. With each of the shifting gears I heard her make, I realized I was more isolated. Melissa was the first real friend I let go of. But it wasn't me doing the separation. Because I valued the presence of the Holy Spirit more, I knew it was He causing the division. Imagine that! Nobody except Big Guy wanted to know more about the Bible or Jesus.

Big Guy and I went to Basil's Diner for breakfast. Old Betty was one of the waitresses and pretty cool to talk with at times. Betty and Melissa hit it off from the start, and she got Melissa a job there. She let me paint some of her apartment when I needed work. The old girl told me her God was in the stars of astrology, and Melissa liked that idea. They both wore special bracelets and earrings and spoke on and on about reading their horoscope in the newspaper.

I had listened to their chatter but told them that stuff sounded pretty bizarre. Who could live according to rotating stars that changed from day to day? I told them of my faith in Jesus. I learned the New Testament Bible was almost two thousand years old. The truths in the Bible didn't change over time. Some interpretations and applications of the truth tended to be flexible, but the truth of God remained. The teachings and the life of Jesus are so valuable that humanity divides time at the birth of Christ. Before Christ is BC and After the Death of Christ is AD. Old Betty and Melissa got quiet; they didn't like hearing those credentials.

Betty encouraged us to take the kittens that were outside mewing in the cardboard box that someone had left in the doorway. She fed them and placed the box on the sidewalk hoping for some passing kindness. We took two of them home, but left the one with three legs. Big Guy and I watched them walk around his living room. We named them Pony

Boy and Lightfoot. Just like Rough and Reddy, the pair before them, the new kittens tore through the house and lunged for the drapes to swing on. Big Guy loved it when they ran and jumped on him, then curled up in his lap and slept. He loved talking and petting those baby cats.

✝

After a month of new mind-altering truth and the supernatural words of the Bible coming alive, I took a breath. The walks to North Hollywood Park without Piper were not the same, and yet they were now never empty. I walked with thoughts of God. Christians lived and died for centuries. They were around me somewhere living in my neighborhood, and I was one of them. I needed to find those people, but I was ashamed of my sinning and thought I wasn't good enough. But I was lying to myself. I really didn't want to deal with my sin. Regardless of whether or not I was strong enough, I was not comfortable with people in general. After all, I lived in a garage. It was more comfortable to deal with sin on my own. I was lying to myself, but I didn't know I was living a lie at the time.

It was either my lie or Satan's lie. But I knew in time that things would happen to those sins. Just like I was unable to stop myself from going to church, I knew God would do something with them. There was no denying the power and presence of God in my life. God and sin don't go together, so something was going to happen. What I didn't know was the deceitful dynamics of the human heart. I was still not seeing clearly that my heart was the center of all the lies I had believed. I was more understanding of how wrapped up the world was in believing lies.

Pulling away from the sins I loved, I continued to fail the tests. Again and again, I found myself in the waters of compromise. My addictions to pot, pills, booze, and sex were stealthy. There was no clean break or one big cut cutting away decades of sinful habits. My new enemy was my confidence. When I walked away from reading the Bible, my mind would either slowly let desire in or flood my thoughts all at once. I found myself wanting to be anchored to a tree reading the

Bible; I could not trust myself. The complexity of my dilemma got me very agitated. My bicycle rides were a good new exercise, but sometimes too fast to think things out. I'd walk to the park with the diary because the slower pace was like medicine.

✝

BEYOND AND WITHIN

I dwell on the everything of God,
The real and astonishing source,
Beyond the blue and blackness of space,
Love His promise to rule heaven and earth,
Planted inside, always in His plan,
Growing in light, fighting darkness,
Amid searching, confusion, came hope.
Gift of peace beyond understanding
Beyond and Within, Beyond and Within.

Forever with the pure before origin,
Stamped with the assurance of love,
Power of proof lives within my breath,
In God's will, I sojourn in His family.
We pilgrims share beyond holy words,
Alive within, mysteries of God,
The gift of gifts, the greatest of gifts,
To know and to serve our Lord Jesus,
Beyond and Within, Beyond and Within.

✝

I wasn't alone; I was with the Trinity. That was big medicine. I was always thinking. I was evaluating what was happening to me, all on my own, but I knew I wasn't alone. My only source of dialogue was with my little red New Testament and talking with God. The Bible's small size was good to carry in my pocket. I would take the Bible and my diary and go to the park for something to do in my restlessness. Sitting under a tree talking with God was still new for me. And I would think, *How did this happen?* I needed answers. *How is life to go on?* I talked to the diary less and to God more. Those were the first diaries where I mentioned "letting go" of the diary. Perhaps the original intention of the diary to be a medicine for my search of identity was no longer as necessary. The Great Physician was in town.

By the end of September, I worked at a carpet-cleaning business in Van Nuys on the phone making appointments. The business owner was a Catholic, and we made religious comparisons. He was a curious guy, always asking questions. That was the first time I was pressed for answers. I found that my hearsay from the radio meant nothing if I couldn't back it up with scriptures. I brought my Bible. At last I was talking to someone about Jesus. When I was asked where I went to church, I could only mention the church where they spoke in gibberish called tongues amid the confusion. There was no good answer I could give for not looking elsewhere for a church. The fight with my sin was too embarrassing to mention. My love for my addictions was keeping me from church and from honesty with myself.

Chance and I had written about thirty-five lyrics and put them to music over the last five years. I asked him for the complete collection and got them on cassette. I wanted something to show for years of paying dues. I needed to have a product in my hand for the seven years of hard work. After a million hours spent, gone, toiled over, and times never to be had again, I needed a piece of hard plastic to hold. The cartridge with audio tape inside, with sounds and words, satisfied my old self-fulfilling life. The old life was like a passing shadowy cloud.

Another roommate moved in, so we had two rooms rented. The house was only a shadow of what it used to be. Big Guy and I lived with strangers, but at least the rent money was good and steady.

After a month of the city tearing down our backyard cement wall, Big Guy and I planned to put up a cheap fence to replace the emptiness exposing us. The world of cars, people, and noise daily fashioned a wicked riot on our senses. In fact, the unfortunate deed ushered in that dirty river of population and progress known as Burbank Boulevard. We planned to put up a used chain link fence wrapped in black plastic and call it a wall. We wanted to just stop the looking at it all and the all that was looking at us; it was the nakedness of it all that bothered us. It was a difficult time for me walking back and forth from the house to the garage. Our privacy was on display, like it or not. I missed my seclusion.

I did a late fast this year, for ten days, which brought a great peace and stillness connecting to the Creator of the universe. Divine awareness was not the intention, but it was unavoidable. True spiritual fasting was a cleansing of my body, mind and soul. My spirit was made stronger with God. Fasting was like a secret I could tell and still keep because no one else did it. No one else wanted my secret. One motive and effect of fasting was like that of praying: to praise, cleanse and to receive the clarity of forgiveness and God's will. No one wanted that either.

Chapter 19: Charismatic Twist or Trendy Oddity

After six weeks, I decided that I would go to church again. After my August twentieth awakening, I never had an inclination to go to a Catholic Church. Perhaps the bad childhood memories of Catholic school or the absence of Bible belief in my supposed Catholic home turned me away. I suppose my exposure to the radio preachers' teaching helped influence my decision.

I learned that the Catholic Church had an enormous organization built on men; the organization culminated with one man, the Pope. The book of Acts 5:29 says, "But Peter and the other apostles answered and said: 'We ought to obey God rather than men.'" The Catholic man-made system put itself above the individual bond of the Holy Spirit with the believers' bible reading. The superstructure spoke in Latin for a few thousand years, keeping people in the dark. The Catholic system included a confessional box, repeatedly visited. Penance perpetuated an endless undue fear of never being good enough for heaven. By asking a priest, a man, for forgiveness and praying to Mary, a woman, that frail human system of religion didn't raise God and Holy Scripture as supreme.

I learned of King David's plea to God in Psalm 25:1–5: "To You, O LORD, I lift up my soul. O my God, I trust in You; Let me not be ashamed; Let not my enemies triumph over me. Indeed, let no one who waits on You be ashamed; Let those be ashamed who deal treacherously without cause. Show me Your ways, O LORD; Teach me Your paths. Lead me in Your truth and teach me, for You are the God of my salvation; On You I wait all the day." That was a direct prayer to God. The apostle Paul prayed for the Philippians in 1:9: "And this I pray that your love may abound still more and more in knowledge and all discernment." Loving biblical truth and learning to apply it in life was Paul's prayer. God's choice to open up a loving association with me was growing, and I wanted more.

My direction, my searching, was only toward that Protestant church where I first went. For the next few weeks, I kept going back to that church. I really tried to get into it. I even bought another Bible at a Christian bookstore. I discovered a new material world. Mixed in with Bibles and books was paraphernalia totally dedicated to a commercial outlook of Christianity. With the Bibles and books came plaques, pictures, wind chimes, stuffed bears, coffee mugs, calendars, and collectables of all kinds. What was I missing, and where had I been? All that was going on in my thirty-six years, and yet I knew nothing about it. It was as if I were living on a different planet. I bought a bigger Bible, and I got some bookmarks and a coffee mug with the face of a man named John Owen. A short message on the mug spoke of Owen, the English theologian, an author whose writings on the seriousness of sin and temptation must be essentially dealt with for godly living. I did begin to try and read more in my new, larger, complete King James Bible. It wasn't the thickest or the biggest Bible on the shelf; it was a medium size. I kept hearing about the King James on the radio, so I wanted to have one. But I found that the King James was harder to read than my small Bible.

When I went back to church on Sunday, I liked carrying the big Bible. I sat alone amid hundreds. I liked hearing the live message about God in the Bible. I turned to the book of Matthew and found the chapter and verse and read along. The King James's old English threw me off. But the print was bigger, and that I enjoyed. At the end of the church service, I hung around with my Bible, waiting, hoping to be friendly.

Standing among a sea of people, I turned to look at someone nearby. A young man was saying something. I was confused because of the strange speaking performance. His articulation was unlike any language I heard live or on TV. The handful of onlookers looked as confused as I was. I asked one of them what was going on and was told the man was speaking in tongues. I knew that I'd seen it there before. Other people in other small groups were also speaking in tongues, whatever that meant. Confusion covered my face and filled my eyes and ears. There were no apparent reasons for what seemed to be a form of playacting. I curiously watched and listened to his exaggerated expression, but nothing else happened—no predictions, no divinations, just mumblings. They must have made him feel good. I asked about that. I wanted to know what came next. Nobody knew what anybody was saying in tongues. So what good was accomplished other than that guy maybe feeling good?

It was implied to me that if I did not do like they did, then I did not possess the Holy Spirit. That was confusing—as if I needed more confusion. The Holy Spirit and nothing but the Holy Spirit's work had changed my life. By Him convicting me of sin and allowing me to understand Scripture, I knew He was with me. I didn't know what spirit that guy was talking about, but I knew God was alive in me. I walked out. I was 98 percent naive and was just trying to be friendly and get into the flow of things. But that stuff was as phony as watching an actor in front of a camera. It wasn't real. That church was weird. I went looking to see if I could fit in, but I walked out; it was just too strange.

Alone in my garage, I tried to get on the next level or into the zone of speaking in tongues. I began small spattering's of the nonlanguage gibberish passed off as a so-called spiritual language. I recognized it for what it was, like I was watching a documentary on oddball TV of a Haitian voodoo ritual. That gobbledygook was so bizarre and off cue, like amateur dramatics. It didn't make sense; it was nonsense. It was as if I were standing there waiting for some kind of magical reaction or unusual deal to happen. It didn't add up. In fact, the idea of it was rubbing me completely the wrong way. Again, it reminded me of the false conveyance in acting. The basic intent was to make non-truth believable. Just like acting was pretending a feeling was real, those nonsense words were nothing real. There was no benefit, no learning. The act of make-believe may have felt good to the pretender. It may have moved an audience into confusion, but it wasn't passing on truthful knowledge. Tongues were too much about showing something off, putting something on display. But I did want to know more about the Bible. I read the Bible's words in the English language out loud. I thought and prayed in English. As I spoke with God, the words were on my mind, in my voice and ears, so I could benefit from the English language. There was no confusion about using the English language; it was perfectly clear. That was that.

The next day and for days to follow, I went back to the small Bible to read and to find answers. About this time, I stumbled on another Christian channel on the radio. These stations, it seemed, never stopped with their programming aimed toward a variety of Christians. I listened to it all, with hopes of knowing more about what had happened to me. When a preacher spoke about being born again and its impact on a person's life, I listened more intently. I went to that church on and off—mostly off—for six months or so, thinking I could somehow fit in. I didn't know what those folks went through in their lives, but I knew about the earthquake that exploded in mine. Something supernatural happened to me that left me a wreck and gave me a treasure. I was living in mental ruin and experienced a calming peace at the same time. It was completely impossible to explain. Long about that bumpy time in my continued Bible studies with myself and the radio programming, I discovered some more truth.

Radio preachers were talking about the first Christians and the early church about two thousand years ago. It seems that the speaking in tongues as they called it was clearly defined in the Bible. I read and followed along. The Holy Spirit way back then gave some men the ability to speak in other known languages. Also, the gifts of healing broken or dead bodies and prophesying the future were present. The miracles and gifts were given during Christ's ministry to validate His power. So were the gifts of the apostles during their lifetime. As they spread the gospel message and showed it was truly of God, those extra gifts were present. However, since the writing of the Bible, those gifts went pretty much silent for a real long time, several hundred years, perhaps centuries. God's Holy Scripture became His evidence of power to convince and change lives through faith reading and hearing the scriptures.

The preachers went on explaining ancient tongues. Other than someone's language that was initially known and spoken, God allowed that person to also speak a foreign language from a different region. Then there was someone else who could interpret that foreign language, even though he never before knew that language. So it went like this. There was someone who spoke Greek who was given the ability to speak Gaelic. Then there was someone else who only spoke Italian but then could understand the Greek guy who spoke Gaelic. And then I got real confused. Because how could the Italian guy who understood Gaelic but didn't speak Greek tell the Greek guy what was going on? Wow! But no known foreign language was spoken at that church. All I heard was the gobbledygook baby talk and nobody was telling anybody what it meant. The Bible taught in 1 Corinthians 14:28, "But if there is no interpreter, let him keep silent in church." That church was total confusion. My gut instinct said again that something was wrong there. I stuck to the radio teachers and trusted the Bible. Church would have to wait.

As my Bible schooling through the radio continued, Christian commentators, pastors, and evangelists intrigued me. Phrases like *water baptism*, *the armor of God*, and *the rapture* drew me in. Like smelling a delicious aroma, my desire for more truth became a searching hunger for more knowledge about God. Jesus is known as the bread of life. The Holy Spirit was feeding me God's word, and I've never stopped eating. God's grace was the only antidote to fight against sin. The Bible's words had the power to battle with sin. The Trinity was God. One person of the Trinity was violently ripping my life, body, and mind off of the earth. He was the Holy Spirit. He was the new sheriff in my town of Depravity. His law found and forced sin out in the open for a fight. Closeness to God was to know victory.

In my dark human streets of awakened ignorance, my solitary mind reasoned badly, making excuses for sin. Certain times of day used to be times to have a beer. Four or five o'clock was an old habit. The tradition of sin knew when to arouse me. Without a group or even one friend to encourage or strengthen me, I crumbled in my transition to godly living. The bar just down the street was calling out, daring me to defy God and have a drink. My flawed logic answered with the foolish compromise of thinking these days of sin would be my last, so why not enjoy them? One sin begot another, and I smoked pot with Emile next door before leaving.

Passing the fenced in weeds of an abandoned Little League field on my walk to the bar, I knew I was wrong. I sat at the bar with my sinful body and mind, but I had new eyes. I saw my changed attitude in the mirror looking back at me with guilt. When I looked at the lined-up liquor bottles, my affection for them shone. But there was a new emptiness in me for what they held. I didn't want their ride up on the way of getting drunk. They looked silly sitting as advertisements for their temporary feeling of good. There was no picture of me when I got sick from too much alcohol. No sign pointing out liver damage. I spun on the stool, drinking a bottle of beer, disturbed with my awareness. There was nothing new at the other end of the room, where a few guys and chicks played pool, laughing and smoking cigarettes. Again the freshness in my eyes witnessed folly that echoed my own. I didn't look at their fun; I saw the trouble. They looked silly sucking on poison smoke. Their posturing, hugging, and kissing displaying their foreplay reflected my lost years. I did the same in life, chasing pleasures for two decades.

None of the old saloon ambiance was the same. It was taken away, and I was given new eyes to see my folly.

Through my poor fight to resist temptation, I learned that I had been changed more than I knew. Realizing my new phase of hypocrisy, I also realized the lie I told myself about coming there to enjoy sin while I could. I would never enjoy a bar again. My barroom years had nourished my sin habit, but now they were being torn apart. Staying was not an option. I don't know why I had a shot of bourbon before I left. I suppose I had one to say good-bye to the old ways when there was a tavern's exciting presence, just one for the road. Walking out of the dark through the door, I stopped in the day's high skylight. Looking up, I couldn't fly up to God, but I was in His sight. The bar was behind me forever. Looking down at how each foot met the concrete sidewalk, I felt my weight. My hypocritical defiance was labeled step by step. Like a pouting child covered in a heavy conscience, I lurched awkwardly homeward under sin's weight. Out of balance with pity on myself and so much sin, I was limited by not being able to shed my flesh. And with so little strength from the Christian life, I was sin almost through and through.

Above me the gentleness of God's gaze, with His laser of love, began carving my self-loathing. Once He was trimming off my mind's affections toward sin, I knew there was nothing He couldn't do. His love and willpower pierced through my immoral, rebellious armor of sin. I saw the decades of unsettled life stretched before me in my walk. Past the overgrown weedy baseball park, I paused and looked up. Sure of who I was dealing with, I again realized the necessity for ripping and cutting away of sin's folly. Even though I knew I was making a stubborn mess of things, I was certain God wasn't. My hope of heaven was seen as my perfect golden meadow, my someday home. Past the mental jousting of those evening doubts, I walked knowing God's care. Earth was going to be a transition of struggle mixed with supernatural joy, and I smiled up at the clouds.

---

†

In late September 1989, Chance and I delivered the new music packages. In his new alliance with the guitar player, they were calling the band the Fables. Again the music project tried to get noticed; we sent out cassettes as well as mentioning their live performance. They pulled together some players for a gig in a club called the FM Station. I called the music-industry A&R people to stay in touch. No one called back. It was another episode of doing our best as long as we were in California's music community.

$\dagger$

BLACK

It's 1989. Everyone tries to wear Black,
Black, a color of mourning the death of a decade,
Public acknowledgment of a dark era,
The grim reaper blended into social acceptance.

Black garb, draped head to toe from undergarments to overcoats,
The blankness of Black, the evil opposite of white, takes hold of
Every level of sight, to fill the yearly change with popular apparel.

It is conscienceless, and it is ironic how the colorless color
Is worn to attract and make a statement. Keeping up with the
Peer pressure is Black, the shroud of a dying society.

Or is society attempting to relate its fear and eventual downslide
Through the sheer ignorance of being the part and parcel outcome
Of the billboard mentality, so easily swayed by visual price tags?
I fear not for this lad. No matter how dark the surroundings are,
There is a glowing light guiding myself and others on the inside.
Jesus is Lord. Lord of my life, please help all to turn from Black.
Follow the Lord of right in the light of Scripture.

$\dagger$

After the slaughter of our backyard wall, after the city poured the new sidewalks, we finally began to gather planned material for a fence. Big Guy and I went to a scrap yard and bought what we needed. We erected the cheap used chain link fence with four-by-four wooden posts. Then we wrapped a layer of tough black plastic on both sides. We covered it with cheap bamboo vertical slats bound with wire. Our new wall was thin and good enough to block the view. Keeping the eyes and the street people out helped to keep our privacy in. But things weren't the same. The old solid wall was all about yesterday. People walking on the new sidewalk poked sticks through the plastic. The pores, links, and shiny black shield of solid synthetic screening would just have to do. Nothing lasted; everything began to be seen as temporary. Everything needed work.

✝

I confess that my new life was off to a very rough and rocky start. Without accountability, my spiritual awareness suffered and was dogged by spiritual warfare. The product of a solo Christian life quickly became a slow compromising transformation. Because I was alone, I was without the assets of what a family man might have. No kids to tend to; no wife to share plans with; no one to do my best for. I only had my selfish self to care for, with a baby's infant love for his or her Father. Over the first few months, I was just able to start thinking consistently of sin being wrong. My heart was surely not as cold toward God. Without the blessings of having my own family, I was far less distracted by the needs of others. That was a good thing.

Each morning began with recognizing the day as a supernatural and earthly life. In prayer, I breathed the serenity of the Holy Spirit. But it was still a torn heart. Sin's battle cries didn't wait or give me a chance to have a second good thought. When I saw the first morning sunlight, I saw the plain truth of my new life, a war with two sides. I knew the loud screaming temptations were waiting. My first few steps through the door outside were pulled with impulses to get high. My old patterns of life were antagonized from appetites within. Cannon blasts came filled with desire and fiery cravings for more than the beauty of a sunrise. From within and around me flashed an enemy raging in defiant combat. Anarchy and turmoil were questioning everything in the first five minutes of my day. My greedy flesh sought temporary added pleasure from sin.

My weak willpower was tested and failed. Sin's strength won the no-contest fight I was grossly ill-prepared for. With smoke burning my eyes, I gazed at the clarity of the two opposing forces. But I was not alone. Both powers were real. The sin that was silent for decades spoke up at last calling me back and the new voice of the Holy Spirit was calling me forward. Each had a vested interest in me. I was never alone again. I'll never be alone for the rest of my life. But I didn't get the big lifelong picture yet. I was still a baby. I did not submit to God's will. I did not resist the Devil, so he did not flee from me. I was found guilty of sin and convicted. I was to suffer the diminishing of the Spirit's lifting joy from my prayer just minutes earlier. The loss hurt. But I never lost the joy completely. My new ally was conscience, and it never left my side. My conscience brought both guilt and innocence. Guilt showed up a lot. However, I also found that I was innocent many times by thinking godly. Guilt and innocence had voices, but they were untrained mental and emotional muscles.

In my Christian youth, I was just starting to put on the eyeglasses of the Holy Word of God. Christ won the war against sin and spiritual death. But seeing the reality of the live battles between good and evil in me and in the world was a truth that affected me differently. Only God can soften and mend a person's heart when the mind is defective with sin. Only God can change a leopard's spots. The conflict in the mind was a daily battle. Conflict roared at times between the "old me" and the "new me." Thank God for an awakened conscience bringing sin's conviction. From conviction I learned what caused the loss of joy and a close togetherness with God. I needed to not just avoid the causes of sin, but to reprogram my mind with God's biblical teaching. I was not learning on my own. Even though sin called, the silent work of the Holy Spirit never left me alone and taught me how to fight sin.

†

CHAOS DRAFTED

The Messiah came. Jesus made His call,
Give back to God, love Him, He gave all.
He must increase, my old life is done.
Oh! Kingdom come, Your will be done.

Chaos Drafted from Hell's lying, evil ledge.
Chaos Drafted, defeat Satan's burning wedge.
Chaos Drafted, brought to the Living Water's edge.
Chaos Drafted, saved by God, His truth I do pledge.

Learning to stand in a good fight to win,
No more stumbling in and out of my sin,
Saying "so long" to my old life of less,
Here with my Lord, with my mouth I confess.

Chaos Drafted from Hell's lying, evil ledge.
Chaos Drafted, defeat Satan's burning wedge.
Chaos Drafted, brought to the Living Water's edge.
Chaos Drafted, saved by God, His truth I do pledge.

Old walls don't stand, old reasons black and blue,
My ceiling over time, my past is burned through.
No more falling, being wrong, wrongly proud.
Conscience is guiding, its siren will ring loud.

†

My head was coming out from underneath quicksand as the realization of God's determined plans for my life hit me again and again. I could breathe, and my eyes were allowed to see truth again over and over. I was in great need of help, which brought a desire to surrender again and again. I wanted the Lord to fix my brokenness. I was learning.

After three months, I was repeatedly amazed. Salvation at thirty-six was happening on the inside as my thoughts were being led in the light of God's Word. When my thoughts were left to stand on their own without communion with thoughts of God, I fell into sin. Only the Bible-led thoughts could lead me in my earth-shattering life against sin. Knowing my priorities didn't mean I accomplished them. My weak muscle for the desire of God was only an exercise that achieved strength in God's good and perfect time. I needed to think of God more. "For those who live according to the flesh set their minds on the things of the flesh, but those who live according to the Spirit, the things of the Spirit" (Rom. 8:5).

Big rains came in early winter. On garbage night, we found a way to keep Harvey, our rabbit, drier. Big Guy and I trolled the streets for solid material to be used as a covering off the flooded ground. Old office partitions made of laminated thick cardboard were laid on top of pallets, with plywood ramps for Harvey to run on. We got a dry bale of hay for him to lie on. The rain poured down so much it overflowed the twelve-inch curbs on the streets and traveled over the new concrete sidewalks. Cars splashed through the swamped Burbank Boulevard, spraying our living-room window. The plastic fence was slapped with waves of water and wind.

Life was inching along like a worm cut in half. Both halves wanted to live, and both were moving; sin and righteousness crawled along side by side. Smoking the last joint and telling myself to keep away from the dealer was good for only a few days. But in my weak moments of wanting to give in to the cravings, I paused. Faced with the choice to sin or wait, I waited, amazed at the second pause that followed. Victorious blasts of strength would empower me and were the greatest surprises. Like a charging cavalry to the rescue came God's Graceful Spirit. A passing veil of the closeness of God was near. I was tutored by the Holy Spirit of God. After another week of giving in to sin and living with my discouraging weaknesses, I saw the price tag drop on what I used to value. I saw my desires as the sins they were, and how sinfulness offended God. As the two opposite sides were warring, the Holy Spirit showed me in my failure how little I loved God.

I held my head in my two hands. Inside was the battle zone from day one, and evil didn't fight fair. My cravings for booze, sex, and getting high were dogging me all at once. Good intentions to refrain from their temptations failed. Even when I enjoyed harmony with the Trinity, a flash of sinful thought would flare up. I can't explain it. When I was praying or reading the Bible, a sinful thought popped up and threw me off my path of concentration. However, I could feel relief from the seriousness of my sin in the name Jesus. I knew the seriousness that comes with the power of God in the calling for Jesus. Seeing the pain He suffered on the cross for me demonstrated His love.

✝

LORD JESUS

Clear-eyed and clean-minded,
Never again being blinded,
Crushing sin when in it creeps,
I got good conscience critiques.

I'm born again, evil can't rule me.
I'm born again, Holy Spirit carries me, caring, caring.

> Lord Jesus, I read Your word.
> Your breath of salvation has spoken.
> Lord Jesus, we go forward,
> Your love's dedication unbroken.

Teach me more in Your truth, Lord.
Help me carry Your word, Your sword.
Holy Spirit leads the way,
Faith in You I trust and obey.

I'm born again, evil can't rule me.
I'm born again, Holy Spirit carries me, caring, caring.

> Lord Jesus, I read Your word.
> Your breath of salvation has spoken.
> Lord Jesus, we go forward,
> Your love's dedication unbroken.

✝

Physical and emotional parts of my life were being voluntarily and involuntarily reevaluated. Seeing the hand of God as the orchestrator placing me in the path He chose for me broadened my considerations of life. Walking through the house, I viewed my status as caretaker of the property with more respect. Cleaning the kitchen more often and even washing other people's dirty dishes in the sink was strange at first. Having been shifted to the new side of life called enlightened, I was being shown to give up boundaries of my self-interest. Confusion about why I hadn't cared enough to do chores for others was cleared up. Seeing my motives as good deeds were gestures in reverence toward God, honoring Him. Pleasing God first helped others. But my two avenues of needed change were unequal. It was easier to do good than it was to be good.

Struggling to explain my new feelings against being around drugs to the roommates was an atypical battle for me. I stood in front of them a completely defenseless hypocrite answering truthfully, "Yes, I still smoke pot. But my goal is for it to be eliminated." And yet I valued my conviction, saying, "My mental addiction is like worship to a false god, which offends God." My roommates laughed at me. At times my confusion seemed to have been balanced by the hand of God. Joy and truth were passed on to me and lived within me as I continued to walk a different path. I watched mixed messages in my earthly body colliding with the supernatural Spirit of truth. Battles with old sin habit's trying to live found reason's not to because of a slow growing love for God.

My acceptance that I was living in the mystery of God didn't bounce as much within. I knew I knew a little and I knew I would know more as God would allow me.

My halfhearted commitments against sin were just that: a massive sinner making unaided, uneducated, halfhearted attempts to stop sinning. The peace of God, which I had occasionally, was coming and going like the movement of a yo-yo. Because of my sinning, I could see that sin hurt my peace, but I could not figure out how not to sin. Just knowing not to sin wasn't good enough. My emotional swings would lead me to question my sanity. How could I knowingly admit the sin was wrong, and then be attacked by the thought of sin, then sin, and then feel guilty about sinning? And feel like a traitor to God watching it all. How could that be anything but part of the mystery of God?

✝

During my transformation, I once more made use of my California experience by auditioning for a play called *A Streetcar Named Desire*. Slipping back into the Hollywood mind-set while living in my Spirit-led renovation brought more challenges with truth. I can surely say there was war in my life. I was a new-thinking man walking and talking to myself about God in my old body. In writing down what that meant for me as a living receptacle of God's truth, the diary became vital. When sin was absent, life was beautiful, with wanting to be closer to God and to stay at His side. Truth about my purpose in life to live for God swelled within by means of tasting real fulfillment and hungering for more.

✝

IN HIS HONOR ON MY GUARD

I've been chosen to see more than this.
I'm a soldier. I will not dismiss
God's Word in the world,
In His Honor on My Guard.

       Pulled from Satan's spell, Drawn from sin's hotel,
       Taken off the road to hell, Saved from fires of hell.

Here in His fight, fighting for all I'm worth,
In His strength, for His Word on earth,
Holy Word in the world,
In His Honor on My Guard.

       He shall call from heavens above
       And to earth, He will judge with love.
       I will sing how the streets of gold are.
       For my Lord, In His Honor on My Guard.

       Pulled from Satan's spell, Drawn from sin's hotel,
       Taken off the road to hell, Saved from fires of hell.

Share His mystery, give the gospel news,
Hear the trumpet blast, see His rendezvous,
King's Word in the world,
In His Honor on My Guard.

       He shall call from heavens above
       And to earth, He will judge with love.
       I will sing how the streets of gold are.
       For my God, In His Honor on My Guard.

I believed the radio preachers right from the start that I should give money back to help support Christ's church. Believers in Jesus Christ who were true born-again people gave back a portion of their blessings. The suggested framework for tithing or giving back to God for all the work of God's church is found in Nehemiah 10:38: "And the Levites shall bring up a tenth of the tithes to the house of our God." Money that is given in an offering to a local church helps the preachers and is for the building and for helping missionaries and needy widows in the church, and advancing the true gospel. Giving is a privilege and has been all through time and all over the globe. Those who are the happiest to give money back to the local church understand the privilege. As I understood more about my privilege of giving back to God what He first gave me, I remained a regular and eager giver. All money and everything was God's. He was giving me the opportunity to give to Him my worship, praise and tithes.

When I didn't go to church, which was often at first, I helped the street people by buying them a meal and coffee. I gave my money directly to them with food. The money issue was a big deal because I didn't have much. But it was clear to me that giving was good and God's command in the Bible. Spending money stupidly on sinful expenses didn't work well together with good giving. Tithing was another avenue of good change exposed by heaven's grace.

The understanding of Scripture and the supervision of the Spirit of God were the best. But all my learning, including that from the radio, came without human feedback to consider. Not going to church was a growing irritation. But my childhood memories of getting dressed up, having big Sunday meals, and visiting relatives were ideas that helped keep church at a distance. My Dad going to church one day and trying to be good, and then being himself the other six days was my hypocrisy also. The idea of church still didn't fit on me. But I saw it for what it was: another avenue of change for the good.

I did learn to let go of girlfriends and not to take on any new girlfriends. Sex outside of marriage was sin. The women I knew didn't agree with what I believed. My sexual promiscuity was both sharing my sin and deliberately showing my sin off. Even though it was in private, it was public with them. That was wrong. Drinking beer and smoking pot were private. Not that that was any better. The public hypocrisy from participating with sin openly seemed to come with more conviction. I could feel the shame and rebellion more. Hiding my sins, I knew they were still sins, but the public ones were the first to be cut out. Excluding fleshly immorality was another avenue of righteousness. The good path to take was uncovered by the Holy Spirit's guidance.

✝

BE SEPARATE, SAYS THE LORD

Boy and girl may be husband and wife,
Fun and laughs, but where's God in their life?
Wait and see that this life is not joking,
Take God's truth, hear what He has spoken.

Who will stand with God? Who will walk away?

Time keeps turning cold hearts from the Rock.
God is love, He will not be mocked.
Turn your head before the sun goes down,
Jesus first, only He wears the crown.

Who will stand with God? Who will walk away?

What fellowship has the light with the dark?
Don't go there, don't get close to the spark.
Come out from and Be Separate, Says the Lord.
Turn away, and Be Separate, Says the Lord.

Who will stand with God? Who will walk away?

Joseph ran when he felt her first touch,
No excuse letting sin lean so much.
Faith will fight, holding God's Word within.
Stay with the Lord, turn from the face of sin.

In December I was four months old in my new life and still crawling. The wheels of time rolled on; the old life was stumbling. The new life was gaining in recognition. I got the part in *A Streetcar Named Desire*. I played the guy living upstairs, Steve Hubbell. Bitten by the acting bug of worldly ambition again, my mind rethought old ideas. During the holiday season, I began considering using the entertainment magazine *Drama-Logue*. Advertising for another composer to work with and my own creative projects making music videos played on my mind.

Ma's care package came full of love. I sent Ma a letter explaining God's greatest gift to humankind, His Son. I told her in my own words that I believed His Son died for my sins and God told me so in the Bible. I was so lonely without the Pie dog. I had nobody close to me to share my mixed-up world with, nobody to reach out to and touch. I didn't know where to go to church on Christmas Eve. I didn't go anywhere. I was not alone. With God within, nobody is ever alone. I stood in the backyard surrounded by the black sky speckled with stars. I stared into all of space and caressed both my edginess and calmness.

My life got so huge with all the good news and information. It would take me ten lifetimes to understand it all. And then it hit me. By receiving God's gift of truth in His Son, Jesus, I was actually getting a glimpse of what's beyond the black space. Some of His eternity was related to me in a surge, and I felt a swell of total fulfillment. I didn't go anywhere, and I didn't do anything; it was a gift. There was nothing left for me to do; everything was done. God, who is eternal, was with me, and we were on a new path. Cheerful thoughts snapped into my mind as if—I repeat, as if—God Himself were speaking to me. Peace was with me, bubbling up again. God was the greatest, beyond all on the earth, beyond the stars and space. God was bigger and better than any battle. He was all victory and always victorious. God was paramount to me because of Jesus dying for my sins on the cross.

Like bright neon signs with brilliant colors in an all-dark desert, I saw again the truths that God is and God is Jesus. Why couldn't I keep that presence, that camaraderie? There, close to me, was the Holy Spirit God, who was a friend. God Almighty, the Creator of heaven and earth, chose to let me be with Him. There's nothing better than that. The awesome brilliance in God's grace to allow me to reflect on His presence was so very special, and yet had one aspect of familiarity. Again the unique aspect was the blast that came in realizing I was allowed to reflect on the perfection of Him and His gift in Jesus.

The familiarity was similar to those first weeks after my concussion. When I first was able to remember something, there also came with the memory the importance to write it down. So I began writing the diary. Again that night, I realized the importance of diary writing. Yes, it was important to me for many reasons, but now there was something bigger going on with the diary. At thirty-six years of age, I was being allowed once again to see the importance of writing the diary and how it might be helpful to others. I sat in the shadows of the trees from the streetlight in silence. Jesus was the biggest and the best news any human being could be with. I was warmly celebrating God's gift, the birth of His Son, Lord Jesus, my Savior. The profound news of the gospel came with profound change and the profound presence of the Holy Spirit. I was with my new family. All I could do was hang my head and stare at the ground. The end of 1989 left me some very peaceful pieces of my puzzle. The mixed-up parts of the puzzle were for God to work out in His good and perfect time. I was being made into something new. I was thankfully given faith to believe in God. I was in the awesome plans and hands of God.

Chapter 20:
Learning Truth, and Fighting Lies and Vices

January brought with it cold nights, as were all those first days of 1990, which only looked new on a small desk calendar. Each piece of square glossy paper appeared daily with an aging number, a Bible verse, and a picture. I enjoyed reading the verses so much I collected every page after tearing them off. Seeing the beautiful photos of God's creation led me to dwell on the infinite Creator. For His pleasure, He made mountains, formed seas, and gave me breath with strength to rip through time. Morning thoughts of my life, with its physical isolation, and my heavenly union were revealed. My slow, awkward stubbornness impeded my ability to heed God's wisdom more fully.

I pushed on a button for help and listened for another lesson. The radio preacher spoke of a person's heart, with one throne chair only big enough for one to sit in. Before the gift of true spiritual awakening, the throne was occupied by the spiritually dead sinner, surrounded with the sins he loved. After being spiritually born again, God, His Master of all authority, was sitting in the throne chair. The sinner could either be defiantly standing with stubborn arms folded or a compliant subject of his Creator King, bowing humbly. I pushed off the button. Bowing my head, I praised my immeasurable God. Only He could soften my hard heart; only He could rule my life with a parent's patient love. Pleading for His will in my life, I prayed.

Again I questioned my prolonged stay in the San Fernando Valley. I searched for answers. Why did I get involved with another play? Why was I thinking about making a music video? I should be so different. I was a Christian; I was born again, and yet I was still me, an obstinate sinner. Even if I were locked in a cave on a Rocky Mountain hillside away from temptation, I'd still be willfully sinning in my mind. I was here, and here is where God saved me. My forgotten lyric title jumped into my thoughts: "Almost Is Addicting." I saw the fiber of my true grit traveling west. The tenacity of me striving for a goal, my perseverance, was explained in the diary; striving was what I was about. I wasn't going anywhere yet. I was living the life given to me, and now priorities were being rearranged by God. Above all I could think or do was the will of God. His plans would surely come to pass no matter where I was.

The *A Streetcar Named Desire* play rehearsals were beginning. I enjoyed being the fun-loving, poker-playing guy living upstairs from

Stanley Kowalski. The play rehearsed and would perform in a small community called Tujunga. A historical building off Foothill Boulevard was where the small cast met. The country-like setting, with small stores and friendly people, was enjoyable. Beyond Sunland and Tujunga was Big Tujunga Canyon Road, which led into the Angeles National Forest. But I drove through what was called Little Tujunga, or La Tuna Canyon, during my involvement. Those cold, dark January nights after rehearsals, in the parking lot I paused looking up for the monthly moonrise, which got steadily closer. Each night the glow got nearer and whiter, and I eagerly waited for the fullness.

Driving through La Tuna Canyon's solid black twisting ravine one night, I was looking up like out of a deep, dark well. The stars above were brighter and clearer, and the white specks were more numerous. High above the road on the canyon walls, moonglow shone on the rocks' vertical craggy faces. Through the tree limbs, white and black shadows cast their eerie, magnetic pull overhead. As I drove under the shadows around the two-lane curves, moonglow flickered and flashed like lightning. Anticipation for when I would see the full brilliant orb grew with each narrow turn. My eyes darted to and fro as I negotiated the spooky road. Carefully I came around a curve lit up like daylight and greeted the giant moon. I slowed and froze in its grandeur. The size and clarity of its surface took my breath away. Like a specter, the ghost captured my gaze, and I pulled over to gawk in its power. Oh, how I enjoyed our get-together. The burst of reflective thoughts from my first post-concussion New York encounters flooded my reunion. Our meeting gave way to a new vein of reinforcing creative energy. I was here in southern California and might never be gone or never come back. Here is where the Holy Spirit began His leading me.

When I arrived at Big Guy's place, the fireplace burned again with lots of fires to heat the house. Without Pie or Rex, just I and Big Guy sat staring at the flames. Sometimes the best friend is one who just sits and says nothing. The quiet held only the crackling snaps and pops from our trash-day street-side wood collecting's. The sight I held in my thoughts was of me tearing the first pages from the calendar of 1990. Those square glossy pictures with numbers that grew fanned my inspiration. Silent artistic thoughts that had been set aside began smoldering. With my recent God-sent transformation, creativity began to glow.

My original eighty-five lyrics that I had brought with me from New York grew to 110 before I registered them for copyright in March 1982. Since then, I enjoyed writing fifty-five more, stemming from class and when the muse of creativity struck. Adding those with the thirty-five I wrote with Chance, my collection had grown into two hundred. Emile had allowed me to type all of them using his word processor. Despite my dyslexic disadvantage, the slavish process of pecking with two fast fingers for six months was worth every poke. Seeing the lyrics printed out was encouraging.

My cache of lyrics on floppy disk wasn't idle too long. After eight years, I once again began seeking other composers to collaborate with. Placing an ad in the *Drama-Logue* entertainment magazine, I looked in the Hollywood area.

I was still working as an extra on films and TV while rehearsing for *Streetcar* in the evenings. Like months earlier, those spells of extra work were very often a classroom to learn the procedure of filming. The continuity of getting the shot sequence wasn't always clear, but a similar technique was used on every set. That knowledge plus seeing how the play was coming together was of value and created an opportunity to use it. During this time, I was contacted by my actor/producer friend Rick, whom I had met on a shoot. He mentioned his short film project called *Heading Back* and his hopes for it going to the Cannes Film Festival. I suggested that I seize the moment with my video camera and put together a music video to enhance his project. He had nothing to lose, and it was my time, my gamble. The time had come; it was my turn to take the video camera and use it. How I could assemble lyrics, music, and motion pictures to make a short three-minute movie was a mystery just beginning to unfold.

Even though my exposure to stage, film, and TV acting was small, it wasn't insignificant. Fortunately I seemed to get a lot of extra work; I was on the go day and night. The money helped me. As I sat around sets, I watched and perceived the meaning or intention of what the director's instructions were to the crew. I wrote down my observations to help me clarify how they put their objective into action. Sometimes my surveying was akin to enjoying a circus-like event. The small or very large world of employees and equipment took control of small portions of the community. Streets were blocked off, police guided traffic, and a small production city emerged. There was a lot to watch, all for the sake of actors pretending and entertainment for viewers. I'd studied how the various crews' lighting, sound, costumes, and cameras performed their duties. Uncle Shawn always used to say if you want to learn, watch someone good doing their job.

The cameramen and their structure of sequence in shooting a scene were fascinating. Measuring distance, filtering light, laying tracks to roll equipment on, when needed they walked with a Steadicam device. With a camera braced on their body, they walked with the actor but the device eliminated most of the bumps. Cameras were one of the most important parts of the unity to simulate truth. Over and over again, I saw how such meticulous detail and great expense went into producing show business. The script, the director, and the actor were all interwoven as fabric into the production cloth of fantasy. Once the actors or the actions' façade was polished in rehearsal, it was released in front of the camera. From hearing the word Action to the word Cut, I saw another stitch of fabrication captured and woven into the illusion of truth. I sat on the sidelines thinking time after time how phony it all was. Yet there was the benefit in how acting transferred a feeling or emotion. Similar to what I saw in theater acting, a performance helped stimulate feelings in the person who was watching. Enjoyment was understood in a variety of entertainments. At theme parks, cruise ships, tours, and on and on, millions and millions of dollars were spent on amusements.

Reality was being replaced in the lives of viewers with temporary imitations of life. Of course, the relaxation that came from entertainment had value; it was like a vacation for emotions. There was an educational element with seeing other lands or ways of life. And with the films' expensive amusements that were offered to the public, there was a cost.

Time and money were exchanged. Television sold commercials. The more a person watched the scripted fiction, the more disconnected he or she became from real life. The more the commercial was seen, the better the odds were that the product was bought. Like sheep grazing, people would watch and be led by the false shepherds on the TV. Whatever Hollywood's values were and whatever opinions were pumped into American homes, all came through entertainment. Films and TV were fun to watch and let the mind relax. All the while, though, images and words were sifted into the viewer's relaxed mind. When all was said and done, life moved on with Hollywood's subtle or overt values absorbed into people's lives.

I thought about how the obvious guiding effects of movies, pictures, and words were like leading a dog on a leash. Surely I wasn't the only one who could see that. It was a personal choice to lend someone's mind to the influences of Hollywood movies and TV. But I thought I could do some of that guiding with my music video, so I did.

---

†

A lyric I wrote with Chance called "Coming Back" was an almost perfect match for Rick's film short *Heading Back*. We both related to past love in our lives. Chance and I changed a few words, and he first remixed the music and then sang the new lyric. Basically the song was about a guy remembering a lost love. In the film, he relived those good times, his love, then cheating and drug deals, before regretting his path that got him in prison.

The first scene that came alive in my head was of a guy stuck in prison remembering the good times. Interpreting the lyrics with my choices of images was captivating my imagination. Like the finished words in a lyric, the final edited video choices would eliminate all other visual possibilities. But first the images needed to be collected. Next was all the planning on paper and scouting for locations. Hunting for sites with Big Guy was more fun than I first conceived. Driving around Los Angeles as video producers, we both felt important, like we were on a mission. Being in public with the camera this time was not like our attempts at Venice Beach. We didn't need approval or other people to participate. I made notes and took some video several times at several places. Big Guy held his arms up asking people to please wait while I worked the camera. Later we watched what I shot, and I could hear him telling people we were shooting a movie and we laughed. Lighting was most important since we didn't have a studio with proper equipment. All my work would be done outside in natural light. So far everything was innocent and off to a good start.

Then I went all the way as far as I was able to become a no/low-budget music video producer. I literally turned the tables around and got behind the camera to shoot actors. I advertised in the *Drama-Logue* magazine as a producer seeking actors to be in my music video. A hundred actors and actresses responded with pictures and résumés. I quickly found a conflict within me as my music video concept was flirting with the similar concept of acting. Acting was the very thing I struggled with because of the lies that were involved with a production of make-believe. I resolved my issue by realizing that my actors would be without lines; there were no words to speak at all. No lies, no false feelings, would be conveyed—just images. I would work with them as human props in my pictured expressions explaining my words. But I saw I was quickly getting ahead of myself and slowed up. I needed to follow through with my part in *A Streetcar Named Desire*.

✝

The cold February desert nights ranged from in the forties dipping into the low thirties at times. We, the players in the play, gathered like playground children. Excited to soon be released for recess for each evening's performance, we were ready. Nightly a small crowd sat on folding chairs placed in the historical building's large living room area on hardwood floors. The small stage at one end was plenty, and I climbed the stairs to my make-believe second-floor apartment. In one scene, we men gathered outside on the big beautiful front porch wearing

T-shirts, freezing and waiting for our cue to enter. We piled through the door pretending to be drunk and sat at the table playing poker, listening while Stanly got all worked up. We pulled him off of Blanche, and the colored lights were torn down as my times in the theater ended with *A Streetcar Named Desire*. Before my last performance, I knew I would again miss the stage and my character.

After the play's closing, I found that God was there to fill the void of any loss or depression. But I had no strong spiritual legs to stand on to fight off temptation. Done with my actor's obligation to stay sober, I felt the energy of restlessness being released. I saw I had empty time on my hands and that my problems with addictions were still a drama in my mind. Any falling into the old habit of drinking beer would just be my weak excuse to help shed my cloak of pretending as an actor. Within the first few post-play days, I wondered how long my sobriety from pot would last. Days seemed like months; my earthly reason to abstain from marijuana and beer was gone. My willpower began walking the high tightrope of denial and balancing to stay up by surrendering to God's will. I found myself learning and wanting the new me more and the old me less. But my two desires, one to sin and one to please God, continued. The splitting up inside of me was an internal battle. A fight waged over what peace I could enjoy with my heaven-bound eternal soul against my physical body with its defective mind. There was no dualism, no equal powers, God ruled over all. Sin was a choice made to move away from God. Satan made it, Eve then Adam made it and the sin nature was passed on to me and my choice.

The mysterious Holy Spirit-led process of changing me was a progression of love. The lifelong Christian endeavor to become more and more like Christ was encouraging, beautiful, and joyful. But living through the baby Christian life was impossible with my own strength. Without heaven's help it would have not only remained impossible, but I would have still been going to hell. Living with the recognition of that long-range battle for the rest of my life was only positive and doable with God in the strength of Jesus. It doesn't get any more exciting than that! Think of it.

Unlike false truth in theater, TV, or film acting, the true drama of God's unfolding plans was the very best I or any true Christian could witness and live in. I was living a blind, sinful life unenlightened, offending God. That same silent, invisible, spiritual battle was going on for thousands of years. I was one of the millions clueless about the spiritual battle going on around me.

Then God out of nowhere saved my soul from hell and gave me His Spirit. But as a baby believer, I was learning in the trenches. There was no staying down; there was always getting up and getting back into the fight. There was no middle ground, only the intense zone of hand-to-hand combat. How can anybody say the Christian life is boring? It is the most exciting, most dramatic way to live, and it is all for the glory of God. That's why the planet is here, and that's why people are on the planet. We are here to live lives in faith through His Son fighting sin to honor God. Our time on earth is really the threshold before two eternities. Cathartic! "He restores my soul; He leads me in paths of righteous for His name's sake" (Ps. 23:3).

✝

STANDING FIRM IN THE LORD

I started shooting cannons,
Heard the war so far away.
Now I'm digging in the trenches,
Burning down lies at sin's café.

Only God can help me now, by the blood of Jesus.
Only God can help me now, by the blood of Jesus.

> Pray the Lord help me, Standing Firm in the Lord,
> Power of His might, Standing Firm in the Lord.
> The armor of God, Standing Firm in the Lord.
> Doing all we can, Standing Firm in the Lord.
> Finally, my brother, be strong in the Lord.

Only God can help me now, by the blood of Jesus.
Only God can help me now, by the blood of Jesus.

Still, bombing burning bridges
Keep the fight, advance the light,
Cut each, every sin to pieces,
Burning evil day and night.

                               †

But I failed and couldn't resist the temptation to sin. The post-play spiritual battle zone of sinning and spells of sobriety lingered in no-man's-land, the gray area between the opposing sides of light and dark. Through my bad choices I was learning more about God's faithful, forgiving and steadfast love. His love was growing my love.

                               †

Seven months after being born again with genuine spiritual awakening, it was March 1990. I had the camera. I had the audacious spirit to go for it. I still lived near Hollywood. The music video was next. Just like when I took the defiant shot of bourbon in the bar, I found that I couldn't just roll over and be an all-new someone so quickly in my transformation. I was still me on earth; albeit with a catastrophic life change, I was still struggling for identity. How was I to be a Christian and earn a living? Even though I felt as if the inclination to make a music video might be a distraction from heavenly matters, I followed the diversion. My naïve reasoning in trying to juggle both my former earthly longings and my new Christian longings showed me again the difficulty of my staying in Los Angeles.

The path of denying old me and living as new me was a new trail of walking a fresh life while hacking off wrong values, all in the same time frame. I wasn't strong enough to deny myself the video work experience, the challenge to create and maybe make money at it. God chose this time and this place to make me spiritually alive. He knew me better than I knew myself. At the edge of that perilous decision to engage in a new project, I was beginning to realize more fully what living in faith meant. All I could do was trust the Holy Spirit.

I likened my predicament to that of a lawyer or a rug salesman. After all, if God came into their lives, would they change their walk in life? Wouldn't they try to cope with their divine awakening as they were trying to make a living? I thought others would manage as I would in trusting God to work out our lives. Considering further what pictures I would place in the video storytelling, I was drawn in. I discovered an area in my mind that needed more investigation. The challenge to represent the message of the lyric with images opened up a huge new world of thought.

With many ideas and plans on paper, I decided to call some of the actors who sent me their pictures and resumes and hold auditions for the music video. Taking advantage of an actress friend's kindness I met in *Harvey*, I used her address in Studio City. Those who answered my ad were invited to dress well and come to be videoed. I used her pool house to tape four dozen actors over a two-day period. They arrived at her driveway, registered, and waited. They entered the backyard one at a time, and I had them wait by the pool. I taped them standing, walking, turning, and smiling a lot near the water. The women kindly sashayed about in their high heels in the blinding sun's pool reflection. A few turned and nearly fell into the water.

In the pool houses large roofed, screened in patio area, I zoomed in for close-ups and profiles. I followed a routine, but was looking for something I didn't know of. My initial interviews were an experiment to learn from. Seeing some of the people face-to-face first and then looking at them in the viewfinder of the camera, I found a noticeable change. Not just in skin tone, but they looked more appealing through the viewfinder. I learned a lesson. Surprises like seeing a visual difference popped up again when I watched the recording of the actors on my TV monitor. Their looks changed again. In hopes of getting the intentions of the writer, me, and my message across, I began to enjoy the production.

Sometimes I saw things in 3D; it was my dyslexic way of thinking out of the box. As I conjured up location images in my mind to tape my actors, I felt I had some kind of artistic advantage by using my mind's eye.

✝

With Rick as the actor, I chose one very pretty young lady to be the actress with him in the *Heading Back* video. We three shot scenes of what Rick remembered as his character sat in prison. Motion pictures of them loving life and then frolicking holding hands, hugging beneath the huge Hollywood sign on the bridge at the reservoir. Elsewhere, for the prison scene, I got footage of barbed wire on a high wall in a secluded parking lot. Rick was shot in another private parking lot with high walls and a windowed roof tower. Rick leaned on the black bars of a large iron gate in remorse at another location. Traveling about with my camera increased the options and ideas for other shots. At night, the images played in my mind and were becoming bothersome. There was no off switch in my subconscious. Following the gist of Rick's script, I needed one more shot before editing: an airport scene, an interior shot with sufficient lighting to video my actors in a drug bust. It was the most daring of all the locations. The LAX Airport was my choice to tape a one-take shot before security caught on. I unloaded people and equipment, looking like we were traveling out of town. I, a one-man crew, previously gave instructions to my team of actors. We just walked in and did it exactly like I planned.

My three actors and I marched in with my camera and tripod, found a group of small lockers with good lighting, and set up the blocking. Once the pattern of movements was established, we rehearsed a few times before the tripod was set up. When I mounted the camera, I still felt like our scene should be within security's allowance. This first shot would be the large view of the entire scene. When the actors took their positions, I stood at the back of the camera recording. I gave a hand signal for action and joined the scene as the fourth actor. As the scene unfolded, Rick went to the locker for the drugs. I and another actor were the undercover police. Wearing my gray three-piece suit from the Salvation Army thrift store, I arrested Rick, and then we walked him out of the shot. My pretty young actress then stepped in, and her look of revenged-woman's scorn said it all as she flipped her hair and walked off. At the end of that scene, coincidentally, a very small boy, a bystander, in a gray suit walked into the empty shot as the camera was rolling. I then repositioned the tripod and shot close-ups and different points of view. The short, young, innocent witness to it all was a perfect fit for a mini-me. I kept the little kid in the shot when I edited. We packed up, leaving in less than thirty minutes. It was a score.

The production fever gripped me. Going on locations, directing actors, and shooting footage for a few weeks generated a greater thirst for more. I had what I wanted for *Heading Back*, but found a new desire for More and More. I was in another version of greed with the More sisters. Still with a full quiver of actors and actresses ready to work, my mind pondered. I reviewed the audition video, especially the close-ups of all the women walking poolside in evening gowns and men wearing their suits and sport coats. I mused about doing another daring video with a few dozen actors.

Chance and I had written a lyric called "Any Moment" about a shy guy meeting lots of women before he met the right woman. The lyric spoke of the possibility of seeing the right one at the right time anywhere and everywhere. Throwing myself back into the planning stage and location hunt, I forged ahead. This time I used one main guy, a few more guys, and almost all of the twenty women. My prop actors, silent actors without lines to speak, were to meet me at several locations. They gathered with me on street corners and in parking lots in Hollywood, Santa Monica, and the San Fernando Valley. I did an action shot at night with cars on the Hollywood freeway, with wild women waving in Gerry's Cadillac convertible. A similar scene was shot during the day at a bus stop on Chandler Boulevard. At every location I showed up in Big Guy's 1979 Ford Monarch, burning oil and showing moderate rust. I always brought a small table and had fresh donuts with soft drinks on ice for my volunteer actors.

In my last sequence of men meeting women, I taped another daring night shot. The short series of "Any Moment" encounters was shot in an underground parking lot of a food store in Beverly Hills. Extremely well-lit and clean, the garage featured large cement pillars. Behind the columns I hid the beautiful women, dressed in vivacious evening gowns. Well-dressed men were tucked behind other columns. One guy even wore a tuxedo. One young lovely Asian woman brought a bodyguard who looked like a Sumo wrestler. That was good security at no cost. Again I commandeered the location with just a camera and tripod. With my newly well-trained director's voice and camera eye, I barked out orders peering through the eyepiece and we rehearsed. The set was empty of public onlookers; the whole place was mine. I roared, "Action," and my prop actors moved about until I yelled, "Cut." Both words echoed. We took a handful of takes before we packed it up and drove out. Before we left, a few strange cars circled in and drove out after witnessing my roadshow. My group of volunteers and I left before the cops came, if they did. A similar bold scene was shot at night on Santa Monica Boulevard at a red light. With four women, two on each side, of my shy actors devilish alter ego actor crossed the busy intersection arm in arm in front of the bright car lights waiting for green. I recorded it three times before we left. Finally the shy star actor found his lovely sweetheart as his car broke down and she was the beautiful blond mechanic wearing blue jeans willing to help.

✝

My mind was becoming more inventive, more devious as I found more ways to tell a story with a picture. I continued to get background footage for two music videos. To show scenes of emotional disruption in the first video, I used a large swimming pool. First, the stillness of the calm water was shot. Then for the argument between my actors, I added waves. I drove around nights looking for condos or apartments with pools and little security. After finding a place, I set up the tripod and camera on the second-floor balcony and started recording. I went down to the empty pool and dipped a new large straw broom in the water, then walked around and around the edge. Pretty soon I got my waves slapping and my raging water shot. Two little kids near the camera looked out their window at me, and we all laughed.

I really loved to think of what images would best enhance the story of words and music. I preferred lots of nature shots and abstract props, actions, and symbols to provoke a feeling. The wilderness expanses of a far view were some awesome shots I collected in Bakersfield and at Castaic Lake. I walked out to an old cement gun turret in the woods near Malibu. I took footage of Chance playing guitar as a cutaway shot in the music video. He brought a ghetto blaster and lip-synched the words.

✝

Mornings Big Guy and I walked 150 yards to Basil's Diner for coffee and thoughts. The stroll was easy, and then to eat quietly, we sat comfortably in a booth. Watching the traffic at Laurel Canyon and Burbank Boulevard was a good slow Mr. Inside, Mr. Outside thing to do. As hindsight appeared it brought creativity to my pen and paper.

✝

BASIL'S DINER

Corner foundation
Seven days a week,
Clockwork locals support the team.
Queen Mary floats tables to grill
Tied to security and hospitality.
Wrinkled, stained-leather bench seats
Gather crumbs, cradle the greenbacks.
All this service with a smile,
Eatables, shuffling on and off time.
Smiles bring patience.
Hot and cold rushes of breezes
Air-condition the appetites.
Favored faces pause and flow.
Peaceful desert cheers farewell.
Register rings true, more cheers each year.

✝

Early afternoons, the old eatery was quiet after lunch. The air-conditioning was cold and came with a slight rattle, a buzz of chatter. Sitting within close eyeshot of traffic, I made notes and explained them to Big Guy. His curiosity helped find the wrinkles in my plans, and his suggestions were good. We drank iced coffee and ate cream pie.

✝

THE EARLY STAGE

Unwrinkled fingers twist
Purple frosted hair,
Atop a sculptured pillar
Of slender skin and care.

Her radiant peace, beaming
Of premature joy,
Inner beauty blended
Waiting for her boy.

Suddenly the view stirred hurriedly.
Formative years danced the floor,
Adolescents in detail,
Then out Basil's diner door.

Life was just seen living
The easy peaceful giving,
Comes as youth is scored,
The Early Stage, in and out the door.

The pilot, the race-car driver,
The ocean diver,
In life's harmony pond,
Looking, waiting to be beyond.

✝

On days with less heat, the burrito stand kitty-corner across the busy street was the place to be sitting outside to eat. The diary would enjoy those times rounding out an earthly sense of harmony when it was happening. Life was moving on so beautifully at times. Both music videos were about three and a half minutes long, costing me about $200.00 total. Up to that point, I worked pretty hard, but I also had a lot of enjoyable experiences in the videotaping. I thought I was on a path of making the most of my time. I was okay up to then. But what I was about to realize more fully was that production had taken my sights off my biblical responsibility. Not keeping my eye on God was a serious and scary move to make.

Going into middle and late April, the editing madness was ahead of me for the first video, "Heading Back." I had no computer or software to help lay out a systematic mechanical structure of exact editing. My finger pushing the on/off button was always with a shade of guesswork. I'd get close to the chosen frames of pictures on the video tape that represented the lyric. Each scene was in seconds, give or take just that, trial and error. I kept rewinding and trying again until I got it right or close enough. Each video had nearly seventy separate three-second shots or edits on average. Then the reedit followed. I lengthened some shots to mix up the variety. It was a first-time event for me, and the tenacity that was needed took all I had to concentrate and reach the end. Editing off-line is a monster. I never saw the trap coming. I only saw the bait to have a product to show off.

By June I began to edit the second music video, "Any Moment." My obligation to make the master and then thirty copies for each actor involved was driving me frantic. It was the first time I worked so diligently in front of machines. After all the shooting through the camera's eyepiece, I then sat down in front of the TV monitor. I needed to view the footage over and over, noting anything worth using and its location. It drove me crazy. That's editing. Two music videos was the goal. Everything was learned for the first time. Watching and choosing the images to tell the picture story of my lyrics was like placing several additional sets of eyes in my brain. With my eyes open, my subconscious would think of and see my choices. Not my mind's eye but the images themselves flashed and raced about for refinement as I stared. As good or crazy or bad as that may sound, it was devastating after very long hours. I tried to lie down for sleep, but my mind would not turn off.

I would lie there in the dark on the bunk bed in the garage thinking, seeing, hearing, and carrying images and sounds with me into eventual rest. Weakness weakened me. Editing was like watching a parade in the rain; it wasn't fun. I was ugly with agitation. I morphed into a bigger sinning Christian. I was miserable. The stimulation needed for my constant focus on analyzing video shots opened up the closet of bad mistakes. Once I began adding more morning pot and caffeine and evening alcohol prior to sleep, they became a routine. Sin came off the hooks of semiretirement, and I wore those addictions like clothing;

they could not be taken off until I was finished. I was stuck in my own quagmire of sin and commitment.

I knew God had regenerated my life. I was justified once and forever through Christ Jesus. *Justified* meant that I was made acceptable, validated by the blood of Jesus as being righteous in God's eyes. I knew how much better my life could be. I was given the light to see Christ—and Him alone—as my Savior. I longed for those quiet times of sitting with just the Bible alone, reading it. I missed listening to the radio preachers. The difference Jesus made in my life a few months ago was so much better than how I was living now. I saw that my choices were causing me to backslide. In my young faith and my faith alone, I trusted God to work it all out. "But the just shall live by his faith" (Hab. 2:4). Now my sin was trying to push away my young relationship with God. Earthly priorities took the place of heavenly priorities.

But through the misery, I began to broaden my opinion of acting into appreciating it much more. Seeing all the faces of the actors, their smiles and movements, all their looks of surprise when I asked for it was real. The locations I chose and the clothing I asked them to wear were all chosen to evoke a more truthful feeling. Then I truthfully found myself as a producer of feelings and emotions that were on tape to be transferred to viewers. I discovered in myself a better balance between truths and make-believe. I began doubting my previous harsh accusations against acting. There were still the issues of vast amounts of money spent on production. And the viewer's cost of both time lost and his or her cash for just a feeling. What about the casual or explicit messages of violence and sexual immorality? But I was clearly moving off my rigid opposition and onto seeing how I got some things twisted up. But the growing force of negative media was undeniable.

My scheduling and promise to meet deadlines were pressing me into eighteen-hour days. I found that I wasn't able to function well. Pot smoking increased into all-day use, and beer was switched for cognac to help me pass out nightly. Morning coffee became a ritual of boiling strong dark espresso grounds into several cups to wake me up. I was bargaining those excuses with the Devil. I was compromising truth with error. And I had the classic of all excuses: I told myself that when I was finished with the video project, I would go on the straight and narrow. I believed my own lie. I talked myself into lying to myself. I was like the parable of the four soils Jesus spoke of in Matthew 13:3–23, all rolled up in one.

Our Lord told of the seed sower casting seed on the ground. The seed was the Word of God, the gospel of Jesus. The types of grounds or soils were the types of hearts in people hearing or receiving the seed, the gospel message. Some seed was cast on the wayside or the path around the field. The footpath was hard-baked from the sun and the routine ways of the world. The gospel seeds scattered on top never penetrated into the hard soul. Before any change of growth could happen, the seeds were snatched away by the birds, symbolic of Satan. Other seeds fell on stony ground with just topsoil. The seed sprang up, but without a depth of understanding. Without a root system and water, the superficial allegiance to Christ could not be sustained. The sun's heat baked the young growth, and it withered away. More seed was spread and fell into thorns and weeds, representing the socially appealing ways of life. Without a genuine commitment to the message of salvation through Jesus and true repentance, any insincere efforts were too weak to last. The love of thorny success, the love of weedy money, chokes out the hollow hypocritical words of a casual sincerity. Then in verses eight and nine, the words of Jesus read: "But others fell on good ground and yielded a crop; some a hundredfold, some sixty, some thirty. He who has ears to hear, let him hear."

I had heard; I was hearing; the gospel seed was mine to fight for in faith. My prayer was made in faith to break up and soften the ground of my hard heart. I knew I needed the watering from the Word of God and longed for more of it. Whatever was to be grown and yielded was all in faith and in God's hands. My longing for God's goodness grew.

As I continued to edit, my good intentions against sinning would last from two minutes to two days before I crumbled. At one point, I questioned my sanity and my belief. I saw again the lies of Satan, the world system away from God and my sins. They were tall and anchored in my flesh. But through it all, I knew I believed and I had faith in God, the Holy Spirit. I had nothing else, and I had everything with the truth in the Bible. My enormous life-changing rebirth event on August 20, 1989, was sealed by the Holy Spirit. He allowed me to see, understand, and believe the Bible's truth. Yet there I was after months into my new life both miserable with guilt and blessed with forgiveness, and I was getting desperate to kill sin. One undeniable fact was the great power of God, the Holy Spirit. This was God living within me. This was God, who created the planets, stars, and all of it. If God the Holy Spirit wanted to slash and tear out my sins one by one or ten at once, He could. He could do anything beyond all my finite imagination. I was a little kid Christian in faith; all I had was the gift of faith and my commission and accountability to exercise it. God alone was the potter fashioning me, His chosen piece of clay.

Finally the editing of the two videos, their labeling, and their packaging was done. All the duplicates for all the actors were mailed out. They worked with me for a copy, and I held up my end of the bargain. To put an end to that lunacy, the camera went to Chance. Driven and beaten up by commitment and obligation, alcohol, drugs, and little sleep, the reality of just me physically against the world was over. I found myself in a corner of emptiness. I had my way and stifled my spiritual growth through compromise. All I could say was I finished what I had started. Even though I wanted to forget that old me, that same old me that had run my life was not that old or gone. The "I" in pride was still there. The old "I" had been lurking and was over to the side, a passenger, patiently waiting for a chance to come back and sit in the throne chair of my heart. My escape from that misery was at hand as I read the bible. I found some relief and comfort listening to my new friend, the radio Christianity programming. As I sat in the garage with its cool, dark, cave-like appeal, I was not alone. God was with me. I waited for more time to be with Him more.

✝

GREAT PHYSICIAN

Reach deep down inside, the box of sin burning,
Past the heart that lied, and water it with learning.

> Humble me, Lord, keep me low, please, oh please.
> Humble me, Lord, on my knees, please humble me.

> My skin crawls, lustful, greedy, cheating, me, me, me.
> My skin crawls, lying, faking, two-faced, backslid me.

Oh, Father God, You gave Your only Son, our Great Physician.
You gave Your only Son, our Great Physician, Great Physician.

> Humble me, Lord, keep me low, please, oh please.
> Humble me, Lord, on my knees, please humble me.

Exposing your sin, obey what you've heard
Hold the truth within, to the light of God's Word

Oh, Father God, You gave Your only Son, our Great Physician.
You gave Your only Son, our Great Physician, Great Physician.

> Oh Lord, keep me on my knees praying, bring what I need.
> Oh Lord, keep me on my knees, let only Jesus lead.
> Oh Lord, break what's proud, hold me from the crowd.
> Oh Lord, break what's proud, praise You, Lord, out loud.

✝

The unbelievable truth that God was real and was with me was too huge to understand and retain without exercising it. I carried my little Bible to read and prayed often for help. My mistakes were many. Initially I thought that the video-production experience would be good to take advantage of while in California. But just because the elements of opportunity lined themselves up didn't mean they were good or the best thing to do. By doing something that appeared to be timely and good, I was keeping myself away from God and doing the best. Doing good wasn't doing my best! The best would have been to continue absorbing all I could about God and the Bible no matter what I did. I also learned how patient and crafty the enemy was. I had no idea at that time that the enemy, too, scouted and chose locations for his shooting at me. I was naïve, to say the least, about how crafty Satan or the world's influence can be when it comes to stealing my time away from God. Oh, how bitter is the medicine of learning the hard way. But as hard as evil tried to keep pulling me down, the Spirit of God never let go of me. My greatest sin, which would hurt me for decades, was the sin of compromise. In my negotiating with sin, I was not just settling for less; I was learning how to be a hypocrite. All for the prideful sake of doing what I wanted. After choosing to put down the Bible and picking up sin, I became more aware of my folly. Stupidly I chose to continue.

✝

While in progress with shooting the two videos, I was intrigued by the idea Glenn gave me about cable TV. I often mulled over thoughts of taking that step of creativity and working it out with Christian artwork. I was a little familiar with TV production in a studio setting from my work as an extra. Working in a TV studio on an original project was something I hadn't done yet. But something was very wrong with my motive to exploit Christian art for my own benefit. It was a repeating ill feeling no matter how I cut it. Even by telling myself it was to praise God, I still couldn't and didn't buy into it. It was like taking something so pure and getting it dirty with the world's ways of business. It just wasn't in me. Christian acting or drama entertainment on the radio was, for the most part, geared for children, with skits of right and wrong. As useful as some may think that may be, I didn't buy it. Validating the world of acting or make-believe by mixing it with the lessons in the Bible was really joining lies and truth. They don't mix. Scripture is the Word of God; it doesn't need anything added to it. Perhaps if parents were more proactive teaching God's truth, imitations of it wouldn't be considered more valuable. But since I'm no parent my opinions are not first hand.

The contemporary Christian songs on the radio pounded out music that sounded just like all the rest of rock-and-roll music. Some of those Christian lyrics I heard in the variety of songs seemed to be centered on the person more than God. Boy and girl Christian love song lyrics seemed as though they were rewritten to include a love for God or Jesus. Some of the praise lyrics may have been secular and then rewritten to include Christ. I know because I thought of doing the same thing and did. My recycled lyrics never started out to honor God. They were unlike my original lyrics, which were intended with devotion for God. My secondhand rewrites just didn't work for me.

Marketing fashionable Christian songs or those the music industry required was an idea that sank in my thinking. It was a very difficult situation for me to understand and support, let alone relate to other artists. What made a so-called Christian song was only its lyrics. It seemed like some Christian lyrics were being marginalized to accommodate Christian Lite. Other lyrics filled other segments of the large pie of entertainment. Blending into the music industry's fabric wasn't an option I took. The way I saw it was that the world didn't need another mediocre or popular song to sing; they needed strong motivation to read the Bible more. I knew first hand that's what I needed. I was beginning to understand my choice to avoid entertainment was that of a more conservative view. I could only hope to write a powerful lyric that might honor God and encourage someone. Lyrics weren't scripture but they could be used to strengthen or weaken bible doctrine.

I made a subjective decision to stay away from reducing the importance of the Christian message. I could only hope that anything I wrote would ultimately respect Christianity and show its distinction from the world. A lyric was similar to what I could hear in the difference of strengths and weaknesses in the preachers' messages on the radio. Weakness or the compromise of truth from the pulpit is in the same boat as lite commonplace lyrics. Perhaps by watering down the message, some preachers/writers were looking for a larger audience. But oil and water don't mix, and neither can a sinful world system be mixed with doctrine lite. Nothing less than the righteous oil of strong biblical teaching will honor God. I would rather be among a few fundamentally strong than the many popular and weak. My opinions really weren't any kind of judgments more a matter of steps in my learning. I was still growing in my faith and knowledge. But God knows the heart of a man and his intentions better than the man. "It is a fearful thing to fall into the hands of the living God" (Heb. 10:31).

†

Still, those thoughts of cable TV and the idea of Christian art were on my back burner. Maybe God would work out my creative ideas for something I couldn't see. Maybe my idea of a Christian art cable show titled *Heaven High* from a year earlier was a project whose time had come. Was I to meet Christian artists and group their work together to show it on a public-access station? One thing was very clear: the old life wasn't completely dead. The confusion for me lay in how God would work it all out. Even if things didn't go the way I saw they might, I knew things would be worked out the way God wanted them. I trusted God; that was a fact. *Trust and obey* was an expression I got half right. God let me trust Him, and I trusted Him in however He would teach me to obey Him. Faith was going to be an exercise in living through how He worked it all out. "Now faith is the substance of things hoped for, the evidence of things not seen" (Heb. 11:1). I hoped God would lead me or bring me to where I could exalt Jesus. Whatever He brought was okay with me.

†

Things were still happening with our Mischief/Fables band project, but they grew more doubtful. New short-term band members were playing in nightclubs with Chance and rehearsing in our garage intermittently. At the same time, new promotional packages were being sent out, including my phone calls to A&R people. We were still trying to obtain a record contract. We tried bumping up our appeal by producing a live gig and taping it to edit. It was good to have ready in case there was interest to see and hear the band. For the second time, a few friends came with our faithful groupie friend Janine to the FM Station in North Hollywood on Lankershim Boulevard. There was always a good crowd there, and I shot a video of the band on stage playing several songs. Chance edited a short tape of the best stuff, but nobody in the industry wanted a copy. It appeared more clearly as though those bridges were burned. Chance stayed away from Big Guy's and went on living in Palmdale with Miss Fortune.

A few composers contacted me from my *Drama-Logue* ad, and I met with them. But I found that my enthusiasm for starting another collaboration was weak and without fuel to follow through with. I was exhausted from earthly endeavors. But there was one tune in my head I kept whistling; it was my first original music. I called Jack Segal and asked if I could meet with him so he could hear my whistling tune and give me his opinion.

I did meet with Jack one evening when he came to my garage. In fact, he brought me his old electric typewriter. The large eighty-pound machine with long, curved metal keys was a gift between friends. Jack wanted me to have a piece of his legacy. No doubt there were hundreds of hours he invested pecking at it, writing his wonderful lyrics. Some of Jack's time spent with his faithful mechanical friend produced songs like "Scarlet Ribbons," recorded by Dinah Shore and Harry Belafonte, and "May I Come In?" recorded by Blossom Dearie. Receiving Jack's piece of old special property was my privilege. In turn, he sat and listened to my whistling. Typical of Jack's honesty, he said it sounded like a dirge. He recommended jazzing it up and making people happy. I wanted to smoke a joint with him, and we did, taking turns holding our breath. He gave me his best wishes before leaving; we shook hands and hugged. I thanked him for all his help and friendship. Jack was my first friend in the music business, and I learned a lot from him.

†

The hectic distractions of my old life on this earth were like living in a rubber room maneuvering among several circus acts. In one hand I was juggling artistic pride, trying to make an honest living showcasing my video through Rick's film project. With the other hand, I tried to hang onto the truth of God. Life was difficult at best and impossible at the least, even hopeless, but for the hand of God holding me. I was learning to let sin go, but I was learning from my mistakes, failures, and stupidity. Perseverance, which was my strength in dedication, was now misdirected at sin and choking me. Even though I knew the best shot for success with the band was gone, my fifteen years of stubbornness kept me in that environment. I knew better, but at the same time, the Devil was not letting up his stealthy attack. It felt as if the view of my messy first months as a Christian was a picture of me in quicksand. My earthly goals became my worst enemy.

All the Devil's or his minions' dark plays were sucking me down against my new motion upward toward the light of God. The evil one wanted to keep me in dimness. I was naïve and didn't realize the depth of my enemy's spiritual warfare experience. I deeply regret not being more serious about that which was going on around me. The Devil could not keep all of me occupied in the world like he had done for so long. As clumsy as I stumbled out of the gate, I was still a child of God. Since the day Christ came into my life and began a personal bond, I have never been let go of by the Lord. During my darkest moments and most unsure times, there was always a sense of knowing trust and living in faith. And there are the times of great faith and complete joy with harmony, all in the Lord's grace and mercy.

Those first nine months, I carried His love with me. I now expressed my love by searching the Bible for the things of God and telling of them. My joy of knowing I was changed was knowledge that could not be contained. I found myself wanting to share that wonderful life in Christ with others. So I told people about Jesus; the neighbors heard it more than once. I also told strangers I met in North Hollywood Park. I sensed their barriers, but I was happy to tell. Even on different telemarketing jobs I worked on, my coworkers heard how the gospel message was changing my life. In my meditation-type walks through the street on my way to the park, I was very much at peace. Those were days of not only struggle and learning, but also days of contentment, trusting the Lord. After my failures and Satan's attacks, Jesus was still with me, still my Lord. I was a slave of Christ Jesus. He bought me with His blood on the cross. Thank God I was His slave.

Living in the garage and also using the house, I enjoyed all the conveniences of home. Reading became a new joy. Conquering the distaste I had my whole life from dyslexia, the Bible was the answer to make reading always enjoyable. And my diary was used over and over to hear about it all. In my small Christian world, I had a boundless God beyond measure. Within all my self-made distractions, I was still not going to church. I knew it would happen as surely as I knew God was leading me through my Red Sea escaping from sin and Satan's tyranny. On my mind, instead of seeking a church, was the idea to spend some money on food for street people and mention God, the Bible, and Jesus. After I talked with some of the homeless at the park, I was walking on air. I liked both helping a stranger and asking if they knew Jesus. I was evolving slowly as a baby Christian, but still was not anchored with a Christian friend to confide in.

It became apparent to me that my work in California was to come to an end. I might not bring home the temporary fame and fortune. But I certainly could bring home the eternally best that heaven could offer in Jesus. A born-again Christian was who I was. I was just finding out and deeply considering the real meaning and values of life as a child of God. I would be growing in His ways, having His standards for what is right and wrong for the rest of my life. Consequently, there was much thought of abandoning the old California dream altogether, having serenity with the satisfaction of knowing I did my best. Maybe I'd be moving on to search for a fresh start somewhere in a place where people lived slower lives.

✝

Just as I was regaining some stillness in my life, the two renters needed to be given their notice to move out. Their drug use had spilled out into the open, where they couldn't deny their heroin use. An ad was placed for replacements.

In my tenth born-again month in June, Gina surprised me on my thirty seventh birthday. Our discussion at first about my abstinence from immoral sex was not what she thought she would hear. But after we went to lunch and the distance in our past relationship was removed, we returned to the garage and I got greedy. In my weakness, I failed in my vice, my sin, of sexual lust. Then after the deed was done, my conscience and my hypocrisy screamed at me. Guilty as I could be, I took my failure out on Gina at first and told her not to come back. I saw her as a weakness of mine from the very beginning, but it wasn't her as a person; it was my sin I despised. Just as my thoughts had been reversed about acting, so were my ill feelings toward Gina. She meant well but was enabling me to sin. My failure was my problem. I explained how my wants of wanting what I want when I want it weren't what God wants. I hoped she would understand me better. After I explained my issue with putting my pride first, she didn't share my priorities in my attempts to put God's way first. We parted as friends, but sex was off the table. Except for Big Guy, the very few friends I had were gone. They were undesirable to be with, and I was no longer fun in their eyes.

I listened to Christian radio hour after hour and began tape-recording programs of the best preachers teaching from the Bible. I wanted the good strong connection with God to be back, but it was faint. I learned that the flame of the Holy Spirit's love and teaching was quenched by the watering of my sins. I had lost portions of my joy. It hurt. How could I be so cruel to God, who loved me? How could I turn my back on my Maker? I learned that God's love was a very sensitive matter. His love was stable; my love was not yet a developed strength. I had grieved the Spirit, and consequently I grieved also. The joy of God began to return slowly only after the confession of my sins and heartfelt sorrow. His love and forgiveness burned higher again through His Holy Word, and I read the Bible out loud; I was being restored. In the warm

July sun, I sat loving the simplicity of the trees that were around me. I loved the sunrises, the gift of life, and the sunsets more than ever. God's strength was again all about me; He would make me stronger and stronger in His good and perfect time. Like a car was made to run on fuel I was made to run on a good bond with Jesus. No fuel no travel, no Jesus no eternity.

Chapter 21: One Year Born-Again

The ongoing mixture of calm and chaos brought about more acceptances with the struggles in my new life. Without the mess of stress from what I brought into my life with artsy endeavors, I was okay with life's ups and downs. But I wanted more goodness and less sin. I bought another Bible on July first; the New King James Version was my fourth Bible. I liked my new version; the words flowed, and the structure had a poetic rhythm. In hopes of better understanding how to live and what it teaches, I went back to the church I started at. I was still leery about the tongues thing, but I didn't know where else to go. Not knowing anyone at church didn't matter; I just wanted to be with church people and the goodness of learning. I was clean and sober for one week. I lived in sobriety and wrote about it in the diary with so much hope and thanks to God. It was a big deal for me to see my life change. Owned by Christ I hoped to be an obedient slave.

My mental strength or willpower coincided with the time I spent holding and reading the Bible. Being on my knees in prayer was mainly a matter of learning to yield or bow to my Lord in my heart. But getting to the thought of prayer was often preceded by the thought of and confrontation with sin. I could not stop myself from all the aspects of sin with marijuana. Earning the money for it, then going to buy it, and lastly immediately smoking it was my joy and misery. As soon as I would go my way in pleasure, the guilt would roll in, roll over me, and convict me in a crushing way. I then would willingly throw out the pot in the backyard. There was nothing else that was like that freedom. After eighteen years of loving and cherishing the drug, tossing it was an undeniable gift of grace I received. I was able to empty out the bag of pot, spilling it over the backyard onto the leaves and dirt and then kicking it around.

That was a very special lesson in freedom and liberation from bondage. Abandoning the drug was what I had only hoped for in the past to get that monkey off my back. The Devil did not want to lose his power over me; he hung on silently long and hard. I knew that God was greater and He would never give up loving and teaching me. When I had stopped smoking pot during acting to memorize my lines, I struggled to set it aside and saw my willpower work. But that was a temporary victory with a deadline. I was further than temporary now in my Christian walk, so I hungered to change and cut the sin out permanently. But as much as I did not want to go buy pot and remembering how I threw it out, I could not stop myself from getting more. Still, the change stayed. After going through the cycle of buying, smoking, being convicted, and tossing it away a few more victorious times, I felt good. When I told Emile and Gerry next door, I was as astonished as they were hearing me tell of my joy in throwing it out. But throwing it away still didn't stop me from wanting it or destroy the sin.

A strange and powerful internal occurrence happened during the first year of battle with sin and Satan's minions. One of the most powerful experiences I ever learned from was when I was in the middle of the fight between weakness and strength, struggling not to smoke pot. Pacing in the yard, I resisted making the phone call ordering more pot as my restlessness grew. I was being emotionally tossed around in the garage like a piece of furniture in a barroom brawl. The Devil seemed determined to have his way with me at the same time that the Holy Spirit was not letting go in their fight. Without my own strength but with the leading of the Holy Spirit, I closed the garage door, knelt on the rug, and cried out to God for help. I can still see myself crying to God for His help, and help happened. After witnessing the two silent, invisible combatants fight within, I then lived through the moments of cleansing supernatural empowerment. The power of answered prayer came; it was liberating, and somehow I yielded my will to sin. God answered my call. I was able to stay still and not leave to make a buy. It was a victorious battle for the Holy Spirit. Then more joy came to me from realizing the power of the Holy Spirit.

Days later, I anticipated the Holy Spirit's power to help me stay home and not go to buy pot. With God, I would overcome my affection for the drug. I knew if I prayed, God would strengthen me. He let me grow in trust, in prayer and obedience. Living in a short period of sobriety, my lust for pot slowly came creeping back. Then I was falsely proud of myself by resisting it. When sin called again, I found that my heart was so much more a liar and wicked than I had thought. Sin roared back for the attention it once got, and I craved the drug. And in my mind, my wicked mind of prideful self-centered affections, I stopped my prayer. I stopped myself from choosing to submit to God's help. In my collapse, I gave in to my affection for that sin. I went and bought the weed and smoked it only once while driving back. Then the guilt was a hundred times worse, and I threw it on the ground among the leaves of the trees once again. But I had failed badly. I had chosen to fail.

I was shocked, blown away at how I could not deny myself but I could deny God. I refused God's help, strength, and love; I turned my back on God just to enjoy temporary sin. My mind clearly said with my conscience that the sin was wrong. But I saw how my heart loved that sin. I was wrong and guilty without excuse, that's for sure. The next day I was still all upset. Once again I continued what was becoming a new habit, which was talking with God about my shame. I admitted I was rotten, proud, and a traitor. That experience showed me my deep–rooted, thirty-seven-year-old, sinful core of selfish will. It also showed me that God is patient and loving. God wasn't like me; I walk out when things don't go my way. God is faithful. I was without another person to be accountable to and felt the cost. Except for the Spirit of God, there was no one on earth to talk to about those things.

Without human biblical leadership, worship, and fellowship, I was a sitting duck for the evil one. Through those failures, I found that if I prayed first and just stayed still, God would give me strength to stay home. I had the Spirit of God within, keeping me a work in progress. I had to learn to get rid of thirty-seven years of built-in garbage. God could have cleaned out my lust in just one thought. Maybe He had done that for others. The depth of my sin was news to me, not news to God. He would do whatever He wanted. God was the potter; I was the clay. I could only hope in faith. "Faith is the substance of things hoped for, the evidence of things not seen" (Heb. 11:1). Because I was such a loner, with fifteen years of experience on how to be alone in my fabric, I was almost at a great disadvantage. I was a human wrestling match, the target for Satan's pain and the object of God's love. I pleaded for God to remove my suffering, as did Paul in 2 Corinthians 12:9: "And He said to me, 'My grace is sufficient for you, for My strength is made perfect in weakness.'"

✝

A LIVING LIGHT

He let me hear there was a Word.
He let me see there was a light.
He let me smell His air of love.
He let me feel His way of hope.
He let me taste His Bread of Life.

God gave what God gave in the glory of His name.
Born again today, His Holy Spirit a flame,
God gave me a faith, Jesus Christ, A Living Light.
Jesus is my strength, Savior, Lord, A Living Light.

> God gave His Son to set my soul free,
> Praise Lord Jesus, give testimony,
> Resist sin with Him, Devil flees from me,
> Bringing willpower, obedience in Thee.

God gave what God gave in the glory of His name.
Born again today, His Holy Spirit a flame,
God gave me a faith, Jesus Christ, A Living Light.
Jesus is my strength, Savior, Lord, A Living Light.

He lets me feed in His Word.
He lets me grow in His light.
He lets me walk in His love.
He lets me know of heaven's hope.

✝

Most amazing of all things was that I started throwing away my sins. But it really wasn't me; it was God the Holy Spirit who was leading me, teaching me, cleaning me up on the inside. As God's grace, His gift of change continued. I mused about His teachings. He gave me more balance, letting me see the sense of truth inherent in a singer's emotions or an actor's or writer's work. I knew more strongly the godly differences between Gina and me, along with her sincere affection for me. But most importantly He showed me my true nature for the love of my sin. And He revealed the true deception in all people found in Jeremiah 17:9: "The heart is deceitful above all things, and desperately wicked; who can know it?"

I saw society's sins and society was in trouble, and it started for all civilization with Adam and Eve's sin in the Garden of Eden. The damage of sin was passed on through generations, and what was supposed to be normal became abnormal. The population in the world grew so abnormal that sinful people legalized the murder of babies. Bad became good, words were twisted and murder was called women's rights. Abortion became the new normal for the majority of people. Surely things were so perverted that there was no hope outside of God's intervention.

But I was curious about my deception and how I went awry. Failing third grade was my first catastrophe, but it was a dyslexic screw-up that started in my genes and stayed hidden. The fun I had in school with sports and friends was overshadowed too long by my bad choices remembering the worst. I thought of my parents' love for each other, but how I focused on their arguing differences too much. I let a severe back injury wrench me off the path of a normal life as I lay thinking on pain killers. And I let all those wounds tear apart the only true love I ever had, with Hope. Rejecting life, I accepted marijuana, drugs and new perceptions of freedom just before completely shutting down my life with the traumatic brain injury. My misaligned foundational and adolescent thinking was then shaped into an uncommon style of a warped point of view, that of a modern Taoist Sage. There was a lot of switching of values that had gone on in the development of my searching personality. That fostered leeriness and a search for social deceptions in the box of what society called normal. As my personality evolved in my own out-of-the-box thinking, I wrote of my critical comments toward others in the search of discovering myself. I had grown into a skeptic until God brought the death of my doubting. Only He could peel away my distrusts and inaccuracies and bring truth. No matter how much or how bad my distorted attitudes or sins were, He gave me a rebirth. And no matter how bad the world misrepresents truth, He is always watching and in control of His creation. Life is all about God and the only things that matter are the Holy teachings of God.

---

†

The old room renters were drug dealers, and so they were now gone. Just I and Big Guy were left, just like it started. You know you get what you pay for. Without their rent money, I needed more work. I was still working telemarketing in the afternoons, earning ten dollars an hour raising donations for different causes. I passed out doorknob flyers in the morning for a local restaurant; it was great exercise going house-to-house. A few people talked to me, and we ended up talking about God and being born again. I got all charged up and realized how inadequately I was expressing myself. Most people didn't care, but some of them knew what I was talking about. As exciting as that was, it never dawned on me to ask where they went to church. I had a growing desire in me to learn more about how to express God's love.

In August I was back on crutches a week or more with a bad left knee from too much walking door-to-door. Lying around thinking, I could see my past tunnel vision and how the California pot of gold had faded. The idea of perhaps getting a $50,000 advance payment on a record label deal didn't matter anymore. I was no longer just saying the words; it really didn't matter, and I knew it didn't. My shifting new life was nonstop into knowing God more and fighting to live in obedience. I saw my life had become more than having the radio knowledge I learned. I was living with God. Seems I learn better when injured and recuperating. Reading the Bible more, I was learning to meditate on the words I read, strengthening myself to fight my vices. In doing so, I was completely sober a solid two weeks in a row.

Then on August 20, it was one year since I became a born-again Christian. It had been a wild ride. I thought of the fact that over and above all my screw-ups, I was loved by God. Jesus came to me like the tip of an iceberg; there was so much more to know in the unseen time to come. The world is like an ocean of deception; its appeal for self-absorption is everywhere, but it couldn't stop Jesus rising into my life. There were times I was disheartened, when I lost a lot of things, when dreams never came true, and I was still alone. Being alone was beginning to bother me. I could deal with it before, but I knew it wasn't right. In my new Christian world with God and Jesus and the Holy Spirit, there was always a spark of hope and joy, knowing better days were coming. With no renters now for two months, Big Guy and I had to pay his sister the rent. My knee was much stronger, so I started painting the inside of the house for Big Guy and future renters. After decades of neglect, it was at last clean and bright for him. He was such a great friend; he loves life more, and with all the attention he received in the last few years, he feels better about himself. He loves those kitties.

Money got tight, so we put an ad in the paper for roommates. I was working at doing side jobs in the neighborhood until a dog bit me. I got eleven stitches in my left arm. I worked a second telemarketing job until another guy rented one of the rooms. A musician from Texas, he went to Guitar Institute of Technology (GIT) in Hollywood. His wrist injury required pain pills, which found their way to me. That was a bad break for me.

I was on and off the wagon of sobriety, Oh God; I thought I was going crazy. In October I was very sick in the garage, but listening to a lot of Christian radio in the dark. By November, I become more selective in choosing the best pastors on the radio. It was through the radio that I first heard a distinct difference in teaching from a few good men. I thanked God for the constant listening and began a list of times when to hear the good ones. Work was slowing down for me, and then the telemarketing company went bankrupt. It turned out that the new roommate was a waste, a drug addict, and we were going to have to evict him. When the rent is cheap in a broken-down house, what do you get but lies? Knowing their lies, I saw how I lied to God. But He always forgave me and I had a hard time forgiving.

I heard of another church in Hollywood advertised on the radio. In December, I searched it out and went. In a business district, the church had a large stage. The whole thing was a performance like I'd never seen before. There was a big band playing, and people were up and down swaying all over, like a party. I went a few times to see if it was always like that. It was. It was too far out into the entertainment aspect of what people wanted to do with their worship time. It looked like it was mostly about external actions, participation in outward expressions. It didn't work for me; I wanted to be quiet so I could listen and learn. The few hymns I heard on the radio were what I wanted to sing, like "How Great Thou Art" and "How Firm a Foundation." I couldn't handle rock and roll in a church setting and never went back. Not once did I think about going to a Catholic church.

By December I got more work on the phone with a different company making appointments to sell condo shares in Florida. We finally paid for a new heater in the house, and we at last had a constant source of heat. Then Big Guy got a notice that he was losing his job. The factory was closing after he worked there two decades. He felt bad and didn't want to move to Virginia to keep his job. I encouraged Big Guy to get tested for being handicapped. People at the factory where he worked helped him look for work also. In the past, I didn't give much thought to Big Guy's overall steady situation, but I was starting to. He drove a car, he had a long-running job, and he had a house to live in. He was far better off with the earthly stuff than I was. I never thought of my friend as handicapped or challenged more or less than others. I knew he was a little off. To me he was different, but so was I. We were friends, and I was glad to be there for him in his insecurity. He was always there for me and the band project because he was glad to help. He felt good when he found out that there was a place for him to go after the factory closed. He would get disability, and he wasn't going to be lost in the shuffle. Job coaches would help him. He was so glad he could stay at his house.

It had been a few years since Big Guy's sister first broke her silence and wanted rent. I think the people who were helping Big Guy with his limited ability to work and employment status got hold of her. Then Big Guy's sister doubled the rent to six hundred dollars, and the bills came to three hundred dollars. There was decades of poor communication and friction between those two. I was glad to be with him, so he wasn't alone.

The timing was terrible, but we had to give the renter his notice to move out. No amount of talk about God and changing his ways would change him. There was a point at which the argument got heated and loud. His offer to pay higher rent was tempting but didn't fix the real problem. I had to get rid of him because of his drug use, and I wanted to protect Big Guy better. I saw my own dilemma as the renter said one thing and did another. I was a first-class hypocrite. The truth that I was a multilevel mess kept surfacing. I hated my compromising. I hated my weakness. I held more tightly onto faith. We had no money and told Big Guy's sister. Of all things, she said she would find a renter for one of the rooms. But we stalled, and it pushed me into looking for a better-paying job.

I began to memorize Bible verses from Ephesians 6:10–20 and

23–24. My struggle against sinning was fierce at times, and I kept reading about the armor of God. There was something special about the words and believing them for protection against my sinful nature and Satan. The weapon of the sword of the Spirit was the Word of God. I wanted the armor to work on me so much that I memorize the passages. I was always intrigued by the memorizing of those Scriptures. Unlike memorized lines for acting, the words of God had eternal worth and consequences. But I didn't know how to apply the Scriptures or live with the armor. It was like having a gun loaded with bullets but not knowing how to aim or pull the trigger. I continued to write Christian lyrics for me only. It was wonderful to muse on the work of God in my life. Looking at how the Holy Spirit was making the new me was a joy. But more thrilling was living it day to day.

It was so cold in the garage again this winter for me, but the silence was worth it. Ma's cookies came, and I sat alone with God at North Hollywood High School sipping on coffee. It was a tribute to the Pie dog; he had been gone nearly two years. I gave the rest of the sweets to Big Guy. By the end of 1990, my life had undergone gigantic supernatural changes, especially the transformations due to what I valued in the Bible's truth. Meditating on the things of God was golden, as in Luke 24:45: "And He opened their understanding, that they might comprehend the Scriptures." Knowing I was with God spilled out of me. I smiled more at the diner people and the people at the burrito stand or walking in the street. Praying before I eat was getting somewhat easier, but I often remembered after a few bites. Sitting on the corner eating, watching people, I thought of what words weren't appropriate in conversation. Foul language was talked about in James 3:10: "Out of the same mouth proceed blessing and cursing. My brethren, these things ought not to be so." The internal changes never stopped. I saw my time on earth slowly manifesting godly changes outwardly. I didn't know what heaven was like, but I heard the radio preachers talk. If I could, I wanted to push time forward at thirty-seven years of age and get there quickly.

Chapter 22: Blessings of the Lord

The first higher rent of six hundred dollars was due on January 15, 1991. Burned out on the telemarketing jobs, I could not really go back into that arena of persuasion over the phone. My conscience said it was not a good deal any longer. Talking someone into buying something he or she didn't want was not good for either of us. I looked for work in warehouses; I needed to be more stable, doing something with my hands.

Reading the Bible and being sober on all fronts, I felt great knowing more about Jesus, Prayer, meditations, and dwelling on God's truth were so healthy for me I wanted more. With the spiritual increase in my life, the Christian lyric writing added to the beginning of the new year. Concentrating on the meaning of the Bible's words one at a time, I found them to be of a cathartic nature. In my growth, I chose a message to please God and what I wanted readers to someday read. I had ten Christian lyrics now, and dwelling on God was medicine.

---

†

A PROVERB A DAY

Opening God's Word with concern,
His will for our life to discern.
With grace in faith, we turn,
Reading A Proverb A Day.

Christ Jesus has risen, Holy Spirit will lead thee.
We're learning to listen, Holy Bible will feed me.
No more drifting away, Lord, we're praying to stay,
Reading A Proverb A Day, reading A Proverb A Day.

My neighbor's alone as he cries,
Lost in the world and its lies,
With Christ he can clear his eyes,
Reading A Proverb A Day.

> Christ Jesus has risen, Holy Spirit will lead thee.
> We're learning to listen, Holy Bible will feed me.
> No more drifting away, Lord, we're praying to stay,
> Reading A Proverb A Day, reading A Proverb A Day.

The good and evil engage,
The planet cries out in rage,
God's love is turning the page,
Reading A Proverb A Day.

✝

Chance and Miss Fortune called. They thought they might want to move back in and were willing to pay the high rent if they did. He wouldn't say how, but just that his life had changed considerably. In considering someone more positive who could pay the rent, I recalled the few women who came to the front door. They were answering the room-for-rent ads. I always refused their entrance in the past. Avoiding my personal involvement with strange women who could disrupt my living arrangements was a good thing. After turning away Gina and a few women from lyric class and the video auditions, I was weak in my abstinence from sex. My inner man's sinful nature contended with thoughts toward sexual sin. Sinful thought designs conflicted with the presence of the Holy Spirit. I was learning to discard old immoral values. Time used to run and I chased it, but that fun was an idea that was done. My most lofty goal was to seek an even consistency at thirty-seven. By the grace of God, I was finally looking for uniformity. Where else could I live moment to moment but in the safety of the Lord?

✝

It dawned on me that my best times were when I was listening to the radio preachers. I logically thought a job listening to the radio would help me to learn more. My motivation for seeking this unique type of employment, if it existed, was simply to learn. In all my life, I never knew that churches did anything other than have people sit and listen. Maybe because the Catholic Church had people sit and listen to Latin was why I never went there. I never considered looking into what churches did or if they had classes for people to learn. Nothing but driving would allow me the time to listen to the Christian radio five days a week. So I started looking for that job and searched the newspaper.

I needed to listen, so I needed to work alone. When I first answered an ad for a driver, I was told it was driving dead bodies in a limousine. I went for it and got it. I first worked on a trial basis for a week, riding with another driver. I would get paid to be a passenger but also to assist with the dead bodies. Apparently the employer had other applicants give their best intentions and then back out. So it made sense that they spend a little money and I put in a little time. I started work for a mortuary for five hundred dollars a week.

So there I was a passenger, an assistant to a limousine driver who was experienced in picking up dead people. And that's what I thought I wanted. We would literally arrive to pick up deadweight. The private home or motel or nursing home in any kind of neighborhood was where we went. I'd only seen a few of my loved ones dead. It was no small challenge to disconnect my feelings when we walked into a house and heard the crying. I was told before I got there not to stare, and I did find it challenging to not look. We bagged up the body and hauled it away. It wasn't as easy as it sounds. The cliché *deadweight* took on new meaning. The cumbersome task of handling the body into the body bag with your hands got my stomach queasy at first. I went back outside in the sun. Lifting the heavy bag with just our handgrips and then maneuvering it onto the stretcher through the room was tough.

We had to deliver the body either to the Los Angeles County morgue or to a private embalmer. Standing in the morgue and seeing how people went about their normal lives was hard to accept. How could the significance of death and dead bodies all over the place be a regular job? But somebody had to do it and make it their way to go through life. Those people were desensitized to the finalization and lifelessness of death, it seemed. As if all bodies were just a weight to move around on gurneys, the normalcy of it all was just their days' work. I remembered my father's face in his coffin, my grandmother's face in hers for the last time. Death was not normal. Now I was getting a glimpse of how Pa's and Granny's bodies may have laid on gurneys in hospital basements. How staff may have wheeled my family like they were pushing vacuum cleaners. They may have paused like these technicians, stopping to gossip with a coworker or ask someone to lunch.

The employees were just doing a job of necessity for a paycheck. Just like me. Maybe they got paid a lot. Maybe the money outweighed the truth. Seeing and dealing with the truth of death and the finality that comes with having a body must somehow become ordinary. Maybe the casual, routine attitude was the effect from watching TV shows, which often showed life end as a mere meaningless last step before it was motionless. I wondered if anyone there thought about where all the souls went to. Did they care what happened to the soul of a person? Was hell and heaven considered? I wondered if some of these dead or alive people were Christians.

Maybe I was overreacting in my understanding the shock of what seemed to be so much casual death. The factory work of processing the dead body was far, far from casual. And the smell of dead people increased with each step into the large cold warehouse of death. I did the job a second day just to find out if I was mistaken. I wasn't. After two days, I quit. The surroundings of death, the bodies in the morgue, all those sights and smells came and left. I was disturbed to say the least and came home to find comfort in reading the Bible. I love picking up God's letter to humankind. There is nothing more astonishing on earth than the Bible.

Amazingly, as I was still new at opening the Word, I turned to a passage that mentioned dead people. "But Jesus said to him, Follow Me and let the dead bury their own dead" (Matt. 8:22). I think Christ meant the spiritually dead, but that was all the encouragement I needed to get out and stay out of that crazy job. Perhaps a mature Christian morgue worker would have used the facility to explain spiritual life in Jesus. But as for me, I was in a shaken state. In general, the dead-people driver tryout ordeal shook me up a bit more than I had imagined it would. I think the emphasis of seeing actual dead people brought home to me the treasures in the teachings of Christ. The reality of death became much more real to me. The death of the body was only a foreshadowing for the soul's spiritual life in heaven or its spiritual death in hell. Nevertheless, the helplessness and uselessness of a dead body became more than sufficiently obvious to me. Life and death on earth were common to us all. The three most important questions on earth are, "Who do you think Jesus Christ is?" and "Where will the eternal life of your soul be?' and Why? The consequences of how a person answers are eternal. For those souls who definitively know Jesus as Savior and Lord, joyful life awaits in heaven. There is no second chance; there is no coming back. Earth is the last step, the threshold, before entering into forever.

✝

Rolling into 1991 with a positive attitude, I kept filing applications for drivers' positions and used Big Guy's car. It had been ten years since I had a real forty-hour-a-week job that lasted. I prayed for help and for the best job. Chance or Miss Fortune, one of them, was in a hit-and-run car accident, so they asked if they could move back into the house in February. That was their story. Something was amiss, but I had no way of knowing the whole truth. They wanted to leave the area of Palmdale so the car would not be recognized, and in this way, Chance and Miss Fortune eased our rent burden. If it was the car that was being hunted, it seemed like it would be found sooner or later. The war against Iraq continued on the news channel. As I watched, I thought of the dead bodies and wondered if some were going to heaven through faith in Jesus. All bodies die; the real rivalry is for the soul. Life on earth is the field of invisible spiritual warfare, and I was living in it. It was easy to lose sight of our moments-to-moments' strength in Bible truth.

Learning why the planet earth and the people are really here is a gift from God. Knowing God through Jesus only appears for some. "For many are called, but few are chosen" (Matt. 22:14). Having spiritual life in Christ we believe. With God, there is no such thing as chance; all of life is in His control and a gift to be lived to His glory. Whoever believes will have eternal life. All are welcome and some will believe. Others without Jesus chose to be now and eternally spiritually dead, nobody can blame God He invites all.

My annual fast began in February. Again I was moved deeply at the fast's special clarity, especially joined with my growth in God's Spirit. I wondered what heaven would be like as my eventual home forever. There must be no greater joy than to be sinless and love God perfectly and to be loved by Him perfectly.

In March I was still looking to find work with a radio. I had no experience as a professional driver, so I knew I would have to give up a little to get a lot. Searching the newspaper again led me to a mail delivery company. I did get that job transporting mail to the movie studios in the early morning hours. At four o'clock in the morning, the drivers would secure their route bundles from the Van Nuys airport. My training route ended up being my daily route, which I found to be unique. The trainer and I made deliveries in Universal City, Hollywood, the Burbank Studios, and downtown Los Angeles business offices. We were allowed, of course, to drive onto the lot of Warner Bros. Studios, which was certainly an exclusive privilege. Sunrise driving down the streets of time through a variety of Hollywood sets was cool.

It was make-believe with a huge bankroll. The enormous efforts to camouflage and dress up the art of deception were an eye-opening experience. I appreciated more fully the effort to create realism and supply the viewer with the best efforts to feel more emotion. Slowly we drove in the predawn glow down a street of the 1920s, with brownstones and storefronts of pre-Depression America. Around the corner, we rotated through the first rays of sunlight onto the set of a Midwestern cowboy town. Avoiding hitching rails, covered wagons, and strategically placed tumbleweeds, I craned my neck to see the sets. Perhaps my cowboy childhood classics were filmed there. Onward through more modern 1950s' days in the metropolis that maybe Superman would protect. Maybe he worked at a different studio. To see just the fronts of buildings, the facades without guts or the insides, gave me the feeling of empty show business that I was to appreciate for many years.

I could relate to the falseness of my own life of hypocrisy. I hated my two-faced life of being a voice against sin and yet being a sinner. I was stuck with the truth that I was sinful but I was blessed with the power of Jesus to do something about it. I was beating myself up pretty good. I can only thank the Lord for never giving up on me. The downside for that particular job was the heavy lifting and the early morning wake-up call. More importantly I found out that the route was a two-man run, so I listened to the driver's radio station with the voice of a guy named Rush Limbaugh. I knew nothing of this singular voice other than it had captured the driver's attention and it wasn't preaching the Bible. The outlook for getting my own route did not look good at all, so I kept looking for a better job.

Back in the newspaper, I found a third job with normal daylight hours, the use of a company car to take home, and fantastic people to work for. They were a wonderful, married Jewish couple with their own business. Able to capture a niche in the market of their particular advertising expertise, they were very generous with my salary and benefits. The man and woman I worked for brought their dog to work. I got along great with the big German shepherd, so part of my job was to walk and run her in a nearby field. At the beginning, it really was the best job ever, and I thanked God. I was a professional driver alone for eight to ten hours a day, Monday through Friday, over the Los Angeles area. My travels also included the beaches and valleys and deserts. Downtown Los Angeles was like a circus, with such a wide variety of sites.

The new Toyota's radio played a Christian station day in and day out. I was riding with the Holy Spirit getting paid to learn about God, Jesus, and the Bible. God's laws in 1 Corinthians 6:9–10 were clear about what not to do: "Do not be deceived. Neither fornicators, nor idolaters, nor adulterers, nor homosexuals, nor sodomites, nor thieves, nor covetous, nor drunkards, nor revilers, nor extortioners will inherit the kingdom of God." Verse 19 says, "Or do you not know that your body is the temple of the Holy Spirit who is in you?" Even though I wasn't all of those things, I understood more clearly the scope of God's intentions to change people's lives. Every mile I drove, I felt further and further into the new realm of Christian living. I was taking notes and talking into my tape recorder about what I valued. Driving was always a benefit for me to release my thoughts, and again, it was exactly what I wanted and needed. I got to see a lot of Los Angeles and put on thousands of miles of motivated driving. That job blossomed into more than I had imagined.

In my travels I saw old hippies, poor street people, and prostitutes young and old. Whites, Blacks, Orientals, Mexicans, and Middle Easterners were all mixed together. Poverty and sin didn't distinguish or care who it called its own. Poor unfortunate, lowly humans sat, lay on, and crossed the Los Angeles oceans of concrete and blacktop. Each new day, they pushed their carts and plumbed the depths of dejection with probing courage. I saw kids on Hollywood Boulevard with earlobe chains and ringed noses fearlessly strolling in a springtime lightning storm. A woman driving a small, very expensive car heading toward large homes stopped next to me at a red light. Tattooed, pirouetting ballet slippers swayed on the neck above her flamboyant clothing. Her red lipstick stuck to her cigarette. Apparent homosexuals were hand in hand, arm in arm, flaunting homosexuality while crossing the street. Challenging what used to be normal and customary in public with their out-of-the-ordinary sin, they paused and kissed.

Growing up as a child in the fifties and sixties, it was common to refer to homosexuals with slang words. Even in the seventies and eighties, I didn't understand why a man or woman chose to be something other than what they were born. I grew up learning the fact that their preferred abnormality was just that: wrong and not right. Eventually I would learn that some homosexuals actually preferred being referred to as homosexuals and others preferred being alluded to as gay. But the usage of the word gay was an oxymoron. Gay meant happy, jovial, but what I saw was an obvious effort at pretending to be happy. The choice to pretend must have caused a constant inner challenge to maintain the immoral façade. Another expression mix-up was with the usage of the words African American and Black. I learned in a rather abrupt way that using either phrase was either accurate or offensive. Again it was a matter of whom you were talking to and their preference. Another similarity and abrupt lesson I learned was when I held the door open for a woman, as I was taught it was the right thing to do. I was shocked when the woman scolded me and forcefully told me she was fully capable of opening the door herself. That was just plain rude. As far as me being kind and gentlemanly, I still held doors open. My act of kindness was there to be had; people could take or leave it, whatever they preferred. Seeing the homosexuals brought to mind the Bible story I heard on the radio about Sodom and Gomorrah. God punished the sinfully wicked as they were living out perverted lives in the streets. "But the men of Sodom were exceedingly wicked and sinful against the LORD" (Gen. 13:13). I also saw drug dealers and prostitutes hanging in car windows negotiating business. The arrogant, unchallenged public displays of sinful pride gave the appearance that there were no rules and no laws and that sin was acceptable. Bad became good. I now knew better how good good was because I could see bad for what it was and how twisted lives got.

The most disturbing thing I saw were the street people lined up along the sidewalks of a deserted part of L.A. With stuffed grocery carts, balancing dismantled cardboard homes, standing in rags, they too gave the appearance of being accepted and discounted. Avenues full of homeless, with or without carts, belongings, or cardboard box shelters, milled about, nearly crushed to death by neglect. Avenue after avenue, hundreds and hundreds of homeless lined my boundless new vision of regular stuff to see. I worked for this company one and a half years. From that first day, my eyes never again saw a day of normal. My old normal was shaken into a bizarre new reality. The TV never showed the truth of the streets in whole, only short glimpses desensitizing the viewers to the injustice. Seeing the whole truth disclosed the shocking reality of a mismanaged society. The people being wasted were the hidden actualities of society's failed priorities for humans. All around, I could see beautiful, big buildings and an overabundance of expensive cars. The only outward signs of compassion for these people were the Salvation Army and the City Mission, which fed and clothed, with messages of inward rescue in Jesus. It was the poor who looked more toward heaven's full, glorious life. I recalled my knee injury causing me to lie still and how my loss helped me see more clearly the ways of God. Perhaps an earthquake would humble more.

Resurrection Sunday came, and Christ Jesus was praised in my Bible reading and on the radio. Sin and spiritual death are conquered through the death and resurrection of Jesus—believe it. "The last enemy that will be destroyed is death" (1 Cor. 15:26). Jesus conquered death on the cross and will reign over it in His kingdom. My savings accumulated, and I bought a second GMC 1966 pickup truck to drive out of Los Angeles. This one had the motor restored, and the body was in very good condition. I hoped to be in New York for Ma's birthday in September for a surprise. I longed to be out of the desert. My Bible was an oasis I could take anywhere; life poured from it.

After two years of struggling with abstinence, I had absolutely no or little expectation for a relationship with Christian women. I was thirty-eight years old, with nothing to offer regarding financial stability. Aimless but for the Word of God and the suspense of heaven, I thought about being single. I recalled Melissa taking her instructions out of the books on miracles seriously. After she completed her course, she was instructed that there were to be no relationships for eighteen months. There was a risk that a romance gone badly could tear me up. I was okay with waiting, but wondered about how long. It had been three years since I had a meaningful relationship with the Irish woman, Jackie. Thinking of her, I thought of her son Glenn making me laugh, and his notion with cable TV rattled in my mind. In the warm month of March, with some stability in my life, I began putting together my old idea of producing a Christian cable show, maybe calling it "Heaven High," as I first thought. I used it as my working title and considered the aspects of bringing together Christian artists in a variety show.

Then without any warning for us to prepare, Chance and Miss Fortune said they were leaving by giving one week's notice. That was a very coldhearted way to treat Big Guy and me after we helped them hide from their troubles. We got stuck with the rent cost and no time to get a renter going into April. Another ad for a roommate went in the newspaper. The new renter moved in within only one week of advertising. I was so thankful. Saving money was a luxury I hadn't had in fifteen years or so. My steady work allowed me to put money into the truck for leaving soon. Big Guy and I built a wood frame camper for my truck in the backyard.

The charismatic church where Chance went first and where I had gone sporadically for eighteen months no longer appealed to me. Yet I still thought of going to church maybe somewhere else. Churchgoing was a void that needed filling. I still found learning and comfort with the radio preachers. It was a weakness I didn't see because I was learning how not to be part of a church group. There were so many half-hour radio segments, and I was getting better at learning who taught better. My prayers, Bible reading, joy, and meditation were increasing, except when I was sinning. I couldn't seem to fix those bad spots.

One evening I went to that charismatic church again. For the first time, I was going to check out what the evening worship was about. However, a small group of five to ten people came to the parking lot and left. There was an apparent mix-up on where the speaker was. A few folks standing around like me were at the wrong location. They said they were going to another one. But one guy said he was going to another church close by. He mentioned the name of a radio preacher I listened to a lot. That name rang a familiar bell in my head that he was the best preacher. After getting directions on how to move about in the once-desert land, I stood there looking at the dark desert sky. My mind's eye, my dyslexic view in 3-D, went up; I could see the flat, brightly lit streets without people, just cars. Homes at night housed the millions of day people. I thought of those outnumbered night "shadow people" living in the streets. The other church was not very far away, so I ventured over, hoping to worship and feeling good about knowing my way.

To my amazement, it was an enormous building. I parked across the street. Friendly people greeted me outside, shaking hands as I made my way into the huge hall. Apparently that was their water baptism night at church. To my amazement, the preacher on the radio was speaking. I suppose I never paid attention to what information followed the teaching on the radio. When the announcer came on, I switched off the radio or turned the dial. I never got the address if he gave it. But I was sure this was the same voice and name of the man I heard on the radio. I liked to listen to his teaching. As I sat in surprise, I watched, listened, and found it to be much more to my liking. I was okay with that place. I even filled out a visitor's card with my name and address. The pastor explained the purpose of that night's ceremony, called water baptism. Then people actually gave their reasons why their old self was getting dunked beneath the water, and the new self-came up. There were no speaking in tongues, gobbledygook, and baby talk. Instead, there were people telling about their union with Jesus speaking the English language. I was sitting in amazement, wanting to also tell my story. I realized that I had been trying to go to the wrong church and going nowhere too long. All the peace and comfort that I enjoyed within harmonized with just sitting in that church. That new church was real to me and right for my thinking.

Apparently there were big and small differences between how people tried to get along with God. Opposed to the discomfort and confusion within the old church, I now sat in peace. With no full-on entertainment church with it's loud rock band music and prancing in the aisles, I sat in peace. I walked out of there that night knowing peace and living much better. I felt more grounded and accomplished with my new life changes in that one direction. From then on, my walk with Jesus Christ and knowing God and the Holy Spirit was on the right path. It was a path of clarity and truth in exposure to God's Word. I may never know anywhere else a church like that outside of heaven. I believe I was truly led by God's patient hand all the way through my own desert to that house of God. The Holy Spirit led me to God's teachings and instructions that would never leave me. Blessed by the Trinity, I drove on, knowing a home I'd go to on Sunday.

A few days later, I drove to the big new church; it was my first Sunday. Again I thanked the greeters and sat in the back. It was another congregational sea of people. Fitting in with people was always difficult, but I was comfortable with so many. Most of them, I supposed, had a lot in common with careers, families, and houses—long-term normal. My lifestyle was so different; it came easy to feel out of place. The only thing I had in common was Christ; we all had the best without the frills of tongues and rock-and-roll music. That first Sunday was a very special time and life-changing experience; I realized I could no longer avoid people. It wasn't like the other church, where I was floundering in miscommunication. That new preacher made sense out of everything he said, and the people loved listening. After worship I bumped around swarms of people with a searching look on my face, and found a bookshop. It was stuffed with happy people who were honestly helpful and warmly understandable. I was among regular people, Christians who knew the God of love. Families were everywhere thriving with love.

So I stayed going to that new church on Sundays for the preaching and the people. I stayed with reading the Bible and praying alone in my baby steps toward merging with others. I continued in the rank of one as a solitary solider for Jesus, except when I went to church. And the church was a school for all ages; I was thrilled. There was an abundance of Christian wealth that I could take in stride. The classes offered to beginning Christians sounded ideal, as well as the camaraderie among the churchgoers. For the first time in my life, I found a school that taught the teachings of God's Holy Scriptures.

In May a church team stopped at my house. They were following up on the card I filled out, where I checked "Would like to talk to someone." They were reaching out to me. They wanted to help answer any questions I had and explain the gospel message. It was a confusing evening with the band showing up for another impromptu rehearsal and dragging their equipment in. But those church folks stayed right on the target of their mission to help. I thought that night was a great time to talk to actual Christians about the Bible. I went again to the church and again and again. I went to the church every Sunday in June. After thinking and praying about all those classes about God offered at the church, I enrolled. I wanted to be with people of like minds. I wanted to have what they had: friendship, camaraderie, and shared joy.

All that I was missing in my early Christian life came in time— all the benefits of fellowship, all the potluck dinners, the desserts, the camaraderie with eating together and laughing, the small groups studying together, praying together, more church classes, orchestras, soloists, singers, more joy of the Christian life, more eating and fellowshipping. I learned more effectively how to live the Christian life by seeing their example at church. I saw it and learned it and lived it out among other Christians in the basic fundamentals of the faith. I made new friends in my class, and we met at the instructor's house with his wife and kids. Seeing their faces at church brought so much joy in just knowing them. One of the greatest sounds in church on Sunday was the silence of listening, followed by the turning of Bible pages. That wonderful soft swishing harmony has the power of the Almighty. "Turning Pages" is a lyric yet to be written.

✝

I was not sure about going ahead with plans for New York. But I still kept investing more into the truck. I was troubled about leaving. I liked the new church, and I was learning. I valued my job and my church and wondered about leaving my church friends. In my troubled thoughts, I'd walk to the park and hoped to talk with the homeless about Jesus. I found resistance instead and was more troubled by their rejection. My unsteady life was again agitated with doubts and questions that only time could bring answers to. Then I was visited by Glenn, that whimsical leprechaun. He was getting more involved with his jazz radio show through public access, and his talk started my wheels turning.

In July, I met Christian artists and organized for the TV cable show featuring a variety of artwork. The producer at the public-access TV station locked in a thirty-minute time frame for my show two months in advance. But making Christianity commercial still did not feel or seem right, it was not right for me. Soon I canceled that show's idea of Christian artists, but I kept the time slot. I still made plans for a variety show and hoped to use a few band players and Chance. With me as master of ceremonies reciting one of my old lyrics, I still needed some non-Christian artwork to work with. Glenn knew a painter.

August brought the calm to walk and think as I evaluated what was happening in my life. One day I talked with a one-legged man hobbling around in North Hollywood Park on crutches. I first observed him at a distance and saw what appeared to be his struggle with moving about. His strength to hold himself up while waiting for the stoplight at the corner was impressive. It looked like his legs were not much use. After the bus left, he drew my interest more intently. Surely, I thought, there was a man who needed comfort in this life and hope for a better life to come. He used crutches really well and carried a backpack in his determination in front of the cars and into the park. I could not stay away and approached the bearded, slightly disheveled man. He was settling himself on the ground. His eyes were light blue and pierced into mine as he looked up. Introducing myself, I put forth my hand. His handshake was scary strong. I felt completely vulnerable at once and at his mercy. He saw the fear in my eyes. There was no way I could free myself. I bet he could have crushed my bones to powder or tied me in a knot. When he let go, despite my surprised look, I uttered words that went right to the point of why Christ died on the cross. My talk went on about the plan of God. He just listened; he didn't say much, even when I asked if he followed my thoughts. I tried to share with him just a few more words of the gospel, but it was awkward to gain his attention.

He was around the park for several days, always coming and leaving by bus. He said he came to the park to get out of the city of Los Angeles. We had small talk for several days with lunch. I then invited him to Big Guy's house to use the shower, and he agreed to come. I drove him there. While he was there, I washed his clothes and gave him some of mine to wear. We also shared a meal before returning him to the park.

I gave him a few bucks, along with having filled his pack full of clean clothes and supplies. I didn't see him after that.

Reaching out and wanting to spread the good news of Jesus was part of why I helped him, and just helping was part of it too. My only regret was that I did not help more people more often. The one-legged man was in my prayers every day. I told my friends at church about him, and he was in their prayers too—we were all in God's hands, trusting, resting in His mighty hands.

Chapter 23: Stay to Learn

I began a second fast, making it a biannual event this time for only five days in August 1991. I celebrated my second year as a born-again Christian. Special clarity arrived with dwelling on my growing love with God. It was like a path slowly broadening in fullness, with an expectation for more fullness into eternity. Communicating with God by reading his letter, the Bible, and praying in meditative thought is a piece of heaven on earth. Keeping the body cleansed, it is strengthened with energy; it is a force within. This second time it was a big surprise to experience greater peace and joy.

I got rear-ended in my truck on my way to work in September. A fully loaded electrical truck plowed into me at a stoplight. My head shot back, slamming into the rear window of the truck. The EMS driver put a neck brace on me right away. I was hurt bad with whiplash, and that led me into therapy. My plans to return to New York in a classic 1966 GMC pickup truck were postponed. Once again, I was engaged with recovery. Repeating injuries is a theme in my life I have learned to live with. I continued to build on a long list of accidents, mishaps, and misfortunes in one form or another. In turn, the extended stay helped me to grow with the church's teaching programs. I met wonderful people and made great Christian friendships. I hoped to find a Christian woman to fall in love with and prayed about that. Learning Scripture was first and indeed the best part of my recovery process. The Word of God is a medicine for life.

Doctors' appointments and lawyer business began filling my agenda. Out of work on disability, unable to drive eight or ten hours a day, I'd go to and fro by riding the city bus. Sitting in the shade somewhere near the bus stop gave me lots of time to read Christian books and absorb God's truth. Slowing down was a blessing in disguise. Sizing up situations with people in the street, I got more familiar with noticing the ways of everyday people. There was a survival edge in the live face-to-face encounters that gave me a sense of a desperate alert at times. My being vulnerable and with limitations was an attitude I carried inside. With my risks grew my awareness that I walked with the presence of God guiding and protecting me. Still I stayed alert. In my backpack were my diary, a few good Christian books, and a small Bible to read at all times.

By the first of October, I weighed 205 pounds. Standing in 115-degree heat, I waited in the shade for the bus. Obviously I was just one more person among the millions, but my diary helped make me unique. Capturing my growing contact with God, I became saturated in Scripture. I loved reading the Puritans' books Richard Baxter, Jonathan Edwards as well as authors on prayer like E. M. Bounds. Dwelling on the power of prayer and meditating on the truth of God would blow me away. None of it was taken lightly. The Holy Spirit's teaching brings profound joy. Those moments sitting on the ground, I would just begin to edge near a glimpse of heaven's joy. A sense of measureless ecstasy seemed to draw me.

The scheduled appointments became a routine, and so did eating at a new variety of small restaurants in my path. Feeding on the Word of God brought joy to my face and to those cooks, cashiers, and waitresses. I enjoyed showing them my books and asking if they knew Jesus. Most of them said no in broken English. Some of them said they were Catholic but couldn't explain what that meant. When I met a Christian, the first thing I said was, "I'll see you in heaven," and we smiled, nodding our heads, pointing up.

Some women friends still called from time to time, but I turned them away and walked the abstinence path. To them, I was an idiot. My flagrant regard toward the women of plan A was a thing of the past, old life. Plan B was to leave Los Angeles and settle down and be normal. But then my plan B got nullified when God gloriously introduced salvation. God's Word said Christians can only marry Christians. That was the new previously inconceivable plan, which now happened to be my new plan C. Plan C with regard to women was a maybe. Maybe find one and only a Christian woman to love and be loved by if it were in God's plans to allow that. I had all I could do to learn to love God more than the world. To let go of everything in the world that would interfere with God was also in plan C. My odds of finding love were greatly reduced. Putting God first filled most of plan C. I figured I had had enough women anyway. I'd just have to learn to wait and accept my new life as the path unfolded.

✝

Rehearsals for the variety art cable show called "Windows" included Chance's three-piece band. Supposedly they would play live, doing lip-synch to his songs. My friend Glenn, with his bag of tricks, arranged with his mom Jackie for me to work with their painter friend, named Danielle. Her talented artwork on large, framed canvas paintings were undiscovered treasures. Her collage-style art brought together instinctive ideas mixed in with likenesses of her photos. Forming unique interpretations of society, she wove her views uniquely with her brush in hand. She gave her permission to video them and allowed me full access. Videoing the paintings was light work, and bringing them to locations, I incorporated them into my shots of Los Angeles County. The music video was based on Chance's song "Social Plagues and Politics." Mixing in Danielle's paintings of crowded streets, homeless people, smog pollution, and crime, I placed the frames accordingly. Her frames leaned against light poles and sides of buildings as I panned live city and suburban life in progress.

By mid-October, we were ready. When the door of the TV station opened, we knew we had only a few minutes before our taping slot of time began. A prop from one of the previous tapings was still hanging nearby in the background, and it happened to be a scene of a window. The three-man band played Chance's songs. I had already shot and edited my two new music videos to be dubbed in. As MC, I recited my lyric "Windows" and hosted between scenes. Everything was dubbed in and put on a master reel. One thirty-minute take, that was the goal we accomplished, and then we walked out. My three-quarter-inch master videotape was in hand to make better half-inch duplicates from. Putting the opportunity and experience behind me was the other goal.

✝

I drove north on the 101 Freeway to Ventura and visited with Melissa and her husband, Wilbur. She got married to a great guy who loves her. Melissa was thirty-nine at the time and had Kiya, a great teenage girl; then Wilbur and Melissa made a baby girl, named Layla. I was working on my thirty-fourth day of sobriety. Being with my old friend and staying sober lifted my love for God. It was awkward at first, and throughout the afternoon, I felt the urge to crumble. But I also knew the certainty of God changing my life. His strength and love caused me to want to please Him more; doing it was all Him.

✝

Two years and three months after waffling through the charismatic chaos experience, I finally felt a sense of belonging at church. I bought a New American Standard Bible. I knew my auto crash was allowed by God as a blessing in disguise to stay and learn. I was so thankful seeing how God led me. There are no accidents because God is in control of everything. Consequently, it turned out to be a wonderful continuous learning experience. Apparently God was not finished teaching me in the school at the church He chose for me.

My first small class of seven new Christians was given a workbook and weekly assignments. Specific questions came with a biblical reference to search out the exact answer. "In the beginning God created the heavens and the earth" (Gen. 1:1). Thumbing through the Bible, I got used to finding my way around in it. "So God created man in His own image; in the image of God He created him; male and female He created them" (Gen. 1:27). Hearing Dave, the class instructor, explain the answers and teach our group encouraged us all. After class, my fellow students and I charged each other up with exciting news of how God was changing our lives. Being with friends, Dave, his wife Jan and their family in their house for potluck dinners brought me closer to my new reality. Looking forward to church and class was like having a family nearby. Those teachings would serve as my foundation my whole life. Those memories of that wonderful church and its people were like an oasis. Revisiting the memory of those classes and reconsidering how my Christian involvement was truly a great gift, I realized that all my evening bus rides to church were times to draw from a well of love. By December, I was considering taking a gospel-delivery class to learn how to explain the good news of Jesus to others. I signed up for a class to begin in spring 1992.

Discovering a great church and participating in wonderful classes had me coasting in sobriety for a few months. Then, out of work and not on guard looking for trouble, I fell to temptation. It's true that idle hands are the Devil's workshop. My sin never left; it just lay low. In my attempts to break patterns of sin, I was throwing out pot several times during my free time on disability. Battling sin was maddening at times in my hypocrisy. Even with my growing union with God, sin still wanted to cause a riot against God's authority. The lifelong battle was becoming more apparent. Shame kept me from disclosing my sin.

After another three weeks of sobriety, an avalanche of sin fell on me. I knew of my sinful nature, and its patterns of struggle were becoming obvious. I was ashamed of my failure in trying to lose the addiction; I kept quiet. But I don't give Satan credit for his part of messing up my life. Instead, I carry the major load of blame. Over and over, I was trying to fight sin with my own strength. The armor of God in Ephesians 6 was known to me, but not implemented by living in readiness. I was not the watchman on the wall looking for the enemy coming. I didn't want to be just reading the Bible; I wanted to live the truth found in it. How could I be so stupid? My sin was followed by my increased hypocrisy, which was of a new nature, a new irritating level, since I was in church. I fell to temptation; whether it was just my sin or enhanced by the Devil, I still fell. Only in faith could I trust in God to mature me in my desire to love Him and live a life to honor Him. "Therefore, laying aside all malice, all deceit, hypocrisy, envy, and all evil speaking, as newborn babes, desire the pure milk of the Word, that you may grow thereby, if indeed you have tasted that the Lord is gracious" (1 Peter 2:1–3).

My truck was declared a total wreck, so I sold it to a junkyard. I got nearly eight hundred dollars from the insurance company. Disability checks were coming in the mail once again in my life. It was Christmas. I treated Big Guy to a big meal at a real nice restaurant. For the first time, I went to church to celebrate and sing praises to the Lord with a few thousand Christians. Being among believers of all ages comforted my realization of the fact that we all had Jesus as Savior in our common love for Him. We all struggled with sin, and we all had the Holy Spirit leading us in our growth. I came home and sat with Big Guy. We drank milk with Ma's cookies from New York.

Then in the garage, I sat alone, complete quiet in my space. Perfectly still, my mind saw the hundreds and hundreds at church singing glory to God. After being with all those families, I was first sad, and then glad. My narcissism had helped disguise my world of chosen aloneness, but my façade was being exposed more. After decades of being off the common treadmill and living on my path less traveled, I found it too was a treadmill. My life already lived was empty except for God. It hurt to be alone, but I wasn't alone. My new Christian view of humanity was breaking down my old selfishness. Only God and my old friend the diary heard of my pain and joy. Another year was nearly here. Someday was my hope. Someday I'd be in heaven with every Christian who ever lived. Together we would praise God every day perfectly in service to

Him doing the tasks that He set forth for us to do. That knowledge of being in heaven and surrounded by God's people forever was such a blessed gift of truth to cling to.

✝

Talking into a computer and having the machine do the typing was very encouraging to learn about in January 1992. Voice-recognition software was an idea my mind grasped onto. Looking forward down the road at Someday-Ville, I saw I was writing a book. Like a great big lyric, I knew the beginning and the middle but not the ending. I wondered about my weird life and why it was so weird. I didn't know, but I knew God knew. Whatever was going to happen was going to happen just the way God wanted it to happen. January also brought the Santa Anna winds blowing in, with heavy rains coming down.

Once again I experienced a type of early retirement by having time and money. Time is time; either you have it, or you may think you don't. How you spend the ticking twenty-four hours is important. Money, on the other hand, is a matter of practicing self-denial or how to keep it longer. You have to avoid the fact that the more you make, the more you spend. The more you practice austerity, the longer your money lasts. The lower your expectation to spend, the farther your money goes. Since it's all God's money to begin with and He issues it out according to His plans, we have the responsibility to spend it wisely. A wise weekly investment and privilege is giving a portion back to God while at the local church. It's His money in His creation, we are His creatures, and everything is for His good pleasure. I was in a good spot except for the fact that I was still a loner. Big Guy was quiet a lot, thinking of his changing work status. He was in a special place in God's plans to bring us together to help one another. But he wasn't close enough for me to connect to and share a meaningful conversation on the deep things of life. I wasn't used to having a close friend I could relate my way of life to, and that was my weakest link in my chain of Christian growth.

My physical therapy was complete and I returned to work in late

January. Being active and productive again was very uplifting. Driving about, I understood better the lifelong process of sanctification, or being made holy. I would never be perfect on this earth—I knew that. But I wanted to be a lot better than I was, and I would have to trust God for doing that. That took faith, and my faith was from Him. I got involved with gospel-delivery classes, and I was doing a lot of memorizing Scripture. Driving around in the work car making deliveries was where I learned my preparation for class. Inside the car was my mobile classroom. I wrote Bible verses on three-by-five index cards. I used a cassette tape recorder to practice memorizing when a preacher wasn't on the radio.

Come February, I got involved with being water baptized at church. During a prerequisite class explaining the significance of the symbolic submergence and rising out of the water, I gained my knowledge. By Christ taking my sin to the grave, I too immersed my past spiritually dead life in water. As Christ arose from death and the grave, I too emerged out of the water in newness born of the Spirit of God. As Christ lives at God's right hand forever, I too will live in heaven serving God. "John came baptizing in the wilderness and preaching of repentance for the remission of sins" (Mark 1:4). Along with others in my class, I was prepared for the ceremony. In the pews observing and praying for all of us were Dave and Jan, my Bible instructors, along with fellow classmates. Led into the water and plunged down, I rose in symbolic newness and looked out into the crowd. I spoke as did the others of my old life being dead. I looked forward to my new life continuing in the sanctification process. Life was to be lived in faith alone and would produce righteous fruit, known as good works.

Heavy rains fell in February. I was driving around on the job when the unbelievable three weeks of rain started. The rain came down so hard, so fast, and so heavy that flooding was occurring everywhere. The previous night, I thought that it was a kind of divine extension of my water baptism. I felt as if the hand of God were involved. I saw a very serious symbolic attempt to cleanse and to start a new life with such a dramatic act. It's weird how my mind works and reasons like that. It rained every year; you'd think I would have been used to it. Reading into a situation more than the facts can lead one astray. It was a desert, so rain was good; it was flat, so it accumulated fast; end of story.

One day at work, I exited the freeway and stopped at the stop sign in the work car. Without warning and totally unaware, another car hit me from behind, albeit slower and with less impact, but I still was jolted back into the headrest. This time it was a worker's compensation case, which meant more doctors and another lawyer. Again I was kept in California for God's purposes even longer. I had lots of time and again was refreshed to realize I was never alone.

In that time off, I stumbled again on the temptation of smoking pot in April. I bought it, smoked it, and threw it out. The Bible says when you deliberately and willfully commit a sin that it grieves the Holy Spirit. Grieving means the flame of God's presence burns lower. "And do not grieve the Holy Spirit of God, by whom you were sealed for the day of redemption" (Eph. 4:30). Experiencing that loss is terrible, but the flame of the Spirit burns on. In my less-frequent times of weakness and failures, one good thing was it drove me more to my knees. Confessing my wrongs was training in humility, driving me more into faith, hoping that someday in God's plans in His might and strength He would give me continuous victory. Consequently, with continued time on my hands and more amounts of it, I was able to delve into the Word of God. The Nave's Topical Bible was a reference guide to the important topics found in the Bible and their corresponding locations. *The Encyclopedia of Bible Difficulties* by Gleason L. Archer helped explain challenging passages for me. The *New Treasury of Scripture Knowledge* was the best source of finding cross-references for each word in every verse. Sitting, praying, searching, meditating was a gift.

In May 1992 I was taking the bus to go to Sunday morning church and Wednesday night classes. The ride with its stops was a good time to think. I still hoped to begin or find a relationship with a Christian woman. That area of growth didn't surface. One family I met through someone in my Bible class was missionaries from Spain. The husband, Rod, was called into ministry. Rod's wife, Kathleen, was the perfect

Christian mom, raising their kids with the Word of God as their guide. Rod's seminary studies increased and required a larger, newer computer. He offered me his old machine, and I took it.

The June results of a third MRI were not good. I was seeing a doctor at the Cedars-Sinai Medical Clinic, who ordered the therapy work on my injuries to continue. Consequently I was let go from my job. They essentially needed their car back and a driver that they could count on, so I lost the best job.

The fourth MRI results in July were also not good. I needed needle-point injections in my right TMJ (templar mandibular joint). My jaw was very painful. That involved me wearing a brace on my teeth while I slept at night so as not to grind my teeth. Recovery was slow but afforded me time to make plans for a trip to New York. I flew home for my mother's birthday on September 5, 1992, and stayed for ten days. It was so good to see Ma again. Nobody in my family or any of my friends understood any of my talk about God. But they got a big taste of what I would be like once I returned on a more permanent basis. Their coldness registered with me but didn't have time to set in on a repeated basis. At least, I got a taste of their rejection. Having my family not be interested in what I did was nothing new with regard to my writing. My ego adjusted to their disregard toward me years earlier. But their indifference toward God was a larger challenge for me to understand. Treating the things of God as trivial was a small offense to me compared to the larger offense it was to a Holy God. Perhaps the process of forgiving them for offending me was a trial sent by God for me to endure. "My brethren, count it all joy when you fall into various trials, knowing that the testing of your faith produces patience" (James 1:2–3). When I flew out of New York, I left behind the news of my new direction in life. People in the airports still looked at people in the same old way, but I looked at them differently. I saw people living lives with the eternal consequences of heading for heaven or hell.

By September, five months had passed since my last battle with marijuana. It was the first time in my life of not indulging in smoking pot or drinking booze for that long, I thanked God.

CIRCUS OF SIN

All I heard was discouraging words.
Where is love, the One I'm thinking of,
To rescue us from this circus,
Circus of Sin?

I've known and had some friends
Who say life is a holiday,
Credit cards, wheeling and dealing,
Lifetime of wishing and stealing.

Last night was the craziest sight,
I heard such discouraging words.
Poets were laughing and dying;
Virgins were laughing and crying.

Trumpet, I listen for the trumpet,
I'm waiting for my Lord
To rescue us out of this circus,
Out of the circus, this Circus of Sin.

†

Back in my California church, the people that I could consider friends were there at church. I'm sure they prayed for me. They all had real jobs, families, and normal lives. My only camaraderie was at church. I loved going to church. I wished I could live there, but I had to live in the world. I knew full well how hard living the Christian life was going to be for me. I knew that I was different from other people in my wilderness of reasons and ways of life. I was the oddball; I always was alone all of my life with my inward learning struggles. Outwardly I could become like a loose cannon at times, not tethered to stability. It was natural for me to be alone in my struggles, and yet I wanted to be with Christians. My natural was colliding with God's supernatural. I was like a ball in a pinball game. I was safe if I wasn't being played. But once I started bouncing around, reflecting my old thoughts and ways, my old nature began to bounce back.

At times it was easy for me to be out of control without accountability. My ongoing childhood dyslexic challenges, family environment of quarreling, traumatic brain injury, and study of Taoism all created my desire to have an identity as an individual. It was both the path given me and my chosen misfortune. I was always an artistic misfit, and now I was seeing the reality of the rut I was in as a new man in Christ.

My dislike for the ways of the world was getting stronger. My head knowledge was more mature than a real mature heartfelt love I had yet to develop for God. There was nothing I could do to rush that love. They say birds of a feather flock together. And sins are probably like that too. You scare one away, and it flies. Cautiously it circles back around to regroup with the others. The stealth of sin's tenacity tried to strangle my patience and practice of fending off my vices. The deception of sin was relentless, it seemed.

I fought my old nature and did not visit old patterns of visiting women and sexual immorality. I was doing well on making progress. In my resolve, I just stayed away. Some still called, but I didn't call back. For a time it seemed I was becoming more vulnerable to sexual temptation. It also was a fight to be fought like other sins. In thinking of calling a former girlfriend, I saw it was just for sexual pleasure and a backsliding, hypocritical thought. There was no desire to openly choose to involve her. Just when I was doing so well being sober and clean, I slipped in my mind before falling in a big way. I began noticing prostitutes in the street at night, like I had seen so many times during the day when driving at work. Sinful thoughts entered through my eyes into my mind. I wrestled with thoughts, I prayed, and temptations left. The weakest chink in my young Christian armor was my isolation. Looking at the situation of singleness through human eyes of hopelessness, I didn't live in faith, trusting God's plans.

Desire overwhelmed me. In my weakness I ignored my conscience, and sin manifested itself and happened. For the first time in my life, I borrowed a car and picked up a woman of the streets. I got busted in a police sting operation and caught with a prostitute. That was one of the greatest mistakes I ever made. I didn't have any excuse. It was nobody's fault but mine. My sin ended up shooting me in my young Christian heart. No one would have known. When I got in trouble, I prayed in quiet. I couldn't believe I did that to my Lord. My rottenness was to my core; my evil desires were so deceitful. I asked God to forgive me. And I asked Him to keep it our secret. When the time was right, I would come forth with the news. He did. There was no public acknowledgment of my sin. The offense was reduced to a misdemeanor, with no further repercussions. I wanted to bring no shame on the church I went to. My class was nearly over, and I did not think it was timely to drop my failure on such a happy event as our completion. Even though that's exactly what I did—I failed—no one knew. Thank God for His mercy. I lived in shame.

I still carried on with my life in and out of church, but it was not the same life. My heavenly flame burned very low. I was shattered inside and had a horrific time dealing with the Holy Spirit's conviction and my guilt. Our joy, our link suffered, and remorse poured in. I had told myself and God that I would postpone the truth so as not to embarrass others, not to hurt them at that time. I probably was lying to myself all along. I was a hypocrite. I was afraid to show my face. I was so embarrassed. I never wanted to just quit being a Christian; I couldn't just quit anyway. Nobody in the Bible who was a Christian quit. If you were truly a child of God, He wouldn't let you quit. Even when Moses killed the Egyptian in Exodus 2:12, God forgave him and still used Moses in His plans. When David first saw Bathsheba, then lay with her in the adulterous act of immoral sex, and then killed her husband, Uriah, God still used David in a mighty way. In Mark 14:66–72, Peter denied knowing our Lord three times. After Christ rose from the dead and met with the disciples, He forgave Peter, instructing him to feed His sheep, three times (John 21:17). I didn't quit; that wasn't part of God's plans. Thanks be to God, I was His, He was mine.

Continuing with the training I was receiving in one class, I was slowly being restored in my rapport, my peace with the Holy Spirit. In our three-person teams, we would return visits to the folks who visited our church. I was completing the circle that started with the church team visiting my house. One such evening at the door of a couple's apartment, we knocked. We introduced ourselves to a young man who retorted to us his proclamation, "What do you Bible-thumpers want?" It was his wife who asked us in, and we talked about the gospel and found that she was already a believer. The husband voiced his disapproval and milled about with his motorized model airplane, explaining its capabilities. As we spoke and prayed silently, the Holy Spirit had done His work. The woman's faith had received refreshing water. The man's hard-hearted soil was plowed and planted with gospel seeds of eternal life. A few years later in New York, I learned that the man had received Jesus and become active like I had been in a team. He was telling others the gospel message, the good news of Jesus. I helped nurture a person to Christ through a gospel outing. Another soul was saved by God.

I don't know why God would want anything to do with anybody like me. As miserable a failure as I was, who sank so low because of my despicable sin and hypocrisy, God still used a bum like me. At the end of the training session, in my guilt and shame I followed through with my prayer promise to God. I confessed my sin to my teachers at church. They felt sorrow because I injured the cause of Christ. I received their chastisement and teaching from the Bible on the wickedness of sin. I was excluded from any more gospel teams. In my sinful act, I had disqualified myself. But more than my pain, I felt the shame I placed on the name Christian. And Paul, a group leader who was a kind, gentle man, was one of the men I let down. He loved the Lord so much he said, "My sin was the nail in the hand of Jesus who gave His life for me." He was so hurt; Christ was hurt, I'm so sorry.

I was ashamed, embarrassed, defeated, and quietly more alone. I realized that by being all alone, I was in a world of self-made chaos. I lived alone in a garage. I was poor, uneducated, injured, at the bottom of the barrel in my life on earth. I had only what I believed in. I had abandoned my old life and lyrics to be given faith in God through His Son, Jesus. Even though cutting out the old dream and filling me with faith was a done deal in God's eyes, it was still a life to be lived out on the path of time on earth.

Once again, God had made me aware of just how active and just how rotten sin is. There was and is evil in me and around me, and the prince of evil and his demons lurking about. It seemed to be pretty obvious that I was not alone in wreaking havoc in my own life. When I looked at how I was unlike all of the people around me, it made me closer to God; only He could love me. Perhaps only heaven could give a family to me. I compared myself to a lonely street person or someone who was suffering from a severe health condition. In my strange way, I was as isolated as they are. Perhaps that's why I'm intrigued by John the Baptist. He lived alone and was a peculiar sort of individual. Matthew says in 3:1–2, "In those days John the Baptist came preaching in the wilderness of Judea, and saying, 'Repent, for the Kingdom of heaven is at hand!'" Verse 4 says, "Now, John himself was clothed in camel's hair, with a leather belt around his waist; and his food was locusts and wild honey." Someday in heaven I'd like to sit with him and find out more.

It was amazing to see myself in a world that offered so much and most of it I rejected. When I was able to reflect on the condition that I was in as far as being so far out of the box from everyone else, I considered myself just an odd recluse. I learned to accept mistakes as a dyslexic child; they were just the ways of life. I learned from the motorcycle crashes that serious injuries happened to the body and mind, but you kept going. My California life was like a bird flying in a tornado, a mix of good and bad. At the end of my old life, I had learned to accept loss and persevere alone. In the greatness of God's mercy, He gave me salvation. In my new life, I learned that I would never be alone; Emmanuel, God, was with me. In my human sinful nature, I am a screw-up. I don't want to be, but the sin in me wants to fight with me.

My closer walk with learning of the ways of God in books was good. Unfortunately, evil also knows its good ways to attack. Getting arrested was, in fact, just my fault. Learning about my patterns of sinfulness is my responsibility. But in Christ, I screw up less and less and desire to please Him more out of love; more love came and more. I prayed for strength to be able to accept losses in this life that would come. I prayed for God's grace and mercy to help me persevere through the lonely times. In God's love, I'm never alone.

✝

In October, I became excited again about the study of God's Word. Restoration in my connection of love with God is a beautiful thing. I got reengaged with Bible study; another class started at church and I was there. Before I could end the year, before I could enjoy any part of the Christmas holiday, I wrote at great length in the diary.

It's hard to be single. To be alone a lot is not easy either. To be unaccountable and not to answer to anyone is also very stupid. The Christian path is the hardest walk a person can do while living on this earth. To do it without any help except from the bond you have with the Lord is tough. The strength I gained from reading the Bible and training at that time was my walk in life. Everyone's walk is different, and I could feel the core of the Christian ethic, which is love for God and forgiveness toward others. I should give to them what God has given to me: forgiveness and love. That's easy to say and it's easy to read, but living it out is tough. In mid-November I smoked pot again after seven months clean. But I saw the sin in me doing it. Not in my heart or love for the sin did I do it. I loved God more and hated the sin more and its effect to grieve my union with God. It was the sin in my mind, a thought planted by Satan, a powerful fiery dart of sin. I was caught in reacting to the desire of pleasing myself and not being proactive in watching out for the cunning ways of evil. The war is constant.

It was a sad holiday season. On my visit four months earlier when I flew in for Ma's birthday, I told my family. "All that the Father gives Me, and the one who comes to Me I will by no means cast out" (John 6:37). Calling them all at Christmas, it sounded like those words created no interest. My small family didn't care how excited I was about Jesus. They didn't want to hear about Christ and His birth or heaven or hell. But I still prayed for God's will to be done, and I knew it would be. Perhaps God would save them or they would chose to know Jesus.

After eleven years of living away from them, things were not the same for me or them. My brother Ken's traditional lifestyle had two children now. He had a young boy named Frank. His one-income family had kept Ken at the same job for about fifteen years. It sounded like he had fifteen or twenty years to go before retiring. Ma was getting ready to retire but was not sure about financial security. But she was thrilled to hear that I might come home after my accident cases were settled. I got my care package with Ma's cookies, homemade bread, and gifts. I sent Ma a Bible. I bought one at church that included a commentary. I went to Christmas service. I relished in the love of the Christian family singing the old hymns and praises to the Lord Jesus. That church was like heaven on earth. All were joyful to be slaves to the Master knowing they were loved and cared for, protected and cherished.

✝

New Year 1993 started my last year in California. It had some surprises aside from knowing that my injury cases were winding down. My walk with Jesus was growing in a more definite and positive way. I was sober all around and not using anything. The stretch of seven months of sobriety began last April and was ripped off before smoking pot just once last November. I lied to myself, telling myself wrongly that I had earned a "party" or that I'd better sin so as not to be proud. The source of my lies and the lies in the world was the faceless face of Satan. I couldn't see him, but I knew his name and his evilness. His evil in people's lives and my sinful heart were indeed a lot to overcome. But God is faithful and God is all powerful. Jesus conquered sin and evil on the cross. The war has been won, I kept telling myself. It's just these battles on earth will take place until Jesus returns to take His elect away. Until then, in His name and the power of the Holy Spirit, the fight goes on in faith.

Two fresh months' sobriety into the new year was a noticeable and major accomplishment in my Christian walk. Reading my propaganda in the diary helped unmask my lie and the lies I saw around me. A changed life was more in my thinking and actions, and that made the accomplishments I read in the diary more acceptable. I found that focusing on the positive Word of God was the best thing. Trusting God was the best thing. Submitting to God and resisting sin was the best thing. All had to be done first in faith; the work followed faith.

We had continual house problems with the new used furnace and repairs on the hot water heater and a leaky roof, broken windows, and so on. I kept busy, as I was still seeing doctors for the second car accident. My next-door neighbor Emile sold his house and moved on. That made four houses in a row that recently changed hands. Big Guy's corner lot I lived at was the last house on the chopping block of sold homes.

At church I was taking a class in defending the Bible called Apologetics. Learning to support my Christian beliefs in the absolute authority of God and explain the truth of the Bible in a systematic way was very interesting. Another class was on the Puritans. I loved that class. The exposure to Christians who were dedicated and serious while in Europe was a new look at how America then got some of its first biblical guidance. For instance, Puritans believe in the doctrine of predestination, or being chosen by God for salvation. Their belief in Scripture alone sounded like the early Protestants following Martin Luther's and others' reforms, like those of John Calvin, believing in Christ alone, Scripture alone, and faith alone. God's irresistible grace was His gift of salvation, giving someone the ability to believe. Common grace was seen in creation and first drew people to God; it was humans' responsibility to then choose to seek God. Seeing God's attributes in creation and not seeking Jesus was a person's ticket to hell. A fallacy was to think a person could choose God on his or her own merit or works. Choosing God without first recognizing God's sovereignty in all situations was robbing Him of His total control and some of His Glory. Elevating humans to the position of choosing God without acknowledging God's higher control drawing them to Him was to supercede God's divine control.

It was shocking to realize how far our nation had fallen from the dynamic blessings of God in the last three hundred and fifty years. Those classes actually taught me to see the opposite direction America was heading from biblical teaching. Murdering babies was now called abortion on demand. Homosexuality was wanted to be thought of as normal, and if you spoke out against it, it was politically incorrect. If the court system and politicians were so blind to the truth, what hope did America have? It was a no-brainer to see that things were going to get worse. God gives and God takes away, and sin has consequences. The John Owen book *Sin and Temptation* made for the best reading. The seriousness, the deadliness, and the dedication that sin has to destroy lives and ruin a Christian's testimony were exposed to me. I love the teaching of the Puritans in their prayers found in the book *Valley of Vision*.

I had nothing to show for nearly twelve years except ten tons of human effort, sweat, pain, and hard work. A portion of my life was all gone but for the memory of a dream I once held. But there was the diary; there were lots of stories in the diary. I tried as hard as I could to nail down that old lyric dream to come true. I always wanted to try my best, and I did. In place of that old stuff, there was the genuine and true best new life. Salvation was a gift from God. What could be more exciting than the Christian life? God's power, His Bible, His help in struggles, His people in church were my friends all headed for heaven.

I personally knew the positive side of knowing God. My supernatural hope was to share it with people back in New York. I plugged into the positive and rewarding aspects of learning in my new life. Church on Sunday and Wednesday night service and class in the evenings—those were my great days and nights. My church was so blessed by

God. Brilliant minds consumed by the Word of God and dedicated to teaching were giving it back to God's people. Blessings flowed out around the world as sermons were sent out through the radio and other media.

✝

In April I still had access to the camera and the equipment to use. I began two more music videos, with Christian themes. "How Great Thou Art" was my first video of all nature shots, without a person in it. Big Guy and I drove around in the desert, canyons, and near Malibu videoing dozens of shots featuring God's creation. "How Great Thou Art" was a favorite of mine ever since I bought a hymnal from the church's bookstore. Editing that video was a privilege, a blessing. It will be a memento I'll look at, Lord willing, for years to come.

"Soul Train" was the second Christian music video, using Chance's song and lyric. It was about one young man who was being saved, freed from the chains of sin and bondage and then water baptized. I looked far and wide until I found the right location in Calabasas for my last shot in the water. I used a small portion of North Hollywood Park with a chain link fence. Best of all was my actor prop, who was Glenn. He wore chains, with a close-up shot on his ankles in the dust. The fence was a backdrop showing his captivity, and then there were several shots of the poor on the streets in their captivity. As I edited in Glenn wearing shorts at Calabasas, he walked into the woodsy stream. Lowered, he dunked himself in the water, submerging fully. The climax came seeing Glenn rise up with raised arms and head praising God.

The two videos were my last access to the camera; they were an effort to turn around my hard work to praise God. My goal was to make a good, clean, and sober effort, as well as a Christian memory. The videos were just for me. Of course, Glenn got a copy for his efforts. And he did put a lot of effort going into the very cold mountain water.

By the end of April, I had gone six months of not smoking pot.

God was so good to me. He so loves. I loved the ceremony at church to worship and praise Christ Jesus on Resurrection Sunday. The name of Jesus, King of Kings, was on everybody's lips and the heart of worship. In the Bible God speaks of earth in a time when He will burn it all up. "But the heavens and the earth which are now preserved by the same word, are reserved for fire until the day of judgment and perdition of ungodly men" (2 Peter 3:7). I sure do believe it.

At that point my bible head knowledge was still beyond my heartfelt love for God. But love was growing; there was nothing I could do to increase my love but trust God. Just trust, keep the faith, and obey. I knew there were levels in love that would mature. In June I got my last disability check in the mail. It was time to go back to work, and I was ready. The doctor results from an independent exam showed I had lost a large percent of my mid and upper back strength. I was a wreck before with the lower back damage from the Harley, and now I was more of a wreck from the two car crashes. But I wasn't totaled yet; God still had plans for me.

In August it was a full ten months of not smoking pot; only God can do that. I had so much energy and life in me—wow, I was blessed, thank God. I started my last fast in California. This was a somewhat sad realization as I sat in the backyard watching the birds flittering about. God gives them what they need, just as He gives me what I need. Of all the first-time adventures and changes in my life, fasting was one of the most powerful. The results were that I was cleansed without food, and with God's Spirit. I praised Jesus; He is all in all.

I walked the streets at night and missed the Pie dog. I saw rats run in the dark on phone lines from palm tree to palm tree. It's one of the lesser-known amazing sights to see in Southern California. Along the sidewalks, there are tall palm trees through which the electric wires on the street run. In the evening, if you look up, sometimes you can see rats running from tree to tree; it's not a good thing. These filthy creatures were smart to live up off the ground and stay off the ground during the rainy season. And as long as they were up there, they traveled on wires to the rooftops, all in an effort of survival. I thought of all the rooftops they could be gnawing into, spreading disease. Who knew what was going on inside buildings and how impossible it was to stop it? Only God knew.

I also participated in an open-air evangelism class at church, going into Los Angeles and actually preaching on the streets of Hollywood with a small group. In 103-degree heat, we would also visit downtown Los Angeles. In the seedier districts and on Hollywood Boulevard, we were with the people. We would also travel over to Korea Town and down by the Farmers' Market, passing out Bible tracks and praying as we stood. Fully engaged, I was speaking to people about Jesus. That is where I found many people interested in Allah, being of the Muslim persuasion. It was an eye-opening experience to how widespread false religion, cults and apathy toward Christ are in America. "Jesus said to him, 'I am the way, the truth, and the life. No one comes to the Father except through Me" (John 14:6). How patient is God? In a few hundred years America went from receiving God's blessings of power and richness to being cursed by lawmakers legalizing sin. The love of Jesus is the only great message to tell. I pray that all come to know Him as Savior and Lord, all those who are called according to His purpose. God will only hold His judgment back so long.

I was doing less writing in my diary these days, and I was picking up the Bible more and more. Anticipation of once again being with my mother and helping her run the house was growing. She would probably be my only family member to talk about God with me. Getting ready to retire after her twenty-six years, she'd need some help doing needed house repairs if she kept it. She needed to make financial decisions, and I was telling her about elder care and long-term care insurance. I also told her the concept of investing in gold as a form of insurance. All she wanted was me back there to break up her loneliness and add to her happiness. My brother's family lived close, how my mom loved to see them all, especially her grandchildren! She was looking forward to having my company. The excitement was in her voice.

I booked a flight to fly out on November 17 for Albany, New York.

The departure date was six weeks short of exactly being twelve years in California. I found myself a little melancholy with just a few weeks left. I learned at church that the Northeast was known as the frozen-over territory due to the negative results of the Great Awakenings of Protestant religious revivals, such as enthusiastic arousals in sermons and large tent meetings. Hopes to engage the routine churchgoer out of a slumber in the 1730s and the early 1800s worked. Strong preaching of the Word of God brought about strong conviction, increasing church membership. The genuine, regenerated, changed lives that resulted from the Holy Spirit's presence within those who were God's elect had a powerful sway on communities. Others who were not genuinely converted jumped on the bandwagon of its popularity. However, without the true working of the Holy Spirit, false conversions grew apparent and dampened the tone of true Christian revival. Hypocrisy eventually spread, embedding a cold or frozen attitude and outlook on Christianity over the New England region. The term *frozen-over* was not meant for the cold climate, but for the people's very cold attitude against Jesus and the Bible. I felt like I was going on a missionary trip to some remote country. On a positive note, the First Great Awakening sparked an attitude of change and helped initiate the American Revolution within the colonies.

I prepared. I packed lots of stuff and finalized the last push on getting out. These were going to be my last few weeks, and it was sad with Big Guy. After seven years of helping each other, I was sorry to think and say to my big buddy that he would once again live alone. I was able to help him with local disability organizations that worked retraining him for employment, and they were able to give him hope. But nonetheless, my good friend and I would soon have to part.

My emotions were felt for Baby Kitty as well. There's something about a pet. She and I became very close after Pony Boy died. I found him on the sidewalk just the other side of our cheap fence. Burbank Boulevard got him. Baby Kitty knew what was going on with me packing up. I sat in the backyard at night with her in my lap. In the dark with just the streetlights filtering through the trees, we stared at our memories. She jumped on and off my lap as I thought of all my turbulent twelve years in sunny southern California.

I wanted so much to fix what I had broken at church with my sin. There was no way in time to go back, just forward with trust in God. I wanted Baby Kitty's brother back, Pony Boy, and I wanted Piper so badly. I wanted to be different than I was; I wanted to be like other Christians. I wanted the motorcycle crashes and car crashes to have never happened. I wanted my strong back and arms and legs again. I wanted a different life. I wanted to please God. I wanted to be what He wanted me to be. I wanted what God wanted. In the next breath I paused, and my runaway self-pity stopped. I knew God was in control of every single aspect in every smallest corner of every area in all of life in all of time in the entire world. Who was I? I was His. I sat there as His piece of clay, still in the great Potter's hands after four years. God was with me, and I was with God. Another peaceful moment came, like so many when I realized the truth. With God, I needed nothing else. He chose me, He knew me, and He would continue to shape me. I would be what He wanted me to be when He wanted it and for whatever His purpose was. It didn't get better than that. We were family forever.

I packed up forty boxes of stuff. The large and small articles were just property. Some of it symbolized my experience. The UPS driver came and shipped them out early in November. I visualized the large trucks rolling across America like western covered wagons going back home, going east. Each valuable life experience had its own box, labeled churches, vices, jobs, dogs, and my physical health. No price could be placed on the special importance of knowledge and understanding gained. I hoped to be adding more experience into each box and add more boxes as God would allow.

I held the Bible. I was reading the best over and over, Ephesians 1:2–6: "Grace to you and peace from God our Father and the Lord Jesus Christ. Blessed be the God and Father of our Lord Jesus Christ, who has blessed us with every spiritual blessing in the heavenly places in Christ, just as He chose us in Him before the foundation of the world, that we should be holy and without blame before Him in love. Having predestined us to adoption as sons by Jesus Christ to Himself, according to the good pleasure of His will, to the praise of the glory of His grace, by which He made us accepted in the Beloved." Wow! According to the good pleasure of God's will—it doesn't get any better than that. Why me? Because "having predestined us to adoption as sons by Jesus Christ to Himself, according to the good pleasure of His will, to the praise of the glory of His grace, by which He made us accepted in the Beloved." Now that's an answer!

Prior to me leaving, I had accumulated one year of not smoking pot. Praise the Lord! That was His tremendous accomplishment, and I thanked Jesus for His strength and the path that He had me on. My best two paths became one in the opposite direction: one path away from sin and the same path were toward God. My Christian walk and understanding unfolded in my obedience, which was Holy Spirit-led and in turn grew deeper. Pleasing Christ was my desire. He was my Savior and my Lord. He cleansed, purified, and led me to deny myself. I knew I would come to sacrifice things ahead, and I prayed for a will that would do so. Christ suffered, and so would I. That's what it is to be a Christian. "For to you it has been granted on behalf of Christ, not only to believe in Him, but also to suffer for His sake ..." A blessing of privilege, it is God's gift to be Christlike (Phil. 1:29).

My thoughts on trusting God were running very high as I neared my departure. I knew I was going home with the greatest gift beyond all of what humankind could conceive or imagine. God is real. I knew that He chose me and that I was to carry and bring the Word of God to others. On the seventeenth, Big Guy loaded his car for me. We took a last walk through the property with Baby Kitty. Memories were jumping out all over the place. I held the cat for the last time and turned to hug Big Guy, my brother. We prayed and we both choked up saying our farewells with love, and then turned for the door. Amid all the hectic noisy LAX airport traffic of unloading people and luggage, we hugged good-bye. He drove into an array of cars and shifted lanes back to the valley house, with God to comfort him in this world. I will always miss my friend Big Guy; he was an angel for sure. I know I'll see

him in heaven, Lord willing. I turned and walked into the next phase
of my path on earth.

$$\dagger$$

THE GOOD NEWS

God broke the barricade
After all the plans I've made.

My faith now fills the sky.
New hopes are fortified.

> When The Good News comes to your heart,
> Christ will thrive and thrive and thrive.

> When The Good News makes peace inside,
> God's love will provide, He will provide.

Carry on, Holy Spirit, God's grace reigns, His grace reigns.
Carry on, Holy Spirit, God's grace reigns, His grace reigns.

Looking back, I clearly see
Jesus Christ, died for me.

He saves by grace, that's for sure.
In His love, crushing sin's war.

> When The Good News comes to your heart,
> Christ will thrive and thrive and thrive.

> When The Good News makes peace inside,
> God's love will provide, He will provide.

Carry on, Holy Spirit, God's grace reigns, His grace reigns.
Carry on, Holy Spirit, God's grace reigns, His grace reigns.

$$\dagger$$

"But when the kindness and the love of God our Savior toward men appeared, not by works of righteousness which we have done, but according to His mercy He saved us, through the washing of regeneration and renewing of the Holy Spirit" (Titus 3:4–5).

"My brother, count it all joy when you fall into various trials, knowing that the testing of your faith produces patience" (James 1:2).

"Being confident of this very thing, that He who has begun a good work in you will complete it until the day of Jesus Christ" (Phil. 1:6).

✝

THE THRESHOLD

Born on God's earth, quickly babes grow
All of great worth, the plan of God flows.
Care for your soul, in God's truth you'll climb,
Step through your life on a path of time.

> To The Threshold of Love,
> King Jesus at the gate,
> To The Threshold of Love,
> Come celebrate, celebrate.
> To The Threshold of Love.

Time's doorway is a slow-fading breath.
A way seems right, but it leads to death.
Seek Father God with each passing light.
Truth in His Son stays forever bright.

> And the world turns, the world turns
> Good is misplaced, bad is embraced.
> Still God calls all; to Jesus by grace.

To The Threshold of Love,
King Jesus at the gate,
To The Threshold of Love,
Come celebrate, celebrate.
To The Threshold of Love.

Your heart is drawn; to God give praise.
Receive the Lord; He will light your ways.
Holy Spirit, You're leading me now.
Jesus is King, every knee shall bow.

"Also He has put eternity in their hearts" (Eccl. 3:11).